gods

# of Old Europe

6500 – 3500 BC

1 Bird-Goddess found at Achilleion,
Thessaly, Greece. *c.* 6000 BC.
Left: front view clearly showing
the bird-like beak and the parting
of the human hair-do

Marija Gimbutas

The Goddesses and Gods of Old Europe

6500 – 3500 BC

Myths and Cult Images

New and updated edition

with 252 illustrations
171 text figures
and 8 maps

UNIVERSITY OF CALIFORNIA PRESS

Berkeley, Los Angeles

To the inspiration
of Franklin D. Murphy
Chancellor of UCLA
1959–1968

THE PREPARATION OF THIS VOLUME
WAS GENEROUSLY SUPPORTED
BY THE SAMUEL H. KRESS FOUNDATION

The line drawings for this volume were done by Linda
Mount-Williams; the photographs were taken by Kálman
Kónya and Miodrag Djordjević.

UNIVERSITY OF CALIFORNIA PRESS
Berkeley and Los Angeles, California

ISBN: 0-520-04655-2
Library of Congress Catalog Card Number 72-82323

© 1974, 1982 Thames and Hudson Ltd, London
Originally published in the United States of America
in 1974 by University of California Press under the title
The Gods and Goddesses of Old Europe: 7000-3500 BC

New and updated edition in paperback 1982
Reprinted 1996

Printed and bound in Great Britain by BAS Printers
Limited, Over Wallop, Hampshire

6 7 8 9 10

Contents

Preface to new edition

Much new material on the mythical imagery of Old Europe has emerged during the ten-year interval between the writing of *The Gods and Goddesses of Old Europe* and the present edition, but the basic concepts have remained unchanged. The new discoveries have served only to strengthen and support the view that the culture called *Old Europe* was characterized by a dominance of woman in society and worship of a Goddess incarnating the creative principle as Source and Giver of All. In this culture the male element, man and animal, represented spontaneous and life-stimulating – but not life-generating – powers. This priority is represented in the present title by a change in word order, from *The Gods and Goddesses* to *The Goddesses and Gods of Old Europe*.

The term *Old Europe* is applied to a pre-Indo-European culture of Europe, a culture matrifocal and probably matrilinear, agricultural and sedentary, egalitarian and peaceful. It contrasted sharply with the ensuing proto-Indo-European culture which was patriarchal, stratified, pastoral, mobile, and war-oriented, superimposed on all Europe, except the southern and western fringes, in the course of three waves of infiltration from the Russian steppe, between 4500 and 2500 BC. During and after this period the female deities, or more accurately the Goddess Creatrix in her many aspects, were largely replaced by the predominantly male divinities of the Indo-Europeans. What developed after *c.* 2500 BC was a mélange of the two mythic systems, Old European and Indo-European.

The analysis of Old European mythical imagery has reconstituted a link between the religion of the Upper Palaeolithic and that of the pre-Indo-European substratum of European cultures; without consideration of the very rich evidence from Old Europe, neither the Palaeolithic ideological structures nor those of early historic Greeks and other Europeans can be well understood. The persistence of the Goddess worship for more than 20,000 years, from the Palaeolithic to the Neolithic and beyond, is shown by the continuity of a variety of a series of conventionalized images. Her specific aspects of power such as life-giving, fertility-giving, and birth-giving are extremely long lasting. Their indentification was made through study of symbolic signs incised on figurines and associated cultic objects, as well as postures, attributes, and associations. More of this detailed evidence will appear in a forthcoming study by the author on signs and symbols of Old Europe. The object of the present volume is to transmit some notion of the variety and complexity of the philosophical ideas of our European forebears.

Los Angeles, California 1981   *Marija Gimbutas*

Introduction

The tradition of sculpture and painting encountered in Old Europe (for a definition of this term, *see* p. 17) was transmitted from the Palaeolithic era. In art and mythical imagery it is not possible to draw a line between the two eras, Palaeolithic and Neolithic, just as it is not possible to draw a line between wild and domestic plants and animals. Much of the symbolism of the early agriculturists was taken over from the hunters and fishers. Such images as the fish, snake, bird, or horns are not Neolithic creations; they have roots in Palaeolithic times. And yet, the art and myths of the first farmers differed in inspiration and hence in form and content from those of the hunters and fishers.

Clay and stone figurines were being fashioned long before pottery was first made around 6500 BC. The vast increase in sculptures in Neolithic times and the extent to which they departed from Palaeolithic types was not caused by technological innovations, but by the permanent settlement and growth of communities. A farming economy bound the villages to the soil, to the biological rhythms of the plants and animals upon which their existence wholly depended. Cyclical change, death and resurrection, were ascribed to the supernatural powers and in consequence special provision was made to protect the capricious life forces and assure their perpetuation. As early as the seventh millennium BC traits associated with the psychology and religion of the farmer are a characteristic feature of sculptural art. This art was not consciously imitative of natural forms but sought rather to express abstract conceptions.

About 30,000 miniature sculptures of clay, marble, bone, copper or gold are presently known from a total of some 3000 sites of the Neolithic and Chalcolithic era in southeastern Europe. Enormous quantitites of ritual vessels, altars, sacrificial equipment, inscribed objects, clay models of temples, actual temples and pictorial paintings on vases or on the walls of shrines, already attest a genuine civilization.

The three millennia saw a progressive increase in stylistic diversity, producing ever greater variety of individual forms. Simultaneously, a more naturalistic expression of anatomical generalities gradually emancipated itself from an initial subordination to the symbolic purpose. The study of these more articulated sculptures, their ideograms and symbols and the highly developed vase painting enabled the author to distinguish the different types of goddesses and gods, their epiphanies, their devotees, and the cult scenes with which they were associated. Thus, it is possible to speak of a pantheon of gods, and to reconstruct the various costumes and masks, which throw much light on ritual drama and life as it was then lived.

Through the deciphering of stereotype images and signs with the help of quantitative and qualitative analyses it becomes clear that these early Europeans expressed their communal worship through the medium of the idol. In the miniature sculptures of Old Europe the emotions are made manifest in ritual drama involving many actors, both gods and worshippers. Much the same practice seems to have been current in Anatolia, Syria, Palestine and Mesopotamia in the corresponding periods, but only in southeastern Europe is such a quantity of figurines available for a comparative study.

The shrines, cult objects, magnificent painted and black pottery, costumes, elaborate religious ceremonialism, and a rich mythical imagery far more complex than was hitherto assumed, speak of a refined European culture and society. No longer can European Neolithic-Chalcolithic developments be summed up in the old axiom, *Ex oriente lux*.

When the magnificent treasures of the Minoan civilization were unravelled in the beginning of the twentieth century, Sir Arthur Evans wrote: 'I venture to believe that the scientific study of Greek civilization is becoming less and less possible without taking into constant account that of the Minoan and Mycenaean world that went before it' (*JHS* 1912: 277). While his remark was amply justified, the question of what went before the Minoan civilization remained to be posed. Now it is becoming less and less possible to understand the Minoan civilization without the study of the culture which preceded it. The study of this culture, to which I have applied the name 'Old Europe', reveals new chronological dimensions and a new concept of the beginning of European civilization. It was not a single small legendary island claimed by the sea some 9000 years ago that gave rise to the fabulous civilization of Crete and the Cyclades, but a considerable part of Europe surrounded by the eastern Mediterranean, Aegean and Adriatic Seas. The many islands were an aid to navigation and facilitated communication with Anatolia, Levant and Mesopotamia. Fertile river valleys lured the first farmers deeper inland into the Balkan Peninsula and Danubian

Europe. Old Europe is a product of hybridization of Mediterranean and Temperate southeast-European peoples and cultures.

European civilization between 6500 and 3500 BC was not a provincial reflection of Near Eastern civilization, absorbing its achievements through diffusion and periodic invasions, but a distinct culture developing a unique identity. Many aspects of this culture remain to be explored. One of the main purposes of this book is to present, as it were, the spiritual manifestations of Old Europe. Mythical imagery of the prehistoric era tells us much about humanity – its concepts of the structure of the cosmos, of the beginning of the world and of human, plant and animal life, and also its struggle and relations with nature. It cannot be forgotten that through myth, images and symbols man comprehended and manifested his being.

Though profusely illustrated, this volume does not claim to present every aspect of the mythical imagery of Old Europe; the illustrations were selected from many thousands, with a view to showing the most representative examples and not just the most beautiful sculptures or vases. Basic information is derived from the systematically excavated sites, which are listed with full chronological details at the end of the book. The documentation of the illustrated objects is contained in the Catalogue.

NOTE ON RADIOCARBON AND DENDROCHRONOLOGICALLY
CALIBRATED DATES AND THE CHRONOLOGICAL TABLE

The discovery and development of the radiocarbon dating technique by Willard F. Libby (*Radiocarbon Dating*, 1952) gave archaeology its most powerful means of discovering the age of prehistoric cultures. Within two decades of its development and implementation radiocarbon analysis had revolutionized earlier conceptions of European Neolithic-Chalcolithic chronology, extending its span by almost two millennia. Prior to this, stratigraphic and typological interpretations had been used to support a theory of the spread of agriculture from the Near East to Europe in the fourth millennium BC. The backbone of this universally accepted chronological outline was the postulated Near Eastern derivation of the Vinča culture with its typical fine ceramics, result of a migration from the Near East *via* Anatolia subsequent to the Troy I period, datable, it was believed, by analogies to historic Egypto-Mesopotamian civilization to just after 3000 BC. Vinča was firmly located within the relative chronology of the European Neolithic-Chalcolithic cultures and so through its supposed historic connection became the datum around which the absolute chronology of European prehistory was estimated. This chronological system is still maintained by a small minority of

13

European prehistorians who were encouraged by the recent discovery in an Early Vinča context of the Tărtăria tablets, which they consider to be an import from Mesopotamia at about 3000 B C.

This chronology was completely discredited by radiocarbon analysis, which by 1970 had supplied 300 dates for Old European Neolithic and Chalcolithic samples, placing the beginnings of the Neolithic in the seventh millennium B C. This called for not only a readjustment in the absolute dating of Neolithic-Chalcolithic culture but also an important rearrangement of the relative chronologies of Europe and the Near East.

However, by the early 1960's it became evident that radiocarbon dates were inaccurate. The accuracy of the process was dependent upon the validity of the assumption (among others) that the radiocarbon content of atmospheric carbon-dioxide had remained constant during geologically recent time. Discrepancies between radiocarbon and calendrical chronologies were soon remarked, following the radiocarbon analysis of wood samples of known age from historic Egyptian and Near Eastern sources; and it has since been demonstrated through the marriage of dendrochronological research and radiocarbon analysis that there have been variations in the level of atmospheric radiocarbon through time, and that these are of two sorts: localized fluctuations, and a long-term trend in which the divergence between the radiocarbon and true ages increases with increasing sample age during the millennia B C.

Dendrochronology is the study of the chronological sequence of the annual growth rings in trees. Within the confines of a particular environment the ring patterns of different tree specimens can be matched and related one to another, a technique made possible by the fact that annual rings vary in thickness due to varying local environmental conditions from year to year. So a master-chronology can be compiled incorporating both living trees of great age and dead, preserved trunks which can be fitted into the ring-pattern sequence. The bristle-cone pine of the White Mountains of California has provided an unbroken sequence extending back into the sixth millennium B C. Radiocarbon analysis of ring samples of known age identified the inaccuracy of the radiocarbon dates; and, with the accumulation of sufficient analyses, was able to supply curves and tables of conversion which permit correction of radiocarbon dates to approximate true age. Dates falling between the third and fifth millennia B C in 'radiocarbon years' require a corrective addition, increasingly large with increasing age, of a few hundred to as much as a thousand years to align them with approximate true age. Direct comparison of the radiocarbon content of historically dated samples from ancient Egyptian contexts with that of bristle-cone pine samples of equivalent true age has independently confirmed the validity of the method. Currently archaeologists including the author of this volume use the 'Suess curve' (named after Dr Hans E. Suess, of UCSD) for correction of radiocarbon dates to approximate true age.

Consequently, European Neolithic and Chalcolithic chronology is undergoing a second revolution which extends the span of prehistoric development by a further millennium. The most important effect of radiocarbon chronology and of this marked extension of it to approximate true age has been to demonstrate the antiquity of European prehistoric culture, and its autonomous growth as the equal rather than the dependent of Near Eastern cultural evolution. Socio-economic developments that 20 years ago were compressed into little over one millennium are now seen to have required at least three millennia to evolve, emphasizing the stability, longevity and cultural continuity of the Old European Neolithic-Chalcolithic civilization.

A chronological table of the cultural complexes of Old Europe appears below. The given years represent true age, i.e. radiocarbon dates converted into true age on Suess' calibration curve.

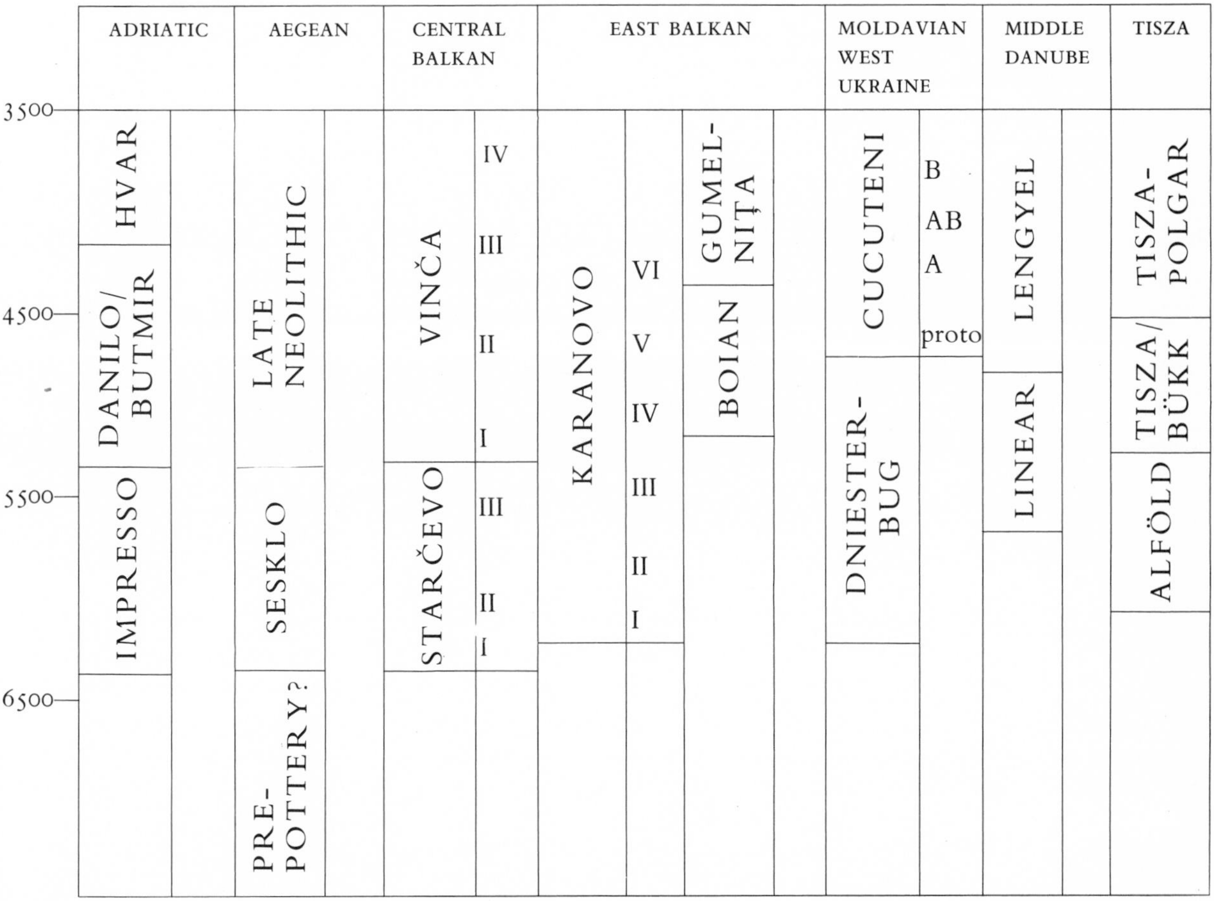

	ADRIATIC	AEGEAN	CENTRAL BALKAN	EAST BALKAN		MOLDAVIAN WEST UKRAINE		MIDDLE DANUBE	TISZA
3500	HVAR	LATE NEOLITHIC	VINČA IV	KARANOVO	GUMEL-NIŢA	CUCUTENI	B / AB / A	LENGYEL	TISZA-POLGAR
	DANILO/BUTMIR		VINČA III		VI		proto		
4500			VINČA II		V / BOIAN			LINEAR	TISZA/BÜKK
			VINČA I		IV	DNIESTER-BUG			ALFÖLD
5500	IMPRESSO	SESKLO	STARČEVO III		III				
			STARČEVO II		II				
			STARČEVO I		I				
6500		PRE-POTTERY?							

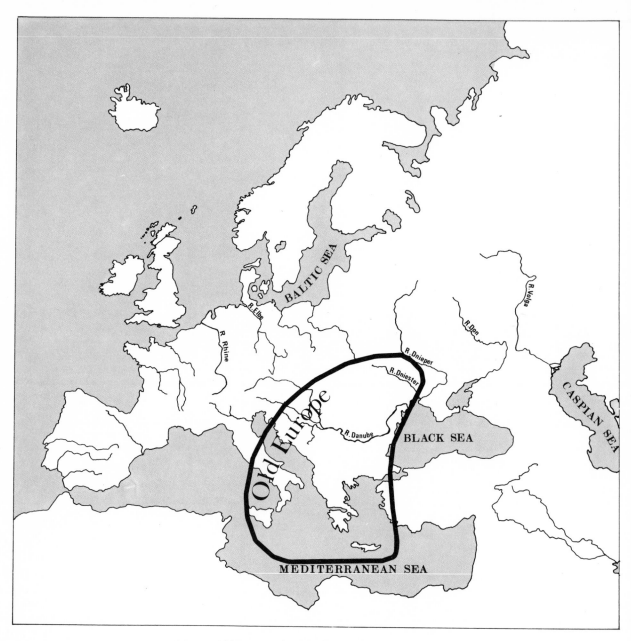

Map I: Old Europe: the area of autochthonous European civilization, c. 7000–3500 BC in relation to the rest of Europe

16

1 Cultural Background

Villages depending upon domesticated plants and animals had
appeared in southeastern Europe as early as the seventh millennium
BC, and the spiritual forces accompanying this change in the economic and social organization are manifested in the emergent artistic
tradition of the Neolithic. The development of a food-producing
economy and subsequent cultural innovations can no longer be
simply explained as an introduction of vaguely designated colonists
from Anatolia or the east Mediterranean. During the seventh, sixth
and fifth millennia BC the farmers of southeastern Europe evolved a
unique cultural pattern, contemporary with similar developments
in Anatolia, Mesopotamia, Syro-Palestine and Egypt. It reached a
climax in the fifth millennium BC.

A new designation, *Civilization of Old Europe*, is introduced here
in recognition of the collective identity and achievement of the
different cultural groups of Neolithic-Chalcolithic southeastern
Europe. The area it occupied extends from the Aegean and Adriatic,
including the islands, as far north as Czechoslovakia, southern Poland
and the western Ukraine. Between *c.* 7000 and *c.* 3500 BC, the
inhabitants of this region developed a much more complex social
organization than their western and northern neighbours, forming
settlements which often amounted to small townships, inevitably
involving craft specialization and the creation of religious and
governmental institutions. They independently discovered the
possibility of utilizing copper and gold for ornaments and tools, and
even appear to have evolved a rudimentary script. If one defines
civilization as the ability of a given people to adjust to its environment and to develop adequate arts, technology, script, and social
relationships it is evident that Old Europe achieved a marked degree
of success.

I

The most eloquent vestiges of this European Neolithic culture are the sculptures, which bear witness to facets of life otherwise inaccessible to the archaeologist: fashions in dress, religious ceremonialism and mythical images.

The inhabitants of southeastern Europe 7000 years ago were not the primitive villagers of the incipient Neolithic. During two millennia of agricultural stability their material welfare had been persistently improved by the increasingly efficient exploitation of the fertile river valleys. Wheat, barley, vetch, peas and other legumes were cultivated, and all the domesticated animals present in the Balkans today, except for the horse, were bred. Pottery technology and bone- and stone-working techniques had advanced, and copper metallurgy was introduced into east central Europe by 5500 B C.

Trade and communications, which had expanded through the millennia, must have provided a tremendous cross-fertilizing impetus to cultural growth. The archaeologist can infer the existence of far-ranging trade from the wide dispersion of obsidian, alabaster, marble and Spondylus shell. The seas and inland waterways doubtless served as primary routes of communication, and obsidian was being transported by sea as early as the seventh millennium B C. The use of sailing-boats is attested from the sixth millennium onwards by their incised depiction on ceramics.

The continued increase in prosperity and in the complexity of social organization would surely have produced in southeastern Europe an urban civilization broadly analogous to those of the Near East and Crete of the third and second millennia B C. The increasing cultural momentum of fifth millennium European societies was, however, cut short by the aggressive infiltration and settlement of semi-nomadic pastoralists, ancestors of the Indo-Europeans, who disturbed most of central and eastern Europe during the fourth millennium B C. The colourful pottery and sculptural art of Old Europe's incipient civilization quickly vanished; only around the Aegean and on the islands did its traditions survive to the end of the third millennium B C, and on Crete to the mid-second millennium B C. The Early Helladic culture of Greece and the Cyclades and the Minoan civilization on Crete, with its wealth of palace art, epitomize the Neolithic and Chalcolithic culture of Old Europe.

REGIONAL AND CHRONOLOGICAL SUBDIVISIONS OF OLD EUROPE

The development of the Neolithic was characterized by an increase in sedentary habits and reliance upon domesticated plants and animals, larger demographic units, a continued growth in artistic and technological sophistication, and a marked regional diversity of material culture.

By 6000 BC, and increasingly through the ensuing millennium, Old European culture can be divided into five major regional variants which display well-developed traditions in ceramic art, architecture and cult organization. The five variant traditions of Old European civilization are: 1) The Aegean and central Balkan, 2) The Adriatic, 3) The middle Danube, 4) The eastern Balkan, and 5) The Moldavian-west Ukranian.

I THE AEGEAN AND CENTRAL BALKAN AREA

Neolithic, c. 7000–5500 BC.

The beginnings of Neolithic art in the Aegean and central Balkan area can be dated to *c.* 7000–6500 BC, along with the emergence of a well-established village society. This earliest Neolithic is known by a different name in each of the modern European countries over which it was distributed, the terminological distinctions reflecting modern political boundaries rather than significant cultural variations. It is known as *Proto-Sesklo* in Greece, where the Sesklo settlement near Volos in Thessaly was the source of Neolithic terminology; *Starčevo* in Yugoslavia after the eponymous site east of Belgrade; *Körös* in southeastern Hungary and *Criş* – the Romanian name for the same River Körös – in western Romania. This complex occupied the drainage area of the Vardar and Morava in Macedonia and southern and central Yugoslavia and the southeastern part of the middle Danube basin, extending as far as Moldavia in eastern Romania. To simplify terminology, this cultural bloc will be referred to as 'the Aegean and central Balkan Neolithic'.

This Neolithic culture left remarkably homogeneous artifacts: bone, stone and ceramic artifacts, including distinctive painted bowls and ring-based jars, all closely resembling each other. Wheat, barley, lentils, vetch and peas were cultivated and among the domesticated animals, sheep and goat were the most numerous, a characteristic feature of the warmer and drier conditions of the Aegean and east Mediterranean. Although the basic economic pattern was faithfully transferred from the south to the middle Danubian basin, Neolithic farmers in northern Yugoslavia, Hungary and Romania had to adapt to a somewhat damper, more heavily forested environment: consequently cattle and pig were increasingly exploited by more northerly settlers, and fishing and hunting usually played a much more important role. The climate was slightly warmer and wetter than it is today. 'Tells', created by the accumulation of cultural debris, attest the permanence of these farming communities on extensive coastal and inland plains in the Aegean area and Bulgaria south of the Balkan Mountains. Further north, they occur less conspicuously, especially in the upper river valleys of central Yugoslavia,

Vienna

Budapest

R. Körös

Kopáncs Hódmezővásárhely
Röske-Lúdvár Kotacpart
Gorza
Nosa

Sarvaš D. Branjevina

R. Sava

Perieni

ALPS

Let

TRANSYLVANIAN

R. Olt

R. Siret

R. Prut

Dniester

Dniester-Bug

Bucharest

Obrež
G. Tuzla Starčevo
Starčevo Padina
Beograd
Cuina Turcului
Lepenski Vir

Smilčić Kakanj
Danilo Obre

Tečić R. Morava R. Nišava

R. Danube

Impresso

**Adriatic
Sea**

Impresso

Gladnice Pavlovac
Rudnik

Zelenikovo Vršnik
Anza

Porodin R. Vardar

Nea
Nikomedeia

Seskl o

BALKAN MTS Azmak
Karanovo

Sofia

R. Marica

Karanovo

**Black
Sea**

PINDUS MTS

Otzaki Souphli
Argissa
Tsani
Tsangli Sesklo
Achilleion Pyrasos

Elateia Chaeronea
Nea Makri

Corinth Athens
Lerna

Amorgos

Aegean Sea

Mediterranean Sea

Knossos
Kato Ierapetra

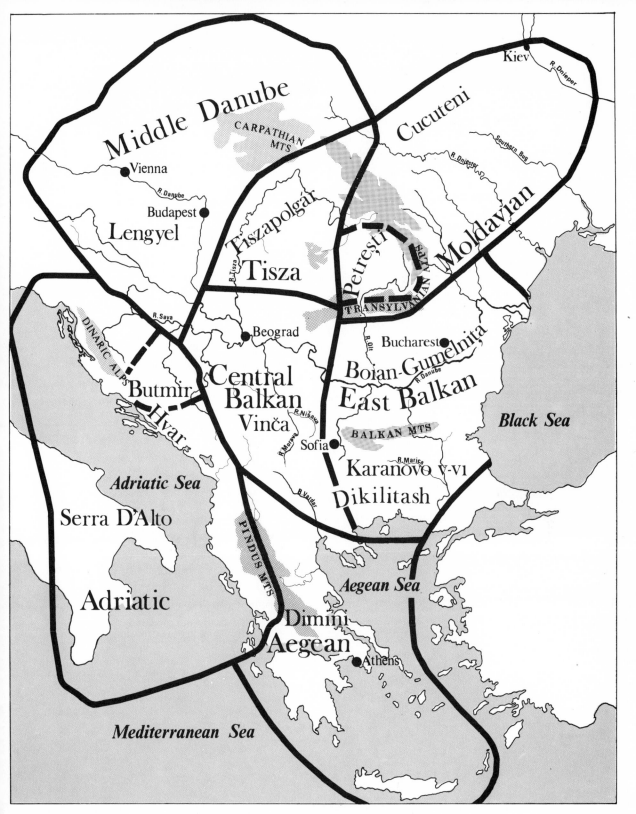

Map II: Distribution of Pottery Neolithic complexes in the Balkan Peninsula and the Danube regions, and sites mentioned in text. Seventh and sixth millennium B C

Map III: Chalcolithic Europe at its climax of development in the fifth millennium B C and its regional groups

Hungary and Romania, where the deposit is usually shallow and more widely distributed. This may reflect a partially horizontal displacement of settlement through time, possibly as a result of semi-nomadic agriculture, involving periodic abandonment and re-occupation of sites. The use of wooden rather than substantial mud-brick structures would also explain the less-marked accumulation of midden deposits in the wetter northerly environments.

II
More than a thousand Proto-Sesklo, Sesklo, Starčevo and Körös (Criş) sites are recorded, of which about fifty have been extensively excavated during the course of the last century. The area of distribution and the names of sites mentioned in the text are indicated in the map. Most of the radiocarbon dates for this complex range from the end of the seventh to the beginning of the fifth millennium BC. Employing the corrective scale produced by radiocarbon analyses of dendrochronologically dated wood samples these dates would yield an approximate true age of 7000–5500/5300 BC.

The process of separating out into regional groups progressed steadily. By 6000 BC, the Sesklo culture of Thessaly and central Greece was typologically distinct from the artifact assemblages of the rest of the central Balkan region. Further north, typical forms of the Starčevo complex persisted into the middle of the sixth millennium, finally undergoing a rapid transition, most clearly reflected
III
in ceramics, to form the Vinča complex.

Chalcolithic, c. 5500–3500 BC.
The Vinča sequence is best documented at the site of Vinča itself, 14 km. east of Belgrade, excavated intermittently between 1908 and 1932 by M. Vasíc. The stratified mound yielded about 12 m. of cultural debris, of which the Vinča remains occupy about 7 m. and the Starčevo, below, a depth of almost 2 m. No other site with such well-defined stratification has yet been discovered, and it has remained the backbone of the skeletal chronology and typology of Vinča assemblages. At Vinča alone, almost 2000 figurines were discovered, by far the greatest number unearthed at a single site. Other important settlements excavated during the last fifty years are indicated on the map, where they are seen to cluster around the modern towns of Belgrade, Vršac-Timişoara, Cluj, Kragujevac,
IV
Priština, Kosovska Mitrovica, Skopje and Štip.

Many settlements of the Chalcolithic period are large, occupying as much as twenty or more acres of river terrace. The houses are of two or three rooms and are organized into streets. Vinča sites such as Pločnik, Potporanj, Crnokalačka Bara, Medvednjak, Selevac, Drenovac, Grivac and Valač must have been townships rather than mere villages.

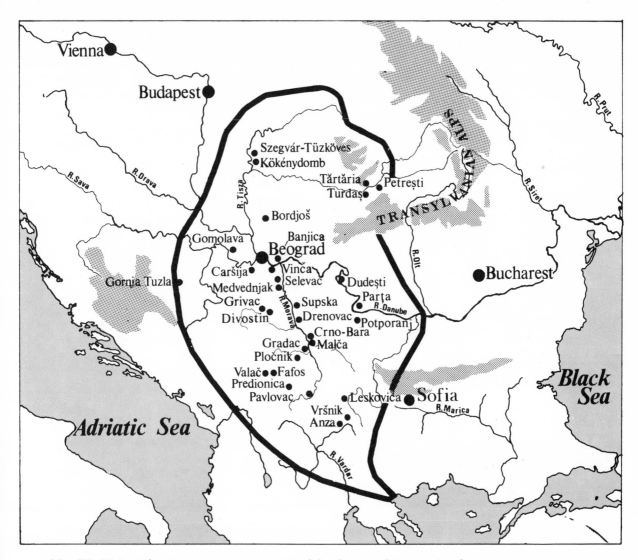

Map IV: Vinča civilization, c. 5300–3500 B C. Areal distribution and sites mentioned in text

Radiocarbon dates converted to approximate true age provide an accurate chronological definition of the southeast European Neolithic and Chalcolithic cultural sequence. This diverges radically from the conservative traditional chronology which maintained that the European Neolithic and Chalcolithic encompassed nothing more than stagnant cultural backwaters, incapable of autonomous innovation and growth. When Professor Vasić first reported the results of his excavation of the Vinča mound in the *Illustrated London News* in 1930, he described the site as 'a centre of Aegean civilization in the second millennium B C'. He believed that the settlement was continuously occupied from about the beginning of the Middle

23

Bronze Age in the Aegean down to the conquest of the area by the Romans. Finally, shortly before he died he asserted that Vinča was rather a colony of the Greeks, and this suggestion continues to be cited in some modern histories of the Balkans. The culture was considered much too advanced, its art treasures too sophisticated, to be of Neolithic or Chalcolithic age, some 7000 years old. The calibrated radiocarbon dates obtained from eight sites of different phases of the Vinča culture (Anza, Predionica, Vinča, Medvednjak, Banjica, Valač, Gornja Tuzla and Divostin) place this culture between 5300 and 4000 B C. The artistic tradition produced in the late sixth and fifth millennium B C in the central Balkan Peninsula is one of the most remarkable and distinctive of European and Near Eastern prehistory.

The discovery of the Tărtăria tablets and other signs inscribed on figurines and pots, coupled with evidence of a marked intensification of spiritual life in general, has nourished a diffusionist explanation. Many would attribute the appearance of the Vinča complex to migration or intensive stimulus-diffusion from the east, in particular from Anatolia. In this context the tablets are believed to have reached the Danube region from Mesopotamia not earlier than about 3000 B C. Despite stratigraphical evidence, typologies, natural scientific dating techniques, and new excavations indicating strong influences from the east Balkans and not Anatolia, some archaeologists persist in viewing the Balkan prehistoric cultures as inferior; and this, even though most of them find no marked cultural hiatus between the Starčevo and Vinča complexes. The first attempts at linear writing appear not later than the mid-sixth millennium B C and the Early Vinča inscribed figurines, spindle whorls and other objects are definitely of local manufacture. The much-discussed problem of the origin of the black-polished and lightly channelled pottery predominant among the Vinča ceramics can be explained by postulating continuous cultural contact and exchange between the central and eastern Balkans: the black-polished wares with channelled decoration were first introduced by the Neolithic inhabitants in the Marica valley of central Bulgaria, during the early phases of Karanovo. The ware spread first to Macedonia and subsequently to the central Balkans during the Karanovo III phase, the true age of which is approximately 5400–5300 B C. Despite constant contact with neighbouring cultures Vinča sculptural art remained markedly distinct from that of other groups. Indeed, the mythical imagery, perhaps more than anything else, reflects the European roots of the Vinča complex.

Due to intensive communication via the prehistoric 'highway' of the Rivers Bosna and Neretva connected by a narrow pass of the Dinaric Alps, a culture of the central Balkan background in Bosnia developed into a separate entity known as *Butmir*, thus named after the Butmir settlement at Sarajevo, excavated in 1893–96; it is noted for its spiral-decorated globular and piriform vases and a significant number of sculptures. The Butmir culture is affiliated with Vinča, but also was strongly influenced by the Adriatic Danilo-Hvar and southern Italian Matera-Serra d'Alto cultures. The key site for chronology is Obre II, excavated in 1967–68 by A. Benac and the author. The site yielded an ideal, uninterrupted four-metre stratigraphy and a series of radiocarbon dates. These place the three periods of the Butmir civilization between *c.* 5100 and 4000 B C.

2 THE ADRIATIC AREA

Neolithic, c. 6500–5500 B C.
The early Neolithic culture of the circum-Adriatic region is known as the Impresso complex, characterized by grit-tempered wares impressed with cardium shells or finger-nails. The simple pottery bowls ornamented in this way and the farming economy which they served are believed to have developed as a result of diffusion, coupled with maritime movement and trade along the Adriatic littoral and off-shore islands. The Impresso culture of western Yugoslavia, western Greece and southern Italy represents only a part of the widely dispersed circum-Mediterranean complex.   V

Impresso sites occupy caves or take the form of open settlements enclosed by a ditch, and their economy was based upon domesticated sheep and cattle, fishing and hunting, and cultivation of wheat and barley. The material culture was poor in ceramic art and sculpture until the production of new forms was stimulated by contact with central Greece, perhaps the result of more extensive maritime activity which is otherwise witnessed by the widespread distribution of obsidian from Lipari, one of the Aeolian islands north of Sicily, and from Sardinia.

Advanced Neolithic-Chalcolithic, c. 5500–3500 B C.
Elaborate red-on-cream painted wares appeared in southern Italy, marking the inception of the *Scaloria* period. This in turn was succeeded by the *Serra d'Alto* period, characterized by baroque handles, 'fruitstand' shapes and other complex ceramic forms. On the Yugoslav coast, there emerged the *Danilo* complex, closely related to Butmir, and characterized by geometrically decorated painted ware and zoomorphic cult vases.

The radiocarbon dates from the earliest Scaloria sites with painted ware cluster around 5500 B C (the average calibrated date is 5550 B C), and for the sites of the advanced stage (Serra d'Alto, Hvar–successor to Danilo) fall within the first half of the fifth millennium B C.

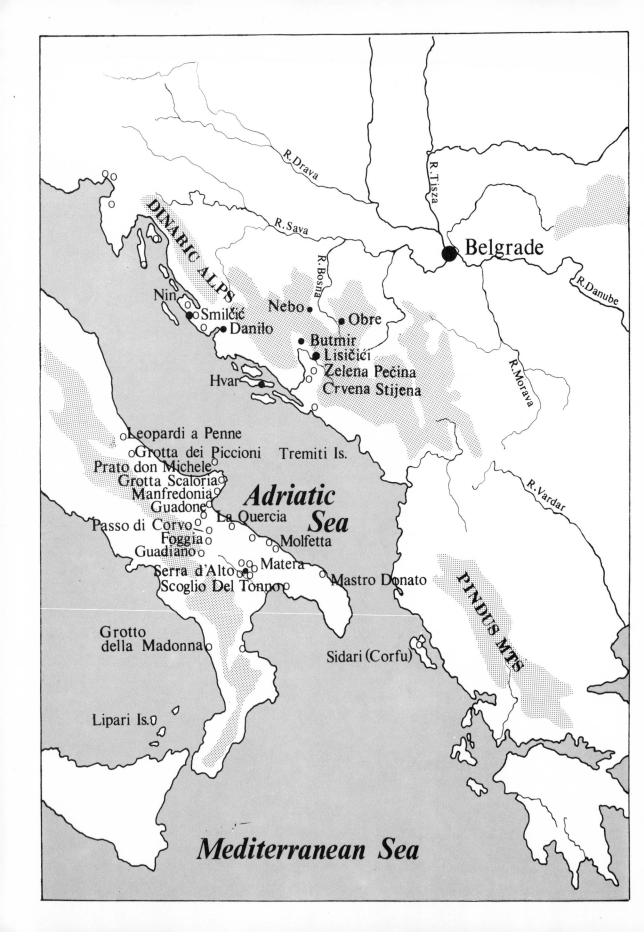

Belgrade

R.Drava

R.Tisza

R.Sava

R.Bosna

R.Danube

DINARIC ALPS

Nin

Smilčić

Danilo

Nebo

Obre

Butmir

Lisičići

Zelena Pečina

Crvena Stijena

R.Morava

Hvar

Leopardi a Penne

Grotta dei Piccioni

Tremiti Is.

Prato don Michele

Grotta Scaloria

Manfredonia

Guadone

La Quercia

Adriatic Sea

R.Vardar

Passo di Corvo

Foggia

Guadiano

Molfetta

Serra d'Alto

Matera

Scoglio Del Tonno

Mastro Donato

PINDUS MTS

Grotto della Madonna

Sidari (Corfu)

Lipari Is.

Mediterranean Sea

Villages in the plains around Foggia and Matera in southeastern Italy were large. The settlement of Passo di Corvo near Foggia occupied approximately 50,000 square metres and included more than a hundred compounds (Tiné 1972). Caves were used as sanctuaries, particularly those with stalagmites and stalactites.

3 THE MIDDLE DANUBE BASIN

Neolithic Central European Linear Pottery, Alföld, Tisza and Bükk complexes, c. 5500–4500 B C.

A fully developed Neolithic culture and economy evolved by about 5500–5000 B C in the Middle Danube Basin and the foothills of the Carpathians. The earliest Neolithic assemblage representing the *Linear Pottery* culture ('*Bandkeramik*') of central Europe and the related *Alföld* group in eastern Hungary reveal strong central Balkan (Late Starčevo and Early Vinča) influence. Nevertheless, the local robust, tall-statured European of 'Cro-Magnon B' type, distinguished by a mesocephalic skull and 'rectangular' face – a very wide mandible and short, straight nose – continued to occupy the area, comprising both the Mesolithic and Neolithic inhabitants. It seems that the local Mesolithic population was gradually converted to an agricultural economy, following the example of the farmers to the south and east. The practice of extensive slash-and-burn agriculture involving periodic resettlement effected the rapid spread of the Neolithic economy among the indigenous population from Holland in the west to Romania in the east. The second stage of Neolithic development is marked by the appearance of the Želiezovce variant west of the middle Danube in Hungary, Slovakia and Austria, the 'music-note' (*Notenkopf*) decorated pottery phase to the north, and the Bükk culture in the Carpathian foothills. The Tisza complex, named after the River Tisza, may have developed from the Alföld Early Neolithic and is contemporary to Early Vinča.

Advanced Neolithic and Chalcolithic Lengyel, and Tiszapolgár and Petreşti complexes, c. 5000–3500 B C.

In prehistoric as in early historic times competitive struggle for occupation of the fertile valleys of the Middle Danube Basin seems to have played a significant role in the culture history of the region. The periodically migrating farmers of the Linear Pottery culture were supplanted by the *Lengyel* complex which has quite different

< *Map V: Adriatic civilization during the Neolithic and Chalcolithic periods, 6500–3500 B C. Butmir sites have a Central Balkan background influenced by the Adriatic civilization. Circles indicate sites of seventh and sixth millennia B C; dots indicate those of fifth and early fourth millennia B C*

architectural and artistic traditions. The Lengyel physical type, the so-called 'Atlanto-Mediterranean', contrasts with the central European Cro-Magnon, although a closely related physical type is known from central Italy. Analogies to the Lengyel complex with its settlements fortified with wide ditches, and its sophisticated painted piriform vases and footed stands, are found in the Danilo complex along the Adriatic coast of Yugoslavia. This may reflect an ethnic infiltration from the Adriatic area to the Sava basin and the region east of the Alps.

VI

The Lengyel sites are distributed over a large territory including eastern Austria, central and eastern Czechoslovakia and southern Poland. The settlements consist of two house types – rectangular timber structures built with upright posts and semi-subterranean dwellings. These villages were located on large flat terraces and surrounded by fortifications, enormous ditches and palisades with towers. Adjacent to their settlement, the villagers cultivated wheat, barley and Italian millet; in addition to tending sheep/goat and keeping dogs they domesticated both cattle and pig and engaged in hunting. Each of these animals also played an important part in ritual practices, judging from the frequent zoomorphic figurines and specially prepared offering-pits which contained aurochs skulls or dog skeletons. Lengyel sculpture retained a unique identity throughout, and so forms a separate unit in the mosaic of Old European art. The classical Lengyel culture in central Europe began some time in the fifth millenium BC, its later period extending into the fourth millennium BC. The ceramic sequence for which a painted period with three sub-phases and an unpainted period with two sub-phases can be recognized, corroborates these widely separated dates.

The *Tiszapolgár* complex in the east Hungarian plain emerged as a successor to the Tisza group. It is also referred to as the Hungarian Early Copper Age because of the occurrence of copper axes, awls and pendants. The complex derives its name from the cemetery of Tiszapolgár-Basatanya in northeastern Hungary with 156 burials near the settlement area. These people of Mediterranean type buried their dead in shallow pits in a crouched position accompanied by large and small vases, copper and shell bead necklaces, copper and gold pendants, flint blades and copper and stone axes. Their ceramic forms – biconical vases and wide bowls on pedestals – are generally related to those of the Lengyel culture, but they did not paint their pottery. The *Bodrogkeresztúr* or Middle Copper Age complex is a continuation of Tiszapolgár and terminated around 3500 BC with the infiltration of the steppe element and East Balkan refugees.

The *Petreşti* group in Transylvania is contemporaneous and culturally closely related to the Karanovo and Cucuteni cultures. Its beginning may have been connected with the northward movement

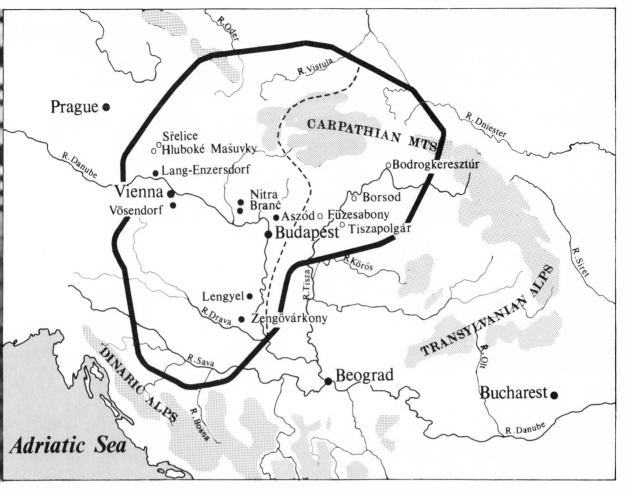

Map VI: Middle Danube and Tisza civilizations. Dots indicate Lengyel sites, circles
Tiszapolgár sites. Fifth and early fourth millennia BC

of the Karanovo people along the River Olt and painted-pottery
peoples from Hungary. The site of Petreşti itself lies near Cluj and its
cultural deposits overlie Early Vinča layers.

4 THE EAST BALKAN AREA

Neolithic, c. 6000 – 5000 BC.

The East Balkan civilization began before or around 6000 BC with
the first appearance of Neolithic occupation along the Marica river
valley of Bulgaria; the most noteworthy sites are Karanovo at Nova
Zagora, Azmak near Stara Zagora, and Kazanlik, all in central
Bulgaria, and Čavdar east of Sofia. In the lowest levels of the tells,
representing the Karanovo I period, rectangular one-roomed houses   VII

29

with wattle-and-daub walls and aligned plank floors were arranged in parallel rows. Their contents proved to be surprisingly advanced, including tulip-shaped vases with a black or white geometric design painted on a red slip, one-handled cups, three-legged cult vessels, marble and clay figurines and a rich bone and stone tool assemblage including numerous mill-stones and sickles of deer antler with inserted flint blades. Plentiful remains of einkorn, emmer, wheat and lentils, and bones of domesticated sheep/goat, cattle and pig confirm the role of agriculture. Although fundamentally related to the central Balkan Neolithic, we have here another distinguishable variant of southeast European Neolithic culture.

The highest Bulgarian tells have a stratigraphic depth of as much as 18 m., composed of accumulated debris from the sixth to the third millennia BC. The stratigraphies defined at the Karanovo, Azmak and Kazanlik tells yield an ideal documentation of the evolution and continuity of material culture over a long period; the Karanovo sequence, phases I to VI, has become universally adopted as a chronological yardstick for the development of East Balkan civilization during the sixth, fifth and part of the fourth millennia BC. A large number of radiocarbon dates from the Karanovo and Azmak tells, representing Karanovo I–III, form an almost perfect sequence; calibrated, they run from the end of the seventh millennium to about 5200 BC.

There was a considerable increase in population during the Karanovo III phase, which must have begun around 5500–5400 BC, when elements of the Karanovo III assemblage were carried, probably by ethnic expansion, northwest into the lower Danube region and southward beyond the Rhodope Mountains to Macedonia and Thrace. In the north the intruders had to confront the settlers of the Central European Linear Pottery culture, who occupied the lower Danube and the Hamangia group on the Black Sea coast.

Chalcolithic, c. 5200/5000–3500 BC.
The East Balkan Chalcolithic is composed of two different cultures: Hamangia on the Black Sea coast, and Marica-Boian-Gumelniţa in Romania, Bulgaria and northeastern Greece.

The *Hamangia* sites are located along the coastal strip of the Black Sea between northern Bulgaria and the western Ukraine. Most information comes from 350 excavated graves of the cemetery at Cernavoda in the lower Danube region (Berciu 1966). Skeletal examination revealed a predominantly Mediterranean population, but with a distinct local brachycephalic component. Their settlements are found on the low terraces of rivers.

The Hamangians practised mixed farming, cultivating wheat and vetch and herding sheep/goat, cattle and pig. The earliest ceramics

Map VII: East Balkan civilization: distribution of Karanovo, Boian–Gumelniţa and Hamangia complexes during the Neolithic and Chalcolithic periods. Hatched area denotes Hamangia complex. c. 5500–4500 BC >

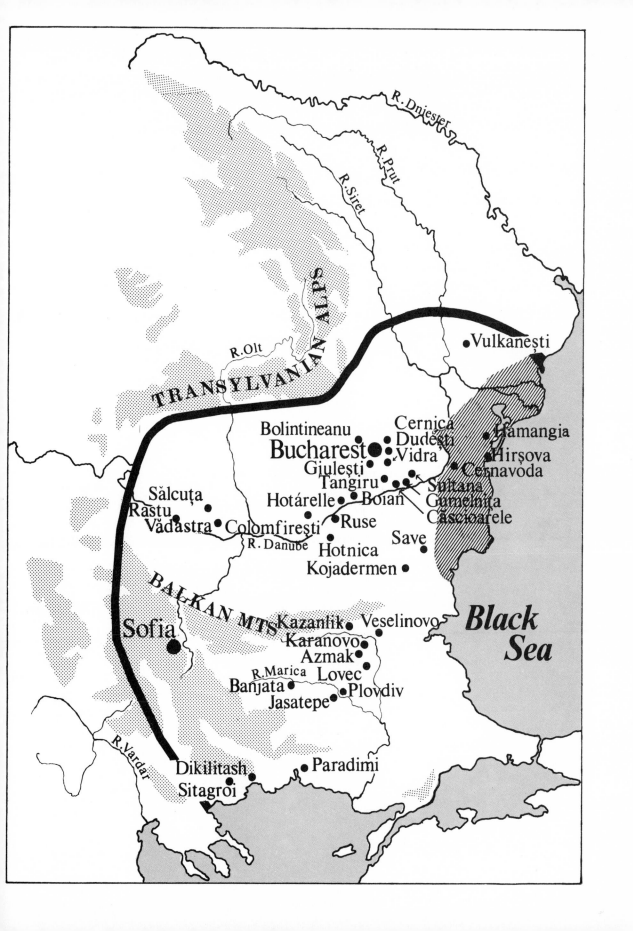

R. Dniester

R. Prut

R. Siret

TRANSYLVANIAN ALPS

R. Olt

• Vulkaneşti

Bolintineanu
Cernica
Dudeşti
• Hamangia
Bucharest
Vidra
Giuleşti
Hîrşova
Tangiru
Cernavoda
Hotárelle
Boian
Sultana
Sălcuţa
Gumelniţa
Căscioarele
Rastu
Vădastra
Colomfireşti
Ruse
R. Danube
Save
Hotnica
Kojadermen

BALKAN MTS

**Black
Sea**

Sofia
Kazanlik
Veselinovo
Karanovo
Azmak
R. Marica
Lovec
Banjata
Plovdiv
Jasatepe

R. Vardar

Dikilitash
Paradimi
Sitagroi

were cardium-impressed. Ornaments, found abundantly as grave goods, include huge bracelets and beads of Spondylus shell. Around the middle of the fifth millennium the Hamangian complex was superseded by the Gumelniţa civilization.

The *Marica* complex represents the southern branch of the East Balkan civilization, named after the River Marica in central Bulgaria.

The *Boian* tradition is a northern variant of the East Balkan civilization. It is named after an island settlement in the Danube south of Bucharest. During its second (Giuleşti) phase, Boian material culture spread as far as Moldavia in the northeast. Skeletons from a large Boian cemetery at Cernica near Bucharest were predominantly of small-statured Mediterranean type. The name '*Vădastra* civilization', derived from a middle layer of the stratified site on the Danube in western Romania, is not a separate culture but a western variant of the East Balkan civilization parallel to the Boian tradition.

The Marica, Vădastra and Boian groups are not different cultures but integral parts of one civilization, which in its advanced stage and climax is known as the *Gumelniţa* civilization.

At least five hundred tells containing Gumelniţa material remains have been recorded in Romania, Bulgaria and eastern Macedonia, of which about thirty have been systematically excavated. The Gumelniţa site itself lies southeast of Bucharest on the Danube and was excavated between 1924 and 1960. Other important sites from Gumelniţa deposits are Căscioarele, Sultana, Vidra, Tangîru and Hîrşova, all in the lower Danube region of Romania, and Ruse, Chotnica and Kodjadermen in northern Bulgaria. In the Marica Valley, in addition to Azmak and Karanovo (VI), known sites cluster around Stara Zagora and Plovdiv. North of the Aegean, the most noteworthy are the recently excavated Sitagroi and Dikili-Tash mounds on the Plain of Drama.

VII

Sedentary Gumelniţa communities occupied compact villages or small townships for a millennium or more, producing deep accumulations of cultural deposit, rich in artifacts. The subsistence economy depended upon the usual crops and domesticates – wheat, six-row barley, vetch and lentils; and cattle, pig, sheep/goat and dog. There was a steady growth in metal-production and trade: copper needles, awls, fish-hooks and spiral-headed pins were produced and, at the end of the period, axes and daggers, a development which is also found in the Vinča, Tiszapolgár, Lengyel and Cucuteni cultures. Workshops of flint, copper, gold, Spondylus shell and pottery have been discovered, implying craft-specialization and general division of labour. Gold was obtained from Transylvania and copper from Carpathian sources.

Gumelniţa fine ceramic vessels are distinguished by the manner in which colour and decorative patterns are blended with exquisite forms, clear evidence of an advanced technique. Graphite painting, which became the dominant method of decoration, required special kilns to provide the prolonged period of reduction necessary to prevent oxidation of the graphite. Shapes range from large decorated storage vessels for grain to cups, profiled dishes, biconical or piriform bowls and amphorae and highly stylized anthropomorphic, zoomorphic and ornithomorphic forms.

Schematism is a characteristic of all East Balkan sculptural art. During the Boian phase, figurine form was bound by rigid conventions, which were subsequently relaxed to permit the increased freedom and versatility displayed by Gumelniţa figurines. Linear signs (possibly writing) were employed by the East Balkan Boian-Gumelniţa civilization throughout its existence.

5 THE MOLDAVIAN–WEST UKRAINIAN AREA

Neolithic, c. 6500–5000 B C.
During the Boreal and Atlantic climatic phases, the black soil region northwest of the Black Sea, intersected by the fertile valleys of the Prut, Siret, Dniester and southern Bug, offered a suitable environment for the inception and development of a Neolithic economy. The *Dniester-Bug* Neolithic culture, comprising permanent village settlements based on agriculture, developed indigenously and was only subsequently influenced from the south and west, in the sixth millennium B C by the Central Balkan (Starčevo) complex, and in the fifth by the East Balkan (Boian) and Central European (Linear Pottery) complexes. The uninterrupted cultural continuum is ideally defined by stratigraphic and typological studies, reinforced by radiocarbon dates, which reveal a Dniester-Bug sequence of three aceramic and five ceramic phases.

Chalcolithic, c. 5000–3500 B C.
The Neolithic culture was succeeded by the twelve consecutive phases of the Chalcolithic *Cucuteni* (Russian: *Tripolye*) civilization. Subsistence was based upon the cultivation of einkorn wheat, domestication of cattle and pig, and intensive hunting of forest fauna and fishing. However, the forest environment made shifting agriculture necessary and consequently there was no accumulation of mound deposits such as are found in Bulgaria and southern Romania. The earliest villages were located on flood-plain terraces and were later established on higher ground during the wetter Atlantic phase. The large Cucuteni villages are always situated on extensive raised river terraces.

VIII

The Cucuteni civilization is clearly affiliated with its southern neighbours of the East Balkan tradition, and forms the northerly outpost of Old European culture, extending as far as the middle Dnieper in the northeast. Ethnically, it appears to have comprised a medley of the indigenous inhabitants and infiltrating Mediterraneans. Southwestern and East Balkan influences played an important part in transforming local ceramic styles, both at the inception and during the evolution of Cucuteni culture, which in its classical period, around 4500–4000 B C, achieved a remarkable artistic maturity in its ceramic products. Characteristic of the Cucuteni peoples are their colourful bichrome and trichrome vases, bowls, ladles, and other pottery forms; equally distinctive are libation jugs, vessels for divination, altars and schematic anthropomorphic and zoomorphic figurines, which reveal an adherence to elaborate ritual practices. Pictorial representations on Late Cucuteni vases are of utmost importance as a source of mythical imagery.

The fortified settlement of Cucuteni in northern Moldavia, after which the culture is named, was excavated in 1909–10 by Hubert Schmidt and in 1961–65 by M. Petrescu-Dîmboviţa. Tripolye on the middle Dnieper was excavated at the end of the nineteenth century by V. V. Khvojka. Almost one hundred years of prolific excavation by Romanian and Soviet archaeologists have made this one of the best archaeologically documented regions in eastern Europe.

The size of Cucutenian (Tripolyean) villages and towns increased during the course of the fifth millennium B C. During the first half of the fourth millennium, the Cucuteni culture developed into an urban civilization. The largest town, near Tal'noe south of Kiev, consisted of about 1,500 houses in an area of 700 acres with a potential population of 20,000 (currently under excavation by N. M. Shmaglij of the Archaeological Institute of the Ukrainian Academy of Sciences, Kiev).

Following the initial excavation of the settlement at Cucuteni, the classical period was called 'Cucuteni A' and the late period 'Cucuteni B'. This terminology survived, although it subsequently required elaboration: an intervening phase is identified as 'Cucuteni AB' and phases preceding Cucuteni A were necessarily termed 'Proto-Cucuteni'. In Soviet literature the 'Tripolye' sequence is divided into A, B and C. The Cucuteni culture continued to the middle of the fourth millennium when it was disturbed and transformed by Kurgen Wave No. 2.

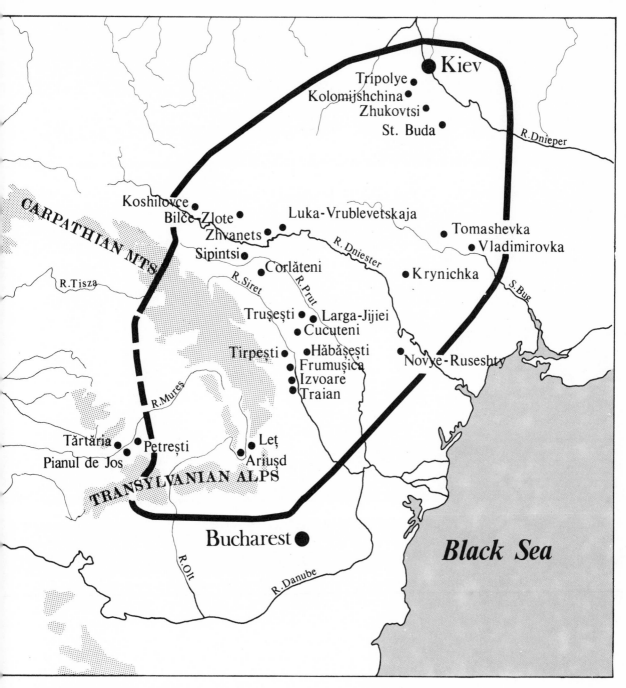

Map VIII: Cucuteni (Tripolye) civilization, c. 5000–3500 BC. The western limit (broken line) is uncertain

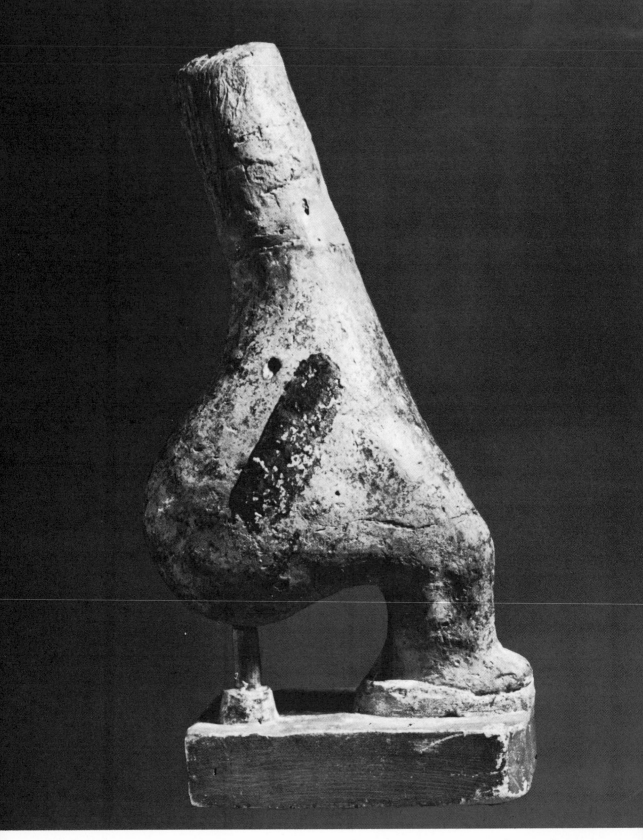

2 Schematized female figure. Hair indicated by incision. Vinča mound. Early sixth millennium BC

2 Schematism

In the earliest level of the Vinča mound, representing the Neolithic Starčevo complex, a ceramic figurine usually described as a 'seated goddess with large buttocks and cylindrical neck' was found. For a female representation it has an extremely reduced form, with no distinction between head and torso, and only a cylindrical neck adjoining the buttocks. Its general shape suggests a bird but there is no indication of wings, beak or bird-legs. Even as a hybrid, perhaps half-woman and half-bird, it needlessly lacks naturalistic detail.

2

This means that we are confronted with the problem of determining the artist's ultimate intention. In the first place we must decide what the sculpture presents, its subject matter; beyond this, we must also try to understand its symbolic content, for only in this way can we hope to comprehend the psycho-social dynamic that inspired its production.

Stratigraphical evidence shows that this figurine dates from roughly 6000 B C, and there are many like it in sites of the same period. Some figurines are even more reduced, rendering the merest outline of human or bird form. Excavation of Neolithic sites has yielded numerous 'bumpy' figurines, often little more than two centimetres long, which archaeologists classify only as indeterminate or ambiguous objects. Examined as isolated, individual pieces they remain enigmatic, their role unknown; but once we identify these miniatures as belonging to a single homogeneous group of figures, they can be recognized as vastly reduced versions of the larger 'steatopygous' figurine-type which will be fully described in later chapters. With these and many larger figures lacking in detail, it is evident that the sculptor was not striving for aesthetic effects; he was producing sculptural 'shorthand', an abstract symbolic conceptual art, images that were emblematic of the divine regardless of the extent of their schematization. The true meaning of the figures can best be sought in the more detailed, less abstracted figurines which reveal the naturalistic detail that betrays subject matter and so brings us closer to understanding the content of the work.

Sculptural 'shorthand', unthinking and repetitive, illustrates the conservative nature of the tradition within which the sculptor worked; each culture translates its basic explanatory assumptions into equivalent form structures and creativity is only expressed in subtle variations from the socially prescribed norms. For the socio-cultural historian it is more important to examine the conventional than the few and slight deviations from it, since his work is to comprehend the inherited and collective – rather than the individual – psyche.

The Neolithic artist's reality – not a physical reality

Both figurine subject matter and the formal repetition of the collectively approved style give an insight into the content and purpose of figurine art. Art reveals man's mental response to his environment, for with it he attempts to interpret and subdue reality, to rationalize nature and give visual expression to his mythologizing explanatory concepts. The chaotic forms of nature, including the human form, are disciplined. While the Cycladic figurines of the third millennium BC are the most extremely geometricized, rigid constraint of this kind, though less marked, characterizes most of the groups of Old European Neolithic and Chalcolithic figures. The artist's reality is not a physical reality, though he endows the concept with a physical form, which is two-dimensional, constrained and repetitive. Supernatural powers were conceived as an explanatory device to induce an ordered experience of nature's irregularities. These powers were given form as masks, hybrid figures and animals, producing a symbolic, conceptual art not given to physical naturalism. The primary purpose was to transform and spiritualize the body and to surpass the elementary and corporeal.

It follows, then, that formal reduction should not be ascribed to the technical inability of the Neolithic artist to model in the round but to requirements dictated by deeply implanted concepts and beliefs. Nevertheless, since we are dealing with an art that has often been termed 'primitive' in a partially pejorative sense, it is necessary to digress briefly in defence of the Neolithic sculptor's ability and to stress that he was not limited to unnaturalistic forms by the inadequacy of his manual skills, the nature of his raw materials or the lack of necessary techniques. In short, old European figurine art was the outcome of skilled craftsmanship, conforming to matured traditions.

The beginnings of pottery manufacture are blurred in the

archaeological record, for the earliest clay vessels and artifacts were unbaked and have not survived. The earliest fired ceramics, including fine burnished and painted wares from the late seventh millennium B C, are articulately modelled and reveal a complete mastery of ceramic technology. Stone and bone was finely carved and ground: Proto-Sesklo and Starčevo villagers in the Aegean area and central Balkans fashioned beautiful spoons of bone and painstakingly ground miniature stone ornaments such as perforated pendants and buttons. The serpentine toad from the site of Nea Nikomedeia in Macedonia is an outstanding work of art of the seventh millennium B C. 171

Stone and bone sculptures are few compared to those of clay, but they show a like degree of stylization, though one might expect them to be, if anything, more schematic still. Two sculptures have been selected to demonstrate this: a typical Early Vinča clay figurine with a triangular masked head, bump for a nose, slanting incised eyes, stump-arms, projecting buttocks and naturalistically modelled breasts 3, 4
and navel; and the marble figurine from Gradac, also of the Early 5
Vinča period. The different raw materials do dictate a differing expression but the figures are alike in style and detail. Both comprise masked heads, arm stumps and inarticulate legs. Other marble sculptures are still more reduced, lacking all facial features. During the fifth millennium, carving in marble became more self-conscious and emancipated itself from the influence of clay-modelling. Bone figures were entirely schematic. A fifth-millennium example of a stylized human figure carved out of bone from a grave in the cemetery of Cernica near Bucharest is a case in point. Its head is 6
broken. The two rounded protuberances apparently portray folded arms. The abdominal and pubic area is emphasized. Although drastically reduced, this little sculpture is probably a portrayal of a Great Goddess in a rigid position, standing in the nude with folded arms, a type encountered in graves throughout the Old European period and in the Cyclades of the third millennium B C. Almost all of the known figurines of copper and gold are schematic, two-dimensional silhouettes of the human body, cut from a flat piece of material.

Throughout the seventh and sixth millennia B C figurine art was clearly dominated by abstract forms such as cylindrical pillar-like necks and a hybrid torso of female buttocks and a bird's body, but at the same time other quite different forms were produced, some of them strikingly naturalistic. An exceptional female figurine assigned to the Sesklo period in Thessaly sits in a relaxed position with her legs to one side, her hands resting on her thighs. In profile the nose is 7,8
exaggerated and beaked but the head and body are naturalistically proportioned, dispensing with the pillar-like neck of earlier sculptures.

3, 4 Female figurine with masked head and stumps for arms. Vinča mound. *c.* end of sixth millennium BC

5 Marble figurine from an Early Vinča site at Gradac, southern Yugoslavia

6 Bone figurine from the cemetery of
Cernica, southern Romania. Late sixth
millennium BC

7, 8 Seated nude figurine from Thessaly.
Sesklo culture, c. 6000 BC

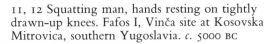

9 Classical Vinča figurine. Schematized above the waist, rounded below. Selevac near Smederevska Palanka, southeast of Belgrade. *c.* 5000 BC

10 Squatting Late Vinča figurine. Incisions indicate dress and punctate design symbolizes snake motif. *c.* second half of fifth millennium BC

11, 12 Squatting man, hands resting on tightly drawn-up knees. Fafos I, Vinča site at Kosovska Mitrovica, southern Yugoslavia. *c.* 5000 BC

THE TREND TOWARDS MORE NATURALISTIC SCULPTURE IN THE CHALCOLITHIC ERA

The gradual trend toward more naturalistic sculpture can be traced in the Vinča statuary. The Vinča mound and other Vinča settlements provide a large group of figurines combining schematization of the upper part of the body with almost naturalistic modelling below. A sculpture from Selevac in central Yugoslavia provides a classic example in this series: the figure has exquisitely modelled abdomen and hips, the legs merging to provide a stable base. The head is schematized, pentagonal, with semi-globular plastic eyes; the arms are represented by perforated stumps. One of the most exquisite sculptures from the Vinča site is a perfectly proportioned squatting woman, unfortunately headless. Another remarkable Vinča sculpture, also headless, from the site of Fafos, depicts a man with knees drawn tightly to his chest, his hands placed on them and his back bent slightly forward. His life-like posture, with the exceptionally accurate modelling of the arms and the hands tightly grasping the knees, is unique in European art of *c.* 5000 BC. 9 10 11, 12

An exquisite rendering of the rounded parts of a female body, especially abdomen and buttocks, occurs occasionally in all parts of Old Europe. An extraordinary series of male sculptures, each individually seated on a stool, is distinguished for perfection in portrayal of the male body, particularly the slightly curving back. 246, 248–250

The excavation of the Butmir site yielded several finely executed heads, remarkable for their realism; the conventional masked features are here replaced by a well-modelled forehead, eye-brows, nose, lips, chin and ears. Unmasked human heads modelled in the round occasionally occur in other cultural groups; even in the Cucuteni area, in which figurine art reached an extreme of schematic symbolism, a few naturalistically rendered human heads were discovered, with eyes, nostrils and mouth shown by impressed holes. Figurines with unmasked heads and human facial features comprise the rarest category of Neolithic and Chalcolithic sculptures.

The finest sculpture was certainly the product of exceptionally gifted members of society, though the varying intensity of individual motivation would also be reflected in the quality of the artifact. Nevertheless the cruder figurines which were the norm were no less rich in symbolic content.

3 Ritual Costume

DECORATIVE MOTIFS ON FIGURINES AS REFLECTION OF COSTUME AND
ORNAMENTS

Decorative motifs frequently occur on figurines to indicate costume,
reflecting the stylistic conventions and characteristics of dress within
the sculptor's society. Late Vinča figurines tell us most about costume
design since they are less abstract than earlier Neolithic figurines and
less conventionalized than those of the East Balkan and Cucuteni
civilizations. Their careful detail, reinforced by less substantial
evidence from East Balkan (Gumelniţa) sculpture, enables us to
reconstruct Old European dress style *c.* 4000 BC.

The usual decorative technique was deep incision, often encrusted with a white paste made of crushed shells, or filled with red
ochre, or black, white or red paint. Alternating dark and light bands,
set either diagonally or vertically, were sometimes produced by this
method, probably to depict a garment made of several broad,
different coloured panels of material sewn together. Plastic relief
decoration was also employed. Applied 'buttons' arranged in one,
two or three rows indicate belts, medallions and necklaces. Both
men and women wore a circular pendant hanging in the middle of
the chest or at the nape of the neck. It may have been an emblem
signifying particular status, or more specifically symbolic of goddesses or gods. The first indications of necklaces on female figurines
are to be traced on the primitive cylindrical Starčevo figurines.
Actual shell, clay, stone and bone heads have been frequently found:
in the Neolithic settlement of Vršnik, near Štip, Yugoslavia, hundreds of shell beads were deposited in a small globular black polished
vase. Numerous beads of shell, alabaster, marble, copper and clay
were recovered from the sites of Chalcolithic Vinča, Butmir, Lengyel, East Balkan, Cucuteni and other cultural groups. Several strings
of beads frequently appear on Cucuteni figurines.

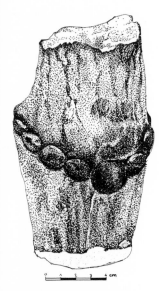

*1 Figurine wearing a hip-
belt made of large and small
discs. Vinča mound. c. 5000
BC*

44

HIP-BELTS

Most captivating are the hip-belts, which have a large button resting on either hip and a third in front of the pubis. The belts were probably fashioned in leather, although some were apparently made of large beads or clay discs. The large buttons may have been manufactured of bone, wood, clay or stone. Mushroom-shaped buttons of white, green or yellow marble, alabaster and calcite, discovered in Vinča settlements, may have served as studs for belts, jackets or other garments of heavy fabric. Figurines wearing large buttons on the hips have been discovered in the deepest layer of the Vinča mound, belonging to the Neolithic Starčevo period, and they continued to be represented in sculpture until the final phase of occupation at the Vinča site. Hip-belts are also portrayed on East Balkan figurines. Female figurines wearing hip-belts appear to be otherwise naked, except for the usual facial masks.

DRESSES

The incised decoration of some figurines indicates long, elegant gowns. They must have been well-fitted to the female body, narrowing at the waist and at the bottom. Breasts, buttocks and legs are well-defined in most sculptures, as if the dress were of light fabric. Commonest are two-piece dresses, consisting of skirt and blouse. The majority of the 'clothed' figurines have incised markings suggesting a blouse of six or more equal panels of material sewn together. It has a simple 'V' neck at front and back and may be sleeveless, short-sleeved or long-sleeved. The blouse or bolero normally extends just below the waist, but seated figurines wear blouses or jerkins extending down to the stool or throne. A suggestion of decorated sleeves appears on some of the most impressive figurines, perhaps implying the portrayal of richly clad goddesses. Above the shoulders a spiral motif is usually encountered, and below it three or more parallel incisions. The Bariljevo seated goddess has a shoulder and sleeve decoration of spirals and two groups of lines. The constricting lines across the middle of the arms and at the wrists of this figure may represent arm-rings and bracelets. A similar constriction appears on the arm of the sculpture from Čuprija, but this figure is unique for another reason: it bears upon its back what appears to be a bag, perhaps a leather pouch for carrying a baby. The bag is suspended over the shoulders and neck by a massive belt or rope which is clearly indicated by an incised applied ridge.

Dress fashions show considerable diversity, and various fabrics and perhaps embroidery can be inferred from the differing zigzag, ladder and net patterns which adorn the blouses. The skirt, discernible on almost all standing and seated figurines in which the

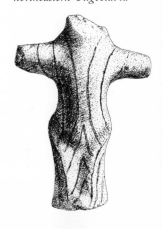

2 Classical Vinča figurine with white-encrusted incisions indicating close-fitting full-length dress. Potporanj site at Vršac, northeastern Yugoslavia

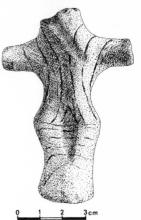

45

13, 14 Late Cucuteni figurine shown wearing five necklaces and a broad belt with fringe at front. Sipintsi (Schipenitz), western Ukraine. Early fourth millennium BC

15 Late Cucuteni figurine wearing two necklaces and a hip-belt above the exaggerated and decorated pubic area. Bilcze Zlote, western Ukraine. Early fourth millennium BC

16 Upper part of large figurine wearing a mask marked with triple lines under eyes and meanders on top and a medallion. Fafos II at Kosovska Mitrovica. Vinča culture, *c.* 4500 BC

17 'The masked lady of Bariljevo' near Priština, southern Yugoslavia, wearing elaborate dress with constricted sleeves and a medallion. Originally seated on a throne. *c.* 4500 – 4000 BC

18, 19 Late Vinča figurine from Crnokalačka Bara near Niš, Yugoslavia, wearing tight skirt of cross-hatched design with 'folds' at bottom. Rectangular panel at back of the shoulders suggests a scarf or is purely symbolic

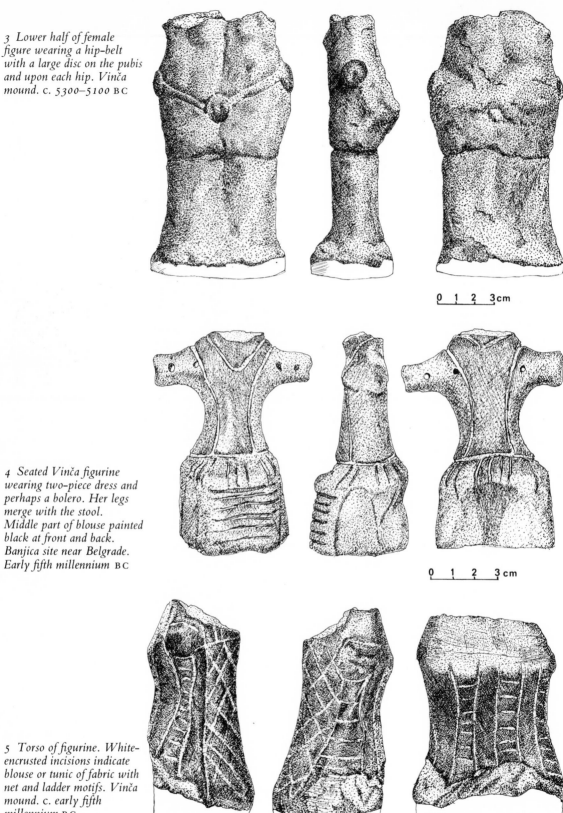

3 Lower half of female figure wearing a hip-belt with a large disc on the pubis and upon each hip. Vinča mound. c. 5300–5100 BC

0 1 2 3cm

4 Seated Vinča figurine wearing two-piece dress and perhaps a bolero. Her legs merge with the stool. Middle part of blouse painted black at front and back. Banjica site near Belgrade. Early fifth millennium BC

0 1 2 3 cm

5 Torso of figurine. White-encrusted incisions indicate blouse or tunic of fabric with net and ladder motifs. Vinča mound. c. early fifth millennium BC

0 1 2 3cm

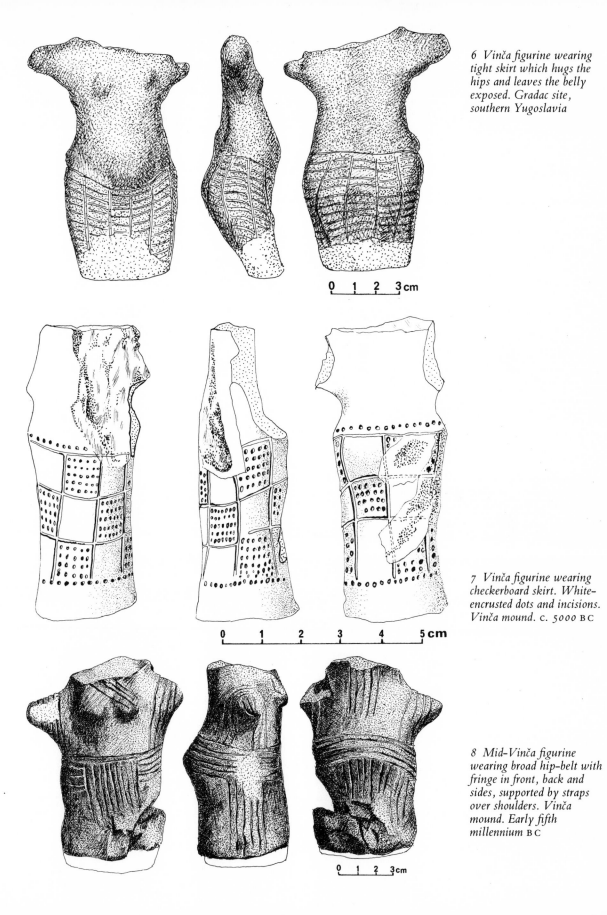

6 *Vinča figurine wearing tight skirt which hugs the hips and leaves the belly exposed. Gradac site, southern Yugoslavia*

7 *Vinča figurine wearing checkerboard skirt. White-encrusted dots and incisions. Vinča mound. c. 5000 BC*

8 *Mid-Vinča figurine wearing broad hip-belt with fringe in front, back and sides, supported by straps over shoulders. Vinča mound. Early fifth millennium BC*

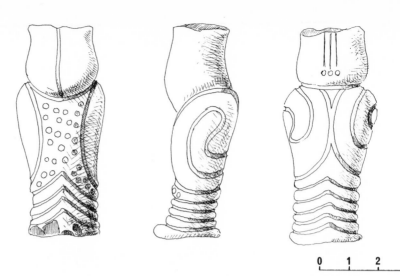

0 1 2 3cm

9 Lower half of a Vinča figurine shown wearing a spiral-decorated narrowing skirt which ends in folds. Dotted pattern in front may represent an apron. Beletinci at Obrež, district of Sremska Mitrovica, northern Yugoslavia

lower torso is preserved, is the most elaborate form of attire. The belly is almost always exposed; the skirt, not necessarily sewn or attached to the blouse, generally begins below the waist-line, hugging the hips. The white encrusted incisions reveal net patterning, horizontal lines divided into sections, checker-boards, dots, spirals and meanders. The skirt usually narrows below the knees, where ornament either terminates or changes into parallel lines. An apron was sometimes worn over the skirt, with a fringe or tassels indicated around the apron sides and at the back. As a rule, Vinča, Gumelniţa and Cucuteni figurines wear hip-belts, sometimes supported by shoulder straps and fringed at the front, back and sides.

The long skirt usually reaches to the toes but in a number of figurines legs and feet are visible, either naturalistically portrayed or with indications of cloth covering. Clear definition of breast and navel suggests that the seated figure from Čaršija wears no clothing above the waist. Below the belly, a dotted apron with tassels or skirt fringe on each side covers her lap. The figure's fat legs seem to be bound, perhaps with thongs or woven bands, but are probably otherwise bare. Other figurines clearly reveal draped cloth and wrappings around the legs and the skirt was possibly slit below the knees and fastened with woven bands, ribbons or thongs. On a fine example from Crnokalačka Bara a skirt is incised with vertical lines, its hem indicated by a horizontal line. Below the hem are two double lines passing around the front of each leg, presumably representing binders of woven material. The costume this figure wears gives an impression of constraint and restricted movement. Many figurines

5, 7

9

8

20

21

50

have curving diagonal incisions over the legs suggesting folds at the hem of the skirt, or ribbons securing and folding up the hem beneath the skirt.

MEN'S COSTUME

Male sculptures are usually portrayed nude in a standing or sitting position, but some wear emblems, pendants or collars. Late Cucuteni figures wear a hip-belt and a band or strap passing diagonally over one of the shoulders and across the chest and back.

One category of Vinča male figurines appears fully dressed in 'sailor blouse' and knickers. A broad V-shaped collar may depict a blouse or something worn over a blouse. Two or three incisions above the shoulders are either a decorative motif or an emblem. A grotesque standing masked man from the Vinča site of Fafos at Kosovska Mitrovica is of considerable interest: he wears padded knickers, and his belly is exposed and his hands, now broken, probably were on his hips.

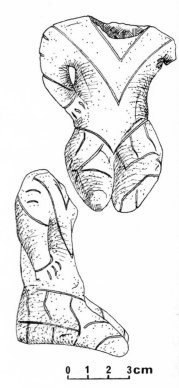

11 Late Vinča seated male? figurine from Valač, southern Yugoslavia, shown in blouse and knickers. White-infilled incisions indicate dress. Broad V-shaped collar painted in red, probably of symbolic nature

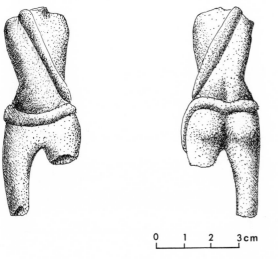

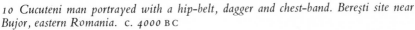

10 Cucuteni man portrayed with a hip-belt, dagger and chest-band. Berești site near Bujor, eastern Romania. C. 4000 BC

12 A decorated shoe, probably leather. East Balkan Gumelniţa complex. Vidra, lower Danube, Romania. c. 4500 BC

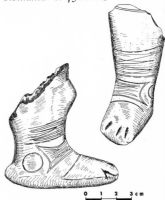

FOOTWEAR

Figurines produced during this period in the Balkan Peninsula do not reveal details of footwear. Some sculptures clearly show bare feet with toes indicated, but in only exceptional cases were shoes portrayed by incision or by modelling.

20 Seated Vinča figure from Čaršija, central Yugoslavia, wearing hip-belt, dotted apron in front and side fringes. Leg-bindings just below knees and calves. Topless except for goddess emblem or V-shaped collar

21 Late Vinča figurine wearing tight skirt. Two double lines passing around legs indicate leg-bindings. Light brown fabric with white-encrusted incisions. Crnokalačka Bara, southeastern Yugoslavia

22 Legs covered by skirt folds characterize this large Vinča figure. Red paint on bare toes. Viňca mound. Mid-fifth millennium BC

24, 25 Grotesque masked figurine with 'padded knickers' and exposed belly from Fafos I at Kosovska Mitrovica, southern Yugoslavia. First half of fifth millennium BC

23 Upper part of a Late Vinča figurine from Pločnik, southern Yugoslavia, wearing broad, red, V-shaped collar. Sleeves constricted below shoulders and three incisions on each shoulder. The mask is marked with V signs and parallel lines. c. late fifth millenium BC

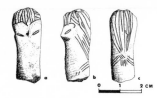

13 *Cylindrical head with long hair neatly combed and bound at the end. Starčevo layer of the Pavlovac site, southern Yugoslavia. Early sixth millennium* B C

14 *Masked head from the Vinča mound showing hair divided into two panels by a hair-band. First half of fifth millennium* B C

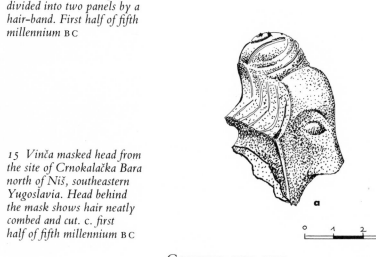

15 *Vinča masked head from the site of Crnokalačka Bara north of Niš, southeastern Yugoslavia. Head behind the mask shows hair neatly combed and cut.* C. *first half of fifth millennium* B C

COIFFURE AND CAPS

Although the face is certainly masked on a majority of the figurines, long free-hanging hair falling down the back to just below the shoulders is often evident behind the mask. Long hair, carefully indicated even on the schematized examples, characterizes the cylindrical figurine heads of the seventh and sixth millennium B C, and special attention to coiffure persisted throughout the duration of the Vinča culture. A masked head from Vinča itself shows the hair divided into two symmetrical panels by a central ribbon, attached, at back and front, to a second ribbon that passes around the crown of the head, disappearing at the back where it is overhung by hair. This hair-style, interpreted as 'plumage' by Vasić, is indicated by incision. Many of the later Vinča figurines indicate hair very neatly combed, parted and cut, descending to below the ears. Some have a band around the crown of the head. A category of Cucuteni nude or semi-nude female figurines has 'pony-tails' which fall to the waist-line and end in a large bun. East Balkan miniature sculptures indicate very

13

14

15

16

54

elaborate coiffures consisting of double-spiral coils round the head. Some figures, male and female, wear peculiar conical caps, hoods or pointed coifs, which are decorated with radial incisions and extend over the mask. The most celebrated of such figurines, wearing a tiered conical cap, is the little man (or woman) from the site of Vinča. Pointed caps must have been widely in fashion during the sixth and fifth millennium BC throughout southeastern Europe. Elaborate coiffure and crown or turban appears only on Bird and Snake Goddess figurines.

SUMMING UP

The costume detail preserved on clay figurines attests a particular richness in the style and ornament of female and male garments during the fifth and early fourth millennia BC. Comparable indication of dress on figurines of the seventh and sixth millennia BC is rare, but sufficient to affirm the presence of hair-styles, hair ornament, bead necklaces, pendant medallions and hip-belts.

In the female costume of the Vinča and East Balkan cultures several dress combinations recur persistently: fully dressed figures wear blouses and tight skirts, or long dresses, and possibly boleros; the others wear either skirts which hug the hips or hip-belts supporting aprons or a long skirt-like fringe, leaving the navel and upper half of the torso exposed. Long, tight and richly ornamented skirts are characteristic of all cultural groups.

At least two forms of attire are discernible on male figurines: some are dressed in decorated blouses with trousers extending below the knees, while others wear only belts or shorts and chest bands. The men's blouses characteristically display broad V-shaped collars.

Necklaces, exclusive to female costume, were strung with beads of Mediterranean or Adriatic shell, stone, bone, copper or clay; equally popular were clay pendants, and arm-rings and bracelets of shell, bone and copper, worn by both male and female figurines.

The richly clad figurines are probably not meant to depict ordinary villagers; they are more likely to personify specific goddesses or gods, or represent worshippers or priests attending rites, garbed appropriately in masks and festive costume.

Much that typifies costumes worn during the fifth and fourth millennia in Balkan Europe can be readily recognized in the illustrations of goddesses and worshippers preserved on Minoan frescoes, statuary, seals and signet rings of the second millennium BC. The exquisite Minoan female costume may represent the culmination of a tradition which began in Neolithic-Chalcolithic Europe. Like the sculptured deities or worshippers of their Balkan predecessors, the Minoan goddesses and their votaries always wear lavishly decorated skirts of various designs and colours. Topless fashions were popular

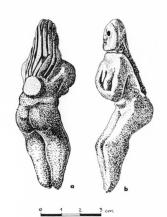

16 Nude Cucuteni figurine with long hair ending in a large round coil. Krynichka, Podolia, western Ukraine. c. early fourth millennium BC

17 Miniature Mid-Vinča masked head, wearing a conical cap decorated with chevrons. Vinča mound. 5000 – 4500 BC

55

in both periods and so were necklaces and arm-rings. Wide-open blouses and bolero-shaped jackets, typical and distinctive in Minoan female dress, had been worn by Vinča and East Balkan women. Individuals having important roles in ritual celebrations and dressed as goddesses and gods were the most extravagantly clad in both periods. However, some difference can be noted: where the Minoan skirt was flounced, that of the Balkan Neolithic-Chalcolithic was close-fitting.

Essentially the same tradition continued from the Bronze Age to the time of classical Greece. On vases of the sixth and fifth centuries BC gods appear in sleeved decorative robes; Dionysus wears one on black-figure vases and so does Andromeda on a *krater* of the fifth century BC, although sleeved robes had become unfashionable by that time (Bieber 1939: Figs. 43, 63). Minoan, Mycenaean and ancient Greek festival attire is an inheritance from the Old European civilization. The parallelism is striking.

What was the origin of the exquisite Old European costume? There is no reason to assume that this surprising sophistication of c. 5000–3500 BC was an imported element, stimulated by Anatolian-East Mediterranean fashions: like the Vinča and East Balkan script and ceramic designs, Old European costume design developed within a local tradition. This is not to say that Europe was culturally isolated from the Anatolian-Mediterranean world, for generalized stylistic similarities imply intermittent cultural contact and exchange.

Only limited comparison is possible between the costume of Old Europe and other parts of the civilized world – Anatolia, Mesopotamia, Syro-Palestine and Egypt – because nowhere else were garments so frequently illustrated on figurines before 4000 BC. A few Mesopotamian figurines, dating from the Halaf and Ubaid periods of the fifth and fourth millennia, display necklaces, belts or short skirts and chest bands (Dales 1963: 21), which are analogous to typical Balkan attire.

During the seventh and sixth millennia BC there was a marked resemblance between European and Anatolian ceramic products, including figurine art and its associated costume fashions. Most of the figurines of this period from Çatal Hüyük and Hacılar in central Anatolia are portrayed nude, but in Hacılar some wear shorts or belts with aprons at front and back (Mellaart 1960: Figs. 6, 9–11, and 14), while others appear to wear blouses or dresses indicated by vertical and horizontal painted lines, display elaborate hair-styles, and wear conical caps (Mellaart 1960: Figs. 13 and 18).

4 The Mask

NON-HUMAN VISAGE

The mask was not invented by the earliest agriculturists; it is as old and as universal as art and religion. Neolithic man followed a tradition established by his Palaeolithic forebears, adapting the mask to his own modes of ritual and artistic expression. Each of the cultural groups included in this study possesses a characteristic style of figurine art, and common to each style is the portrayal of masked faces devoid of realistic facial features.

Cucuteni art evidences little interest in the human head. Early Cucuteni figurine heads are disproportionately small and schematic in relation to the body, and later become almost disc-shaped, with two large eyes, or frequently – on male figurines – only a single eye. The eyes, holes pierced through from the back of the head, are the only indication of facial features; there is no mouth. The uniformity of this figurine type, found widely distributed over the western Ukraine and east Romania, suggests that enduring conventions, rooted in popular religious beliefs, dictated aesthetic values.

13, 14

The heads of East Balkan figurines are typically either beaked and narrow or unnaturally broad, with large noses and perforations in the mouth and ear areas for attachments. To us they appear unfamiliar, even ugly (cf. Pl. 207), presenting an uncomfortably non-human visage suggestive of a mask.

THE VINČA MASK

The Vinča artist attached particular importance to the mask and it is the distinctive and unusual features of his sculptural masks that render Vinča statuary so unique. The Vinča figures, modelled less schematically and displaying a greater variety of forms than their East Balkan, Middle Danubian or Adriatic counterparts, are the key to the interpretation of Balkan Neolithic-Chalcolithic sculptures.

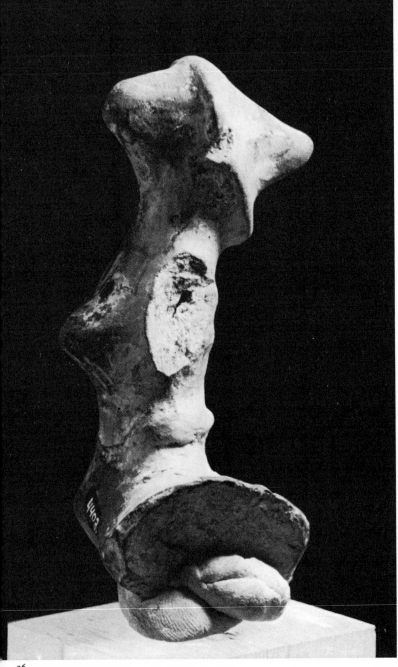

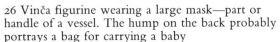

26

27

28

29

26 Vinča figurine wearing a large mask—part or handle of a vessel. The hump on the back probably portrays a bag for carrying a baby

27 Naturalistically depicted masked head from the Vinča mound. 5000 – 4500 BC

28 Late Vinča head with coiffure and coffee-bean eyes. The truncated lower part of the face ending in a sharp triangle shows it to be a mask. Predionica near Priština, southern Yugoslavia. c. 4500 – 4000 BC

29 Vinča head from the site of Crnokalačka Bara, southern Yugoslavia. c. 5000 – 4500 BC

30 Mask modelled in relief upon the neck of a vase from the site of Gladnice, near Priština, southern Yugoslavia. Starčevo culture. Early sixth millennium BC

31 Animal mask (ram?) from Vinča site at Gradac, southeastern Yugoslavia

32 Stylized animal mask from Late Vinča site at Pločnik, southern Yugoslavia, marked with triple lines. 4500 – 4000 BC

Vinča figurines are demonstrably masked; on many of them the mask is clearly outlined, its angular projections extending clear of the face which it conceals. It is this evidence, supplied by the detailed three-dimensional modelling of the Vinča heads, which sustains the more equivocal assertion that the schematic East Balkan and Cucuteni figurines are also masked.

In very few of the Vinča figures is the face depicted in the round: most conform to a stylized facial representation which clearly suggests a mask. The evidence for this being strictly formal, the purpose of this chapter is to display the range of variation of the masks and to delineate their formal evolution within the life-span of Vinča art and of its ancestry.

It is almost unbelievable that during the thirty or more years in which essays treating Vinča art have appeared, there has been no sustained reference to the mask, its most captivating element. The contours of the mask are evident in profile view of many of the better preserved heads. The facial triangularity or pentagonality, or the protruding angular 'cheek-bones' have been remarked by Vasić, Srejović and others, but that this points to a mask and the dominant part it played has only been acknowledged incidentally.

26, 27

Srejović (1965: 35) ascribed the flat decorative faces of the Vinča figurines to a trend towards stylization: 'The elaborate ornamental patterns and shading had to compensate visually the loss of the three-dimensional, sculptural representation of the human figure.' But there was no need of 'compensation' in this sense, for the Vinča artist was amply capable of producing fine sculpture in the round. It is in these figures that the elaborated mask representation reaches its most complex and dramatic form.

The Vinča artist was clearly not motivated to show individualized facial features. Nevertheless there does exist a variety of so-called 'naturalistic' heads, some of which show neatly combed hair and 'dreamy' half-closed eyes. Do these nonconforming examples represent realistic facial modelling, without the imposition of a mask? One of the best known and most naturalistic among them is the 'little man of Vinča', wearing a conical cap. His face is well-proportioned, with fully detailed facial features. However, viewed from the back even this exceptional figure reveals an unnatural protrusion of the 'cheek-bones': it too may be masked, despite the appealing humanity of its features. Other similar small figurines portraying men with pointed heads, wearing caps or hoods, are clearly masked. The same is true of the distinctive, exceptionally well-modelled heads found in the Kosovo Metohije province near Priština, products of the Late Vinča period. One of the most aesthetically pleasing is the head from Fafos. Another example is the head from Predionica, near Priština: its hair is indicated, the eyes are 'coffee-bean' shaped. The massiveness of the nose, dominating the face, gives a false impression of masculinity, the coiffure being that of a woman. One is struck by the uncompromising lines of the jaw: dominated by the nose, the lower part of the face is truncated immediately below it, lacking any indication of a mouth. The cheek-bones and chin project unnaturally. A head from Crnokalačka Bara is rendered with semicircular plastic eyes, large nose and sculpted hair. The clear demarcation of forehead and hair, the stylized spiraliform ears and the rows of stabbed impressions, which may have facilitated some sort of attachment, all imply that this is a masked head. The spiral of the ear is an extension of the facial mask. Animal masks with horns or ears from the Vinča culture are exquisitely stylized.

28

29

31, 32

EVOLUTION OF THE VINČA MASK

In the Neolithic period masks were modelled in relief on cylindrical figurines or upon the necks of large vases. Cylindrical Proto-Sesklo, Sesklo and Starčevo figurines wearing clearly defined masks are known from the sites in eastern and western Thessaly and from Yugoslavia. They are diamond-shaped, oval or roughly triangular with the lower part rounded. One of the finest examples of a mask modelled in relief on a vase was unearthed at the Starčevo settlement at Gladnice in southern Yugoslavia. A cylindrical sanctuary idol from Porodin, southwestern Yugoslavia, wears an impressive beaked mask with huge semi-spherical eyes, modelled in relief. These forms suggest that the masked design was an early tradition of southeastern Europe which was sustained through the millennia, and integral with the spiritual foundations of the society it nourished.

In the mid-Vinča period (7.5–6 m. deep in the Vinča mound) the masks become pentagonal, incorporating the characteristically protruding angular 'cheek-bones', a long and more clearly defined nose and huge incised or raised semicircular eyes with bow-shaped brow-ridges.

The pentagon or broad triangle remained the basic facial outline throughout the Late Vinča period. Some masks, dominated by large, slanting semi-spherical eyes with a border of exaggerated lashes, incised and white-encrusted, give an impression of 'all-seeingness'. Others, with apparently half-closed or closed eyes and no indication of eye-lashes express a pensive or dreamy mood.

At its culmination Vinča art applied a pictorial method to its sculpture, and masks acquired an extravagant appearance due to the arbitrary imposition of an inorganic expression. Decoration took the form of incision and painting and the ornamentation of masks became a pursuit with its own artistic interest, independent of the sculptural presentation of the mask. This reoriented interest in mask

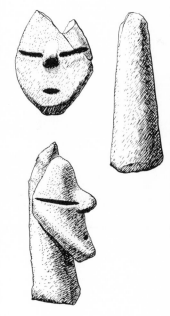

0   3 cms

18 Mask and phallic stand from Achilleion, Farsala, Thessaly. Sesklo culture. c. 6000 BC

34 Chimney-shaped figurine with beaked mask of Bird Goddess originally attached to the roof of shrine model. Porodin near Bitola, southern Yugoslavia. Central Balkan Neolithic. Early sixth millennium BC

35 Masked and crowned head on a cylindrical neck. Fragment of a statuette from the Neolithic mound of Porodin near Bitola, southern Yugoslavia. Central Balkan Neolithic, Starčevo complex. Early sixth millennium BC

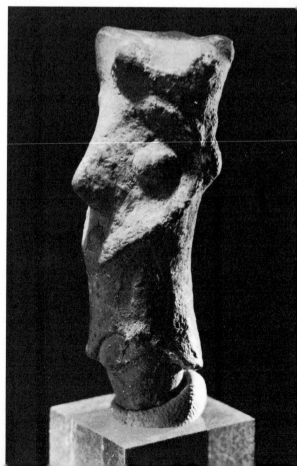

33 Female figure wearing a pentagonal beaked mask. From Vinča mound. Classical Vinča period. 5000 – 4500 BC

36 Black burnished Vinča head (mask) with enormous semicircular eyes, white-filled incisions and red painted bands at top corners and centre. Medvednjak site. Smederevska Palanka, southeast of Belgrade. *c.* 5000 BC

38 Net and two-line ornamented mask from Predionica, near Priština, southern Yugoslavia. Vinča, 4500 – 4000 BC

39 A monumental head, striated triangles above eyes, triple lines below. From Predionica, near Priština, southern Yugoslavia. Viňča, 4500 – 4000 BC

37 Upper part of a figurine wearing a large mask with slanted semispherical eyes and eyelashes marked by white-filled incisions. Crnokalačka Bara, southeastern Yugoslavia. Vinča, *c.* 5000 – 4500 BC

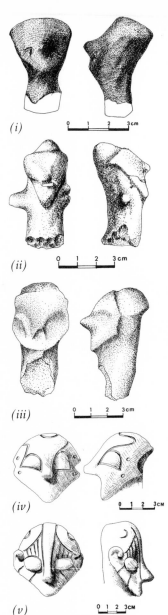

(i)

(ii)

(iii)

(iv)

(v)

19 Typology of central Balkan Starčevo and Vinča masks: (i) roughly triangular (Starčevo); (ii) triangular (Early Vinča); (iii) pentagonal, undecorated (Mid-Vinča); (iv) decorated pentagonal with semicircular eyes in relief (early Late Vinča); (v) pictorial with almond-shaped eyes (Late Vinča)

surfaces dictated the modelled form, and masks consequently assumed the shapes of very broad triangles, or peaked ovals or lozenges. This development is evident in masks found at the sites of Valač and Predionica, located in Kosovo Metohije, southern Yugoslavia. Almond- or egg-shaped slanted eyes typify this series of masks of the Late Vinča culture, and the diamond shape replaces the pentagonal. Many of these pieces have a strictly geometric ornamentation, usually striations, diagonal incisions, with the mask divided into equal sections by the centrally placed line of the eyes. Vertically-striated triangles above the eyes and several deep white-infilled incisions below the eyes replace the long lashes of the other masks. This motif probably derived from an ideographic marking. The most striking sculptures, symbolizing the ultimate development of Vinča art, are the monumental, almost life-size heads from Predionica, each wearing a mask ornamented with large, elliptical-shaped eyes. The ornamental design and the peaked, striated triangles and incised diagonal lines above and below the eyes relate them closely to the type discussed above. But these faces are better proportioned; like the best of modern sculpture they give an impression of monumental solidity. The widening of the mask follows the slanting line of the eyes, while its projection at the eye corners is suggestive of ears. Was it the sculptor's intention to portray on the mask an animal or half-animal, half-human creature? Though we cannot know for certain, we feel that the creature is endowed with an awe-inspiring power, the very essence of the significance of the mask – a proposition which will be discussed in later chapters.

It will be seen, then, that the Vinča masks can be subdivided into five main developmental stages: *i.* Roughly triangular, belonging to the Starčevo and earliest Vinča periods (appearing from a depth of 9.3–8.3 m. in the Vinča mound). *ii.* Triangular, belonging to the Early Vinča period (as high as 7.3 m. in the Vinča mound). *iii.* Undecorated pentagonal, typical of the middle phase of Vinča development (from *c.* 7–5 m. deep at Vinča). *iv.* Developed pentagonal, with large, raised semicircular eyes; ornamented (5–3 m. deep at Vinča). *v.* Pictorial with almond-shaped eyes (see Fig. 19).

DECORATION AND PERFORATIONS FOR ATTACHMENT

Frequently occurring perforations of the mask and a flattened crown of the head imply that the figurines carried some sort of organic attachment which has not survived. Plumes, fruits, flowers, woven bands and other materials could have been employed in this way, and we may legitimately try to imagine these sculptures colourfully adorned with elaborate crowns. In fact, on a few figurines there is a suggestion of a crown or halo. Since a majority of the Vinča masks

64

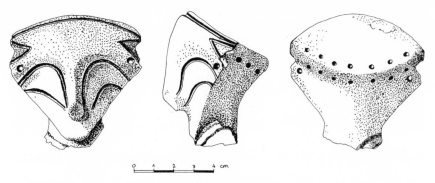

20 Terracotta head of a figurine from the Vinča mound wearing a broad, triangular stylized mask. It has seven pairs of perforations for attachments which have not survived. Late Vinča

appear to imitate bird-like features, the employment of plumage as decoration would not be unnatural. Ethnographic data from the Balkan Peninsula lend support to this assumption, for even today masks used for annual festivals are decorated with plumes. In contemporary western Bulgaria, for instance, bird masks have very elaborate crowns of colourful plumage, while other masks bear rams' or bulls' horns. Minoan figurine masks are crowned with birds, horns, poppies, pomegranates, or even snakes with their heads projecting above the crown (cf. bell-shaped idols from Gazi, Karfi and Gortyna: Alexiou 1958, Pl. E–H). The decoration of masks must have varied considerably depending on what kind of divinities, devotees, or animals were represented. It is possible that some masks served multiple purposes, the transformations being effected by varying decoration. A head-dress could easily be fashioned for the mask, to be renewed annually, perhaps within the context of the farming community's seasonal ritual festivals. The pierced arm-stumps which frequently occur on standing figurines of the Bird Goddess type could have served for the attachment of wing plumes; but generally, perforations through the shoulders, arms and hips were probably intended to permit the figures to be hung up in the home, in shrines or trees, perhaps also to be used in ritual swinging. Swinging is known from ancient Greece in the festival of *Aiora* (Nilsson 1950: 331–32). A relevant scene is depicted on an Attic red-figure skyphos where a satyr wearing a ceremonial head-dress is swinging a young girl. A swinging figurine attached to pillars portrayed in clay has been found in Hagia Triadha, Crete, now in the Heraklion museum. Indeed, a number of Neolithic-Chalcolithic figurines are shown in a half-seated, half-standing position believed to be connected with swinging, in the spring, as a fertility rite (Marinatos 1968: 7–9).

65

Masked figures appear on Minoan sculptures, vases, signet rings and
seals. A goddess and worshippers in the ritual dance scene on the
ring from Isopata near Knossos, Crete, wear insect masks. The
Gorgon Medusa head became a terror mask, although the Corfu
pediment of about 600 BC proves that Medusa was originally a Great
Goddess (Bieber 1939: 35). A satyr-like masked man with padded
knickers and fat belly, a well-known figure from Greek comedy, is
encountered on a Late Mycenaean seal from Cyprus and on the
Minoan steatite vase from Hagia Triadha (Webster 1959: 10). His
costume closely resembles that of the masked and padded figure
from the Vinča site of Fafos. Animal-headed demons walking upright, as depicted on Mycenaean frescoes and gems (Mylonas 1966:
126), must be humans wearing masks. On a Minoan ring from
Phaistos (Webster 1959: 8, fig. 4) a human mask is shown between
two goats. Portrayal of the mask alone was as important as portrayal
of masked creatures, for it was the receptacle of invisible divine
forces. On the many vases used during the Dionysian festival of
Lenaia a mask on a post decorated with dresses represented the god
himself. The priests or priestesses and the worshippers of ancient
Greece and Italy wore masks; the satyrs and the maenads who danced
in frenzy at Dionysian festivals, were masked; everyone who danced
for the god and made music was masked. Each different mythical
persona was represented by a different mask. Masks of centaurs are
known from the sixth century BC (Kenner 1954: 12). A liturgical use
of masked participants, the *thiasotes* or *tragoi*, led ultimately to their
appearance upon the stage and to the birth of tragedy. Masked figures
survive in Greek comedy of the fifth century BC. In their drama the
comic poets used choruses of animals, birds, fish and insects, and
hybrid creatures or sirens (Sifakis 1967; 1971), which were not an
invention of the sixth and fifth centuries BC but trace their origins to
the Mycenaean and Minoan era and to Old Europe. Players danced
with wooden masks in honour of Artemis Corythalia in Italy, and
in the temple of Artemis Orthia in Sparta were found clay masks of
the seventh and early sixth century BC. They were made in imitation
of wooden masks used in the performances and dances and songs
dedicated to Artemis. This analogy, and the shape and decoration of
Vinča masks, strongly suggest that the mask representations on clay
figurines are replicas in miniature of wooden masks.

Masks and masked figures, life-size or in miniature, of Ancient
Greece, Minoan Crete and Old Europe, imply liturgy and drama
whose emphasis is theatrical. It is quite conceivable that all three
belong to the same tradition. Masked figurines are mimetic representations of rituals and mythological scenes.

24, 25

5 Shrines and the Role of Figurines

The abundance of clay statuettes portraying costumed, masked women and men implies that the Old European peoples re-enacted rituals, but it is necessary to look elsewhere in the archaeological record for the ceremonial accoutrements of the cult, in order to reconstruct its practice more precisely.

CLAY MODELS OF SHRINES

The miniature clay house-models produced throughout the Neolithic-Chalcolithic period are particularly important, presenting details of architecture, decoration and furnishing that are otherwise unavailable to the prehistoric archaeologist. Some of these models, discovered under the corners of excavated house-floors or by the central post supporting the roof, must have been used in a sacrificial ceremony to celebrate the erection of the structure. Several examples were discovered in such a context at the Starčevo settlement of Röszke-Ludvár near Szeged in Hungary (Trogmayer 1966) and at Branč, a Lengyel site in Slovakia (Vladár 1969: 506). A divinity was modelled in relief on the gable.

In the Neolithic mound of Porodin near Bitola in southern Yugoslavia several house-models of a unique type were excavated: each has a cylindrical 'chimney' upon which are modelled the masked features of a beaked and large-eyed goddess with a necklace encircling her neck and spreading over the roof. The models have elaborate doors, either of an inverted T shape or with angular cut-outs, and probably represent temples dedicated to a particular goddess. A house-model with a bird's head and incised plumage found at the Early Vinča site of Turdaş in Transylvania, must signify the same concept. The model of a sanctuary from Vădastra in western Romania has divine protectors in the forms of a ram and a bull. The two temples have pitched roofs and stand upon a high podium decorated with a spiral and lattice pattern.

21 Clay model of a Bird Goddess' sanctuary. Turdaş, Romania. Early Vinča, c. end sixth millennium BC

67

A model discovered in 1966 on a river-island settlement of the Gumelniţa culture, at Căscioarele in southern Romania, has caused the interpretative confines of the prehistorian's understanding of Neolithic-Chalcolithic structures and cult practices to be readjusted (Hortensia Dumitrescu 1968). The red-baked, polished clay model was found lying close to a large house (10 × 7 m.) divided by partition walls into two corridors. The wooden construction of the house was not preserved; but traces of its peculiar structure, the presence of a sacrificial place with a 'bench' (altar) two metres away, and numerous cult vases of unusual shape, including *askoi*, suggest that it was a sanctuary. It is impossible to say, however, whether or not the model had been within, or should be associated with, the house structure near which it was found. The model is 24.2 cm. high and 51 cm. long at the base. It consists of a large substructure, like the stereobate of a classical Greek temple, which supports four individual temples, each of which has a wide-arched portal and is crowned with horns on the gable and above the four corners. The entrance to each temple has a narrow border in relief, suggesting a door-frame, from which two ribs project obliquely upwards between the lintel and the roof, perhaps indicating the wooden supports of an arcade leading to the temple. There is no further architectural detail within the temples. The front surface of the substructure is decorated with irregular horizontal incised lines and ten round holes. The model temples presumably illustrate real structures at least three metres in height; add to that a substructure corresponding to that of the model, and we have a temple complex ten or more metres high. The horizontal lines might depict flights of stairs or a terrace-like structure, but the presence of holes, which should represent entrances, remains inexplicable. Mrs Dumitrescu interprets the incised lines as an indication of wood construction, in which case the holes could represent entrances into the podium, where staircases would lead up to the level of the temples. In addition, there was probably a stairway access on the outside of the podium, and on top there must have been a terrace to accommodate a worshipping congregation. Temples supported on terraced substructures are known from Sumerian architecture at the end of the fourth millennium BC. As the closest parallel to the Căscioarele model Mrs Dumitrescu cites the temple from Susa, depicted in a stylized engraving on a cylinder seal of the proto-urban period, c. 3300 BC. It has a large substructure with entrances and apertures. On top there is a rectangular temple which has two gates and is decorated with three bull-horns on each side (H. Dumitrescu 1968: Fig. 7). Radiocarbon tests gave the dates 3668 ± 120 and 3535 ± 120 BC; calibrated, they take us back to the second half of the fifth millennium BC. So the Căscioarele edifice may ante-date the Sumerian temples by one millennium.

The model from Căscioarele is not unique. Within the area of distribution of the East Balkan civilization many fragments of similar models, usually smaller, have been known for a long time. A 'two-storey house' discovered in the site of Ruse, on the lower Danube in Bulgaria, possesses architectural similarities to the Căscioarele model (Georgiev–Angelov, *Ruse*: 58, Fig. 20). The surface of the lower part is incised with roughly parallel lines and pierced by round apertures; while the second storey, the main temple, has a structure of vertical posts and horizontal beams. This model was fragmentary, particularly its upper part, and the reconstruction may not be entirely correct. Structures with wide-arched portals standing on terraced stereobates are depicted by other clay models excavated from the same settlement of Ruse during 1948–49 (*id.*: Fig. 90) and from Izvoarele in Romania. The detail on these models suggests that the temple's foundation need not invariably have been of wood, but might consist of steeply terraced earth. A quadrangular clay model of a temple with wide-arched portals on all four sides was recently discovered in a Late Neolithic context in the site of Krannon-Duraki in Thessaly (Michaud 1970).

22 Clay model of a temple on a stereobate. Izvoarele, southeastern Romania. East Balkan civilization. Copper Age, c. 4500 BC

Architectural remains encountered during excavations at Varvarovka, a Cucuteni-Tripolye settlement near Kishenev, Soviet Moldavia, were considered to represent the collapse of two-storey rather than single-storey structures. A clay model of a two-storey sanctuary, the second floor comprising the temple, was discovered in 1969 near Kiev in the Ros river valley. (The model is housed in the Archaeological Institute of the Academy of Sciences in Kiev.) There are entrances on both floors, and in front of the large portal or gate of the main temple is a platform adorned with bulls' horns. Vertical wall-posts are indicated in relief and the arched roof is supported by horizontal beams.

Miniature clay models of shrines from the Bug Valley in the western Ukraine have been known since the beginning of the twentieth century. The model from Popudnia, a Late Cucuteni (in Russian 'Tripolye C') settlement north of Uman, was discovered by Himner in 1912 (Himner 1933). It is usually interpreted as a building resting on piles because the model stands on cylindrical clay legs. By analogy with other models of shrines, some of which are illustrated in this volume, it may be assumed that the presence of these supports is meant to stress the importance of the sanctuary's elevation above the ground. Hundreds of Cucuteni houses have since been excavated, none of which was built on piles. The Popudnia model consists of the main room and a vestibule or enclosed platform. Between them there is a rectangular entrance with a threshold. On the right side stands a large rectangular oven, raised on a platform, and benches. On the bench to the right of the oven, a female figurine

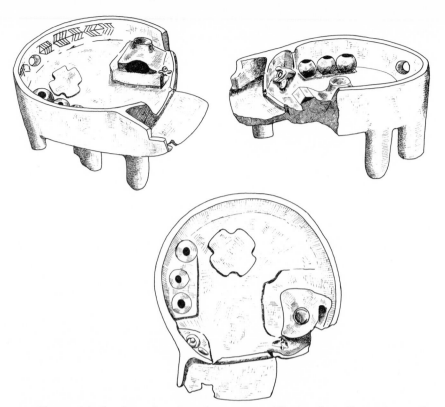

23 Clay model of a shrine from Popudnia, western Ukraine. Late Cucuteni. c. mid-fourth millennium BC

with hands on her breasts was found; by the other wall, again on a raised level, a sculpture of a woman grinding grain. Near the quern-stone is a small depression to accommodate the ground grain. By the same wall stand three large pear-shaped vases. A raised platform in the shape of a cross decorated with grooves around the edges lies near the centre of the shrine. Such cross-shaped platforms also occur in the actual houses of the Cucuteni settlements and are known to be places for votive offerings (documented in the settlement of Vladimirovka: Passek 1949, 85, 89). Interior walls are decorated with bands of black-painted geometric designs consisting of lozenges flanked with chevrons. The model, of reddish clay, was constructed in parts which were then glued together and baked. It has no roof, allowing the observer to view the interior arrangement of the sanctuary. Many other models of Cucuteni shrines from Vladimirovka and Shuvkovka are roofless (Passek 1949: 100, 125). The model found in the classical Cucuteni site of Vladimirovka has exterior and interior walls. The floor of the main hall and of the vestibule is painted in red, white and dark brown concentric circles and semicircles, and there are zigzag bands around the entrance, the round window and along the top of the walls.

23

70

One of the most exciting discoveries in Romania was the temple unearthed in the village of Căscioarele in a layer immediately below the Gumelniţa stratum in which the large clay model of the edifice was found. The carbonized wood revealed radiocarbon dates in the region of 4000 BC (Berlin Lab. dates: 5980 ± 100 BP, 5860 ± 100 BP and 5570 ± 100 BP). Calibrated, they equate with the early part of the fifth millennium BC. Vases found standing on the hardened clay floor are of late Boian style of the East Balkan civilization.

The sanctuary is rectangular in plan, 16 × 10 m., divided into two rooms by a row of six posts. Only one room has a painted 24 interior, its walls being cream on a red background, in the form of curvilinear and angular designs of thin ribbons and larger bands. A terracotta medallion, nearly circular in shape, decorates the western wall. It is painted with a band of red spirals bordered with a thin line of cream paint on a brownish-green background. Two pillars were found in this room. The larger one is about 2 m. high. It has a hollow interior and was probably modelled around a tree trunk which was then removed after the clay hardened, because no traces of wood remain. The pillar, like the walls, was painted three times and each set of the painted geometric designs is different. The pillar was 31 encircled by posts, but does not seem to have had any architectural

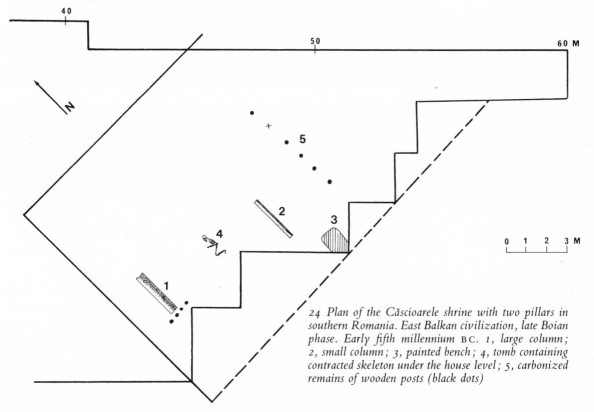

24 Plan of the Căscioarele shrine with two pillars in southern Romania. East Balkan civilization, late Boian phase. Early fifth millennium BC. 1, large column; 2, small column; 3, painted bench; 4, tomb containing contracted skeleton under the house level; 5, carbonized remains of wooden posts (black dots)

function. Nearby, a skeleton of an adult in a crouched position was discovered. Another, thinner pillar (only 10 cm. in diameter), but of the same height and also hollow inside, was found close to the interior wall. It is painted with cream ribbons, 8–12 mm. wide, on a reddish-brown background. Next to it was a terracotta bench, c. 40 cm. high and painted with curvilinear ribbons of cream paint. Many fragments of large *pithoi* decorated with excised motifs, and vases, painted in white on a lustrous brown background, were found above the floor (V. Dumitrescu 1970).

In the Cucuteni (Tripolye) civilization, remains of a temple were found in the site of Sabatinovka II in the valley of the Southern Bug (Makarevich 1960*b*; Movsha 1971). It dates from the Proto-Cucuteni period ('Early Tripolye' in Russian terminology). The rectangular building occupied about 70 sq. m. A narrow entrance was located on the long side. The entrance area was paved with flat stones and the rest of the floor was plastered with clay. A bone figurine was found at the entrance. Each part of the building served a different cult purpose. About halfway in, towards the right, there was a large oven, at the base of which a female figurine was found. Beyond and to the right of the oven was a group of vessels, including a dish filled with burnt bones of a bull and a channel-decorated pot with a small cup inside; to the left of these stood a brazier (an incense burner?), a group of five saddle querns and a row of five terracotta figurines. All of the figurines were of the same type, seated, with bodies leaning

25 *The shrine of Sabatinovka in the Southern Bug Valley, Soviet Moldavia. Early Cucuteni. The shrine occupies 70 square metres and its walls are built of wattle-and-daub. 1, stone pavement; 2, clay oven; 3, dais (altar) of clay; 4, clay throne; 5, clay figurines; 6, group of vases including a dish filled with burnt bones of a bull*

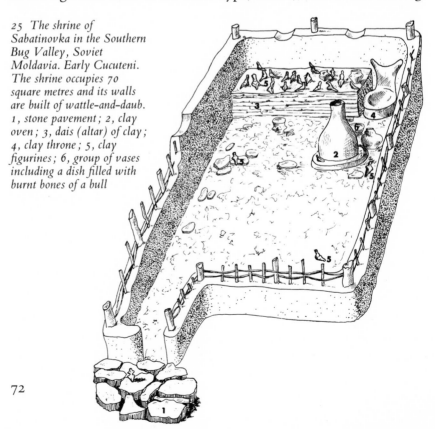

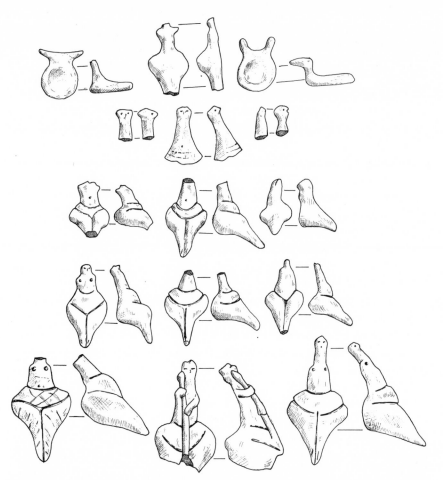

26 Clay figurines found on the altar of the Sabatinovka shrine, all originally seated on horned thrones (several of these are illustrated in top row); they are all characterized by massive buttocks – to aid the sitting position – and snake-shaped heads. One figurine (bottom centre) holds a baby snake or a phallus

backwards. Farther inside and opposite the entrance, was a large altar measuring 2.75 × 6 m., covered with four or five layers of clay plaster. Sixteen female figurines were found at its southern side, all seated on horn-backed stools. In the corner, behind the altar, was a clay throne or chair. Its seat, one metre wide, was originally covered with split planks. The total number of the figurines found in this sanctuary was thirty-two. All of them are schematically rendered with fat thighs and a snake-shaped head. A few were perforated through the shoulders, but have no arms except one who holds a baby snake or phallus (Fig. 26, bottom row, centre). The association of quern and grindstones with figurines portrayed in a seated position suggests magical grinding of grain and then perhaps baking of sacred bread. There was an overseer in control of the proceedings, probably a priestess or priest, seated on the full-size chair near the altar.

In the Classical Cucuteni settlement of Kolomijshchina I in the middle Dnieper region a raised red-painted altar, 70 cm. in diameter, was discovered in the centre of one of the houses (No. 6), near the oven. Twenty-one figurines, all in seated position, were discovered in the altar and oven areas; eighteen were female and three male.

Altars in the shape of a dais, built of clay and covered with wooden planks, or in the form of wooden tables, occur in all parts of Old Europe, in association with beehive-shaped or domed ovens. They are not always accompanied by figurines or ritual vases; owing to bad preservation excavators were in many cases able to identify only the burnt remains of some structures and groups of figurines, or an accumulation of assorted vases (examples: Vinča sites at Medvednjak, Divostin, Crnokalačka Bara, Anza).

Human sacrifice accompanied by animal sacrifice and offerings of other objects was performed in open-air sanctuaries. In a Late Cucuteni site at Tsviklovtsi, Podolia in the western Ukraine, the cremated bones of a youth aged about twenty were found, together with those of a bull, marten and sheep near an offering pit which contained eighteen vessels, grindstones, whorls, net sinkers, and an antler pick. Above another pit filled with charcoal and ashes stood a rectangular altar. There was one more pit plastered with clay, in which, together with layers of ash, stood a large storage jar with remains of wheat grains. At the base of the pit, a stone polisher, an awl, and fragments of dishes and cups were discovered. This sacrificial area was adjacent to the excavated village (Moshva 1971). Sacrificial pits filled with animal bones or skulls, charcoal, ashes and pots have also been found within the settlement area. In the Lengyel settlement of Brańč near Nitra in Slovakia, deep conical pits with walls and bottoms lined with clay were located at one end of large, two-room houses. In one pit, nearly 2 m. deep, there was a bull's skull with horns. Many layers are to be seen in the sacrificial pits: offerings were solidly covered with clay and then with loess. The sterile layers in between the remains of sacrifices perhaps signify annual intervals (Vladár 1969: 507).

Worship with offerings or mysteries took place in natural caves as ritual pottery and graffiti testify. Neolithic paintings were discovered in 1970 in a cave at Porto Badisco, south of Otranto in Apulia (Graziosi 1971). These include spirals, snakes, stylized half-snake, half-human creatures, quadriform designs and lozenges, horned animals, men holding bows, and geometric symbols executed in black or ochre-red. Pottery found at the site is of Adriatic Serra d'Alto style, followed by a few ceramic articles of later Piano Conte style. This suggests the cave was in use during the latter part of the fifth and during the fourth millennium BC.

PARALLELS WITH MINOAN-MYCENAEAN SHRINES

The Old European and Minoan shrines show a striking similarity.

27 Contents of the shrine at Gournia, a Late Minoan town in eastern Crete.
1, earthen tripod; 2, tube-shaped clay vessels decorated with snakes and horns; 3, terracotta figurines (whole and fragments of the heads) one entwined by a snake

74

Analogous shrine equipment and votive offerings cover a wide period from Chalcolithic or even Neolithic Old Europe to Classical Greece. I shall mention here a few closely related examples.

The Late Minoan I shrine of the provincial town of Gournia in eastern Crete is situated at some distance from the palace on the summit of the town hill and had a road leading to it. The shrine was small, only 4 × 3 m., with rudely constructed walls. A raised dais ran along the southern wall to the right of the entrance. In the centre stood a low plastered earthen table with three legs, and around it three curious tube-shaped vessels and part of a fourth. They have a vertical row of three or four snake-like loops on either side, a bigger handle on the back, and above this a pair of horns of consecration; one of these vessels is entwined by two snakes. The other objects include a bell-shaped female idol with raised hands and a snake around the body, two heads of other Snake Goddesses, three arms, hands and bases of other figurines, two snake heads, four small birds, and a fragment of a clay *pithos* (Nilsson 1950: 80–82). Clearly the Snake Goddess was invoked and worshipped in this small shrine. Its equipment has much in common with the snake-decorated vases and Snake Goddess figurines of Old Europe.

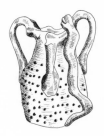

28 Perforated vessels covered with coiled snakes from a private house of Late Minoan I–II periods, in the Palace of Knossos

The snake cult is evident also in the palace at Knossos. At the entrance to a little room in a private house in the southwestern part of the palace dating from the Late Minoan I and II period stood a large jar. It contained a number of clay vessels, including tubular ones of terracotta provided with two pairs of cups, a terracotta stand, the upper part of which is divided into four compartments, two small jugs and vessels of unusual form over which snakes are coiled. The last-named are perforated like strainers and probably served for invoking rain by allowing water to run through the holes. In all areas of Chalcolithic Old Europe vessels with perforations frequently occur; generally they are made of a thick clay with rough and uneven holes. Some are zoomorphic or ornithomorphic and others have perforations in the snake coils.

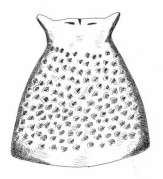

29 Horned stand with perforations from Turdaş, Transylvania. Early Vinča. c. 5200 BC

At Mycenae recent excavations revealed a little room filled with terracotta sculptures of which nineteen were human idols of both sexes up to 50–60 cm. high, and seventeen were coiled snakes (Taylour 1970: 274).

A small shrine, only 1.5 m. square, was found by Sir Arthur Evans in the palace at Knossos and dated to the Late Minoan III period. On the stamped clay floor were many bowls and vases. Inserted into the pebbly surface of a raised dais was a plaster tripod on which stood some cups and jugs. On a higher platform with a pebbled floor and plastered front, two pairs of horns of consecration made of white stucco with a clay core were set up. Leaning against one of them was a double-axe of steatite with duplicated blades. Each of the horns

40 Clay model of a sanctuary consisting of two temples supported on a substructure and topped by a ram's and a bull's head painted in red. Vădastra II, southwestern Romania. East Balkan civilization, Chalcolithic 4500 BC

41 Clay model of a sanctuary with a hole on top for insertion of goddess' image (see Pl. 34). Her necklace is shown in relief around the hole. Inverted T-shaped entrances on all sides. Porodin, southern Yugoslavia. Early sixth millennium BC

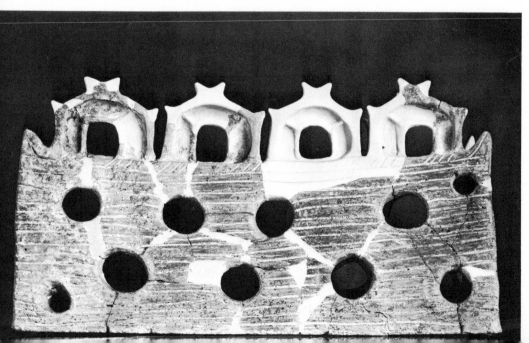

42 Clay model of an edifice from Căscioarele, lower Danube region, portraying a large substructure supporting four temples. East Balkan civilization, Chalcolithic. Late fifth millennium BC

43 Stylized replica of a
sanctuary, probably used as
an altar decoration, from
Truşeşti, northeastern
Romania. Classical Cucuteni.
End of fifth millennium BC

44 Altarpiece in the shape of
a bird with plumage
indicated. Truşeşti. Classical
Cucuteni. End of fifth
millennium BC

45 Altarpiece in the shape of the goddess with
upraised arms. Truşeşti. Classical Cucuteni

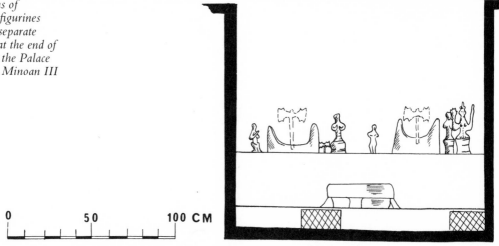

30 Tripod, horns of consecration and figurines standing on two separate raised platforms at the end of a small shrine in the Palace of Knossos. Late Minoan III period

0   50   100 CM

31 Design on the painted larger pillar at the entrance to the Căscioarele shrine. Early fifth millennium BC

had a central socket which was meant to receive the shaft of the double-axe. On either side of the horns stood terracotta figurines comprising three bell-shaped idols, and two votary figures, one male and one female. The female figurine probably portrays the main goddess of the shrine (Nilsson 1950: 80). The double-axe most likely represents the epiphany of the Great Goddess since she assumed the shape of a butterfly rising from the horns of a bull (see chapter 8). Obviously the Great Goddess was worshipped in this little shrine.

The two-pillared sanctuary of Căscioarele has many parallels in Cretan towns and palaces as well as in Mycenaean Greece. A pillar or two in a shrine was the most frequent attribute of a Minoan sanctuary. At Koumasa, for instance, the sanctuary was composed of several rooms, one of which had a wooden column in the middle; a cylindrical idol and a table for offerings stood *in situ* (*Arch. Anzeiger* 1907: 108; Nilsson 1950: 102). Pillar rooms are known from virtually all Cretan palaces. At Knossos they are present in all phases of the site. The oldest pillar room was found in the building which belongs to the initial stage of Middle Minoan I. In it two rectangular pillars were found, each about two metres high, and carved from a single slab of limestone. Near the southern wall opposite the space between the two pillars was a circular pit. In the hillside west of the palace at Knossos is situated the 'little palace', the foundation of which belongs to the beginning of Late Minoan. It has three pillar rooms. The western room has two pillars, one of which is completely preserved and consists of a base and two gypsum blocks. Between the pillars a shallow stone vat with a smaller sunken square in the middle had been let into the ground. At the 'royal villa' of Knossos, in a building of Late Minoan II date, north of the main room there is a pillar room, 4.15 × 4 m., paved with gypsum slabs. In the centre stands a pillar composed of two gypsum blocks. A sunken channel forms a rectangle around the central pillar, about midway between it and the walls. The house near the southeastern angle of the palace at Knossos contains a most interesting pillar room from Middle Minoan III. In the middle of the rectangular room stands a pillar, consisting of six blocks with a double-axe engraved on one of the upper blocks. A truncated pyramidal gypsum block was found close to the foot of the pillar which probably served as the base for a double axe. From this side of the pillar to the wall runs a foundation with many flat stone bases which may have served as stands for vessels. On the other side of this wall an ivory knot was found, and in the ante-room stood a six-legged offering table (Evans, *Palace of Minos*, I, 146ff., 441; II, 396, 407, 515; Nilsson 1950: 237–40). Pillar rooms were revealed in the palaces at Phaistos, Hagia Triadha, Mallia and Zakro. In the palace at Hagia Triadha a square pillar stood in the middle of a rectangular room. A quadrangular channel surrounded the pillar as in the 'royal villa' at Knossos. In the neighbouring room many votive figures were found. To the northwest of the palace two pillars stood in one of the rooms used for burials in the Late Minoan III period. An outdoor Cretan pillar shrine is reported from Phylakopi on the island of Melos, a Middle Minoan III town. (Nilsson 1950: 241, 242.) On the mainland, an interesting pillar room came to light at Asine, in a room complex known as the 'Mycenaean palace'. Standing in the centre of a fairly large room, 7×5 m., two column bases were found. In one corner there was a bench or ledge made of undressed stone slabs. On this ledge a quantity of male and female figurines, vessels and a stone axe once stood, some of which had fallen to the floor, (Persson and Frödin, *Asine*: 298, 308; Nilsson 1950: 111, 112).

The worship of stalagmites in caves from the Neolithic period to Minoan Crete and Ancient Greece was very likely related to that of pillars. In Grotta Scaloria, in the Gargano Peninsula of southern Italy, a beautiful painted pot dating from about 6000 BC was standing by a stalagmite (Archaeological Museum of Foggia). A cave east of Heraklion dedicated to Eileithyia, goddess of childbirth, contained a stalagmite and a relatively smaller one next to it. In many other caves on Crete, at Psychro, Kamares, Arkalokhori and elsewhere, the artifacts and symbols attest the worship of the Great Goddess (Alexiou 1969: 79).

From the large number of pillar shrines, the engravings of double-axes on limestone pillars in Minoan palaces, and the presence of stepped or conical supports with holes for inserting the shaft of a double-axe, an emblem of the Great Goddess, it is apparent that the pillar cult was associated with the worship of this divinity. Pictorial representations on Minoan-Mycenaean gold rings, in which a tree grows out of the shrine enclosing a pillar, indicate that

32 Gold ring from Mycenae. On the right: a small shrine with an enclosed pillar from which grows a plant. On the left: a plant grows out from the body of a wild goat

79

pillar and plant are symbolically interrelated, both symbolizing the power of life or the power of the goddess. This symbolic notion is strengthened by other representations on Minoan-Mycenaean gold rings in which the column is flanked by male animals, usually lions or griffins (replacing the dogs that flank the tree in Chalcolithic Old Europe). The same animals flank the goddess in her epiphany as a butterfly, *i.e.*, a woman with a head of a butterfly associated with bull's horns and a double-axe symbol. A pillar shrine portraying a similar group of symbols can be recognized in a fresco in the palace at Knossos; here the raised central column is fitted into a socket of bull's horns, below which is the ideogram of the Great Goddess: the 'split egg', two semicircular rosettes divided in the middle (Alexiou 1969: 82, Fig. 30). Other columns of the same fresco also had bull-horn sockets. The Minoan and Old European pillar was not an axis of the universe, not the *axis mundi* of the Altaic and northern European cosmologies, but an incarnation of the Great Goddess in her aspect as the source of life-power.

139

Most students of Minoan culture are bewildered by the abundance of cult practices. Shrines of one kind or another are so numerous that there is reason to believe that not only every palace but every private house was put to some such use. Characteristic of these domestic cults are the horns of consecration and the tables for offerings which occur almost everywhere (Nilsson 1950: 110). To judge by the frequency of shrines, horns of consecration and the symbol of the double-axe, the whole palace of Knossos must have resembled a sanctuary. Wherever you turn, pillars and symbols remind one of the presence of the Great Goddess or the Snake Goddess. This situation is related to that found in Neolithic and Chalcolithic Europe: in houses there were sacred corners with ovens, altars (benches) and offering places, and there were separate shrines dedicated to certain goddesses.

SHRINE EQUIPMENT AND OBJECTS RELATED TO CULT PRACTICES

Excavations in Old Europe are continually bringing to light altar-pieces, bucrania, libation vases, partitioned bowls, ladles, peculiar zoomorphic or ornithomorphic vases, and other elaborate artifacts that could have found useful service only in temples or domestic shrines. Life-size bucrania, real or modelled in clay, were raised high on wooden posts and mounted on altars or attached to the gable of a house or temple. At Vinča itself and at Jakovo-Kormadin west of Belgrade, life-size and highly stylized bucrania have been unearthed. In Cucuteni settlements a series of life-size altars or altar 'screens' have been found. One of the most spectacular, from the settlement of Truşeşti in Moldavia, appears to be a stylized replica of the façade of

0 1 2 3 4 5 CM

33 Miniature terracotta thrones from Ruse. East Balkan civilization. (Karanovo VI). Mid-fifth millennium BC

34 *Reconstruction of a cult
table supporting a series of
vases ; found at the classical
Petreşti settlement at Pianul
de Jos, Transylvania. Mid-
fifth millennium* B C

a sanctuary, with a wide-arched central entrance and side entrances   43
indicated by oval holes. Above are two symbols shaped like an M,
differing in size but each capped with a basin-shaped lid which may
represent sacrificial vessels. Other large altarpieces from Truşeşti take   44
the shape of a Bird Goddess or a goddess with upraised arms.   45

Numerous miniature tables, thrones, chairs and stools were
modelled in clay. They seem to have been manufactured in conjunction with figurines, to provide domestic comforts for divinities. In   33
exceptional circumstances the remains of full-sized furniture have
been discovered. In the Petreşti settlement of Pianul de Jos at
Hunedoara, a fire, which possibly occurred within a structure
housing a shrine, preserved parts of a roughly triangular table which
was plastered with clay and displayed a decorated panel in relief.   34
Careful excavation showed that richly decorated pedestalled vases,
dishes, a jar and several lids must have been standing on this table
and a large storage jar under it, before the fire broke out. At Medvednjak, a Vinča settlement in central Yugoslavia, in a rectangular
shrine 5 m. long, two large groups of ritual vases were uncovered
next to the burnt remains of a wooden structure, probably an altar
table (1970 excavation by R. Galović, unpublished). One of the large
pots was packed with smaller vases of various sizes and shapes and
was covered with a lid. Another house of the same settlement yielded

81

a ritual group consisting of three bull-legged vessels and a figurine. Beside the wall, about 1 m. from this group, was a biconical pot filled with grains. Towards the middle of the room, near the oven, lay a heap of 150 clay balls with a bull-legged vessel and a pot on top; another pot, full of grain, stood close by.

A particular type of vessel seems to have been used in sacrificial ceremonies. It consists of a shallow bowl sunk into a flat slab which may be triangular, standing on three legs, or rectangular and four-legged. Such vessels are decorated by incision, encrustation and painting; they sometimes have animal-head protomes projecting from the corners and legs, and may take a human shape. Some of the most impressive are supported by massive bull-legs or rest on standing or crouching animals. The bull or deer models from the East Balkan civilization are outstanding illustrations of this type of vessel. Libation vases make up another series of cult vessels; these may be jug-shaped, spouted, zoomorphic, bird-shaped or anthropomorphic, and are of fine fabric. They are variously ornamented, according to local styles, being either incised or decorated with red, graphite, or polychrome painting in complex curvilinear and meandroid designs. Clay ladles, exquisitely shaped and decorated, occur in great numbers in all parts of Old Europe. Those found at the Classical Cucuteni sites are beautifully painted. In the East Balkans some have anthropomorphic handles portraying masked faces.

The abundant production of small zoomorphic containers or lamps with projecting animal heads usually of rams, snakes or bulls and with various engraved ideograms suggests that they served as votive offerings to particular deities, just as similar objects were sacrificed during the Minoan and Helladic Bronze Age and in the later Eleusinian Mysteries. Literary records mention incense burners and oil lamps among the objects sacrificed to Demeter of Despoina in Lykosura (Nilsson 1957). Traditionally, incense burners and lamps were used as far back as pottery in Europe: on close observation the painted Neolithic ring-based and footed vessels exhibit loss of slip on the interior surfaces owing to some unusual use to which these vessels were put, possibly burning (cf. study of ceramic technology of Anza pottery of c. 6000 BC by Elizabeth Gardner).

In Cucuteni and East Balkan ceramic art sophisticated anthropomorphic vase supports are found. They take the form of either a single human figure (headless, or else with one or two faces) or a group of interconnected bowed figures. The human body, particularly the shoulders and arms, provided an appropriate sculptural motif for monumental stand-supports modelled by Cucuteni artists. A notable example from Frumuşica incorporates five well-proportioned human figures standing erect on a single base, the upper part of their bodies connected by their embracing arms. The raising of a vessel is a common practice in ritual celebrations, usually associated with fertility magic and pleas for future prosperity. The Bulgarians have retained a New Year's custom in which the three eldest women of the family thrice raise the trough containing the sacred New Year's bread-dough (Rybakov 1965). There are statuettes portraying women seated on a stool and holding conical containers for water. A remarkably well-preserved example from Bordjoš in the lower Tisza valley shows a naked woman sitting stiffly, both hands firmly holding a dish on her lap. Another example, a seated figure holding a bowl and a dish with a ladle, comes from a Cucuteni site at Nezvisko in the western Ukraine (Rybakov 1965: Fig. 3). The Early Vinča settlement of Fafos yielded a sculpture of a seated, masked woman performing a magical rite over the vessel which she is holding.

94

92

A very distinctive sculpture of a male figure was discovered during the excavation of the Tisza settlement at Szegvár in south-eastern Hungary. He wears a flat mask and in his right hand holds a sickle extending over his shoulder. On both arms bracelets are indicated in relief, five on the right and one on the left. A broad, decorated belt is incised round the waist of his stout body. This figure has attracted much attention, and recently Kalicz (1970) termed the period of the Tisza culture 'L'époque du Dieu a la faucille', the epoch of the Sickle God, a dominant male deity. Makkay (1964) considers this figure an ancestor of the Greek god Kronos. His dignified posture, and his mask, sickle and festive attire, proclaim his important status; his authoritative possession of the sickle implies that he, as central figure of the cult, is presiding over its rites. In ancient Greek festivals devoted to Artemis and Demeter the sickle was still displayed, symbolizing victory (Nilsson 1957). A curved stick of copper or gold known from the third millennium in the Near East and the Caucasus was an insignia of power, a symbolic value inherited from an early agricultural era, when the sickle was regarded as a sacred cult instrument. There is archaeological evidence of composite sickles, flint blades set in wood or bone, and of their utilization for reaping from earliest Neolithic times. That they were used as cult or ornamental objects in ritual festivities is revealed by sickle imitations which were produced in copper in east central Europe about 5000 BC. The Szegvár figure would seem to be exemplifying the novel and valuable products of a copper technology still in its infancy. Bracelets made of round copper wire are known from both the Tisza and Vinča cultural complexes, and an enormous copper sickle, 54 cm. long, has been discovered in Hungary at Zaerszentmihaly. The sickle was an isolated find but its shape is very much the same as that belonging to the statuette, suggesting that they are contemporaneous. The Szegvár male sculpture is unique, the other Tisza figurines being female.

46, 47

48

46, 47 Seated masked man holding a sickle. Arm-rings on both arms. Szegvár-Tüzköves, Tisza culture. *c.* 5000 BC; detail of the upper part of the sculpture (46)

48 Copper sickle from Zaerzentmihály, western Hungary. Isolated find, presumed to be of same age as figurine shown in Pls. 46, 47

Flutes and triton shells appear in Neolithic and Chalcolithic settlements; only in exceptional circumstances are other musical instruments such as citherns or lyres preserved. Fragments of bone flutes or pipes were discovered in the author's own excavation at Anza, Macedonia, belonging to the period prior to 6000 BC (Gimbutas, 1972). Triton shells were found in Lengyel settlements. The above examples are but reminders of the use of musical instruments in cult ceremonies as in Minoan Crete and in the Cyclades (Zervos, Crete: 391, 445, 704). A priestess holding a triton shell is depicted on a Minoan seal from the Idaean Cave standing at an altar topped with the horns of consecration with the tree of life representing the goddess' epiphany in the middle. Flute-playing is constantly mentioned or pictorially depicted in mythical scenes of Ancient Greece. The tradition must stem from a very early period. The role of music and dance in the religious ceremonies of Old Europe cannot be fully assessed until marble sculptures like Cycladic lyre- or flute-players, wooden frames of lyres or citherns or their portrayals on frescoes or elsewhere are discovered.

35 *Minoan seal from the Idaean Cave. Priestess (?) holding a triton shell. On the right, an altar topped with horns of consecration and a tree in the middle*

VOTIVE OFFERINGS: INSCRIBED FIGURINES, VESSELS, SPINDLE-WHORLS AND OTHER OBJECTS

Man had to persuade the divinity he worshipped to be propitious to him. Hoards of votive figurines, miniature vessels and other objects are constantly being recovered in Neolithic, Chalcolithic, Minoan, Mycenaean and Greek caves and sanctuaries, as well as those of Old Europe. The maker's name, the name of the goddess, or a sort of contract or promise, was sometimes inscribed on a figurine, plaque, spindle-whorl or miniature vessel. Approximately one out of every hundred figurines was incised with the signs of the Linear Old European script (not religious symbols and not ideograms). Since other objects, such as spindle-whorls, miniature vessels, plaques and dishes or bowls, were similarly inscribed, they too must have been votive offerings.

Various signs are found on the front, back and sides of Old European figurines. Minoan figurines were similarly inscribed, and an idol from the Middle Minoan palace of Tylissos bearing Linear A signs is reproduced here for comparison. Some characters of the script, notably a triangular sign in conjunction with vertical lines, are repeated quite often on figurines and other objects. On the Vinča figurine here illustrated, other signs – a meander and chevrons – are also engraved; these are not script signs, but ideograms of the Snake and Bird Goddess, as we shall see from the discussion in the chapters that follow. Inscribed spindle-whorls are known from many Vinča and East Balkan sites, spindles having been among the votive offer-

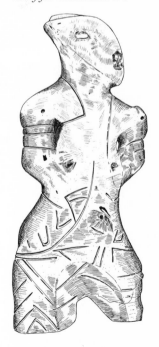

36 *Late Vinča figurine with inscription on one side. c. late fifth millennium BC*

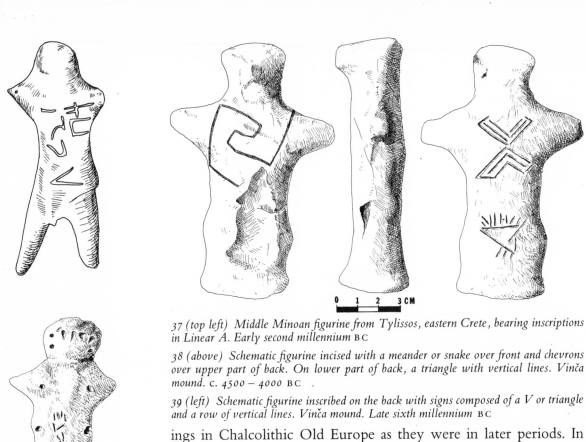

37 (top left) Middle Minoan figurine from Tylissos, eastern Crete, bearing inscriptions in Linear A. Early second millennium BC

38 (above) Schematic figurine incised with a meander or snake over front and chevrons over upper part of back. On lower part of back, a triangle with vertical lines. Vinča mound. c. 4500 – 4000 BC

39 (left) Schematic figurine inscribed on the back with signs composed of a V or triangle and a row of vertical lines. Vinča mound. Late sixth millennium BC

ings in Chalcolithic Old Europe as they were in later periods. In Greek times their association with the cult of Artemis is evident and the notion of 'spinning the thread of life' is very likely to have originated when spinning was still in its infancy and was regarded as imbued with a magic power. Inscribed miniature vessels are abundant; in the Vinča mound no less than 368 were found and many bore inscriptions of various kinds. Such vessels bear the same type of linear sign as do the spindle-whorls and figurines. They are not decorative motifs and not symbols. The miniature vessels, usually very small and crudely made, were meant to imitate large vases and were dedicated as gifts to goddesses. On the rims and walls of larger bowls and dishes inscriptions also occur. They cannot be interpreted as potter's marks, since they are not single geometric signs, but a sequence of linear signs.

One of the best examples of Old European script comes from the Chalcolithic site of Gradešnica near Vratsa in western Bulgaria, which is contemporaneous with the Early Vinča period of the same culture in Romania. On a shallow dish from this site, signs of writing appear on

40 Miniature vessels bearing inscriptions (dedications?), from the Vinča mound, found 7–6.5 m. deep. Early fifth millennium BC

both sides. On the inner surface there are four rows divided by horizontal lines, and on the outside is a schematized anthropomorphic figure, around which the familiar script signs are grouped. Analogous grouping of signs is known on an object from an Early Vinča site of Sukoro at Székésfehervár in western Hungary. On a round plaque from Karanovo VI in central Bulgaria, signs consisting of straight lines were incised between the cross arms of the quartered disc (V. I. Georgiev, 1969).

Although script signs on figurines, spindle-whorls and miniature vessels were known and collected from the beginning of the twentieth century (Schmidt 1903; Vasić 1910, 1936; Roska 1941), discussions concerning the possible existence of a Neolithic-Chalcolithic script only began after the three Tărtăria plaques or pendants had been discovered in the Mureş river valley of western Romania and were published by Vlassa in 1963. These plaques, of which two are perforated, were found in association with scorched human bones, twenty-six schematic Early Vinča clay figurines, two alabaster figurines, a clay 'anchor' (possibly a fragment of a figurine or horns of consecration with a figure in the middle), and a Spondylus-shell bracelet in an ash-filled, sacrificial pit located in the lowest layer of the site. The pit was covered by two occupation horizons: immediately above was a level of the Petreşti group and above this was a Coţofeni habitation level of the fourth millennium BC. By analogy with calibrated radiocarbon dates for Early Vinča layers at other sites, the date of the lowest occupation level cannot be later than the early fifth millennium. The Tărtăria inscribed objects are genuine Vinča artifacts, produced two thousand years earlier than the development of Sumerian civilization and about three thousand years before the appearance of Minoan Palace culture.

One of the Tărtăria tablets shows the outlines of two animals and a tree. One of the animals in this symbolic scene is clearly a goat. The association of goat and tree suggests that the Tărtăria ritual burial may have been performed as part of the rite of annual death and resurrection. In Minoan Crete and in the Near East, the goat was prominent as a sacrificial victim in the festival and the tree symbolized a new life. This also implies the fact that Old European writing was associated with religious functions.

Inscribed votive objects clearly prove the existence of Old European Linear signs and, in general, the very early incidence of writing. From the available material at the present time it is seen that the beginnings lie in the period of transition from the Neolithic to Chalcolithic (Late Starčevo–Early Vinča in central Balkans), c. 5500–5000 BC. More work on the script still awaits the dedicated scholar (but see Milton Winn, Dissertation, UCLA 1973 for analysis of signs; to appear in book form in 1982).

41 Inscribed spindle-whorl from Dikilitash near Philipi, northeastern Greece, East Balkan civilization. c. 4500 – 4000 BC

42 Shallow vessel from Gradešnica near Vraca, western Bulgaria, bearing inscriptions on both sides. (a), outer side with signs around the symbolic figure; (b), inner side with four lines of signs. c. 5000 BC Vinča culture

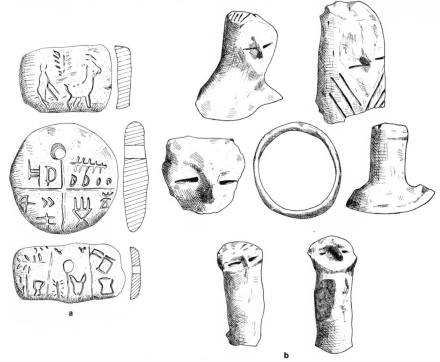

43 Objects found in a sacrificial burial pit at Tărtăria, western Romania. a, inscribed plaques, the upper one showing two animals (goats?) and a tree, suggesting a sacrifice in celebration of the return of new life; b, alabaster figurines, a pillar (phallic symbol or fragment of a clay figurine) and a Spondylus bracelet. c. end of sixth millennium to c. 5300–5000 BC

44 Inscribed clay objects, perhaps weights, from Sukoró-Tóradülö east of Szekesfehervar, western Hungary. 5000 BC

SUMMING UP

Clay models of temples, known from all parts of Old Europe, probably represent communal sanctuaries, dedicated to certain goddesses. These include rectangular structures with portals and wide entrances and four interconnected temples raised high on a stereobate or an earthen terrace.

Shrines whose actual remains have been found take the form of rectangular houses divided into two rooms one of which was furnished with an oven, an altar (dais), and sometimes a separate sacrificial area. These seem to be domestic shrines. The pillar shrine at Căscioarele, located in the middle of the village, was probably a communal sanctuary. The ceremonial accoutrements included life-size bucrania, altar screens, large *askoi*, *pithoi* and other beautifully decorated vases.

Figurines are found on altars, simple platforms like benches, usually built of clay and covered with planks, arranged at the end or corner of the domestic shrine, not far from the oven. This finds close analogy with the Minoan domestic shrines in which figurines are found standing on a dais. Figurines, ostensibly performing some ritual, are encountered also in other places, near the oven, by the entrance, beside grindstones and elsewhere. Figurines also served as votive offerings; they are found in sacrificial burials and, where used as gifts to certain divinities, were inscribed.

88

6 Cosmogonical and Cosmological Images

A striking development in art at the inception of the agricultural era was its persistent representation of a number of conventionalized graphic designs symbolizing abstract ideas. These ideograms, recurring on figurines, stamp seals, dishes, cult vessels, and as part of pictorial decoration of vases and house walls, were used for thousands of years throughout Old European civilization, and help to expand our understanding of its cosmogony and cosmology, and of the functions of the deities it sustained.

The symbols fall into two basic categories: those related to water or rain, the snake and the bird; and those associated with the moon, the vegetal life-cycle, the rotation of seasons, the birth and growth essential to the perpetuation of life. The first category consists of symbols with simple parallel lines, V's, zigzags, chevrons and meanders, and spirals. The second group includes the cross, the encircled cross and more complex derivations of this basic motif which symbolically connects the four corners of the world, the crescent, horn, caterpillar, egg and fish.

THE FOUR CORNERS OF THE WORLD, THE MOON AND THE BULL

The cross, with its arms directed to the four corners of the cosmos, is a universal symbol created or adopted by farming communities in the Neolithic and extending into present day folk art. It is based on the belief that the year is a journey embracing the four cardinal directions. Its purpose is to promote and assure the continuance of the cosmic cycle, to help the world through all phases of the moon and the changing seasons. Graphite-painted East Balkan dishes have cross and cosmic snake designs which recurrently present identical compositions of 'the universe'. The hooks or branching lines *45* attached to the four arms of the cross reinforce its dynamic expression. These vital signs are encountered on the bases, the insides of dishes, on figurines and stamp seals. *46–48*

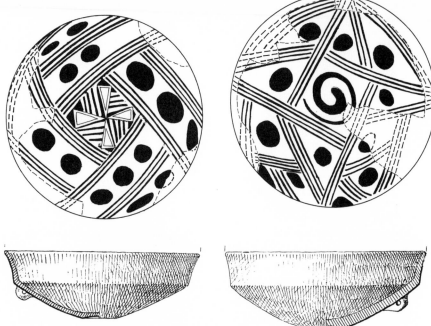

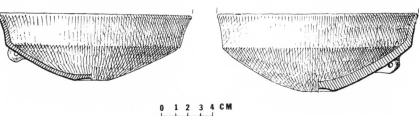

45 Graphite-painted dishes with cross and snake motifs in the centre of the cosmos. Tangîru mound, Romania. East Balkan civilization. Mid-fifth millennium BC

0 1 2 3 4 CM

46 Fourfold signs incised on central European Linear Pottery dishes. Bylany and other sites in Bohemia. End sixth–early fifth millennium BC

0 1 2 3 4 5 CM

The cross and its various derivative symbols are frequently encountered in the incised or painted ceramic decorations of each Neolithic and Chalcolithic group. Their consistent appearance on dishes, bowls, vases, stamp seals and the crowns of figurines strongly suggests that they are ideograms necessary to promote the recurrent birth and growth of plant, animal, and human life. They are symbols of the continuum of life which had to be ensured. Painted or engraved on the bases or insides of dishes they must have served as good-luck symbols as they still do in the European peasant culture. Life is present only where there is no stagnation and the regularity of nature is not obstructed by the forces of death. In Egyptian hieroglyphics the cross stands for life or living and forms part of such words as 'health' and 'happiness'. A related concept could have dominated the minds of early European farmers. A smooth transition from one phase to another spelled happiness. The fourfold compositions, archetypal of perpetual renewal or wholeness and the moon in the symbolism of Old Europe, are associated with the Great Goddess of Life and Death, and the Goddess of Vegetation, moon goddesses *par excellence*.

The symbols of 'becoming' – crescents, caterpillars and horns – accompany fourfold designs. They do not depict the end result of wholeness but rather the continuous striving towards it, the active process of creation. A painting on a Cucuteni dish from Valea Lupului shows stylized horns of four bulls, each quartered by crossed lines, with a crescent or a caterpillar in each section, a symbol related to the idea of periodic regeneration. There is a morphological relationship between the bull, on account of its fast-growing horns, and the waxing aspect of the moon, which is further evidence of the bull's symbolic function as invigorator. The worship of the moon and horns is the worship of the creative and fecund powers of nature. In Western Asia of the fourth to second millennia, the cross was usually associated with the lunar crescent and was an alternative symbol of the moon (Briffault 1963: 343, Figs. 8–12). Painted on a Classical Cucuteni vase from Truşeşti are quartered disc designs having a cross inside with knobbed extremities, probably symbolizing four phases of the moon, hooked to a horn. A portrayal of the head of a bull with the lunar disc between its horns occurs in relief on a vase from a Late Cucuteni site of Podei. The disc is quartered by crossing lines possibly indicating the four phases of the moon. In the lower section of the vase, the bull's horns are shown upside down, perhaps to symbolize the dead bull. In this and many similar portrayals we may recognize the sacrificial aspect of the act of creation. The Great Goddess, as we shall see later, emerges from the dead bull in the shape of a bee or a butterfly. The life process of creation and destruction is the basis for immortality.

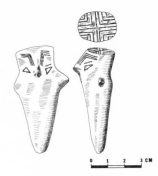

47 *Schematized figurine having crown engraved with quartered design, found in a clay silo filled with wheat grain. Medvednjak, Vinča site near Smederevska Palanka, central Yugoslavia. c. 5000 BC. Note chevrons above eyes*

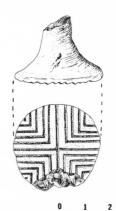

48 *Pottery stamp bearing a quartered design. Multiple chevrons in each section. Ruse, lower Danube. East Balkan civilization. (Karanovo VI). Mid-fifth millennium BC*

51

49 Quatrefoil design painted on the inside of a Late Cucuteni dish: four bull's horns enveloping a quartered disc with a crescent or a caterpillar in each section. Valea Lupului, Moldavia, northeastern Romania. Mid-fourth millennium BC

50 Quartered discs emerging from bull's horns (only one horn is visible.) Polychrome painted Classical Cucuteni vase. Truşeşti, northeastern Romania. Late fifth millennium BC

51 Painted Late Cucuteni vase with bull's head in relief. The bull's outsize horns encircle a quartered disc. Dark brown on white. Podei at Târgu-Ocna, northeastern Romania. Mid-fourth millennium BC

52 Horned terracotta stand (one horn broken) with female breasts. It has a hole on top between the horns. Medvednjak, Vinča site at Smederevska Palanka, southeast of Belgrade. *c.* 5000 BC

53 Terracotta figurine of a bull with exaggeratedly large horns (both broken off). Vinča culture. Fafos, southern Yugoslavia. Fifth millennium BC

The sacredness of the bull is expressed in particular through the emphasis on horns. They are sometimes as large as the whole animal figurine. Replete with a mysterious power of growth, the horns have become a lunar symbol, which is presumed to have come into being in the Upper Palaeolithic Aurignacian when reliefs of naked women holding a horn begin to appear (*cf.* the relief from the cave of Laussel in southern France). In the mythical imagery of Old Europe the bull was as dominant as elsewhere in the Mediterranean world. Terracotta figurines of bulls in the Cucuteni civilization usually have conical bosses on the forehead or a piece of copper set between the horns (a figurine with copper on the forehead was unearthed at Bolboch, a classical Cucuteni settlement near Kishenev). The heads of bulls with rosettes on the foreheads known from Minoan and Mycenaean art inherited this Old European tradition. Horns of consecration, so frequent in Minoan art, were already present in the Vinča and East Balkan civilizations. Hundreds of horned stands with a central hole for the insertion of some divine image made of perishable material are found in Vinča sites. In one case the breasts of the goddess are indicated on the stand. The abundance of these stands would suggest their association with some sort of myth-enacting ceremony, and the beginning of this symbol probably goes back to the primordial sacrifice with the underlying concept that out of the sacrificed bull's body a new life emerges. The schematized bull horn represents one of the basic philosophical ideas of Old European religion; perhaps this is why they are so numerous – as numerous as horns of consecration in the Palace of Knossos. The tradition of expressing the same idea in shorthand continued in the Proto-palatial period of Crete. The so-called 'sheep-bell' figurines with a suspension ring, two horn-like projections and eyes or a masked face depicted on the body, found at Knossos, Poros, Tylissos and Vorou (Platon 1949: 833f.) probably represent a divinity in combination with the horns symbolical of a sacrificed bull. In Neo-palatial Crete, the horns of consecration are always associated with the epiphany of the Goddess in the shape of a double-axe (a butterfly), a tree or a pillar.

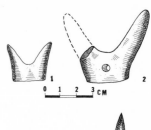

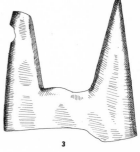

49 *Miniature terracotta horns of consecration from 1, 2, Ruse, Gumelniţa complex; 3, Vinča. Fifth millennium* BC

THE SNAKE

The snake and its abstracted derivative, the spiral, are the dominant motifs of the art of Old Europe, and their imaginative use in spiraliform design throughout the Neolithic and Chalcolithic periods remained unsurpassed by any subsequent decorative style until the Minoan civilization, the sole inheritor of Old European lavishness. The Chalcolithic Butmir, Cucuteni, and East Balkan peoples created large bulbous vessels, adopting the snake-spiral as the basis of the entire ornamental composition. This art reached its peak of unified symbolic and aesthetic expression *c.* 5000 BC.

'Symphonies of snakes' appear in colours and in graphite or white-encrusted incisions on cult vases, lamps, altar tables, hearth panels and house walls. Concurrently, almost naturalistic models of snakes were produced by all the cultural groups of Old Europe in bone, wood or clay. A coiled pottery snake, decorated with incised zigzag and punctate designs, was found at the Early Vinča settlement of Predionica. The entire inner surface of a ritual dish with holes from Kukova Mogila in Bulgaria is covered by a snake coil. The zigzagging outer coil contrasts with the inner spiral and suggests the radiating sun. A formidable horned snake modelled in relief winds around a Neolithic pot from the site of Suvodol-Dibel in Pelagonia. Snakes, their bodies marked by dots or comb-like stamps, have been found incised on a number of vases from the Vinča mound. The Vinča settlement of Potporanj at Vršac yielded curling snakes carved out of bone, with triangular heads and eye-holes. Snake ornamentation dominates the ceramics of the Neolithic Linear Pottery culture in central Europe and that of the Bükk group in the Carpathian foothills, ranging in expression from naturalistic portrayals to elegantly curving geometric designs. Snakes modelled in relief, sometimes with fine naturalistic detail, meander across the inner surface of dishes discovered in graves at the Dvory and Žitavou cemetery of Železovce, a variant of the Linear Pottery culture in western Slovakia. Similar snakes, but painted in black or brown on orange piriform vases, are frequently encountered during the Late Cucuteni period. The snake coil also appears on Cucuteni stamp seals.

The mysterious dynamism of the snake, its extraordinary vitality and periodic rejuvenation, must have provoked a powerful emotional response in the Neolithic agriculturists, and the snake was consequently mythologized, attributed with a power that can move the entire cosmos. Compositions on the shoulders of cult vases reveal pairs of snakes with opposed heads, 'making the world roll' with the energy of their spiralling bodies. Tension between the two is emphasized, since it is not just one snake that begins the movement. This motif occurs in various degrees of schematization during the Neolithic and Chalcolithic eras. The more naturalistic tendency is to distinguish the heads and bodies of snakes and their tails, which end in widespread triangles, a contrivance to fill the space between the discs or ovals. The organization of the motifs demonstrates that the imagery is genuinely cosmogonic: the disc and snake compositions appear in bands occupying the middle of the vases, associated with belts of the upper skies containing rain clouds, divine dogs and fawns. The belt of earth is characterized by plant motifs. On some vases snake coils in the upper bands have diagonal stripes, probably to indicate torrents of rain. In some cases the snake is portrayed winding across the cosmic double-egg.

94

The involved ornamentation of Cucuteni and East Balkan ceramic painting is a symbolic glorification of nature's dynamism. Its graphic expression is organized around the symbol of the snake, whose presence was a guarantee that nature's enigmatic cycle would be maintained and its life-giving powers not diminish. The snake was the vehicle of immortality. Some vases flaunt a gigantic snake winding or stretching over 'the whole universe', over the sun or moon, stars and rain torrents; elsewhere the snake winds above or below a growing plant or coils above the pregnant mother's belly. Snakes coil in concentric circles covering every protuberance, the buttocks as well as the female abdomen. The sanctity of protuberance is indicated by the special attention given every convex roundness of the female body – even a knee is encircled. Similarly, the snake is usually present on a bull's rump or shoulders. The phallus, as well as ithyphallic vases and lids, is also accompanied by snake coils. The snake was stimulator and guardian of the spontaneous life energy, and this anatomical association, so frequent that its symbolic meaning cannot be doubted, demonstrates the power that was attributed to bodily protuberances as its source.

In the Neolithic mound of Porodin in Macedonia numerous ceramic snakes were discovered. Originally they were attached to vessels, perhaps water containers, used in ritual ceremonies. A reconstruction of such a vessel is here reproduced. Similar snake- or phallus-shaped 'elongated heads' have been discovered in Ramad, Level III, a sixth-millennium village in Syria (Contenson 1971: 285).

The phallus, horns, snake, water bird, and water are closely interrelated in myth and cult. The mystery of life lies in water, in oceans, deep seas, lakes or rivers. Gods are born from water. Dionysus comes from water, as do the Bird Goddess, Athena, or Aphrodite. On pictorial Cucuteni vases and Tisza altars we see bird-clawed or horned goddesses borne in the womb of mythical waters. The universal snake winds around the universal egg like a continuous flow of water. To the poets and philosophers of ancient Greece water was the primordial element, able to produce life, stimulate its growth and nurture it with damp warmth. This concept of the genesis of the universe from an elemental aqua-substance surely extends back in time to the Neolithic-Chalcolithic era.

54

196

61, 62

55

110, 92

56

50 Snake and disc motifs as ornamental belts on the shoulders of a Classical Cucuteni vase from the site of Hăbăşeşti, Moldavia, northeastern Romania. a, vase; b, ornament around the shoulders.

95

54 Pottery snake from Predionica at Priština, Yugoslavia. Early Vinča. End of sixth millennium BC

55, 56 Pottery bowl with holes and a snake coil inside shown in relief. Probably used in ceremonies of rain invocation. Kukova Mogila, central Bulgaria. Karanovo III complex, East Balkan civilization. End of sixth millennium BC

57 A horned snake with large eyes from Dibel, a Late Neolithic settlement near Bitola, western Macedonia. Pottery relief on the shoulder of a vase

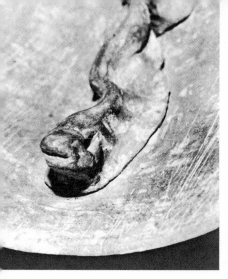

58, 59 Snake in a dish from the cemetery of Dvory nad Žitavou, western Slovakia (detail). Early fifth millennium BC

60 Painted snake on a Late Cucuteni vase from Bilcze Zlote (detail). First half of fourth millennium BC

61, 62 Snake heads as decoration
of cult vessels. Terracotta.
Porodin, southern Yugoslavia.
Neolithic Starčevo complex.
c. 6000 BC

63, 64 Horned head in association with snakes (head of a Snake Goddess) shown in relief on a vase from Tell Azmak, central Bulgaria. East Balkan (Karanovo I) civilization. *c.* 6000 BC

65 Anthropomorphic terracotta figurine of a crowned Snake Goddess from Kato Ierapetra, Neolithic Crete. The legs are formed like snakes. Disconnected lines cover the breasts and shoulders and extend over the lower back

66 Vinča lid with punctated snake-meander, and chevrons on top. *c.* 5000-early fifth millennium BC

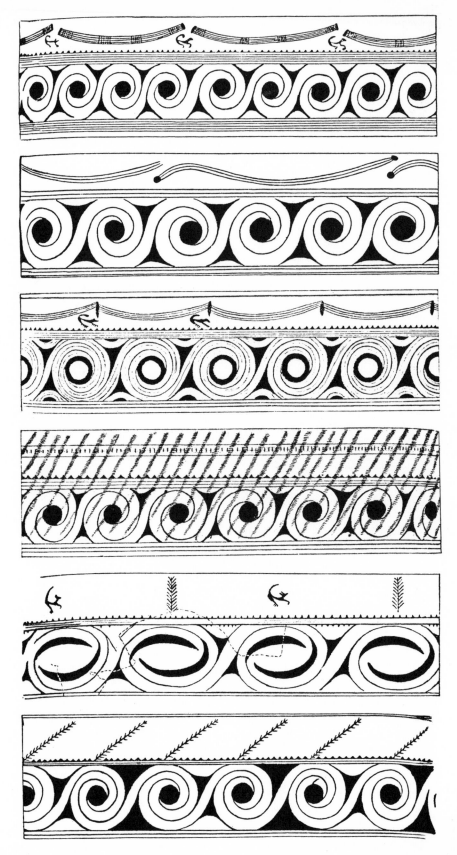

51 Running snake-spiral belts, rain clouds, divine dogs and plants on painted Late Cucuteni vases from Sipintsi, western Ukraine. c. mid-fourth millennium BC

The mythical water snake and the water bird are vehicles of an energy which has its source in water. In Old European symbolism these images are intimately related, as will be seen from the next chapter. The snake winds on the wings of a bird and is depicted on the beaked Vinča lid.

From the Early Neolithic to ancient Greece the snake appears in an anthropomorphic shape as a Snake Goddess. Her body is usually decorated with stripes or snake spirals, while her arms and legs are portrayed as snakes, or she is entwined by one or more snakes. Her anthropomorphized image occurs on vases enveloped by a snake. On a vase from the Neolithic stratum of the mound of Azmak in Bulgaria, her face is human but her eyebrows resemble horns. Monstrous horned heads with anthropomorphic features and bird-clawed or snake-like hands reappear in Pre-palatial Crete (*cf.* Alexiou 1958: Pl. IA, 10). Snake spirals, agglomerations of snakes or hybrids, half-snake and half-human, with spiralling extremities are painted in black on the cave walls of Porto Badisco in Apulia (Graziosi 1971).

52 Cult vessel with two snake heads attached to front corners. Porodin, southern Yugoslavia. c. 6000 BC

THE PRIMORDIAL EGG

Stories of creation known to European and non-European peoples represent stages of a long process of development. Because of their 'primeval' character they are considered to be very old. The actual record of this 'primordial stage' of creation myths is limited, since not everywhere in prehistoric cultures were they expressed in images. Ethnological parallels from fishing and hunting societies indirectly prove the Palaeolithic origin of the cosmogonical ideas centring around water, water bird, egg, doe, and woman. During the Neolithic and Chalcolithic the stories of creation were quite complex, as can be seen from vase paintings and frescoes.

The primal element of the universe was conceived as water. The abstract paintings on Cucuteni vases further reveal the formation of the world and the beginning of life from an egg in the midst of which a germ resided. The egg is enveloped in water, represented

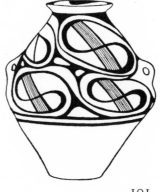

53 Snakes coiling across 'rain torrents'. Painted abstract design on a Classical Cucuteni vase from Vladimirovka, Southern Bug Valley, western Ukraine. End of fifth millennium BC

54 Snake winding across double-eggs enveloped in flowing water: painted compositions on Late Cucuteni dishes from Tomashevka, western Ukraine. c. mid-fourth millennium BC

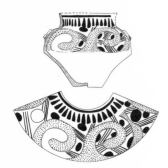

55 Snake 'adagio' on a graphite-painted Gumelniţa vase from the Tangîru mound lower Danube region. Above, reconstructed vase with profile indicated on left side; below, exploded drawing of decoration.

by parallel lines. The symbol of life energy – the snake – winds across or around the cosmic egg. The beginning of life within an egg is caused by the orbiting of two snakes or fawns. The animals are always in opposition, which creates a tension. It would appear that a cross or an X within an oval conveys the same idea. The germ is shown as a dot or a lens. A lens within the enfolding egg layers is sometimes shown flanked by spirals, a probable association with floral motifs; this symbolizes the rudiment of a living organism taking its form from flower buds or grains. A germ within an egg or a vulva may sprout into a plant with buds or with bean-like projections. The idea of a primordial egg or vulva is likewise expressed by sculpture. The Lepenski Vir sandstone sculptures dating from around 6000 BC are almost all egg-shaped and one has a vulva engraved in the centre.

Ancient mythologies – Egyptian, Babylonian, Hindu, Greek – have preserved myths of the universe as a cosmic egg from which gods arise and which was created by a cosmic snake or bird. Ancient Greek myths obviously enlarge on elements that are closely allied to cosmological representations on Balkan Neolithic and Chalcolithic ceramics. Athenagoras in the second century AD recorded the following myth: First all was water. From the water emerged a snake with the head of both a lion and a bull, and between these was the face of a giant, Herakles or Khronos. The Giant created an egg, and the egg split in two. From the upper part came the sky and from the lower part, the earth (Lukas 1894: 230). Some 5000 years before Athenagoras the myth could have gone like this: First, all was water. From the water emerged a cosmic snake with a horned head. The snake (or the bull, or the giant) created the cosmic egg. Then the egg split in two.

A cosmic egg may also be laid by a mythical water bird: this myth is almost universally known between Africa and the Arctic zone; it is recorded in ancient civilizations and was known among hunting and fishing tribes. In an Ancient Egyptian myth, the cosmic egg was laid by a Nile goose which was worshipped as the 'great chatterer', the creator of the world. According to the Orphic story, uncreated Nyx (Night) existed first and was regarded as a great black-winged bird hovering over a vast darkness. Though unmated, she laid an egg from which flew gold-winged Eros, while from the two parts of the shell Ouranos and Gaia (Heaven and Earth) were created. The beginning of the myth must lie in the Palaeolithic era. Engraved and sculpted images with silhouetted egg-shaped buttocks are frequent in western and central Europe from the early Aurignacian and on into the Magdalenian period. The more realistically rendered figures have bird's heads and long breasts (Marshack 1972: 305ff.).

56 Cosmic snake and cosmic egg compositions painted on Late Cucuteni vases from Sipintsi, western Ukraine. c. mid-fourth millennium BC

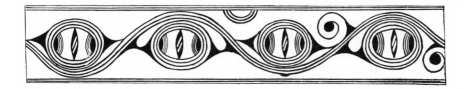

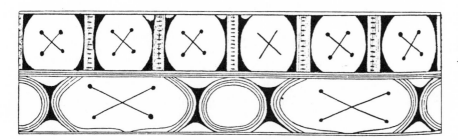

57 Quartered egg and disc motifs on black-on-red-painted Late Cucuteni vases from Sipintsi, western Ukraine. Mid-fourth millennium BC

58 Design over the body of Cucuteni vase, showing eggs with a germ (lens) in the centre flanked with spirals. Dîmbul Morii at Cucuteni, northeastern Romania. c. 4000 BC

103

67 A plant within an egg or vulva. Late Cucuteni painted vase from Bilcze Zlote, western Ukraine

68 Stone sculpture from Lepenski Vir, northern Yugoslavia, in the shape of an egg with an engraved vulva design. Early sixth millennium BC

69, 70 Bird-shaped vase with the head of a doe (?) The Vinča site. *c.* 4000 BC

71 Bird-shaped vase with wings. The body is rounded like an egg. Cascioarele site, southern Romania. Gumelnita layer. *c.* 4000 BC

59 *Large Vinča* askos *from Anza, Macedonia. Reconstructed. c. 5300–5100 BC*

The idea of a water bird, or a form of anthropomorphized bird, as a creator of the cosmic egg is clearly represented in Neolithic figurine art. It must have been a dominating theme among the cosmogonic myths.

Vessels taking the form of a bird are an early tradition in the Balkans. *Askoi*, vases of water-bird shape, occur at Nea Nikomedeia, a site which dates from no later than 6000 BC. The same tradition was followed throughout the Balkan Peninsula and the Danube region during the sixth millennium and later. The most peculiar aspect of these representations is that the jar is shaped not simply in the form of a bird, but that of a bird carrying an egg within its body. Such a vessel is usually rounded like an egg. With the *askos*, the Neolithic artist expressed a female divinity in the form of a bird-shaped water jar containing an egg as a fluid substance. She represented the universal creative force. Another image having a similar kind of potentiality is the doe. Vases in the shape of a deer have an egg-shaped body. Some bird-shaped vases rounded to resemble an egg have teriomorphic heads. Such a peculiar combination can be seen on a vessel from Vinča: the body is shaped like an egg, the neck belongs to a crane or grebe, and the head to a cow or a doe.

69, 70

The symbolism of a bird carrying a cosmic egg recurs considerably later, in Cycladic, Minoan and Helladic art: the bodies of flying birds painted on Early and Middle Minoan vases are seen to contain a large egg.

61

In the Palaeolithic period the myth of the genesis of the world from a cosmic egg laid by a bird gave rise to an important series of so-called steatopygous figurines. The name is derived from 'steatopygia', which is defined as an excessive development of fat on the buttocks, especially of females. Archaeologists erroneously adopted this name for the figurines, thinking that they represented a natural portrayal of women with abnormally large buttocks. This is a false interpretation. 'Steatopygous' images continued from the Magdalenian epoch into the Neolithic and beyond.

60, 61 *Designs of birds with large eggs inside them, painted in black on a white ground on Minoan vases*

1   2

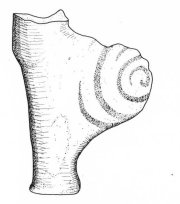

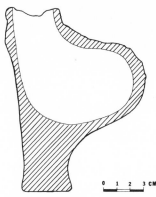

62 Figurine with an egg
(hollow) inside the buttocks
and a snake winding around
them (shown in relief).
Donja Branjevina near
Deronj, northern
Yugoslavia. Starčevo
complex. Central Balkan
Neolithic. Early sixth
millennium BC

This large group of standing or stooping figurines represents the sculptural realization of the concept of the Bird Goddess, abstracting and fusing elements of human and bird form. Her body contains an egg, and even the most schematic representation must be a conventionalized expression of this idea. From the seventh to the fifth millennium BC these figurines conservatively display the same features. They are not truly obese; above the waist they are universally slender, their breasts of normal or even much reduced size. Except in very small figurines, the buttocks are usually hollow and shaped like an egg. The label 'steatopygous' is applied also to seated figurines whose buttocks are exaggerated and flattened for a practical reason: to balance them on a chair or dais.

Interest in steatopygia increased in the nineteenth century with the first descriptions of steatopygous Hottentots and Bushmen, both women and men. However, Hottentot ladies have no place in the art of Old Europe and it is erroneous and misleading to describe Neolithic and Chalcolithic figurines as steatopygous. The hybridization of woman and bird endows the figures with a greater dignity, the dignity of the supernatural, and it is unfortunate that the term ever became associated with Palaeolithic and Neolithic figurines.

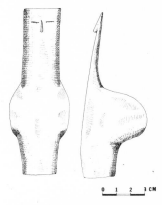

63 Figurine representing a
bird-woman hybrid with
egg-shaped buttocks. Čavdar,
east of Sofia, Bulgaria. East
Balkan Neolithic. Early
sixth millennium BC

THE FISH

The usual symbolism connected with the fish ranges from its being an emblem of the vulva, or the phallus, to a symbol of the soul or the 'mystic ship of life'. By microscopic analysis of engravings on Late Magdalenian bone objects Marshack has recently shown that fish (salmon) and snake typically appear in the context of a seasonal manifestation representative of early spring and frequently in association with new shoots, young animals and ibexes (Marshack 1972: 169ff.). The fish is also inseparable from the form of a phallus since the phallus offers a visual and kinesthetic comparison with the fish and snake (cf. a bâton head from the Gorge d'Enfer in Dordogne:

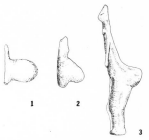

64 Schematic representations
of the Bird Goddess with an
egg in the buttocks. 1,
Lepenski Vir (Starčevo
complex); 2, Neolithic,
Crete; 3, Karanovo I,
Bulgaria

107

73 Egg- or fish-shaped sculpture of sandstone from Lepenski Vir. (A hybrid woman and fish?) *c.* 6000 or early sixth millennium BC

72 Egg-shaped stone head of a Fish Goddess. Lepenski Vir II

74 Fragment of a vessel in the form of a fish. Vinča civilization. Mala Grabovnica near Leskovac, central Yugoslavia

75 Anthropomorphized Fish Goddess of stone with head, arms and breasts chiselled out. Mouth and eyes are those of a fish, the nose is human. Lepenski Vir II. Early sixth millennium BC

76 (*Opposite*) Stone sculpture of a fish-faced water divinity from Lepenski Vir. Zigzags, diamonds and chevrons represent streams of water. Early sixth millennium BC

id.: 330). An engraving in the Magdalenian cave of Lortet shows fish nuzzling a reindeer's genitals (Hentze 1932: 113). Many thousands of years later, in Greek Geometric art, the fish continued to be portrayed hanging on the genitals of horses; the fish is also placed within the womb of the Bee Goddess painted on a Boeotian vase around 700 BC. Its role there must have been related to the idea of cyclic regeneration, since the goddess is shown in the shape of a bee and is associated with the head of a sacrificial bull.

141

In Neolithic art the fish assumes the shape of an egg and is anthropomorphized. This is exemplified by the sculptures recently discovered at Lepenski Vir near the Iron Gates in northern Yugoslavia (Srejović 1969). There, in the late seventh and early sixth millennia BC, fishing and hunting peoples had dug their houses into the bank of the Danube, houses which had trapezoidal floor plans and contained rectangular hearths sunk below the floor level, lined with stones, and outlined with thin slabs of stone set vertically in a pattern of continuous triangles. Large stone sculptures were placed in the lime-plaster floors in front of the hearths. Fifty-four of these monumental sculptures, most of them twice as large as a human head, were found, and fifteen of them reveal half-human, half-fish features. Geometric ornament is pecked on many of them, while others are plain. All appear to possess aspects of either the human figure, the fish, or the egg, and were probably selected for this reason. The shape of the river boulder had a significance of its own; the artist did not alter this, but only gave it the features of the mythical being he venerated. He added the mouth and large round eyes of a fish and

72, 73, 75, 76   the nose and eyebrows of a man. The mouth with downward-drooping corners makes the facial features stern, even dramatically tense. But it is doubtful whether this painful grimace was really what the Lepenski Vir artist sought to portray; the sternness results from a peculiar combination of fish and human features and does not necessarily reflect the artist's conscious intent. In his book on Lepenski Vir, D. Srejović calls one of the egg-shaped and fish-faced sculptures 'Danubius'. The name implies a male river divinity, but does the sculpture really represent a male and awe-inspiring god?

76   Geometric motifs engraved on stone sculptures, such as zigzags, interconnected lozenges each with a dot in it, chevrons and labyrinthine designs on round stones with depressions (probably used for sacrifice) are related to the symbolism which appears on aquatic divinities associated with cosmogonical imagery. The Lepenski Vir statuary seems to represent a divinity of a feminine gender – one of the sculptures reproduced here has female breasts – which incorporates aspects of an egg, a fish and a woman and which could have been a primeval creator or a mythical ancestress. Standing at the hearth she was probably a guardian of the house.

Only here, in this Danube gorge in the region of the Iron Gates, have these remarkable monumental sculptures so far been found, and they may well be specifically connected with the cult practices of a people whose main concern and subsistence was fishing. Fish effigies, however, have been found elsewhere in the Neolithic sites where farming activities were evident. Even in the flourishing civilization of Vinča the fish must have played a part in mythical imagery, since some cult vessels were formed in the shape of a fish.   74

7 Mistresses of Waters:
the Bird and Snake Goddess

The presence of the Bird and Snake Goddess is felt everywhere – on earth, in the skies and beyond the clouds, where primordial waters lie. Her abode is beyond the upper waters, *i.e.*, beyond meandrous labyrinths. She rules over the life-giving force of water, and her

65

image is consequently associated with water containers. On Cucuteni vases, the goddess' eyes, or her eyes and beak, appear above represen-

66

tations of water or falling rain. The eyes of the Bird or Snake Goddess even stare from the very centre of the world – a sphere with a mythical

67

water stream in the centre. Her cosmic character is emphasized by

68

a series of abstract compositions painted on Cucuteni vases.

The Snake Goddess and the Bird Goddess appear as separate figures and as a single divinity. Their functions are so intimately related that their separate treatment is impossible. She is one and she is two, sometimes snake, sometimes bird. She is the goddess of waters and air, assuming the shape of a snake, a crane, a goose, a duck, a diving bird. The combination of a water snake and a water bird is a peculiarity of the Old European symbolism representing divine ambivalence.

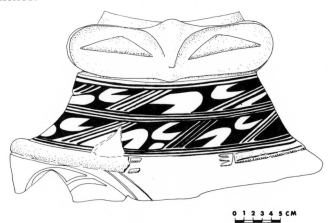

65 Part of vessel with a representation of a masked East Balkan Bird Goddess. Sultana at Olteniţa, Romania. Gumelniţa complex. c. 4000 BC

112

66 Pictorial representations of the Bird Goddess' face in association with water streams on Late Cucuteni vases. Tomashevka and Staraja Buda sites, western Ukraine. First half of the fourth millennium BC

THE INVOCATION OF RAIN, THE BEAR AND THE IDEOGRAMS OF THE BIRD GODDESS

Parallel lines, V's, chevrons, belts of zigzags, and groups of parallel lines are frequently found on figurines, stamp seals, cult vases and vase lids. Their consistent appearance on figurine masks and bodies, anthropomorphic vases, miniature cult vessels and zoomorphic containers suggests the existence of a coherent system of symbolic expression: the relationship between the depiction of rain torrents, the mythical bear and the Bird Goddess is obvious.

The desiccation of the climate during the sixth millennium BC shown by palaeobotanical and geological research (clearly revealed by results of the author's own recent excavation at Anza, Macedonia) is also reflected in symbolic communication. The centuries-long lack of water resulted in the creation of symbolic images related to streams and mythical creatures considered to be the source of water. The Mistress of Waters, the Bird Goddess, and the bear, who seems to have been also connected with water, are very frequent images all over the Balkan Peninsula, particularly in its driest regions, Greece,

67 Composite pictorial representation of a Bird or Snake Goddess' eyes and water streams. Staraja Buda, western Ukraine. Late Cucuteni

68 Abstract compositions of the Bird Goddess' eyes and beak (or only her beak) in association with a cosmic egg. Painted on Late Cucuteni vases. Sipintsi, western Ukraine. Early fourth millennium BC

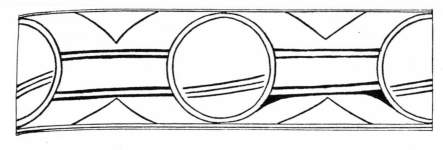

69 Bird Goddess' eyes and beak above groups of straight painted lines (falling rain?) as found on ritual footed vessels painted in dark brown on orange-red. Anza III, Macedonia. Central Balkan Neolithic III. c. 5500 BC

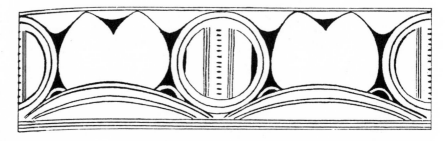

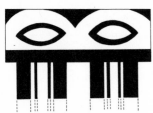

70 Beaker with black-painted design of eyes associated with hair portrayed like snakes or falling rain. Tsangli, Thessaly. Late Neolithic, mid-sixth millennium BC

Macedonia, southern Yugoslavia and the Adriatic seaboard. Even the pottery decoration reflects an 'obsession' with rain and water symbolism. Floral and spiral motifs of the earlier Neolithic were replaced in Sesklo, Danilo, late Starčevo and Vinča complexes by rigidly geometric decoration: bands or groups of vertical or diagonal parallel lines, striated and punctated bands and chevrons. The goddess' eyes emerge in association with rain torrents or lines representing water. Stamp seals of this period reveal the same tendency: almost all of the known seals are engraved with either straight lines, wavy lines or zigzags. Torrents of water shown as vertical zigzagging lines in separate panels depicted on an early Vinča funnel-shaped vase

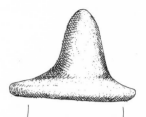

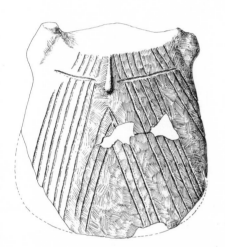

71 Painted black-on-red ornamental motifs, probably symbolizing rain, on Late Starčevo vases from northern Yugoslavia. c. 5500 B C

72 Clay seals engraved with zigzag and parallel lines from Starčevo and Karanovo I sites: 1, Grabovac, Yugoslavia; 2, 3, 5, Čavdar, western Bulgaria; 4, Rug Bair, Macedonia. c. 5500 B C

73 Zoomorphic pottery lid with clusters of diagonal incisions (streaming rain?). Early Vinča. Parţa, Timişoara district western Romania. c. 5000 B C

74 Pottery lid in half-human, half-animal form with beaked nose, depression for mouth (source of water?), and incised markings, from Malča near Niš, southern Yugoslavia. Early Vinča, late sixth millennium B C

0 1 2 3 4 5 cm

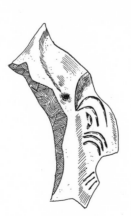

0 1 2 3 4 CM

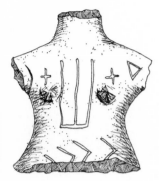

75, 76 Torsos with inverted Vs (75) and crosses (76) above breasts, triple verticle lines and chevrons. Sitagroi III, Macedonia. C. 4000 BC

77 Head of a Bird Goddess with pointed beak and lozenge-shaped eyes. Rug-Bair, Macedonia. Early Vinča, c. 5300–5100 BC

78 Bird-headed figure (a vessel protome) with an ideogram on the body composed of chest bands and chevrons. The Vinča site. c. 5000 BC

may be related to the ritual of rain invocation. On masked Vinča heads or zoomorphic lids the incised parallel lines merging on the nose ridge and the forehead give an impression of torrents of water running down the mask.

The 'cat-headed' Vinča lids have puzzled archaeologists since the discovery of the Vinča site. They certainly do not portray cats, since the cat was not known in prehistoric Europe. Are they bears? Birds? The puzzle can be solved only by studying all the accumulated symbols. They have large incised, usually semicircular, human eyes, ears, bird's beak and a V or chevron engraved above the beak. Bands of striations, punctuated bands, or parallel lines clearly show their connection with water. They are not given mouths, but sometimes have a round depression below the beak, as on many other bird masks from which 'water flows in all four directions'.

The relationship between water and the bear is further indicated by bear-shaped cult vases, abundantly represented in the Danilo, Sesklo, Butmir and Lengyel cultures. The Danilo bear-shaped vases are solidly covered with belts of zigzags, chevrons and striated diamonds, symbolic of flowing water. Large paws of bears from the Butmir settlement at Obre, probably once part of a water container, are also decorated with incised parallel lines.

The presence throughout the Neolithic and Chalcolithic periods in Europe and Anatolia of V's, chevrons or cross signs on female breasts or immediately below them, or on arms supporting breasts, suggests an identification of rain with milk, an old and widespread belief which induced people to see women's breasts or cow udders in the clouds. This belief still extant among the Arctic hunters points to its origin in Palaeolithic times. V's are marked on the breasts of a painted clay figure of a goddess from shrine VI in Çatal Hüyük (Mellaart 1967: 182, Fig. 50, Plate 79), and many of the Proto-Sesklo goddesses of Thessaly have red-painted V's on their breasts or chevrons incised on their hands. There appears to have been an association between a female divinity and divine moisture from the skies. A beaked figurine from Porodin has, in addition to her normal breasts, breast-like protuberances on the neck, perhaps to invigorate the influence of her magical breasts. The double-headed Bird Goddess from Vinča has breasts marked with V's and her body is covered with a meandrous design. Among Cucuteni vessels, breasts sprout from basins held by a female figure and from jars; they are usually depicted in the centre of bands or parallel lines symbolizing rain torrents. Two of the many figurines found in the Chalcolithic levels of the Sitagroi tell in northeastern Greece illustrate the arrangement of these rain- or milk-invoking symbols. Unfortunately, they are headless but other East Balkan figurines bearing the same signs have bird heads. Note that there are three parallel lines between the breasts and chevrons on these figurines; an identical sign of three lines connected on top by a horizontal line recurs on the figures in Early Vinča reliefs. On the neck of an anthropomorphic vessel from the Bükk site of Kenezlö in northeastern Hungary, there is a mask with three lines incised between the eyes and three more below the mouth. The body is incised with zigzagging and meandering lines, simulating 'torrents of water': tiny arm stumps suggest the goddess' wings. Signs of three interconnected lines engraved on human figures are present in the Magdalenian era of the Upper Palaeolithic. Rectangles consisting of three lines connected at the ends appear engraved on a human figure on the bone point from the Abri Mège at Teyjat (Dordogne). The human image, probably an abstract rendering of a goddess, has a tiny head, double ovaloid vulva with two lines below it, a serpentine decoration along the sides and strokes down the legs (Marshack 1972: 315). The serpentine stroked design along each side seems to be a snake or water image. The symbolic connection with the abstract Snake or Bird Goddess images of the Neolithic is apparent.

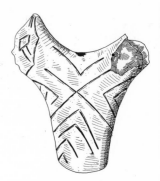

79 Double-headed Vinča stand with hole in the middle incised with crossed chest bands and chevrons. Crnokalačka Bara, southeastern Yugoslavia. c. 5000 BC

Chevrons (multiple V's), two, three or more parallel lines and a crossed chest band characterize the bird-headed or bird-masked figurines. These signs are either incised or painted on their masks, heads, arms or body. A crossed band with chevrons appears incised on the chest of a bird-shaped figurine from Vinča, and a similar chest-band sign, associated with symbols of three connected lines, occurs on the body of a double-headed Bird Goddess. The chest-band sign is also found incised on double-headed stands and consistently occurs in combination with chevrons on bird-headed or bird-masked figurines, clay stamps and flat plaques. An Early Vinča anthropomorphic lid from Parţa bears, below the goddess' eyes and nose, an X, probably signifying chest bands, and a chevron appears in the upper segment. A Tisza pot with a spout, probably used as a libation vase in ritual ceremonies, has the same ideogram incised on one panel; a second panel contains four groups of three parallel lines and a third panel large meanders. An altar table from Vinča, supporting a female figure seated in front of a vessel, probably portraying a water-invocation scene, was also decorated with V's, a chest band and meander motifs. Unfortunately, the upper part of the seated figure is lost. Another altar table from Fafos portrays a bear- or bull-legged altar table. The woman holding the vessel seems to be wearing a mask representing a bear or a bird. The altar is decorated with chevrons. A rain-invocation or water-divination scene can be recognized in the sculpture from Bordjoš in northern Yugoslavia, representing a nude woman seated on a stool with a large basin on her lap. The stool is decorated with a meander design. From what follows we shall see that the meander symbolizes water.

80 Clay seal bearing an ideogram of a Bird Goddess: crossed chest bands and chevrons. Predionica, Early Vinča site near Priština, southern Yugoslavia. End of sixth millennium BC

117

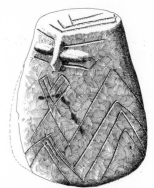

81 Lid, bearing symbols of Bird Goddess: chevrons and incised chest bands. Early Vinča. Parţa site, western Romania, end of sixth millennium BC

77 Late Vinča vase with panels still showing the 'rain-torrent' motif. Meander panel on the other side. The Vinča site

78, 79 Zoomorphic Vinča lids with a bird's beak and incised bands of 'streaming rain'. Vinča site: Early Vinča (78), Late Vinča (79)

80, 81 Bear-shaped vase, incised with bands of zigzagging lines and striated triangles. Smilčić site near Zadar. Danilo culture. Second half of sixth millennium BC

82 Bear's paw decorated with bands of parallel lines. Obre II, Early Butmir. Early fifth millennium BC

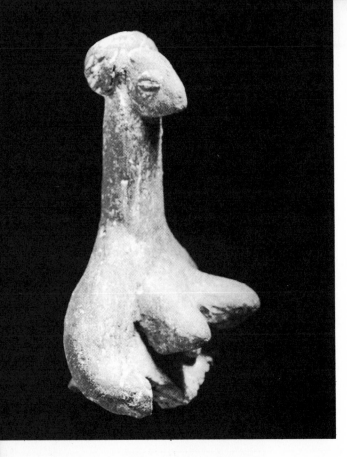

83, 84 Bust of a bird-headed goddess with long cylindrical neck, cap or hair bun, large breasts and incised chevrons over lower arms. Thessaly. Ayca Anna (Meg. Vrysi) at Tirnavos, Sesklo. *c.* 6000 BC

85 Upper torso of a figurine with cylindrical head and bird's beak. Porodin, southern Yugoslavia. Central Balkan Neolithic, Starčevo complex. Early sixth millennium BC

86 Double-headed goddess. Early Vinča. Rastu, western Romania. End sixth millennium BC

87 Anthropomorphic pot suggesting a bird-shaped water divinity. The goddess' mask is marked with chevrons and triple lines. Kenezlö, Bükk group, northeastern Hungary. End sixth millennium BC

88 Jar featuring breasts set in 'rain torrent' bands. Early Cucuteni, Negresti, northeastern Romania. Late fifth millennium BC

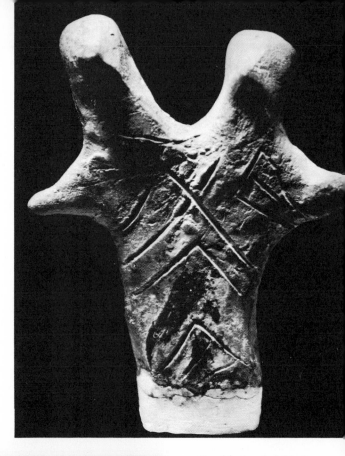

89 Head of a Bird Goddess with chevrons incised above the beak and on top of the head. Kálojanovec, central Bulgaria. *c.* 5000 BC

90 Double-headed Bird Goddess marked with chest-band sign, chevrons and signs consisting of three connected lines. The Vinča site. Early fifth millennium BC

91 Altar table with figure of a woman holding a vessel. Both damaged. Possibly a rain-invocation scene. Bird Goddess' symbol on front face of altar. The Vinča site. 5000 – 4500 BC

93 Cult vase with spout. The incised panels
show: left, the X and chevron design;
right, large meanders. In between, three
connected parallel lines. Borsod, northeastern
Hungary, end sixth millennium BC

92 Altar table in form of an animal-masked
woman holding a vessel decorated with
meandering bands. Legs are bear- or
bull-shaped. Early Vinča. Fafos I, southern
Yugoslavia

94 Seated nude woman holding a large basin.
Possibly a rain-invocation scene. Elaborate
diamond-shaped design incised on the side of
stool. Tisza culture. Bordjoš, northern
Yugoslavia

82 Terracotta head with Bird Goddess' mask decorated with meanders over the top and parallel lines (rain torrents?) round the eyes. Potporanj, northeastern Yugoslavia. Classical Vinča. Fifth millennium BC

THE MEANDER SYMBOL OF COSMIC WATERS

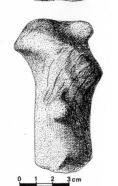

83 Upper torso of an Early Vinča figurine with a large meander incised over the body and face (mask). Potporanj at Vršac, northeastern Yugoslavia

84 Figure of water-bird incised with meanders on back and wings, V's in front. Perforations pierce the body at neck and tail. The Vinča site, Classical Vinča

The meander was incised on figurines with bird-masks or bird-heads, snake-arms or snake-legs, and on masks, cult vessels and altars in all cultural groups of Old Europe. Vinča statues representing dignified personages, some seated and some standing, wear a disc-shaped pendant and have the meander symbol marked either on the abdomen or on the back or front of the skirt. The same type of incised pattern occurs on the forehead of more elaborate masks, at the upper right corner of the mask, or between the eyes and extending down the bridge of the nose. The front and the back of the two-headed Vinča goddess from Gomolava is decorated with a large meander, while a meander incised on the back of a water bird from Vinča reflects its association with a bird divinity and with water.

The enlarged or double meander motif must have originated as two opposing lines – like two snakes with their heads meeting but not touching – subsequently elaborated into an enormous meander design which appears incised on body, pediment and throne. Double meanders and double snakes were also incised upon discs. Frequently the meander is associated with striated triangles, chevrons, bands of parallel lines and semicircles; zoomorphic lids from Vinča sites and an oval plaque from the Vinča settlement of Banjica serve as examples. The double meander, incised with white-encrusted lines at the centre of the latter must have been a sign of essential importance in the cult of the goddesses.

A Linear B tablet (Gg 702) from Knossos, deciphered by Palmer (1965), informs us that the labyrinth must have been a symbol of the abode or 'palace' of the 'Mistress of the Labyrinth' (*da-pu-ri-to-jo-po-ti-ni-ja*). This palace or cult place, *i.e.* the labyrinth, is thought to be depicted on a tablet from Pylos. The Pylian 'labyrinth' is more complex than the meanders of the Vinča, Gumelniţa, Tisza, Lengyel, Bükk and Cucuteni civilizations, and dates from 2000–3000 years later, but the link between them is nevertheless apparent. The role of the labyrinth in games and dances was still strong in Roman, Hellenistic and even later times. Comparison of the interlaced movements of an Ancient Greek dance known as the *Geranos* ('crane') to the labyrinth structure (Harrison 1894: CXXVIII) leads to an understanding of the connection between the labyrinth and its Mistress, the prehistoric Bird Goddess. The crane may have been one of the incarnations of a water divinity, and the Neolithic figurines with flattened posteriors, stiff legs and long necks probably represent cranes or water birds of a similar kind. Water birds with long legs and necks are depicted on Cucuteni vases and similar bird-forms have been found modelled in clay. Indeed, all the evidence seems to indicate that the divinity associated with the meander had the attributes of a water bird.

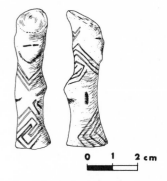

85 *Schematized figurine (a stand) with meanders and chevrons in front and at the back of the neck. Masked head with peaked hat. Early Vinča. Turdaş site, Transylvania*

Panels of labyrinthine design associated with gate and water-stream symbols appear on anthropomorphic vases and figurines of enthroned goddesses from Szegvár, a settlement of the Tisza culture located near Szentes in Hungary. There is a systematically repeated arrangement of the incised motifs on these artifacts. The body and throne of the seated Szegvár goddess is covered with meanders organized in vertical and horizontal panels, interspersed with parallel vertical lines and narrow panels of zigzags. Although the panelled design is suggestive of a garment made up of many pieces of cloth sewn together, it is unlikely that the entire decorative composition was merely a copy of an embroidered costume. The design appears to symbolize several levels of mythical waters. Corresponding symbolism is encountered on vessels from the Tisza sites of Szegvár and Kökénydomb, cult vases which were apparently used in ritual or festivals dedicated to the water divinity. The Szegvár footed vessel is divided by vertical lines into four alternating broad and narrow panels containing different patterns of incised labyrinthine meanders. Six holes at the top and bottom of the narrow front panel must have had some special significance associated with the functions of the goddess. Incised patterns on the cylindrical body of the vase from Kökénydomb seem to show meanders superimposed upon gates. On the upper part of the cylinder is a sign composed of seven horizontal lines with six dots below and a vertical line above branching into three dots on top.

86 *Lower part of standing Vinča figurine bearing meander sign in front. Agino Brdo site near Belgrade*

87 *Lower part of broken terracotta portraying an enthroned goddess. Meanders incised on the sides of the throne. The Vinča site. Classical Vinča*

95 Vinča mask with vertical lines and a meander framed with V's incised above the right eye. Crnokalačka Bara, southeastern Yugoslavia

96 Pentagonal Vinča mask with meanders above eyes and snakes below. Medvednjak, central Yugoslavia *c*. 5000 BC

97 Bird Goddess from Vinča with a medallion in the centre of the chest bands, another at the nape of the neck, and a meander on front and back of skirt and on top of mask, *c*. 4500 – 4000 BC

98 Fragment of a clay disc incised with meanders and spirals. The Vinča site. *c*. 4500 BC

99 Upper torso of a Vinča figurine wearing a pentagonal mask. A meander symbol is added above the nose. Medvednjak, central Yugoslavia

100, 101 Double-headed goddess from Gomolava, northern Yugoslavia. Meanders incised at front and back. Perforations probably for attachment of perishable materials (wings, plumes?). Vinča, mid-fifth millennium BC

102, 103 The Szegvár enthroned goddess. Tisza culture. Szegvár-Tüzköves at Szentes, southeastern Hungary. *c.* 5000 BC

104 Footed vase decorated with meander panels and six dots at top of panel. Tisza culture. Szegvár-Tüzköves, southeastern Hungary

105-107 Large vase in shape of an enthroned goddess decorated with meanders, gate symbol and zigzags; a comb sign featuring three dots on top, six at bottom, is incised in the upper part. Tisza culture. Kökénydomb at Hódmesövásárhely, southeastern Hungary. End sixth millennium BC

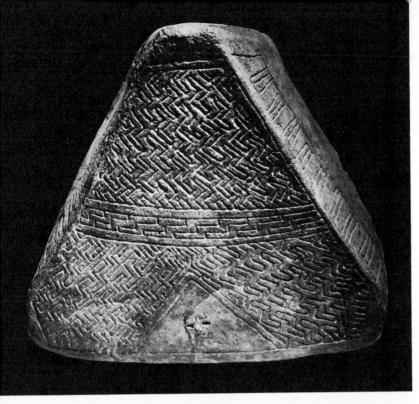

108, 109 Altar depicting several spheres of the universe. It probably portrays a cosmogonical myth (birth of water divinity – horned snake?). Tisza culture. Kökénydomb, southeastern Hungary

110 Vase with large meander pattern on upper part and figurine of goddess between snake spirals in the middle band. Painted in dark brown and white. Late Classical Cucuteni. Traian, northeastern Romania. *c.* 4000 BC

The richly incised decoration on the Tisza altar from Kökény-domb may relate to cosmogonical myths. Its triangular front is covered by meanders and divided into two levels by a horizontal band of meandering lines. In the centre of the lower register two eyes and a nose are set in a triangle. Two vertical lines above the nose may symbolize horns (a horned Snake Goddess?). Groups of parallel lines arranged in threes form panels along each side of the altar. The decorative organization suggests several levels of cosmic waters with the goddess' abode or birthplace at the lowest level. Furthermore the triangle may represent a schematic rendering of a female goddess.

Similar and symbolically identical designs are found on white-encrusted East Balkan Boian and Vădastra vases and models of shrines, and on the Cucuteni polychrome painted wares from Moldavia. An outstanding model of a shrine, 40 cm. high, very probably dedicated to either the Bird or the Snake Goddess was unearthed in the settlement of Vădastra, in the lower Danube region. Its façade, solidly covered with zigzagging labyrinthine meanders in relief, has a gate in the centre. Several necklaces in relief adorn the goddess' neck. The head, as the illustration shows, is reconstructed. The model is hollow inside. The whole complicated symbolic design, resembling that on the Szegvár ceramics and identical with finds from sites which are separated by the Carpathian Mountains and a distance of about 600 km., must have been reinforced and maintained by common mythical beliefs and imagery.

88 Early Vinča zoomorphic lid (broken at the bottom) incised with meanders, chevrons and parallel lines. Aiud, central Romania

89 Oval clay plaque with a meander incised in the centre, surrounded by chevrons and semicircles. Early Vinča. Banjica site near Belgrade

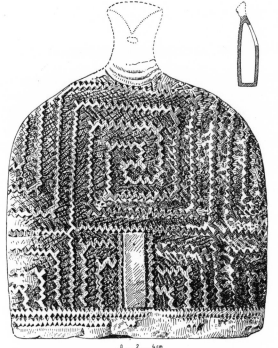

90 Tablet from Pylos marked with labyrinth pattern. c. 1200 BC

91 Model of a temple decorated with excised meanders filled with white paste. Vădastra, southwestern Romania. First half of fifth millennium BC

131

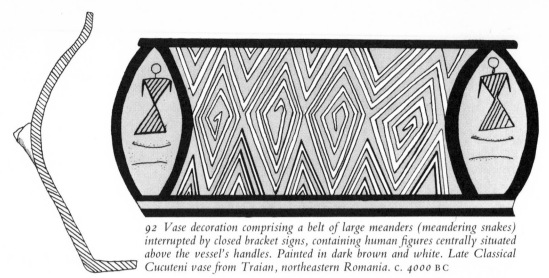

92 *Vase decoration comprising a belt of large meanders (meandering snakes) interrupted by closed bracket signs, containing human figures centrally situated above the vessel's handles. Painted in dark brown and white. Late Classical Cucuteni vase from Traian, northeastern Romania. c. 4000 BC*

92, 110   The Cucuteni painted vases represent etiological myths, perhaps depicting the birth or abode of a water divinity. This divinity has an anthropomorphic form enclosed in a bracket-shaped design which in turn is contained within a belt of large rhombic meanders. This type of narrative motif was encountered on several vases from the Traian settlement in northern Moldavia. The reconstructed part of such a vase shows four large snake meanders and a standing goddess consisting of two opposed triangles, her figure framed by a closed bracket-like symbol. The fully reconstructed vase from Traian illustrates the organization of the cosmos: meanders occupying the upper levels and below them the goddess' abode with her image framed by spiralling snakes. Human figures consisting of two triangles and with bird-clawed hands are familiar to Minoan art (Alexiou 1958: Pl. IA). These and other compositions connect the labyrinthine motifs with the mythical water sphere beyond or below which the goddess resides. Many cult vessels are decorated with the meander pattern and must have served the water cult either as containers for holy water or when invoking the water deity.

THE ORIGIN OF THE BIRD GODDESS AND HER IMAGE DURING THE NEOLITHIC

The meander and chevron were not invented by the early agriculturists. Symmetric and rhythmic meanders and bands of chevrons are encountered on Magdalenian bone and ivory objects. The motifs appear in association with each other and with bands of parallel lines. Even infinite, 'endless' interconnected meanders are already present on Upper Palaeolithic sculptures and ornaments. Best examples come from Mezin, an early Magdalenian or 'Kostenki IV' site on the bank of the Desna in the Ukraine, excavated in 1908/9. The ivory figurines bearing chevrons and meanders appear to portray water

112 Marble sculpture with long phallic neck and pronounced buttocks. Slightly stooping position reminiscent of a bird. Attica, Greece. Typologically Proto-Sesklo

111 Small Vinča figurine with female breasts, bird's beak and male genitals. The Vinča site

113–115 Figurine of Bird Goddess from Anza II, Macedonia. c. 5800 BC

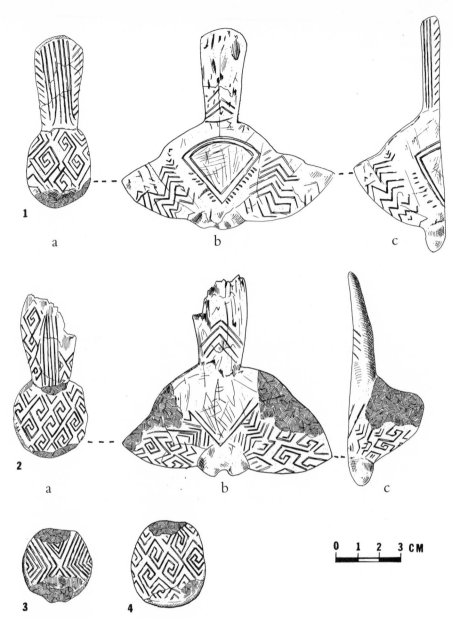

93 Upper Palaeolithic ivory
figurines decorated with
incised meanders, chevrons
and parallel lines. a, back;
b, front (exploded design);
c, profile. Bottom row: lower
parts without necks. Mezin,
western Ukraine. c. 14,000
BC (chronology not
firmly established)

0   1   2   3 CM

birds with long necks. They unquestionably have characteristics of
a bird and must be grouped together with the schematized female
figurines or female human and bird hybrids of the Magdalenian
Petersfels type (Marshack 1972: 284, 306–308) and with the Neolithic
'steatopygous' figurines described in the previous chapter. Water
birds, such as the crane, heron, wild goose, wild duck or grebe, were
sacred to the northern hunting tribes. Together with the bear and
the elk they were venerated throughout the prehistory of northern
Eurasia, and in myth have not lost their importance to this day. For
the northern hunters the water bird was the major food supply, and

the well-being of the people depended to a great extent on its regular return from the south in the spring. The divinity symbolized by a water bird must have been a giver of nourishment. Portrayals of water birds in stone and bone are known from Upper Palaeolithic sites in Europe and Siberia. It is the notion of hybridization of bird and woman which led to the creation of a rigidly schematized type found in Mezin and Petersfels. The geometric signs were necessary to invigorate the effectiveness of these amulets. Chevrons emphasize the avian character, and the meander, the mythical waters or the energy of waters and their mistress, the snake.

Chikalenko regards the Mezin meanders as a new artistic design, hitherto unknown to the art of mankind, which shows in graphic form the understanding or feeling of rhythm and symmetry. He further calls this art 'rhythmographic', akin to music and dance. 'In fact, in the beginning it is the dance of a hand upon a smooth surface – a hand armed with a chisel – in order to eliminate unwanted smoothness. Then, subsequently, there arises a play, an amusement, a sport' (Chikalenko 1953: 534). He sees here the beginning of pure art, where rhythm and symmetry existed in a most naked form with no concealed accessories. 'This art', he says, 'does not imitate anything in its designs, nor does it express any idea.' In view of the consistent and persistent association of the meander and the water bird and the water snake, it is difficult to see mere amusement or sport in the chiselling of endless meanders by the Palaeolithic artist and to concede a completely independent discovery, divorced from religious belief, for this motif. I feel there was an inspiration – the rippling of water, the sinuous movement of a snake, or a dance imitating water birds – and a linking of the divinity with its own aquatic sphere.

The 'bisexualism' of the water-bird divinity is apparent in the emphasis on the long neck of the bird symbolically linked with the phallus or the snake from Upper Palaeolithic times and onwards throughout many millennia. This 'bisexualism' may derive from the fusion of two aspects of the divinity, that of a bird and that of a snake, and not from female and male principles. The image of a phallic Bird Goddess dominates during the seventh and sixth millennia in the Aegean area and the Balkans. Sometimes she is a life-like erect phallus with small wings and a posterior of a woman, which, if seen in profile, is readily identifiable as a bird's body and tail. Or she may take the form of a nude female figurine with a disproportionately long and massive neck which obviously represents a phallus, as in a marble figurine from Attica. 'Bisexualism' is reflected in bird-shaped vases with cylindrical necks and in containers shaped like a bird's body attached to a female human figurine having a cylindrical head. The concept of the fusion of the sexes occasionally reappears in representations of hermaphroditic figurines of the Vinča culture having

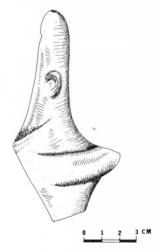

94 Proto-Sesklo terracotta figurine with neck in the form of a phallus and with bird's wings and tail. Tsangli, Thessaly. c. 6000 BC

135

male genital organs and female breasts. Such figures have beaked heads and sharply protruding posteriors, notably in the Early Vinča complex.

Bird-woman hybrids vary in the degree of their schematization. One may be a bird with the breasts of a woman; another may have wings and the body of a bird, but the head of a woman. In an overwhelming majority of cases, she is a hybrid having female buttocks outlined in the shape of a bird's body, female breasts, a bird's beak, a long neck and either wings or arm stumps. Her erect posture, with the upper part of the body bent forward, is that of a bird. A figurine from Anza demonstrates typical hybridized features of the Bird Goddess: the torso takes the form of a bird's body and even the wings are indicated; yet the figure has naturalistically rendered female buttocks.

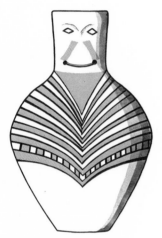

95 *Early Vinča Bird Goddess from Anza in the form of a large vase. Anza IV, Macedonia.* c. *5300– 5000* BC

THE 'LADY BIRD' AND THE 'LADY SNAKE' OF THE CHALCOLITHIC ERA

When the Old European civilization reached its cultural peak around 5000 BC there emerged a sophisticated image of the Bird and Snake Goddess. She is now either an exquisitely shaped vase wearing a mask or a lady wearing an elaborate dress and a mask.

The Early Vinča settlement at Anza in Macedonia yielded a number of vases with the goddess' eyes moulded in relief on a cylindrical neck. All were grouped together on the floor of a house. Associated with another house was a vase, 92 cm. high, with a goddess' face engraved and painted on the neck. Below it, a pendant necklace is indicated in relief. The body of the vase was solidly painted in red and cream bands meeting in the centre. An overwhelming majority of all the figurines found in this settlement belonged to the standing or enthroned Bird Goddess. She seems to be the most important goddess of the Vinča people since her image dominates in all known settlements. Of all the articulate sculptures from the Vinča site, more than forty per cent had ornithomorphic features.

The goddess' epiphany expressed in bird form finds its most evocative manifestation in the famous Vinča 'Hyde vase', a gracefully floating duck, which has two rounded protuberances on the top of its head and wears a mask. This *askos*, about 40 cm. long, is hollow inside, and its yellowish-orange walls are surprisingly thin. The surface is channelled throughout, apparently imitative of rippling water. Wings and plumage are indicated by raised arches and black painted bands. Another vase representing the goddess from the same site and phase and having a similar rippled surface of orangy colour, takes the form of a standing female with bird's posterior and wearing a large pentagonal mask. Known as the 'Venus of Vinča', she has human breasts, abdomen and legs. Each of the arm stumps has two perforations, probably for the attachment of wings. An outstanding ornithomorphic vase unearthed in Grivac in central Yugoslavia, has nearly life-like characteristics of a bird with plumage indicated by engraved parallel lines along the whole length of the body, but the stout legs are shaped like those of a woman (Kragujevac Museum). The missing lid probably bore the masked head of the goddess.

The eyes and arched brow-ridges of the goddess persistently recur on necks and lids of East Balkan and Cucuteni vases. The numinous   119 nature of the dominating eyes, which together with the arch of the eyebrows and beak or nose (usually connected with the brow-ridges in the shape of an anchor or letter T) contribute to the bird-like character, persist throughout several millennia in the archaeological record. They are familiar throughout the fourth and third millennia BC and are well known from the early settlements of Troy. The owlish features may stem originally from the representation of the horned head of a snake.

A type of late Vinča figurine of the Bird Goddess depicts a woman wearing an elaborate dress and a bird's mask. Where the mask   120, 121 represents the head of duck or other water bird, these became master-pieces of detail during this period. The chic coiffure of one East Balkan Bird Goddess consists of a pony-tail or a peaked cap, others   124 wear a double spiral or snake coil. A spiralling snake may also be   127 engraved on the neck or the upper part of the body of a figurine, as for example on the masterful little sculpture of a masked goddess from Vădastra in Romania. A meander was excised on the back of   125 her neck and filled with white paste. Snake spirals, meanders, dotted bands or parallel horizontal painted bands often decorate the costume of the standing or seated Lady Snake.

At all periods and in all regions of Old Europe one, three or six holes or notches were frequently cut into the throat of the Snake or Bird Goddess. One, three or six holes or notches (and sometimes   126, 128 seven, perhaps by mistake) also occur on vases decorated with meanders or parallel lines symbolizing water (see Pls. 77, 104–107; Fig. 84). Three lines or a vertical line in the middle of the V sign are associated with the figurines of the Bird Goddess only (see Pls. 93, 95, 105–107, 121; Figs. 75–77, 82, 88). The Snake and Bird Goddess usually wears three or six necklaces (see Pls. 124, 131; Figs. 85, 91) and three arm rings (see Pl. 121). Six chevrons cover the upper part of the gracile Lady of Cucuteni. The number 'three' and its   129, 130 duplication apparently possessed a certain symbolic significance where the goddess was concerned. The Minoan bell-shaped idols with snake hands on breasts are decorated with painted horizontal bands in groups of three (Evans, *Palace of Minos*, IV, 1, Fig. 120: 7) and, in Minoan and Greek art, three columns are associated with birds, and with Athena. Three figures, three lines and three dots

116, 117 Cult vase in form of a duck, with a human masked head and wearing a crown. Channel-decorated and painted in black bands. The Vinča site. Mid-Vinča, first half of fifth millennium BC

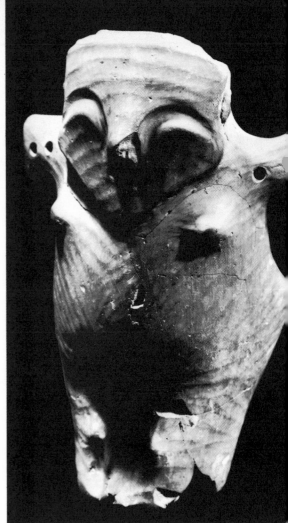

118 Standing Bird Goddess in the form of a vessel. Channelled surface, orange colour. The Vinča site. Mid-Vinča, first half of fifth millennium BC

119 Eyes and beak of Bird Goddess from the neck of a vase. Ruginoasa, Cucuteni A site, northeastern Romania, c. late fifth millennium BC

120 'Lady Bird' from Vinča. Late Vinča

121 Late Vinča Bird Goddess wearing duck's mask. V sign with a vertical line on the chest. Supska at Čuprija, central Yugoslavia

122, 123 Bird Goddess' mask in the form of a duck's head. Late Vinča. Vinča mound

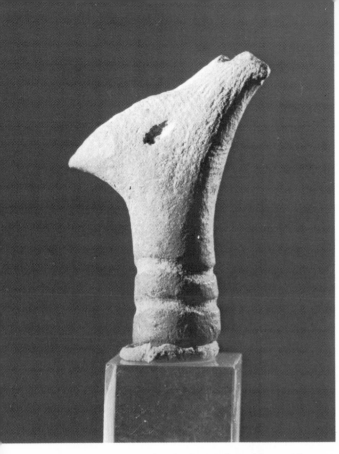

124 Miniature head of a Bird Goddess with a tuft or crest and channels for necklaces. Sitagroi mound (Period III), northeastern Greece. East Balkan civilization. *c.* 4000 BC

125 The Bird or Snake Goddess from Vǎdastra, lower Danube, Romania. Relief design includes snake coils in front, meander at the back

126, 127 Heads with snake-spiral coiffure. Sitagroi mound (Period III), northeastern Greece

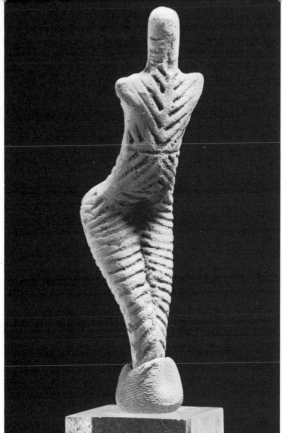

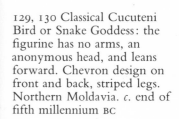

129, 130 Classical Cucuteni
Bird or Snake Goddess: the
figurine has no arms, an
anonymous head, and leans
forward. Chevron design on
front and back, striped legs.
Northern Moldavia. *c.* end of
fifth millennium BC

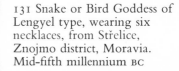

131 Snake or Bird Goddess of
Lengyel type, wearing six
necklaces, from Střelice,
Znojmo district, Moravia.
Mid-fifth millennium BC

128 Snake or Bird
Goddess of Cucuteni
type from Bernovo
Luka, western Ukraine.
Proto-Cucuteni.
Characterized by six
notches on the neck.
Mid-fifth millennium BC

consistently appear on Corinthian and Boeotian sculptures and vase paintings. A sculptural masterpiece of the seventh century BC was discovered in the temple of Poseidon on Isthmia. It is composed of three feminine figures standing on a round base and supporting a large vase encircled by a snake. In each compartment between the figures, heads of rams with large winding horns appear (Museum of Corinth). Proto-Corinthian vases frequently display water-bird figures in association with three vertical lines, undulating lines and a net pattern. A Boeotian Snake Goddess dated to 575–550 BC is depicted with hair falling on her shoulders in three clusters. Her arms are snakes, her dress and tiara are decorated with dotted lines (Higgins 1963 : 3). A snake-headed figurine holding a baby snake (or a loaf of bread) from the Hellenistic period in Corinth has a headdress decorated with three discs.

Each cultural area of Old Europe had its own method of portraying the Snake and Bird Goddess, but the symbolic signs and the general conception of the image were the same throughout. (For classical representations of the Vinča civilization, see Pls. 97, 120, 122, 123; for those of the East Balkan civilization, see Pls. 125–127; for those from the Cucuteni and Lengyel cultures, see Pls. 128–130 respectively). These examples are from contexts widely separated in time and space, reflecting the pervasive symbolic importance of the 'Lady Bird' or 'Lady Snake' motif in the mythical imagery of Old Europe.

THE SNAKE AND BIRD GODDESS AS NURSE

In contrast to the Indo-Europeans, to whom Earth was the Great Mother, the Old Europeans created maternal images out of water and air divinities, the Snake and Bird Goddess. A divinity who nurtures the world with moisture, giving rain, the divine food which metaphorically was also understood as mother's milk, naturally became a nurse or mother. Indeed, the terracotta figurines of an anthropomorphic snake or bird holding a baby are encountered at various periods and in many regions of Old Europe, and in Minoan, Cypriote, and Mycenaean cultures as well. This is exemplified by the Dimini seated Nurse or Mother, striped like a snake and with a spiralling snake over the abdomen, from the site of Sesklo, as well as by an anthropomorphic figure wearing a bird mask and holding a baby similarly masked, from Vinča. Bird-headed figurines frequently have humps on their backs, and may very well be stylized renderings of sacks for babies.

132 Bird-masked woman holding a bird-masked baby. Plastic decoration of
a large vase. Mid-Vinča. The Vinča site

96 Enthroned Goddess holding a child. Striped and spiral-painted, she may represent a Snake Goddess. Sesklo site, Thessaly. Late Neolithic

RECAPITULATION

The Snake and Bird Goddess was a predominant image in the pantheon of Old Europe. As a combined snake and water bird with a long phallic neck she was inherited from the Magdalenian culture of the Upper Palaeolithic. Though usually portrayed as a hybrid, this divinity could also be a separate Snake Goddess or Bird Goddess. She is the feminine principle.

Her status is shown by crossed chest bands and a medallion hung round the neck, as well as by an elaborate dress and head-gear. Her avian characteristics are stressed by a forward-leaning or stooping posture, arm stumps with perforations for the attachment of feathers, letter V signs and multiple chevrons over her body or mask. V's, chevrons, and crossed chest bands became the ideograms of the Bird Goddess and appear on figurines, stands, stamp seals, plaques, cult vessels, altar tables, and other cult objects. The snake characteristics were emphasized by parallel or zigzag lines, dotted bands, and most frequently, by snakes spiralling over the body and by a 'snake-spiral' coiffure.

The upper and lower waters which she controlled were represented by labyrinthine meanders and snake spirals. As a source of rain she was invoked as documented by the sculptures of nude rain-invoking women holding large basins, altar tables in the shape of animal-masked women holding vessels, bear-shaped cult vessels, and a persistently recurring decorative motif made up of rain-torrent parallel lines, zigzags, and dotted bands. The bear must have been connected also with the mythical source of water, a motif probably inherited from the Palaeolithic era. Rain-bearing and milk-giving motifs were interwoven. Rain torrents and breasts appear on jars and basins used for rain invocation, and the goddess appears as a snake-masked and bird-masked nurse holding a snake- or bird-masked baby. Her abode or birthplace is beyond the upper waters.

The epiphany of this goddess mainly took the form of a snake, a water bird, a duck, goose, crane, diver bird, or perhaps an owl. In sculptural representations she is shown as an ornithomorphic vessel wearing a mask with human eyes and a bird's beak. Her numinous eyes and a triangular beak, or the snake, appear in cosmological representations which shows that she was a Mistress of life-generating cosmic forces. As the Egyptian Great Goddess Nut, she was the flowing unity of celestial primordial waters. As an owl she was also connected with the aspect of death.

THE BIRD GODDESS AND SNAKE GODDESS IN MINOAN CRETE AND IN ANCIENT GREECE

The Indo-European infiltration into the western Ukraine, Moldavia, and nearly the whole Danube region in the fourth millennium BC resulted in the enthronement of important local goddesses and gods and most conspicuously, the universal water divinity in the shape of a snake or bird. The great tradition of sculpting 'Lady Bird' figurines

97 Minoan Snake Goddess or her devotee with a bird's beak painted on leg of an altar table. Phaistos, Proto-palatial period, early second millennium B C

ceased in east central Europe. Only occasionally does her image re-emerge at the end of the fourth millennium and the early third millennium, notably in Troy and in the Baden complex in eastern Hungary. The situation was different in Minoan Crete, the Aegean Islands and in all areas where Minoan influence was strong, including the Greek mainland.

Minoan and Minoan-Mycenaean art generally abounds in birds, snakes, and women with wings or with snakes crawling up their arms or on top of their heads, the epiphanies and the anthropomorphic images of the goddess inherited from the Old European pantheon. In the Proto-palatial period (2000–1700 B C) the Snake and Bird Goddess is a familiar representation on cult vases, dishes, and altar tables. She is a beaked lady with snake curls or crest on her head and has snake arms as depicted on a stem of a round altar table and a dish in Phaistos. Peculiar Pre-palatial (Early Minoan) anthropomorphic vases with hollow breasts, owl-like eyes, and many necklaces, decorated with bands of zigzags and meanders, as found at Mallia (Zervos 1956: Fig. 116) or Mochlos in eastern Crete (*id.*: Fig. 187), considered to be 'divinities of the sea', probably originate in the Chalcolithic Old European water divinity. During the Palatial period in Crete, the Mistress of waters appears as a sophisticated lady, best known from the ivory and faience statuettes called 'Snake Goddesses', one holding snakes in her hands, another with snakes intertwined around the abdomen and breasts, and both having exposed breasts. The snake, like the bird, was a form in which the goddess became manifest. Nilsson in *Minoan-Mycenaean Religion* provides evidence of the presence of idols with bird-like attitudes and terracotta birds in Minoan shrines (Nilsson 1950: 330 ff.). The large bell-shaped idol from the Shrine of the Double Axes at Knossos has a bird perched upon its head, which probably is an image of the Bird Goddess. In the shrine of Gazi, three idols carry birds on their heads. A bird perches on an earlier Proto-palatial altar from the sanctuary of the Dove Goddess of Knossos. Another expression of the same idea is the small gold model of a shrine from shaft-grave IV at Mycenae, where birds perch on the horns of consecration. There are two pieces of gold leaf from shaft-grave III at Mycenae representing a nude woman with her arms held in front of her breast. One figure has a bird apparently in flight upon her head, the other has birds attached to her elbows by their tails. In the shrine of Gournia in eastern Crete three terracotta birds were found together with the anthropomorphic images of Snake Goddesses. Three terracotta birds were also discovered in the southwest wing of the palace of Hagia Triadha. A room at Palaikastro yielded three female figures and a lyre player in a group with six terracotta birds, and on an ivory plaque from the same Late Minoan I palace, a beautiful winged

146

water bird is portrayed with a crest of three feathers (Zervos 1956: Fig. 528). Three small terracotta birds were found in the cave at Patso among other votive animal figurines. The number three, it would seem was not accidental and was indeed connected with the mythical number of three which in the Neolithic and Chalcolithic era is evidenced by the continuous recurrence of three or six holes on the mouth or neck of the goddess, or three parallel lines or three chevrons. Birds portrayed on vases are exclusively water fowl, sea-gulls, ducks, cranes, or diver birds. Their bodies, wings or necks are decorated with striations and chevrons or snake zigzags (cf. Zervos 1956: Figs. 734 and 738; Zervos 1957: Fig. 336). Jugs of the Neo-palatial period of Crete are shaped like water birds and the painted decoration on them is conspicuously symbolic of flowing water, including chevrons, striations, bands of dots and groups of three vertical lines (cf. Zervos 1956: 571, 727, 729, 731).

Mycenaean art abounds in winged bird-woman images and snake-headed figures with round eyes, standing or seated on a throne and frequently wearing a crown; during Late Mycenaean (Late Helladic III) times, small terracotta figurines with cylindrical bodies and wings become very common (Mylonas 1956). The posture of the standing figures, leaning forward, their buttocks naturally upraised or of the half seated and seated figures, is surprisingly similar to that of the Neolithic-Chalcolithic figurines. Some of these Mycenaean figures are multiple, double-headed or double-bodied, a familiar trait of Vinča art. Painted on the figurines are usually vertical, some-times undulating stripes, reminiscent of the symbols of rain water or the sinuous movement of water snakes on Neolithic-Chalcolithic figurines, cult-vases or altars, and thrones which accommodate seated figures and are decorated with striations or undulating patterns. Since these forms and decorative motifs have no direct antecedents in the earlier Mycenaean (Indo-European) period, their appearance can best be explained as a re-emergence of the enduring, local pre-Indo-European tradition. It is feasible that these forms, which during the intervening period are absent from the archaeological record, were produced without a break but in a perishable material; alternatively, the Snake Goddess and Bird Goddess may have been secretly wor-shipped for some time after the advent of the Indo-Europeans, before manifesting themselves again in graphic and sculptural form at a later date.

The Bird Goddess or memories of her original image continued into the Iron Age. Meanders and water birds re-emerge in the art of the Geometric period and the Bird Goddess herself appears in the art of Ancient Greece as Athena; the bird-form has been shed but Athena is occasionally winged and the bird is her attribute. She sometimes appears in the semblance of a sea eagle, a gull, a swallow, a vulture, or a dove, thereby perpetuating the Minoan-Mycenaean tradition. On a Corinthian *aryballos* dating from about the beginning of the sixth century B C, a bird with a woman's head is shown perching behind Athena and at the side of the goddess is clearly written *Fous*, a variant form of a name given to the Diver-bird, *Aithuia*. In Megara there is a cliff called the cliff of Athena Aithuia, Athena the Diver-bird (Harrison 1961: 303; Nilsson 1950: 492). In the earliest known vase-painted representation of the rape of Cassandra a large human-headed bird stands behind the figure of Athena (*JHS* 1884: Pl. XL). In the time of Aristophanes it was a popular belief that Athena appeared as an owl in the battle against the Persians. He says: 'We conquered toward evening, for an owl flew through the ranks before the battle began' (Nilsson 1950: 493). A small red-figure jug in the Louvre shows the owl armed with helmet and spear, while on a black-figure vase at Uppsala a big owl perches on the altar towards which a ram is led to be sacrificed (*JHS* XXXII, 1912: 174, Fig. 1). On a black-figure vase from the British Museum a bull is led to sacrifice, followed by a procession of men towards the altar on which a bird, a sea-gull or a duck, perches. Next to the altar stands Athena, equipped with a shield and spear, and behind her is none other than the snake (Stengel 1890: Pl. I, *4*). The ram and bull sacrifice to the Bird and Snake Goddess is of great antiquity, since in the settlements of the East Balkan and Vinča civilizations, cult vases with the protomes in the shape of a ram's or bull's head and figurines portraying a ram 133–135 with three(!) horns or a neck decorated with groups of three horizontal lines were found in association with the images of the Bird and Snake Goddess. A small votive cult vase from Vinča was incised with 136 V's and chevrons, the ideograms of the Bird Goddess, and so was the 137 ram-headed vessel from Banjata in Bulgaria. The animal's head was incised with chevrons and horns – with parallel lines. Another aspect of the Greek owl which may have its beginnings in the Neolithic era is her association with the craft of spinning and hence with the sheep. A series of terracotta plaques show an owl with human arms spinning wool (Nilsson 1950: 493–4; an illustration in: *BCH* XXXII, 1908: 541, Pl. VII, 3). An *askos* from an Early Helladic II site at Zygouries near Corinth has a spout formed in the shape of a horned ram's head (Museum of Corinth).

Portrayals of Athena on black- or red-figure vases of Ancient Greece reveal her intimacy not only with birds but also with snakes. A snake crawls on or is concealed under her shield, or appears by her side, equal in height and majesty, as her double (Harrison 1961: 306). Why are Athena and the snake related in this way? Is this imagery not an inheritance from a deeper antiquity, from times when the cosmic Bird Goddess had as her counterpart a cosmic snake? Her association with the snake is old and intimate; the Minoan house goddess also appeared as a snake and as a bird, and the same associations go at least three millennia farther back.

How did Athena become a goddess of war, while the Minoan and Old European Bird Goddess was not? Why, too, it may be asked, is the chief war deity of the Greeks female? The answer is: Athena, as a direct descendant of the Minoan palace goddess and as the distant heir of Old Europe, became Indo-Europeanized and Orientalized during the course of two millennia of Indo-European and Oriental influence in Greece. The protectress of a city naturally became engaged in war. The name Athena is pre-Greek. The town Athenai is named after the goddess (Nilsson 1921; 1950: 489ff.).

Aphrodite Urania, born from the sea, was portrayed as flying through the air standing or sitting on a goose or being accompanied by three geese in the Greek terracottas of the sixth and fifth centuries BC; like Athena, she maintains certain Old European features of the Bird Goddess. Homer regarded Cyprus as her true home, but pre-Phoenician Cyprus was within the sphere of Minoan culture. There is strong reason to believe that 'Aphrodite' was a goddess-name originally common to the language of both islands. It is also believed that the Cretan name 'Ariadne', 'the very Holy One', was an early Hellenic description for Aphrodite herself (Farnell 1927: 18).

And who was Hera, the obviously un-Hellenic goddess of the ancient Greeks? In myths and legends she frequently appears together with Athena; the two are almost inseparable or are rivals. In Paestum, the temples of Athena and Hera stand next to one another. Although Hera married Zeus (the Indo-European Thunder God) during the Bronze Age (probably before the thirteenth century since in the Linear B tablets both names appear side by side), archaeological records reveal her as one of the most revered and pre-eminent goddesses. In sanctuaries and pictorial representations, Hera is shown in the central position; she occupies the throne, not Zeus who stands at her side. The sanctuaries dedicated to Hera were built in valleys at the estuaries of rivers, near the sea, and surrounded by pastureland. Such locations of Hera temples can be observed in Perachora at Corinth, Argos in the Peloponnese, on the islands of Samos and Lesbos, at Foce del Sele in western Italy, Sybaris, and elsewhere (Simon 1969: 40f.). She was the guardian of seamen and ruler over the pastureland. The votive offerings in her sanctuaries include terracotta snakes, horned animal figurines, calves, anthropomorphic idols with large eyes and decorated with spirals and meanders, and shrine models imitating the plan of a Doric temple or an apsidal house with walls or roof decorated with bands of meandering lines, striations or parallel vertical lines (examples of the latter from Perachora and Argos are reproduced by Simon 1969: 39). She, 'the Noble One' and 'Giver of All', was sculpted and described as tall and beautiful Hera or Roman Juno. More significantly, Homer called her βοῶπιζ, 'the cow-eyed'. Her hair curls like snakes in many of her portrayals, and a snake winds or zigzags vertically in the middle of her skirt (*cf.* a wooden relief from the Heraion II in Samos, *c.* 610 BC, Simon 1969: 50; or the Boeotian bell-shaped idol of *c.* 700 BC housed in the Louvre, portrayed with long snake curls and a panel in front in which the snake as a band of criss-cross lines is framed with zigzags and parallel lines and then flanked with water birds holding snakes in their beaks); or else her anthropomorphic image with curly hair, eyebrows in the shape of horns, and upraised hands is flanked by a snake (as painted on a plaque from a proto-Attic votive deposit in a house of the Geometric period in Greece: *Hesperia* 1933, 2: 604). According to Herodotus, Hera was taken over by the Greeks from the Pelasgians, the indigenous people in northern Greece. Her name, *e-ra*, as it appears in the Linear B tablet, is not of Indo-European origin. Homer and Plato connected her name with the air. Ludwig Preller in 1854 in his book on *Greek Mythology* described Hera as a feminine aspect of the sky, the air, which encompasses the aspect of female fertility. His definitition does not run counter to the functions of the prehistoric Snake Goddess, the ruler of all cosmic or heavenly waters. Archaic features to be found in portrayals of Hera betray much that links her with the Old European Snake Goddess. Both, Hera and Athena, are true heiresses of the Old European pantheon.

133

134

133, 134 Head of a ram, protome from a ritual vessel. Originally painted in red and white, it has three horns in the back of the head. Found in association with ornithomorphic vases. Anza, Macedonia. Early Vinča. *c.* 5300–5000 BC

135 Head of a ram, part of a ritual vessel. Distinguished by two groups of three parallel lines (chevrons) on the neck. Sitagroi mound, Macedonia, Greece. East Balkan civilization. *c.* 4000 BC

136 Classical Vinča ritual vessel with a ram's head at one end. It is covered with incised V's and chevrons. The Vinča site

137 Ritual vessel with ram's head at one end. There are incised chevrons on the animal's head and parallel lines on the horns and body. Baniata, central Bulgaria, East Balkan civilization

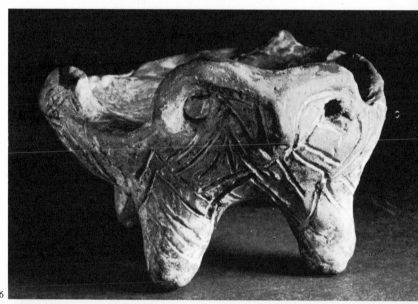

136

137

8   The Great Goddess of Life, Death and Regeneration

The 'Fertility Goddess' or 'Mother Goddess' is a more complex image than most people think. She was not only the Mother Goddess who commands fertility, or the Lady of the Beasts who governs the fecundity of animals and all wild nature, or the frightening Mother Terrible, but a composite image with traits accumulated from both the pre-agricultural and agricultural eras. During the latter she became essentially a Goddess of Regeneration, *i.e.* a Moon Goddess, product of a sedentary, matrilinear community, encompassing the archetypal unity and multiplicity of feminine nature. She was giver of life and all that promotes fertility, and at the same time she was the wielder of the destructive powers of nature. The feminine nature, like the moon, is light as well as dark.

THE ANDROGYNOUS AND CORPULENT GODDESS WITH FOLDED ARMS OF THE NEOLITHIC PERIOD

The Neolithic 'virgin' is almost as corpulent as the Palaeolithic 'Venus', particularly in central Anatolia and around the Aegean. Typical seventh-millennium sculptures from Çatal Hüyük in central Anatolia take the form of a massively fat woman, either standing or seated, supported by leopards. She usually either holds her hands up to her large breasts or rests them on the heads of accompanying animals (Mellaart 1967: 184, Figs. 52, 53). During the sixth millennium the goddess becomes more vigorous and less obese with her shoulders, upper arms and breasts accentuated. The forearms are folded and the hands are placed on or below the breasts. These characteristics are not found on figurines portraying the Bird Goddess. Folded arms are a characteristic feature of goddess figurines from the Hacılar, Sesklo and Starčevo complexes of central Anatolia, the Aegean area and the Balkan Peninsula. Throughout the Neolithic period her head is phallus-shaped suggesting her androgynous nature, and its derivation from Palaeolithic times (*cf.* phallic females: Marshack 1972: 292–93).

152

Five clay sculptures of vigorous and fat, but not steatopygous, ladies with phallic heads and folded arms were found in the largest early building at Nea Nikomedeia in northern Greece, a settlement dating from *c.* 6300 BC (Rodden 1965: 88). The content, size and central location of the building imply its use as a shrine. The shrine also yielded three toads carved from green and blue serpentine, probably representing the shape of the goddess manifest. One of the best preserved figurines from Nea Nikomedeia is a powerful erect   138
woman with broad shoulders, folded arms and hands on breasts. The head takes the form of a slightly flattened cylinder with a prominent pinched-up nose and slit-eyes incised in applied clay eyeballs. The hips and buttocks are constru ted from two stout, almost cylindrical pieces which were modelled individually and pegged together before firing. On top of the figure's head is a round protuberance suggesting a head-dress similar to the round or conical caps found on central Anatolian figurines. Other phallus-shaped heads reveal a circum-cision around the top and central hole suggesting that the cylinder   139
head was meant to be a phallus and was set in a female torso. This type of head was modelled separately and pegged to the torso before the clay hardened. Some of these 'pillar' heads have obvious facial features – incised eyes, pronounced nose and brow-ridge, but no mouth. In a number of them the hair is shown. Another category of phallus-shaped heads is characterized by facial features of animals.

Some phallic heads are no more than blank pillars. Almost all the figurines of the Hamangia culture have cylindrical phallus-shaped heads without any facial features. Their deployment in graves, and the folded-arm posture, suggest an association with death or regenera-tion. Some standing figures of *c.* 5000 BC with huge torsos supported by strong stump legs and breasts cushioned with the arches of massive arms are true sculptural masterpieces. The Hamangian figurines are related to sixth-millennium Hacılar sculptures which also have very strongly built bodies, muscular upper arms, huge abdomens and   98
thighs, and folded arms. Elaborate ones wear a conical cap and full dress. One class of figurines reveals the goddess dressed in a loincloth   99
and cap, holding a leopard cub.

Mainland Greek figurines, as well as the Hamangian, are formally related to those found at Hacılar, emphasizing the analogies that exist between the European and central Anatolian portrayals of this god-dess. A beautiful long-haired 'virgin', her head perfectly preserved, and several fragmentary torsos with extremely massive shoulders   143
and upper arms were found at Sesklo. Many Neolithic marble figurines in a standing or seated position from the Aegean area also have phallus-shaped heads with or without a prominent nose. Others   100
have modelled heads with facial features and a cap and some of them may represent masked heads. Horizontal forearms, massive arms and   141

153

138 Figurine of a goddess with phallus-shaped head and hands on breasts. Nea Nikomedeia, northern Greece. *c.* 6200 BC or earlier

139 Phallus-shaped head of a figurine with a pinched-up nose, slit eyes, deep incision near the top, and a canal down the middle. Rudnik, southwestern Yugoslavia. *c.* 6000 BC

139

140

138

140 Pillar-headed goddess with folded arms. Her back is flat. Hamangia culture, cemetery of Cernavoda, eastern Romania. *c.* 5000 BC

141 Marble figurine with folded arms and wearing a cap. Sparta, Peloponnese. *c.* 6000 BC

142 Marble figurine of a goddess with folded arms, columnar neck and a large pubic triangle. Aegean area, exact provenience not known

143 Upper torso of a goddess with massive shoulders and arms. Hands in typical position on breasts. Sesklo, Thessaly. *c.* 6000 BC

144 Marble figurine with exaggerated pubic triangle and schematized arms. Tell Azmak, central Bulgaria. Early sixth millennium BC

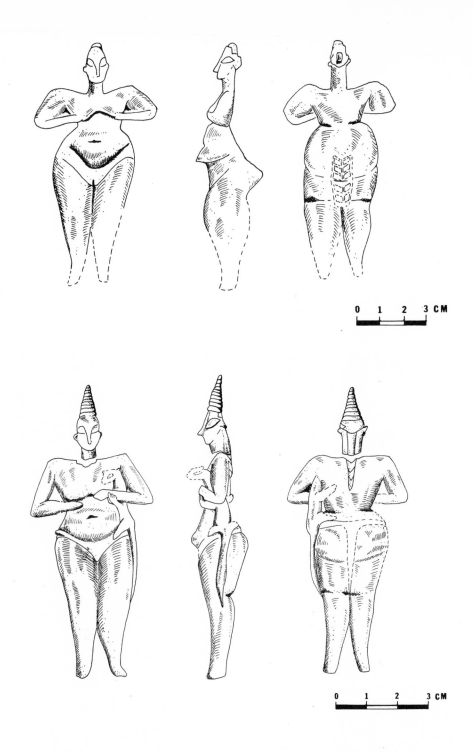

98, 99 Two strongly built and youthful goddesses with folded arms, wearing a cap and loin-cloth, from Hacılar, central Anatolia. One of them holds a leopard cub. c. *6000* BC

shoulders, and the huge abdomen of the marble figurines are typical of the Great Goddess. The physical strength of the female body was an ideal. The Old Europeans never held in esteem the meagre feminine appearance fashionable in our own day.

The marble idols with long cylindrical necks from the Cycladic islands of Amorgos and Naxos are usually sitting or squatting with arms folded. The most rigidly schematized ones resemble a pear or a violin and have been dubbed 'fiddle-shaped idols'. From the Aegean area numbers of very schematic white marble figurines are known – some mere cylinders or cones, and some adjoined to a schematically modelled body (Zervos, 1963: 341, 346, 350). Schematized white marble figurines are also known from the Neolithic strata in central Bulgaria. The beautifully carved sculptures from the mounds of Kazanlik and Azmak have schematized arms and heads and an accentuated supernatural pubic triangle.

THE CHRYSALID GODDESS WITH FOLDED ARMS OF THE CHALCOLITHIC PERIOD

The image of the goddess with arms folded became increasingly stereotyped during the fifth and fourth millennia BC. She is portrayed standing or seated, arms tightly pressed to the body, breasts barely indicated and legs schematized and usually narrow at the end. The masked head has supernatural features. East Balkan sculptures have flattened oval masked heads with large semicircular eyes, a nose, and from two to ten impressions or holes below the mouth. Holes on either side of the head support ear-rings of copper or gold. Cypriote clay figurines with large pubic triangles from the third millennium also have enormous ears with holes for ear-rings. Marble seems to have been especially cherished in Bulgaria as a material for fashioning Great Goddesses, and some marble figurines are over 30 cm. high. Sheet gold was also used for figurines and a fine example comes from Ruse in northern Bulgaria. Regardless of the material used, clay, bone, marble, or gold, the Great Goddess always appeared in a rigid pose, the pose of a chrysalis. Only in exceptional cases is her appearance more animate; the superb figurine from Neolithic Lerna in the eastern Peloponnese reveals a headless nude body of nearly naturalistic proportions.

Cycladic marble figurines of the third millennium BC obviously represent the same divine image. Their stiffness betrays the same chrysalid character. Folded arms, small breasts, tapering lifeless legs and supernatural heads continue ideological and stylistic traditions of several millennia. Oval or triangular heads, probably representing masks, were sometimes painted red. Cycladic figurines were placed in graves. It used to be thought that they were connected with

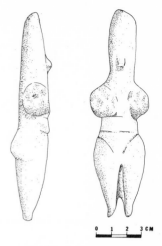

100 White marble figurine with a massive phallus-shaped head and folded arms. Cyclades. Typologically it can be dated to c. 6000 BC or earlier

145–147, 152
101, 102

146, *102*

102

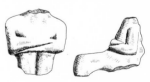

101 Fragment of a seated marble figurine with folded arms from Ruse, northern Bulgaria. East Balkan civilization. c. 4500 – 4000 BC

ancestor worship or were companions or concubines leading a dead person to the other world (Hogarth 1927), but it is now apparent that they must represent the Great Goddess of a deeply rooted Old European tradition. Analysis of the reproduced illustrations of this goddess reveals only a very gradual stylistic change during the course of nearly four millennia; the image of the Great Goddess remains remarkably stable.

149–151, 153   To the same category belong Cucuteni, Vinča and Gumelniţa
103   figurines with schematized arms and an accentuated, even enormous, pubic triangle. In the East Balkan civilization, particularly in the Gumelniţa complex, schematized bone figurines with a pubic triangle, ear-ring holes, two dots or depressions on the back (*trigonum lumbale*) probably representing eggs, and arm stumps or 'perforated arm stumps' which are stylized renderings of folded arms, are found in both settlements and graves.

Great Goddess figurines were placed in graves singly, in pairs or even dozens. Exquisitely decorated vases portraying cosmological scenes were also offered as gifts to the dead. The grave inventory from the cemetery of Vykhvatintsi in Moldavia yielded five vases, three clay figurines of the same type, shell beads and a spindle-whorl. The presence of a spindle-whorl suggests the aspect of a spinning goddess, *i.e.* the Goddess of Fate. The spindle is an attribute of the east Mediterranean Great Goddess and is also an aspect of Artemis as portrayed on Corinthian vases (Tucker 1963: 56, pl. 20: 3).

102 Marble statue from Blagoevo at Razgrad, Bulgaria. East Balkan civilization. c. 4500 – 4000 BC

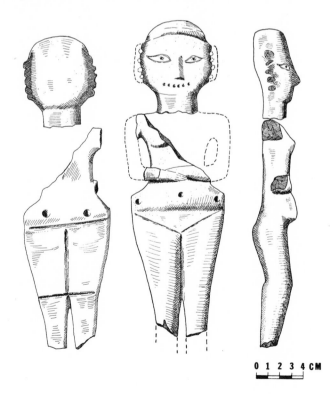

0 1 2 3 4 CM

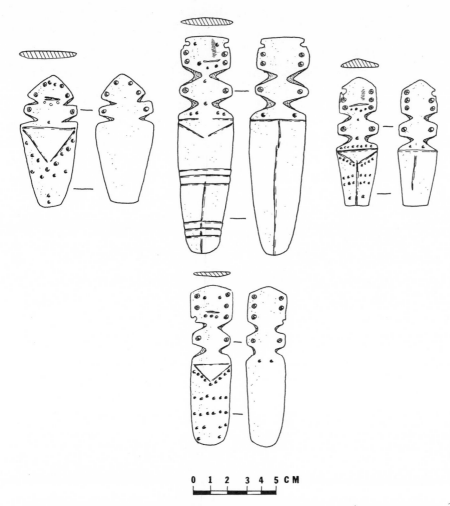

103 Schematized bone figurines from Ruse, northern Bulgaria. c. 4500 – 4000 BC

The large size of many figurines (in the Cyclades some are nearly 150 cm. high) suggests that they are portrayals of a goddess. The supernatural triangle and the nudity do not reveal her sexuality. Breasts and belly are not stressed. Through the act of engraving an enormous triangle in the centre of the sculpture the artist perhaps visualized the universal womb, the inexhaustible source of life, to which the dead man returns in order to be born again. In this sense the Great Goddess is the magician-mother. The folded and pressed arm position (the attitude of the embryo in the matrix?) is typical of the dead buried in the cemeteries of Old Europe. Babies and children squeezed into egg-shaped *pithoi* for burial had arms tightly pressed to the body, a natural foetal position. A *pithos* was a womb as was the grave pit from which the child or adult could be born again. For this purpose miniature vessels filled with red colour were laid in graves (Georgiev and Angelov, *Ruse*, 1957: 127). The colour of blood was as effective as the real blood necessary for restoration of life.

159

145

146

145 Torso of a terracotta figurine with folded arms from Pianul de Jos, Transylvania. *c.* mid-fifth millennium BC

146 Marble figurine from the tell of Sulica near Stara Zagora, central Bulgaria. East Balkan civilization. *c.* 4500 – 4000 BC

147 Marble figurine with folded arms from Borets near Plovdiv, central Bulgaria. East Balkan civilization. *c.* 4500 – 4000 BC

148 Cycladic marble figurine. Syros. Early third millennium BC

149, 150 Elongated terracotta figurine with large pubic triangle from the Late Cucuteni cemetery of Vykhvatintsi, Soviet Moldavia. Early fourth millennium BC

151 Triangle-centred flat bone figurine from Lovets near Stara Zagora, Bulgaria. East Balkan civilization. *c.* 4500 – 4000 BC

152 Terracotta figurine with folded arms from Neolithic Lerna, eastern Peloponnese

153 Flat figurine with breasts and enormous triangle as centre of focus. There is a hole on top for insertion of a goddess' head. From Vinča

154 Marble figurine of a goddess with a baby on top of her head. Cyclades. Early third millennium BC

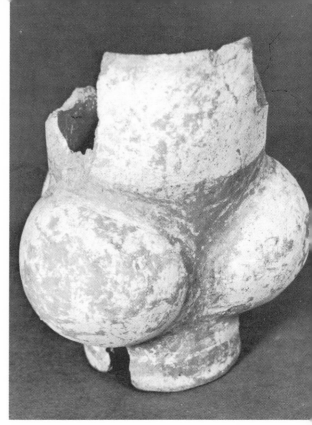

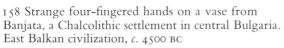

158 Strange four-fingered hands on a vase from Banjata, a Chalcolithic settlement in central Bulgaria. East Balkan civilization, *c.* 4500 BC

159 Anthropomorphic vase with the egg-shaped thighs and pubic triangle characterizing the Great Goddess. Muldava, central Bulgaria. East Balkan (Karanovo I), civilization. *c.* 6000 BC

160 Late Cucuteni 'binocular' vase from Bilcze Zlote, western Ukraine. Early fourth millennium BC

106 A double-egg motif (goddess' buttocks?) in graphite painting on the inside of a dish. Pietrele near Bucharest. East Balkan civilization. c. 4000 BC

107 Double-egg motif with a snake winding across. Dish painted black-on-red on inside. Late Cucuteni. Petreni, western Ukraine. Fourth millennium BC

109, 110

The persistence of magical hands either sculptured in relief or painted is a continuing tradition for several thousands of years. In the East Balkan civilization in particular, the large four-fingered hands occur in relief or are painted on large vases having a hypnotic quality. Superposed stylized figures with enormous arms and hands are shown on a Cucuteni vase from Petreni; they occupy the entire height of the frieze, alternating with quartered discs and rain torrents (Rybakov 1965: Fig. 36).

Vinča and East Balkan figurines of women in squatting position with emphasized upraised egg-shaped thighs evidently depict a natural birth-giving position. The masked woman in a contracted position from the Vinča settlement of Medvednjak, southeast of Belgrade, has one hand lifted to the mouth, in the manner of the Goddess of Sultana. Incised on the buttocks and thighs are spiral lines and circles with a dot in the middle. A small sculpture from Căscioarele in southern Romania shows a woman in nearly identical squatting position (Dumitrescu, 1966: Pl. 88). A beautifully moulded female figurine sitting on a stool shaped like an exposed vulva was unearthed during the 1971 excavation in Drenovac, a Vinča site at Svetozarevo in central Yugoslavia. A Pre-palatial pot from Mallia in Crete has incised on it a likeness of the naked goddess with legs spread to show the pudenda (Alexiou 1969: 85). The exposure of the genital region must have been symbolic of birth-giving. The pregnant womb is conspicuously absent in representations of the goddess in her birth-giving function.

The two large eggs or circles on the back of the body of the Great Goddess represent her potential. They stand for the source of subsequent development and thus could be called symbols of 'becoming'. The egg is readily observable on vases that were probably connected with the cult of the Great Goddess. Anthropomorphic vases have egg-shaped thighs and buttocks. Lids, dishes, bowls and jars are incised or painted with egg motifs, and pots frequently have a double-egg shape. Typically Cucutenian are the so-called binocular vases. In all probability they served in rituals dedicated to the Great Goddess; symbolic figures depicted on them include dogs, deer and moon crescents, her constant companions.

The double-egg symbol found on the back or the front of the East Balkan and Cucuteni figurines is one of the most frequently encountered. The two dots just above the buttocks (known to science as *trigonum lumbale*) may have originated the idea of showing the eggs in this particular place. If such a figurine is sectioned one actually finds a double-egg inside. They stand here for a universal life source, not for human foetuses. Countless anthropomorphic vases carry the twin egg symbol and it is found, in abstract compositions, on large Cucuteni vases. This symbol is associated with or surrounded by water

166

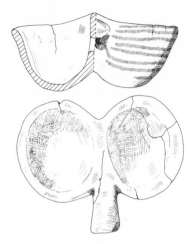

0 1 2 3 CM

108 A double-egg (or buttock)-shaped bowl with a handle, painted in concentric semicircles. Pietrele near Bucharest. East Balkan civilization

109, 110 Double-eggs within the bellies of figurines which have double-egg motifs incised on front and back. Classical Cucuteni. Novye Ruseshty, Soviet Moldavia. End of fifth millennium BC

111 Vase in the shape of buttocks. Sectioned multiple motif painted in white on red. Classical Cucuteni. Izvoare, Moldavia

0 1 2 3 CM

112 Sectioned multiple egg design with crescents and 'rain torrents' painted in black-on-red interior of a bowl. Late Cucuteni. Koszylowce, upper Dniester Valley, Ukraine. Fourth millennium BC

113 Decorative motifs on shoulders of late Cucuteni vases. 'Sonatas of becoming': sectioned and splitting eggs, crescents, full moons and snakes. Sipintsi, western Ukraine. Fourth millennium BC

167

snakes, crescents or schematized does or fawns. A true 'fabric of becoming' is expressed in painting on a Cucuteni bowl from Koszylowce: the sectioned egg motif is surrounded by smaller and larger moon crescents amid the water bands. Sectioned or ruptured egg motifs, painted in three or more concentric and parallel lines, occur in the main zone of the vase decoration. They alternate with diagonal bands made up of parallel lines (rainwater torrents?), above which runs the whole procession of animals associated with the goddess.

The sectioned egg motif is firmly woven into the ornamental pattern of vase decoration. In the fourth millennium BC, the conjunction of the egg, double-egg, lens, crescent, snake, and spiral motifs on vases of the Cucuteni civilization reached a rare level of exquisite design. In the abstract and composite designs, dictated by mythical thinking, a harmonious combination of germ cell and cosmic snakes and fawns is apparent. The sign of a sectioned double-egg as an ideogram of the Great Goddess persisted into Minoan-Mycenaean times. The motif reappears as a decoration on the festival attire of the goddess in a procession holding a double axe in each hand, on one of the frescoes of the Late Minoan Palace of Knossos, and painted on Middle and Late Minoan vases. It can also be seen carved out of limestone as frieze decoration in the Middle Minoan III Palace at Knossos, and at Mycenae as part of the decoration above the doorway of the Treasury of Atreus.

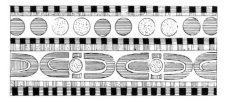

114 Pattern painted in blue, red, yellow and black on the hem of skirt worn by goddess. From a fresco representing processional scenes in the western wing of the palace of Knossos. Late Minoan. The ruptured-egg motif in the lower band is significant

115 Egg-and-germ-splitting motif painted in two rows on a Late Minoan amphora from the Royal Tomb of Isopata at Knossos. Vertical lines may symbolize a snake

116 Half-rosettes and triglyphs – motif on a limestone frieze from the northwestern angle of the palace of Knossos. Middle Minoan III

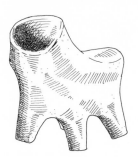

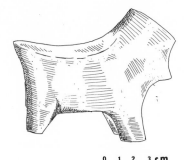

117 *Ritual vase in the shape of a dog. The Vinča site, Early Vinča period*

119 *Dog on the lid of a steatite vase from early Minoan site of Mochlos. Third millennium* BC

118 *Lid handle in the form of a dog with human mask. Gorni Pasarel, central Bulgaria. East Balkan civilization.* C. 4000 BC

120 *Mythical dog painted in black on a large pear-shaped vase from Varvarovka, a Late Cucuteni site near Kishenev, Soviet Moldavia. Fourth millennium* BC

The epiphanies

1 *The dog, a double of the Moon Goddess*

Dog, the howler by night, was the goddess' principal animal. How important a role it played in the mythology of Old Europe is emphasized in figurines of marble, rock crystal and terracotta, portraying the animal as a whole or its head alone in the form of cult vases shaped like a dog, or dog-figurines attached to vessels or forming the handles of vases or cups. The handle of a graphite-painted vase from Gorni Pasarel in central Bulgaria shows a dog wearing a human mask. Its body is notched on the back and front probably to emphasize the dog's aggressive characteristics. A large vase discovered at the Cucuteni site of Podei has a handle of a dog with forelegs stretched out and the hind part of the body raised up as if about to attack. A close parallel, about one thousand years later in date, from the Early Minoan II site of Mochlos shows a sculptured dog on the lid of a steatite vase decorated in zones of striated triàngles. Four dogs are portrayed holding the neck of a large black vase found in the Lengyel settlement of Střelice in central Czechoslovakia (Vildomec, 1940). Ferocious-looking dogs with three-clawed paws, fur bristling and tails raised, flying through cosmic space, appear painted in black or chocolate brown on late Cucuteni ochre-red vases, notably on large pear-shaped *pithoi* and on binocular pots. Masterfully schematized, they aptly portray the dynamism and gracility of the animal's body.

121 *Animal with caterpillar frieze painted in black on a large vase from Krutoborodintsi, western Ukraine. Late Cucuteni*

169

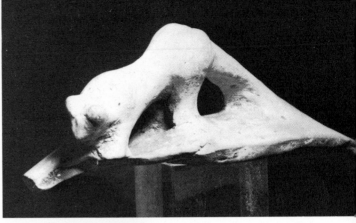

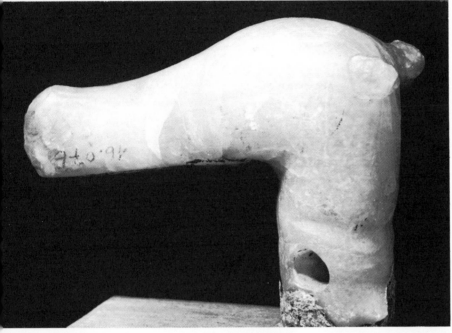

161 Reclining dog. Pietrele, southern Romania. East Balkan culture. (Gumelniţa-Karanovo VI). Mid-fifth millennium BC

162 Dog in attacking position, the broken-off handle of a vase. Late Cucuteni. Podei at Târgu-Ocna, northeastern Romania. Early fourth millennium BC

163 Dog's head of rock crystal. Crnokalačka Bara, Vinča civilization, 5000 – 4500 BC

164 Late Cucuteni vase bearing a design divided into three metopes, each including a dog and caterpillars Valea Lupului, north-eastern Romania. Early fourth millennium BC

165 Dogs fly above 'the cosmic disc's course'. Design painted in black on the ochre-red surface of a piriform vase. Late Cucuteni. Bilcze Zlote, north-western Ukraine. Early fourth millennium BC

The menacing dogs obviously belonged to the Moon Goddess who, like the nightmarish Hekate of early historic times, was worshipped by dogs barking at the moon, and whose principal sacrificial animal was the dog. Their lunar character is stressed by crescents depicted around or below the figures of dogs. Other Cucuteni vases display processions of dogs, a deer, a billy goat, a nanny goat, and a woolly caterpillar in the 'upper sphere' above the main zone in the centre of the vase, the central motif of which is the sectioned egg and the ideogram of the Great Goddess. Dogs are portrayed leaping high on either side of a tree, perhaps a life-tree, the symbol of all life, wild and cultivated. The representations of the life-tree guarded by ferocious animals on Cucuteni vases are the earliest in European art, and later persisted through all of prehistoric and early historic times. The guardian dogs, however, were replaced by lions, he-goats or other male animals. In folklore, the Old European mythical dog has lasted to this day. In the Balkan countries it is believed that eclipses of the sun and moon are caused by dog-headed monsters. In Macedonia, a *Chetvorok*, a dog with a whorl of hair over each eye, making him appear four-eyed, is the enemy of a vampire. Hence we have several aspects of the dog: dangerous, nocturnal and punitive on the one hand, and a protector against the forces of evil on the other. The northern European belief in the existence of a corn spirit in the shape of a dog or wolf may also have originated in the Neolithic period. In fact, dog's original role in myth may very well be derived from its importance as a guardian, protecting man's home, his seedlings and young crops against the early farmers' own herds and wild animals – as was rightly observed by Bogaevskij (1937) and after him by Rybakov (1965).

122 *Dogs flanking a caterpillar. Painting on the upper part of a vase from Valea Lupului, northeastern Romania. Late Cucuteni. Height, 52.8 cm. Fourth millennium* BC

123 *Dogs guarding the life-tree. Paintings on Late Cucuteni vases from Sipintsi, western Ukraine*

2 The doe, a double of the Goddess of Regeneration

The prestige of the deer in symbolism is not simply connected with its appearance – beauty, grace, agility – but also with the phenomenon of the cycle of regeneration and growth of its antlers. The latter aspect lay deep in the mind of Neolithic peasants. Deer's antlers play an important role: reliefs of stags with enormous antlers are frequent on vases of the Starčevo complex. Even in miniature figurine art there were attempts to portray stags. The role of a deer in Old European myth was not a creation of Neolithic agriculturists. The importance of a pregnant doe must have been inherited from a pre-agricultural era. The northern people in the hunting stage still believe in the mother of the universe as a doe-elk or wild reindeer-doe. Myths speak of pregnant women who rule the world and who look like deer: covered with hair and with branching deer's horns on their heads (Anisimov 1959: 28, 49ff.; Rybakov 1965, 2:35). In the Upper Paleolithic era, similar images probably existed all over Europe.

166

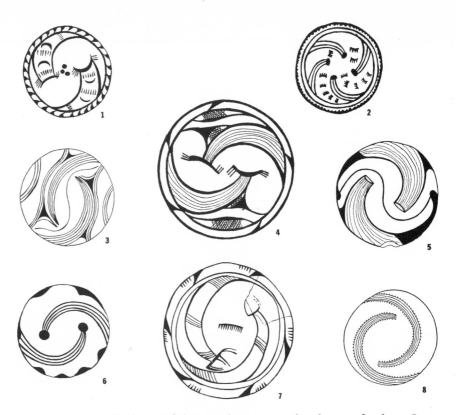

124 Does in the shape of moon crescents (?) turn in opposite directions. Painted black on red on the inner surface of bowls. 1, Tomashevka; 2, 4, 7, Staraja Buda; 3, 6, 8, Sipintsi; 5, Podolia. Western Ukraine. Late Cucuteni. Fourth millennium B C

167, 168

Exceptionally beautiful are cult vases in the shape of a doe. Outstanding is the large vase from Muldava in central Bulgaria. As a sculpture, the Muldava deer of the Neolithic period competes with the ceramic models of deer made some five thousand years later, for instance with those of the proto-Geometric or Geometric period of Greece (*cf.* a sculpture of a doe from a grave of the tenth century B C in the cemetery of Kerameikos in Athens: Kübler 1943: Pl. 26). As an animal sacred to Artemis and Diana, the doe continued to be sculpted in ancient Greece and Rome (Hoehn 1946: Pls. III, V, VI, Figs 17 and 21). The body of the doe of Muldava is decorated with crescents in a negative design; hence the animal is shown to be closely related to the moon symbolism.

124

In the pictorial representations on Late Cucuteni bowls the schematically portrayed body of a deer is transformed into a crescent. Like snakes or tails of comets, two deer whirl in opposite directions over the spherical surface of the bowl. Heads like crescent moons and small crescents repeated on abstract bodies emphasize the lunar characteristics. The comb-like signs encountered on some representations may symbolize the udders of a doe, the source of rainwater. Painted in parallel lines, the bodies of the deer give an impression of rain clouds, while through the middle a snake winds. In some portrayals deer antlers and crescent moons merge together as they spin

172

166 Stag with oversized antlers. Relief on a fragment of a storage vessel from Csépa, southeastern Hungary. Early sixth millennium BC

167, 168 Ritual vase in the shape of a doe. Muldava, central Bulgaria. East Balkan civilization. Karanovo I. Early sixth millennium BC

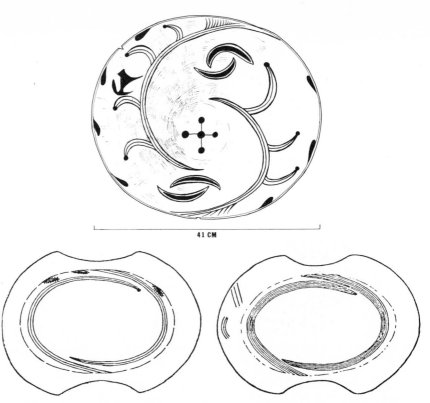

41 CM

125 *Deer or deer antlers spinning around a central cross-sign form an abstract pattern on the inner surface of a deep bowl. The goddess' dog appears on one side. Two pairs of crescents, rudimentary symbols of 'becoming' are on opposite sides. Late Cucuteni. Bilcze Zlote, northwestern Ukraine. Early fourth millennium BC*

126 *Two schematized deer or snakes spin in opposite directions in egg-shaped containers, associated with caterpillars and triple lines. Late Cucuteni. Sipintsi, western Ukraine. Early fourth millennium BC*

125

126

around a cross with knobbed extremities showing the four cardinal points of the world. Two pairs of opposed crescents and the goddess' dog can also be seen. Geometricized to a shape beyond recognition, two deer, like water snakes or rain clouds, spin within egg-shaped containers. Through association with the egg and water their role as instruments of the Goddess of Regeneration is clear.

3 The toad and the turtle: the goddess in the shape of a human foetus
The goddess as life-giver assumed the shape of a toad. A hybrid of woman and toad carved out of greenstone or marble or made of clay is found in Central and East Balkan civilizations, the Proto-Sesklo, Starčevo, Vinča, Karanovo and Gumelniţa complexes. In schematized versions her outspread legs and pubic triangle are accentuated while her head is just a cone or is entirely neglected. The beautifully carved figures of green and blue serpentine from Nea Nikomedeia are certainly frogs or toads but they are either stylized, or have a hole in the head, probably to accommodate the insertion of a goddess' human head. That these toads or frogs represent the Great Goddess is suggested by their formal similarity to a group of peculiar female figurines from Hacılar. These combine a toadlike trunk with a woman's chest, head and coif. Like the standing virgins they hold their hands on their breasts.

169, 170

171

127

174

169 Anthropomorphized toad with raised arms from the Vinča site. *c.* 5000 BC

170 'Birth-giving Goddess' in the shape of a toad. Marble figurine from Anza, southeastern Yugoslavia. Central Balkan Neolithic. *c.* 5800 BC

171 Stylized toad carved out of blueish serpentine from the Neolithic settlement at Nea Nikomedeia, northern Greece. End of seventh millennium BC

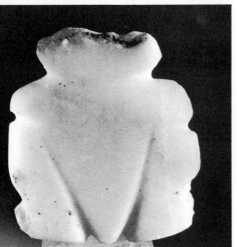

172 Two figures with raised arms and parted legs shown in relief on a Vinča vase from Gomolava, northern Yugoslavia. Snakes appear between the two figures and to the left of the larger figure. Early or mid-fifth millennium BC

173 Goddess' image on the neck of a large vase. Her feet take the form of handles. Szentes, southeastern Hungary. End sixth millennium BC

174 Terracotta turtle from the Vinča site

The life-giving goddess, her legs widely parted, appears in relief on the walls of Çatal Hüyük shrines, frequently in association with bulls' heads or bulls' horns (Mellaart 1967: 102–3, 109, 115–16, 127, 134–35). Bulls' heads with enormous horns, or the horns alone, were attached to walls or to special pediments, and in several shrines one or more huge bull heads were placed just below the goddess as if to assert and strengthen her powers. The belly of the goddess is usually marked with a circle or concentric circles. Although no shrines of comparable antiquity or state of preservation have been found in Europe, it can be surmised from reliefs of the goddess with upraised arms and outstretched legs on sixth-millennium vases of the Proto-Sesklo and Starčevo complexes that her image was as frequent there as in Anatolia. The relief of a figure with widely parted legs and upraised arms on a Starčevo potsherd from the site of Sarvaš in northern Yugoslavia is undoubtedly related ideologically to the Çatal Hüyük shrine reliefs. Pottery bearing reliefs or incised representations of figures with upraised arms and parted legs is found from Thessaly and Macedonia to northern Hungary and Germany, where the goddess is schematically engraved on vessels of the Bükk and Linear Danubian complexes of the fifth millennium BC (many illustrations of these are given by Gulder 1962). The stylized toad

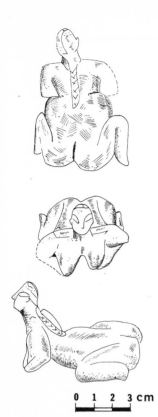

0 1 2 3 cm

127 Great Goddess in the shape of a toad. Statuette from Hacılar, west central Anatolia, a sixth-millennium settlement

129 Shrine from Çatal Hüyük, central Anatolia, with 'Birth-giving Goddess' in relief above bull heads. Seventh millennium BC

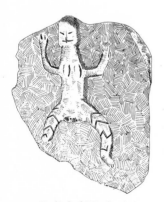

128 Relief of 'Birth-giving Goddess' on a pottery fragment from Sarvaš, northern Yugoslavia. Central Balkan Neolithic. c. early sixth millennium BC

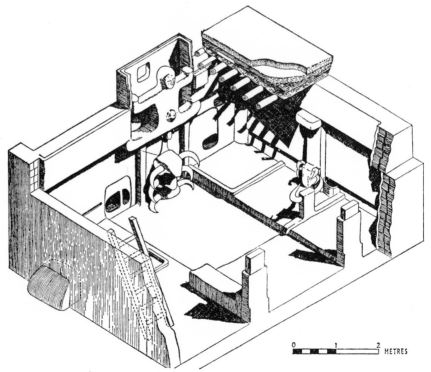

0 1 2 METRES

motif on central European Linear Danubian pots is so frequent that Butler in his monograph of 1938 assumed this creature to be 'sacred' (Butler 1938: 56). That the upraised arms and outstretched legs had a magical significance is evident from pottery reliefs of two figures associated with snakes on a Vinča vase from Gomolava. Parted legs and pubic triangle, in shorthand resembling the letter M, became the ideogram of the Great Goddess. The M sign occurs on vases, engraved or painted, and in combination with the image of the goddess' face on *pithoi* from Szentes in southeastern Hungary. The face, incised on the neck of the *pithos*, is flanked by snakes. The handle ends are modelled as upraised human arms and a small M sign is incised on the underside of each arm, below the hand. Vases bearing such representations in engravings or reliefs could have played a part in the cult of the dead. The mysterious power over life processes which the toad is thought to possess consistently recurs in the consciousness of the European people long after the dissolution of Old Europe. Thus the toad appears painted on amphorae of Palatial Crete. Of particular interest is the 'Lady Toad' from Maissau, a Bronze Age urnfield in lower Austria, which dates from around 1100 BC (Gulder 1962). This terracotta has a human face, female breasts and an exposed vulva on the underside of the nearly natural-istically portrayed animal. Terracotta, bronze, amber and ivory toads are known from Etruscan, Greek and Roman sanctuaries and graves. A bronze sculpture of a toad with an inscription was found as a votive offering at Corinth and a beautiful tiny figurine of a toad carved out of amber was discovered in a grave at Vetulonia at Poggio alla Guardia in Italy. Its being carved in amber, an imported and expensive material, proves the high esteem in which the toad was held during the Early Iron Age. Ivories from the sixth-century BC sanctuary of Artemis Orthia at Sparta in the Peloponnese include toads and turtles as votive offerings. The turtle cult was no less ancient and significant than the toad's: a terracotta turtle was found in Vinča and another comes from Dimini at Volos in Thessaly (National Museum, Athens 37: 6019). At Grivac, a Vinča site in central Yugo-slavia, a representation of a turtle with a pig's head came to light (Kragujevac Museum, Inv. 4, 288).

Toads made of wax, iron, silver and wood are to be found to this day as votive offerings to the Virgin Mary in churches in Bavaria, Austria, Hungary, Moravia and Yugoslavia; ethnographers have recorded more than a hundred instances in Bavaria alone (Gulder 1962:26). Some of these ex-votos have human heads, others bear the sign of a vulva on the underside, while many have a cross on the back. Examples from the eastern Alps are of astonishing antiquity. They were intended as a protection against barrenness and to ensure safe pregnancy. Toad's meat was eaten until recently to invoke labour

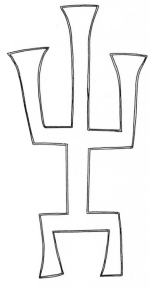

130 Schematized 'Birth-giving Goddess' engraved on a potsherd from Borsod, northeastern Hungary. Bükk culture. End of sixth millennium BC

131 'Birth-giving Goddess' in the shape of a toad. Engraving on the base of a Linear Pottery dish from the settlement of Kolešovice in Bohemia. End of sixth millennium BC

132 *Amphora decorated with a uterus symbol and toad, first palace of Phaistos, southern Crete. Middle Minoan I*

pains, toad's blood was used as an aphrodisiac and dry toads were hung up to protect the house against all evil. Such beliefs suggest a benevolent goddess, but the toad as a nocturnal and mysterious creature can cause madness, can take away the milk and suck the blood from humans while they sleep. In Baltic and Slavic (*i.e.* Indo-European) mythologies, she is the main incarnation of the chthonic magician goddess. In the Indo-European mythologies she is basically an incarnation of a goddess of death, while in the south, where Old European (*i.e.* pre-Indo-European) mythology was firmly rooted, the most prevalent beliefs concerning the toad are those connected with birth, pregnancy or the womb (uterus).

European peasants still speak about a travelling uterus in the woman's body. Similar beliefs are recorded in Greek and Roman times. Hippocrates, Plato and Aristotle compared the uterus to an animal which moves in the lower part of a woman's body (Blind 1902: 69; Gulder 1962: 36). If this animal is not satisfied, it may move up and hinder breathing, and cause fright or other disorders.

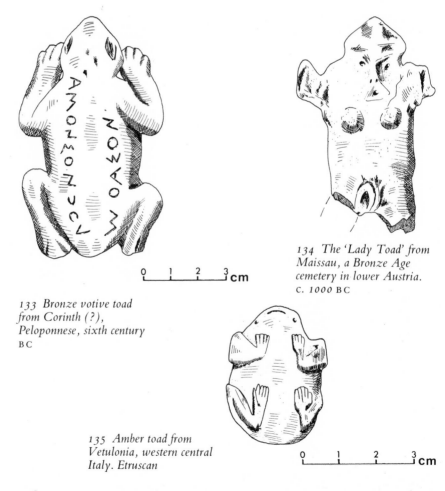

133 *Bronze votive toad from Corinth (?), Peloponnese, sixth century* BC

134 *The 'Lady Toad' from Maissau, a Bronze Age cemetery in lower Austria.* C. 1000 BC

135 *Amber toad from Vetulonia, western central Italy. Etruscan*

178

Egyptians also knew of the travelling uterus (Reinhard 1917: 340). Who is this animal moving about in a woman's body? Equipped with documentation from present folk, medieval, Greek, Roman and Egyptian beliefs, Gulder (1962) in his treatise on the Maissau toad presented a very convincing interpretation: this mysterious animal, must, he concluded, be a toad. The foetus was a toad which crawled into the womb (the real cause of conception was not known in pre-history). Neolithic or even Upper Palaeolithic man must have seen the human embryo at the age of one or two months: it is about 3.5 cm. in length, has a big head, two dark points for eyes, black holes for a nose, two depressions for ears, a long opening for the mouth and stumps for arms and legs. Such a creature can easily be taken for a toad! And this is what apparently happened far back in time, probably more than ten thousand years ago, and the belief has still not completely died out. The idea that a toad causes pregnancy may have originated before the Neolithic period since representations of toads (or lizards) engraved on bone artifacts are known from the Mesolithic Maglemose culture.

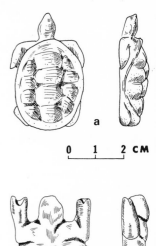

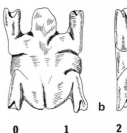

136 Ivory toad (a) and turtle (b) from the Greek sanctuary of Orthia at Sparta. Sixth century B C

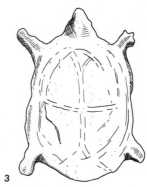

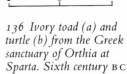

137 Modern votive toads and wax turtle. 1, Munich; 2, upper Austria, 3, Austrian Alps

1   2   3

4 The hedgehog: the goddess in the shape of an animal uterus or foetus
Another hybrid is the 'Lady Hedgehog'. We reproduce a lid in the shape of a hedgehog which bears the unmistakable imprint of a goddess' face (mask). The importance of the hedgehog in mythical imagery is well attested and terracotta figurines of hedgehogs are recorded in Vinča, East Balkan and Cucuteni sites. A beautifully carved alabaster hedgehog, dedicated to Artemis Brauronia dating from around 600 B C is housed in the Brauron Museum in Attica. In European folk medicine the hedgehog plays an exceptional role: a wound rubbed with hedgehog fat is believed to heal instantly, and also to rejuvenate and beautify a person. Superstitions and proverbs point to the hedgehog's prominent role in sexual life. A hedgehog is

176

177, 138

175 Head of a hedgehog.
Terracotta from Crnokalačka
Bara, southeastern Yugoslavia.
Vinča civilization. *c.* 5000 – 4500
BC

176 Terracotta hedgehog from
Căscioarele, southern Romania.
East Balkan civilization
(Gumelniţa-Karanovo VI).
Mid-fifth millennium BC

177 Pottery lid in the form of a
hedgehog with goddess' face.
Vidra, southern Romania. East
Balkan civilization.
(Gumelniţa-Karanovo VI).
Mid-fifth millennium BC (*see*
Fig. 138)

a nocturnal animal; it does not emerge during daylight and when startled in its nightly forages it rolls itself up in a ball, from which sharp spines stick out in every direction. No wonder it is endowed with magical powers.

A key to understanding why the Great Goddess chose the hedgehog as her double again lies in parallels of ex-voto images. In southern Tirol, instead of an imitation toad, a so-called *Stachelkugel*, a 'spiky ball', was brought to churches or chapels and also placed in graves. Such balls made of wood and painted red, are usually 8–19 cm. across, round or oval in shape, and are called 'uteri'. About fifty years ago many such *Stachelkugeln* were to be seen; now only old ones still remain (Gulder 1962: 25). The prototype possibly derives from the uterus of a cow, which after parturition remains swollen and covered with warts (known in German as 'Igeln', 'hedgehogs'). Indeed in some areas of southern Tirol the cow's uterus is called 'Igelkalb', 'hedgehog's calf' (*id.*: 30). The association of a cow's uterus with the hedgehog is certainly not recent and may date from the period of the beginning of animal domestication. The archaeological evidence shows the Great Goddess' epiphany in the form of a hedgehog to be not later than the fifth millennium BC. Votive offerings in the shape of a uterus – flat and oval clay objects with a ridged surface – occur among the Etruscan and Roman antiquities.

138 *Profile of terracotta hedgehog from Căscioarele, southern Romania. East Balkan civilization. See Pl. 177*

5 The bee and the butterfly: the bull-born Goddess of Transformation and Regeneration

Before we discuss the epiphany of the Great Goddess in the shape of a bee or a butterfly we must mention the ancient belief that bees are begotten of bulls. One of the earliest writers to mention the bull-born bee is Antigonos of Karystos, about 250 BC, who says:

> In Egypt if you bury the ox in certain places, so that only his horns project above the ground and then saw them off, they say that bees fly out; for the ox putrefies and is resolved into bees.
>
> (Antigonos, *Hist. mir.* 19; quoted by Cook *Zeus* I, 514; Ransome 1937: 114).

The most appropriate time for this method of reproducing bees was said to be when the sun entered the sign of the bull (Taurus). Nearly three centuries later Ovid speaks of Aristaeus, the 'Honey Lord' who was weeping because all his bees had died, leaving the honeycombs unfinished. On the advice of his mother he captured Proteus, the magician, who told Aristaeus 'that he must bury the carcase of a slaughtered ox, and that from it he would obtain what he wanted, for when the carcase decayed, swarms of bees would issue from it. The death of one produced a thousand lives'. (Ovid, *Fasti* I, 393; quoted by Ransome 1937: 112). In his fourth *Georgic*, Vergil (70–19

139 Onyx gem from Knossos portraying the Bee Goddess flanked by winged dogs. Bull's horns and 'double axe' (butterfly) above the goddess' head. c. 1500 BC

140 Early Minoan three-sided bead seal of yellow steatite portraying the goddess in the shape of a bee. The other two faces show a head and the foreparts of two dogs respectively. Kasteli Pedeada, southeast of Knossos

140

179

BC) likewise recounts this method of obtaining the ox-born bees. A further explanation of vital importance is given by Porphyry (AD 233 to c. 304), who writes:

> The ancients gave the name of *Melissae* ('bees') to the priestesses of Demeter who were initiates of the chthonian goddess; the name *Melitodes* to Kore herself: *the moon (Artemis) too, whose province it was to bring to the birth, they called Melissa, because the moon being a bull and its ascension the bull, bees are begotten of bulls. And souls that pass to the earth are bull-begotten.* [My italics]

(Porphyry, *De ant. nym.*: 18; quoted by Ransome 1937: 107).

From this passage we learn that Artemis is a bee, *Melissa*, and that both she and the bull belong to the moon. Hence both are connected with the idea of a periodic regeneration. We also learn that souls are bees and that *Melissa* draws souls down to be born. The idea of a 'life in death' in this singularly interesting concept is expressed by the belief that the life of the bull passed into that of the bees. Here we have the very essence of the meaning of sacrifice which is also applicable to Neolithic and Chalcolithic Europe as well as to the Minoan civilization.

The image of the Great Goddess in the shape of a bee appears on the head of a bull carved out of bone from the Late Cucuteni site of Bilcze Zlote in the western Ukraine. Her upraised and bifurcated arms are definitely those of a bee. Her head is a dot and the conical lower body (without indication of legs) is clearly an imitation of a bee's body. Similar representations, though less schematized, are known from Minoan, Mycenaean, Geometric and Archaic Greek art. Many gold rings of Minoan workmanship from Crete and Greece portray the bee-headed goddess or the same goddess holding bull's horns above her head. A steatite bead-seal from Kasteli Pedeada, southeast of Knossos, shows the goddess with legs parted and a long conical projection which obviously is the lower part of the body of a bee. Her arms are upraised and the head is human. The other side of this seal portrays a bull's head. Greek jewelry of the seventh to fifth centuries BC from Rhodes and Thera includes gold plaques of the 'Bee-Goddess'. She has a pair of 'hands' in addition to her wings, and there is a rosette on either side of her ridged abdomen. The famous painted Boeotian amphora dating from c. 700 BC portrays the 'Lady of the Wild Things', or the 'Mistress of Animals', as she is usually called, flanked by two lions, a (decapitated) bull's head, a bottle-shaped object (a uterus?), birds and swastikas. It is significant that she has the arms of an insect. Zigzagging hair and a serrated line around the lower part of the body suggest the hairy body of a bee. In this case the titles 'Mistress of Animals' or the 'Lady of the Wild Things' are

misleading. She is here the 'Goddess of Periodic Regeneration'. She is shown with a fish inside her, a symbol of fecundity related to water. The loose bull's head is that of a sacrificed bull. The bull is dead and the new life begins. The swastikas (wheels, concentric circles, rosettes) turn, the snakes crawl, the beasts howl (by the middle of the third millennium B C lions had replaced the more ancient dogs). The epiphany of the goddess is inseparable from the noise of howling and clashing, and the whirling dances. Kuretes, the male devotees of the goddess, dance vigorously, 'rattling their arms' as Callimachus, the Greek poet of *c.* 260 B C, says in his *Hymn to Jove*: 32. Vergil, describing the noise made to attract swarming bees, says 'they clash the cymbals of the Great-Mother' (Vergil's fourth *Georgic*: 63). At Ephesus, Artemis was associated with the bee as her cult animal. In fact, the whole organization of the sanctuary in classical times seems to have rested on the symbolic analogy of a beehive, with swarms of priestesses called bees, *melissai*, and numerous eunuch priests called 'drones', *essênes* (Barnett 1956: 218).

Why was the bee chosen for the symbol of regeneration? We may ask the same question where the Egyptian beetle or scarab is concerned; it too symbolizes the moon and eternal renewal. The reason probably is because both have antennae like bull horns and wings in the form of a lunar crescent. The periodic swarming and buzzing of bees, when a new generation is born, and the creative activity associated with the production of honey must have greatly impressed our forefathers who regarded it as the food of the gods. This is suggested by the famous gold pendant from a tomb at Mallia in Crete dating from the early second millennium B C, a superb piece of Minoan goldwork, in which two bees hold a honeycomb in the shape of a disc. Three other discs are suspended on the wings and at the point where the bodies of the two bees join (Matz 1962: 126).

Known portrayals of bees from antiquity are made of metal, usually gold, or take the form of engravings, reliefs and paintings. Hitherto, probable representations of bees painted or indicated in relief on vases from the Neolithic and Chalcolithic periods of Old Europe have been either completely overlooked or confused with the

142 Frieze (partly reconstructed) of Bee Goddess (?) painted on Proto-Sesklo vase. Otzaki, Thessaly. c. 6400 – 6200 BC

143 Schematized Bee Goddess on a potsherd from Holašovice, Linear Pottery site in Czechoslovakia

144 Bee Goddess, a pottery relief from Truşeşti. Classical Cucuteni. Second half of fifth millennium BC

145 Genii dressed in bee skins hold jugs over horns from which a plant grows. Mycenaean gem

portrayals of schematized toads or 'dancing figures'. The image of the goddess in the shape of a bee or some other kind of insect has a very long history: earliest representations occur in the Neolithic Proto-Sesklo and Starčevo complexes. A creature with wing-like arms and a protruding cone between the parted legs painted in cherry red on a white background on a jar from Otzaki, a Proto-Sesklo site in Thessaly, may be one of the earliest representations of a 'Lady Bee'. Schematic figures with upraised arms and bifurcated heads have long been known in the Starčevo complex of Hungary. What may be a headless bee appears in relief on a large vessel from the same site of Kopancs. Headless bees portrayed on rosettes are known from the Artemisium of Ephesus (more than 5000 years later) where they were probably used as charms. In Roman times, headless bees together with headless toads also occur on rosettes used as talismans to avert the evil eye (Ransome 1937: 110). A figure of a goddess in the shape of a bee (?) is painted in red on a Tisza dish from Ilonapart at Szentes. Her bee-like attributes are a bifurcated insect-type head, legs and a sting ('a tail'). Schematized figures of bees, having the characteristic ridged body, are quite frequent on Linear pottery. Analogous representations often appear in relief on Cucuteni vases. On a Mycenaean gem of Minoan workmanship two lion-headed genii clad in bee skins hold jugs over horns from which a new life springs in the shape of a plant. What do these jugs contain? – probably 'food of the gods' produced by the bee. That mead was used as a libation is well known from Classical Greek writers. Sacrificial honey was among the 'sober offerings', the *nephalia*, but it was also known as an intoxicant. Honey was always considered to be a food that conduces to a long and healthy life. Pythagoras, whose life spanned the greater part of the sixth century BC attributed his longevity to a constant use of honey in his diet. Honey was a healing substance. Glaucus, the son of Minos and Pasiphae, was restored to life when buried in a honey jar.

The apiculture of the Minoans is documented by hieroglyphs, representations of actual beehives, engraved images, and myths. The Greeks, who like the rest of the Indo-Europeans knew only of wild honey, inherited bee-keeping from the Minoans. They borrowed even the most important names: *sphex* ('bee'), *simblos* ('hive') and *propolis* ('kerinthos') (Ransome 1937: 64). They also inherited the mythical image of the Great Goddess as a bee, the Goddess of Regeneration, the image of her virgin priestesses or nymphs as bees, and many other myths and beliefs connected with the bee and honey. The Cretans on the other hand, must have held bees in high esteem from the beginning of the Neolithic era.

The fact that we have been considering the bee rather than the butterfly does not imply that in ancient mythology the bee was the more important of the two; both were equally ancient and essential in the symbolism associated with the goddess. The difficulty is that in schematic prehistoric reliefs or paintings of the goddess we can recognize little more than an insect head or insect hands. Whether she is 'Lady Bee' or 'Lady Butterfly' cannot be determined. In most Neolithic reliefs, such as that from Kotacpart, the image of the   180 goddess can be interpreted as representing either a bee or a butterfly. The scene on the gold ring from the grave of Isopata near Knossos, dating from *c.* 1500 B C, includes four female figures in festival attire, perhaps portraying the goddess and her devotees, usually assumed to be *melissae*, or bees. Their heads and hands are certainly those of an   146 insect, but we cannot be sure of what kind.

0 |————————————————————————————| 1 CM

146 The gold ring of Isopata near Knossos portraying goddess (right) and three wor-shippers. The heads and hands are those of an insect. C. 1500 B C

185

147 *Gold chrysalis from a chamber tomb at Mycenae. c. 1500 BC*

148 *Seal impression from Zakro, eastern Crete, portraying goddess with the wings of an eyed butterfly. Middle Minoan III*

The motifs of chrysalises, butterflies, and 'double-axes' are well known to the student of Minoan-Mycenaean art. It was indeed Sir Arthur Evans who published a series of chrysalises, butterflies, and goddesses related to chrysalises or with butterfly wings (Evans 1925). He interpreted the chrysalis as an emblem of a new life after death. Common white and other species with eyed, indented wings occur repeatedly in Minoan and Mycenaean art. In a chamber tomb at Mycenae a detailed example in the form of a gold chrysalis bead was found by A. J. B. Wace. It has eyes, and the wing cases and articulation of the abdomen are indicated. In Shaft-grave III at Mycenae, Schliemann discovered gold pendants in the shape of chrysalises associated with golden butterflies, as well as butterflies embossed on the plates of what had been scales (Evans 1925: 56, Fig. 48*a* and *b*: 59, Fig. 52). The Mycenaean butterflies are an inheritance from Minoan Crete, where they are known from the Middle Minoan III and later periods. A seal from Zakro in eastern Crete reveals the goddess with a human head, large wings of an 'eyed' butterfly, and animal or bird legs.

The epiphany of the goddess in the shape of a butterfly in Minoan-Mycenaean religion cannot be doubted. We may ask now how far back she can be traced.

An upper torso of a female figurine with schematized butterflies incised beneath the breasts was found at Passo di Corvo, a neolithic settlement of the sixth millennium BC north of Foggia, southeast Italy (Tine 1972: 330). The figurine probably belongs to the late 'Impresso' period, Masceria de la Quercia complex. Another emblem of regeneration or birth-giving resembles the letter M. It was incised randomly on the back and front of the torso. The phallic top of the figurine's head was encircled by a spiral, probably a snake. The uplifted face of the figurine was masked and impressed dots around the neck suggest a bead necklace. The accumulation of symbols allows one to regard this figurine as a Great Goddess in her function as the Goddess of Regeneration.

The shape of a butterfly emerges on Çatal Hüyük frescoes (Mellaart 1967: Pl. 40) and is incised on European Neolithic pots. The butterflies on Danubian Linear Pottery jars even have dots on them, possibly to represent the 'comma'-type butterfly. These schematic butterflies are the prototypes of the Minoan 'double-axes' which we find portrayed between the horns of a bull. The emblem of the Great Goddess in its origin has nothing to do with the axe; it antedates the appearance of metal axes by several thousand years. In the second millennium BC, because of their increasing importance axes were made in imitation of a butterfly (therefore double-bladed). When finally the butterfly became a double-axe, the image of the goddess as a butterfly continued to be engraved on double-axes.

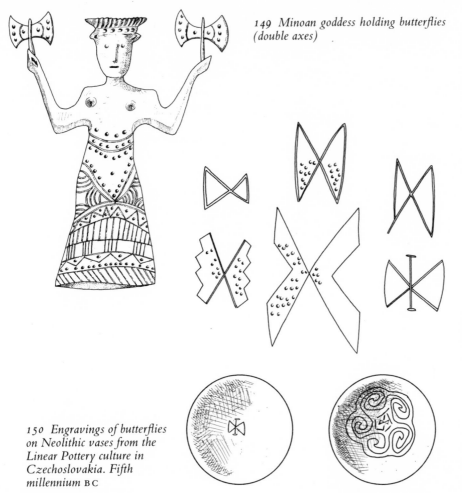

149 Minoan goddess holding butterflies (double axes)

151 Bucrania and ritual horns surmounted by a 'double axe' (butterfly). Painting on a Mycenaen krater from Salamis, Cyprus

150 Engravings of butterflies on Neolithic vases from the Linear Pottery culture in Czechoslovakia. Fifth millennium B C

152 Painted representation of goddess with wings in the shape of a double axe on a Middle Minoan III vase from Knossos

Moreover, on painted Minoan vases there is frequently an anthropomorphic image of the goddess having wings in the shape of a double-axe, an echo of the goddess' epiphany in the shape of a butterfly. The Tomb of the Double-Axes at Knossos was, in fact, a shrine of the goddess (Evans 1925: 61). The process of transformation from a butterfly to a double-axe must have been influenced by the similarity of shape between the two or by the influence of the nearby Indo-Europeans (Mycenaeans), to whom the axe of the Thunder-god was sacred since it was inbued with his potency. Whereas the Indo-European axe was the weapon of a male god, the Minoan double-axe was never shown in such a context. It appears as an emblem held by the goddess in each hand in frescoes and on schist plaques.

Caterpillars appear on Cucuteni vases, both in a procession of the goddess' animals (see Fig. 121) and in association with her dogs (see Pl. 164). Short zigzagging creatures with round heads at both ends above the belt of spiralling snakes probably were meant to represent

153 Painted representation of goddess with wings in shape of a double axe (resembling a butterfly) on a floral stem. Late Minoan I, island of Mochlos, Crete

178 'Bull-horned goddess in the shape of a bee' rendered on a stylized
bull's head of bone. Bilcze Zlote, northwestern Ukraine. Late Cucuteni.
Fourth millennium BC

79 Gold plaque of Bee Goddess
from Camiros, Rhodes. Seventh
century BC

80 Bee Goddess. Relief on a
potsherd. Kopáncs, southeastern
Hungary. Central Balkan
Neolithic. Sixth millennium BC

81 Remains of a bowl showing
Bee Goddess painted in red on
white background. Szentes,
southeastern Hungary. Alföld
Neolithic

82 Late Cucuteni vase from
Podei, northeastern Romania. The
caterpillar in the band around the
neck is significant

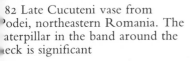

caterpillars. Crescents with dots around them, in association with bull's horns within the sections of crossed lines, such as we have seen painted on a Cucuteni dish (see Pl. 49), could also be caterpillars. The moon crescent, the caterpillar and bull's horns are closely connected.

Since caterpillars and butterflies appeared in Old European symbolism, it is reasonable to assume that there were chrysalises too. The chrysalis, if inarticulately presented, can be easily overlooked. Some horizontally ridged greenstone pendants from Early Neolithic settlements (such as were unearthed in the earliest site of Anza, Macedonia, dating from the end of the seventh millennium BC), as well as certain forms of shells used as beads, could be interpreted as representing chrysalises. The shape of a chrysalis does not necessarily have to appear in lifelike representations. The figurines of the chthonic goddess of the Chalcolithic period seem to have the chrysalis as an underlying idea. These figurines are usually schematic and groups of horizontal lines are incised on the narrowing lower body (cf. Fig. 103). The narrow skirts of the Vinča ladies, which usually end in horizontal lines or bands (see Fig. 8), may likewise be related to the idea of the chrysalis. An odd painting on one of the shrines of Çatal Hüyük of the seventh millennium BC seems to represent a honeycomb with chrysalises, bees or butterflies (Mellaart 1964: 129).

Even to the scientific observer today, the transformation of an ugly caterpillar into a beautiful winged creature seems like a miracle. But even more astonishing is the fact that man, equipped with only the patience to observe, recognized all the stages of the drama and incorporated it in his symbolism at least seven or eight thousand years ago.

6 The bear: the goddess as mother and nurse

A strange animal-headed figurine with two turban-shaped ears, female breasts, and its single unbroken arm resting across the abdomen was found at the Starčevo settlement of Porodin. In Vinča sites a number of bear-headed figurines were found, representing either epiphanies of the goddess in animal form or her worshippers. Some are seated on a throne and decorated with crescents. The famous sculpture known as the 'Lady of Vinča', broken from a throne or seat which was not recovered, is probably a refined portrayal of the goddess wearing an animal mask. Painted in alternating black and red bands and wearing a pentagonal stylized mask with huge black eyes, she has her right arm held diagonally across the front of her body, the hand touching her left breast. Her shoulders are broad and on the upper arm are four incisions which may symbolically assert her status.

A Vinča figurine, representing the bear mother or nurse, from Fafos in southern Yugoslavia shows a seated woman holding a cub,

188

183

184, 185

193

190

183 Goddess with animal (bear?) mask seated on a throne from the Vinča site. *c.* mid-fifth millennium BC

184, 185 The 'Lady of Vinča'. Terracotta of a masked goddess originally seated on a throne. Late Vinča, 4500 – 4000 BC

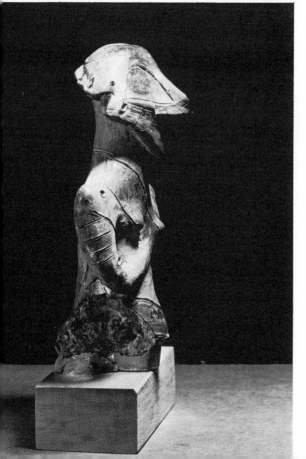

186, 187 Bear cub (?) from Pavlovac, southern Yugoslavia. Vinča, *c.* 4500 – 4000 BC

188 Anthropomorphic figurine with animal (bear?) head from Porodin, southern Yugoslavia. Central Balkan Neolithic, early sixth millennium BC

189, 190 Terracotta of a mother and child from the Early Vinča site at Rastu, western Romania. *c.* 5000 BC or earlier

191, 192 Vinča figurine portraying bear-masked woman with a pouch on her back. Site of Čuprija I at Supska, central Yugoslavia

193 Goddess, holding a baby, both
wearing bear masks, from Fafos II at
Kosovska Mitrovica, Yugoslavia. Vinča
culture

194 Headless 'Madonna' from Gradac,
central Yugoslavia. Classical Vinča.
Fifth millennium BC

195 Vase fragment with representation
of animal-masked 'Madonna' in relief,
from Zengövárkony, a Lengyel
settlement in southwestern Hungary.
Fifth millennium BC

her face concealed by a bear mask. The maternal devotion of the female bear made such an impression upon Old European peasants that she was adopted as a symbol of motherhood. Bear cubs with large heads were also modelled. The Vinča sculpture from Gradac in central Yugoslavia of a mother holding a child with the head of a bear cub is unfortunately headless but she probably wore an animal mask. Similar figurines were found at Fafos, Drenovac and other Sesklo and Vinča sites. The animal-headed 'Lengyel Madonna' from the settlement of Zengövárkony in southwestern Hungary cuddles a shapeless infant in her arms. Sculptures in which the mother holds a large child include the figurine from the early Vinča site of Rastu in southwestern Romania, which is remarkable for its perfect proportions. Unfortunately, both mother and child are headless and the right arm and legs of the mother are broken off. The preserved hand of the missing arm touches the left breast at which the child was suckling. The back of the figurine is covered by incisions including V's, meanders and crescents. Analogies with other Vinča sites that have yielded calibrated radiocarbon dates place the Rastu sculpture in the early fifth millennium BC.

186, 187

194

195

189, 190

189

Some east and central Balkan clay figurines of the fifth millennium BC are dubbed 'hunchbacks' because of their schematically rendered humps. Their heads are either masked or amorphous. The mystery of the humps is explained by an articulated bear-masked Vinča figurine carrying a bag suspended on a thick rope over the neck. Apparently she is a bear nurse. Hundreds of such schematized bear-nurse figurines imply the role of the goddess as a protectress of weaklings or of a divine child. They are especially numerous in the Karanovo complex of central Bulgaria.

191, 192

RECAPITULATION OF VARIOUS ASPECTS OF THE PREHISTORIC GREAT GODDESS

The image of the Great Goddess of Life, Death and Regeneration in anthropomorphic form with a projection of her powers through insects and animals – bee, butterfly, deer, bear, hare, toad, turtle, hedgehog and dog – was the outward symbol of a community concerned with the problems of the life and death cycle.

Even if the goddess' corpulence and association with wild animals implies an Upper Paleolithic origin, her image during the period of early agriculture must have been transformed. The domesticated dog, bull and he-goat now became her companions, and she ruled both wild and cultivated life. Because her main function was to regenerate the life forces, the goddess was flanked by male animals noted for their physical strength. The animals are European; neither leopards nor lions flank her as they do in Anatolia and Mesopotamia.

Her accentuated pubic triangle may have been linked with the concept of the 'Great Mother's womb' (to adopt the term used by Dieterich, Neumann and Eliade) or the 'lap of the subterranean queen', but she was not entirely feminine. She was androgynous in the Neolithic period, having a phallus-shaped neck; divine bisexuality stresses her absolute power. The divorce from the male attributes occurred at some time during the course of the sixth millennium BC.

In her chthonic and frightening aspect she must have been a Mother Terrible perhaps yearning for human and animal blood, as indicated by her epiphany in the shape of a ferocious dog.

There was no isolated image of a Mother Terrible; the aspects of death and life are inextricably intertwined. She was deployed in graves to stimulate and perpetuate the procreative powers of the deceased. The European Great Goddess, like the Sumerian Ninkhursag, gave life to the Dead (another name for Ninkhursag was *Nintinugga*, 'She who gives life to the Dead'). Her magical hands and music were for the release of the life forces. The symbols of 'becoming' – eggs, crescents, horns, and crosses within circles and concentric circles – were engraved or painted over her body or on votive vases. Both an egg split into two halves and twins were concepts emphasized throughout her many representations. Around 4000 BC a layered and split egg became the emblem of the goddess and continued in evidence throughout the Minoan and Mycenaean period. The constant portrayal of twin crescents, or two does with opposed bodies reflects the magical potency of a splitting pair.

In her incarnation as a pregnant doe, a chrysalis, caterpillar, butterfly, bee, toad, turtle, or hedgehog, she was a symbol of embryonic life and regeneration. In this fundamental notion lies her association with the moon and the horns. As a bee or a butterfly she emerges from the body or horns of the bull; as a bear she takes care of all young life.

As a supreme Creator who creates from her own substance she is the primary goddess of the Old European pantheon. In this she contrasts with the Indo-European Earth-Mother, who is the impalpable sacred earth-spirit and is not in herself a creative principle; only through the interaction of the male sky-god does she become pregnant.

HEKATE AND ARTEMIS: SURVIVAL OF THE OLD EUROPEAN GREAT GODDESS IN ANCIENT GREECE AND WESTERN ANATOLIA

The question now arises as to what happened to the prehistoric goddess after the third millennium BC. Did she disappear after the advent of the patriarchal Indo-European world or did she survive the dramatic change?

In Minoan (non Indo-European) Crete the Great Goddess is seen in representations on frescoes, rings and seals. She is shown in association with bulls, or bull-horns, 'double-axes' (butterflies), he-goats or lions. On a stamp from Knossos she appears as a lady of nature untamed on top of a mountain flanked by two lions and a male human worshipper. On a gold ring from Isopata near Knossos the butterfly- or bee-headed goddess is, as we have seen, surrounded by worshippers in festive garments wearing insect masks (see Fig. 146). She is represented on frescoes accompanied by worshippers, women or men in festive garments with upraised arms. Gigantic dogs portrayed on steatite vases or on cylinder seals (Matz 1962: 130) are probably the companions of the same goddess. She or her animals, particularly the bulls, dominate the ritualistic scenes throughout the Palace period of Minoan Crete.

In Greece, as in India, the Great Goddess survived the superimposed Indo-European cultural horizon. As the predecessor of Anatolian and Greek Hekate-Artemis (related to Kubaba, Kybebe/Cybele) she lived through the Bronze Age, then through Classical Greece and even into later history in spite of transformations of her outer form and the many different names that were applied to her. The image of Hekate-Artemis of Caria, Lydia and Greece, based on descriptions of early Greek authors, vase paintings, and finds in actual sanctuaries dedicated to this multifunctional goddess, supplement and verify our understanding of the appearance and functions of the prehistoric goddess. Written sources pour blood into her veins of stone, clay, bone or gold.

In name and character she is a non-Greek, a non-Indo-European goddess. The name of Artemis is known from Greek, Lydian and Etruscan inscriptions and texts. Its antiquity is demonstrated by the appearance of the words *A-ti-mi-te* and *A-ti-mi-to*, the dative and genetive case of her name, on Linear B tablets from Pylos (Bennett 1955: 208–9). *Hekate (Hekabe)* was Asiatic, not known to the Greeks in name. She was *Enodia* in Thessaly, perhaps an earlier name later replaced by Hekate. Whether Artemis and Hekate appear as two goddesses or as one, they both belong to the moon cycle. Hekate, gruesome and linked with death; Artemis, youthful and beautiful, reflecting the purity of untouched nature and linked with motherhood.

In Caria (western Turkey) Hekate was the primary goddess. Mysteries and games were performed in her sanctuary at Lagina. In Colophon, dogs were sacrificed to her and she herself could turn into a dog. West of Lagina was Zerynthos, from which Hekate derived her name of Zerynthia. In Samothrace, there was a cave called Zerynthos associated with Hekate. Dogs were sacrificed there and mysteries and orgiastic dances were performed. Hekate and her dogs are described as journeying over the graves of the dead and above the sacrificed blood. In the days of Aristophanes and Aischylos she is the mistress of the night road who leads travellers astray, of cross ways, of fate, and of the world of the dead, being known by both names, Hekate and Artemis. As Queen of the Ghosts, Hekate sweeps through the night followed by her baying hounds; as Enodia she is the guardian of crossroads and gates. Her sanctuaries stood at the gate to a hill-fort or at the entrance to a house. Pregnant women sacrificed to Enodia to ensure the goddess' help at birth (Wilamowitz-Moellendorf, I, 1959: 69–174). There is no mention in Aischylos of Hekate-Artemis assisting at birth. Clay figurines of the goddess in a seated position were sacrificed to her (*id.*: 171). A terracotta medallion found in the Athenian Agora portrays a triple-bodied Hekate-Artemis with stag and dog flanking her. She holds a torch, whip and bow-and-arrow (Thompson 1960: 367). Sophocles in Antigone mentions Enodia as Persephone, the ruler of the dead. The torch of the goddess probably relates to the fertilizing power of the moon since Hekate's torches were carried around the freshly sown fields to promote their fertility. Statues of Roman Diana show her crowned with the crescent and carrying a raised torch. Hekate is responsible for lunacy and, on the positive side, is Giver of Vision.

The Lady of free and untamed nature and the Mother, protectress of weaklings, a divinity in whom the contrasting principles of virginity and motherhood are fused into the concept of a single goddess, was venerated in Greece, Lydia, Crete and Italy. She appears as Artemis and under many local names: Diktynna, Pasiphae, Europa ('the wide-glancing one'), Britomartis ('the sweet virgin') in Crete, Laphria in Aetolia, Kallisto ('the beautiful') in Arkadia, or Agrotera ('the wild'), and Diana in Rome. She, 'the pure and strong one', was surrounded by nymphs, flanked by animals, and as huntress dominated the animal world. Games with bulls were among the rituals of this goddess. She was present everywhere in nature, above all in hills, forests, meadows, and fertile valleys, and often was therioform, appearing as a bear or doe. The Arkadian Kallisto, her companion and double, was said to have assumed the form of a bear. The stag is her standing attribute in plastic art; she is called 'stag-huntress' in the Homeric Hymns. Her companion Taygete was transformed into a doe and in the legend of the Alodae she herself assumes that form. Pausanias' records (8.37.4) that in the temple of Despoina in Arcadia her statue was clothed with deer pelt. Near Colophon lay a small island sacred to Artemis to which it was believed pregnant does swam in order to bear their young (Strabo 14.643, cited by Otto 1965: 84). Well-bred Athenian girls of marriageable age danced as bears in honour of Artemis of Brauronia, and during rites of cult-initiation girls 'became' bears, *arktoi* (Bachofen 1863:24). In paintings on vases, the worshippers of Artemis wore animals masks while dancing. The girls and women of Lakedemonia performed orgiastic dances to glorify Artemis. Fat men, padded and masked as comic actors, participated in fertility dances for Artemis (Jucker 1963). We can recognize their ancestors in the masked and padded men of the Vinča culture of *c.* 5000 BC (see Pls. 24, 25).

Offerings to Artemis include phalli and all species of animals and fruits, for she was protector of all life, bestowing fertility on humans, animals and fields, and the sacrifice of any living thing was appropriate to her. According to the legend adapted by Sophocles, the most beautiful girl of the year, Iphigeneia, had to be sacrificed to the goddess. The possibility of human sacrifice is suggested by the fact that Artemis herself is called Iphigeneia in *Hermione and Ageira* and that human sacrifice was performed for Laphria who was also Artemis (Wilamowitz-Moellendorf, *ibid.*: 181f.). Mutilated beasts, from which 'a member was cut off', were sacrificed to Artemis in Boeotia, Euboea and Attica. In Asia Minor, in the great spring festival of Cybele, the shorn genitals of her priests were consecrated to her (Persson 1942: 106). He-goat and stag were particularly appreciated sacrificial animals, and also the hare, a moon animal. In nearly all shrines dedicated to Artemis spindle-whorls, loom weights, shuttles and *kallatoi* have been found and from inscriptions in sanctuaries it is known that woollen and linen clothes and threads wound on spools were offered as gifts to her (Rouse 1902: 274, 296). On Corinthian vases, Artemis and her priestesses are seen holding a spindle (Jucker 1963: Pl. 20.3).

She appeared at births as the birth-giving goddess, Artemis Eileithyia ('Child-bearing'). Figurines in a seated position were sacrificed to her. Diana also presided over childbirth and was called 'Opener of the Womb'. As the Bear-Mother she nursed, reared and protected the newly born with the *pietas materna* of a bear. *Tithenidia*, the festival of nurses and nurslings in Sparta, honoured her name.

This goddess, as Otto (1965) poetically observed, mirrors the divine femininity of nature. Unlike the Earth-Mother who gives birth to all life, sustains it, and in the end receives it back into her bosom, she reflects the virginity of nature with its brilliance and wildness, with its guiltless purity and its strangeness. And yet, intertwined with this crystal-clear essence were the dark roots of savage nature. Artemis of Brauronia aroused madness. Her anger caused the death of women in childbirth.

It is no mere coincidence that the venerated goddess of the sixth and fifth centuries in Ancient Greece resembles the Goddess of Life and Death of the sixth and fifth millennia BC. Mythical images last for many millennia. In her various manifestations – strong and beautiful Virgin, Bear-Mother, and Life-giver and Life-taker – the

Great Goddess existed for at least five thousand years before the appearance of Classical Greek civilization. Village communities worship her to this day in the guise of the Virgin Mary. The concept of the goddess in bear shape was deeply ingrained in mythical thought through the millennia and survives in contemporary Crete as 'Virgin Mary of the Bear'. In the cave of Acrotiri near ancient Kydonia, a festival in honour of Panagia (Mary) Arkoudiotissa ('she of the bear') is celebrated on the second day of February (Thompson 1961–62). In European folk beliefs, she still moves within pregnant women in the shape of a wandering uterus or a toad. Each of her feminine aspects, virginity, birth-giving and motherhood, as well as her Terrible Mother aspect, is well represented in figurine art throughout the Neolithic and Chalcolithic eras of Old Europe.

9 The Pregnant Vegetation Goddess

A goddess symbolizing earth fertility was the natural response to an agrarian way of life. Her image harbours no accumulation of symbols from the pre-agricultural era as do those of the Great Goddess and Bird Goddess. She develops her own character in the course of time, but her intimate relationships to the Upper Palaeolithic Pregnant Goddess is obvious.

The seed must have been recognized as the cause of germination and growth, and the pregnant belly of a woman must have been assimilated to field fertility in the infancy of agriculture. As a result, there arose an image of a pregnant goddess endowed with the prerogative of being able to influence and distribute fertility. The belief that woman's fertility or sterility influences farming persists almost universally in European folklore. Barren women are regarded as dangerous; a pregnant woman has magical influence on grain because like her, the grain 'becomes pregnant'; it germinates and grows.

The Pregnant Goddess can be deciphered either by means of her *quasi* ideogram – a dot in a lozenge, or a lozenge within a lozenge – incised or painted on her belly, thighs, neck or arms, or by the naturalistic portrayal of a pregnant female with hands above the belly. She is related to the square, the perennial symbol of earthbound matter.

The pregnant figurines of the seventh and sixth millennia BC are nude, while the pregnant ladies of the fifth and fourth millennia are exquisitely clothed except for the abdomen, which is exposed and on which lies a sacred snake. In this series a high degree of stylization is observed: the abdominal part of the body is emphasized and the other parts are modified. Some figurines take the form of bottle-shaped amulets or rattles, obviously not representations of the goddesses, but necessary in magical proceedings to obtain fecundity.

197–199

196, 200, 201

202, *154*

196 Pregnant Goddess in full attire with a snake winding above the belly. From Medvednjak. Vinča. 5000 – 4500 BC

197 Small pregnant figurine with hands held over the abdomen. Porodin, southern Yugoslavia. Early sixth millennium BC

198 Upper part of figurine depicting a nude and pregnant woman (Pregnant Goddess?) with hands held above the belly. Porodin, southern Yugoslavia. Early sixth millennium BC

199 Pillar-headed pregnant figurine of Hamangian type. Cernavoda cemetery, Dobruja, c. 5000 BC

200, 201 The 'Fat Lady of Sitagroi', Macedonia, with a double spiral (two snakes) above the belly. East Balkan civilization. c. 4500 BC

202 Bottle-shaped figure (amulet) of a Pregnant Goddess (?). Sitagroi, Macedonia. East Balkan civilization. c. 4500 BC

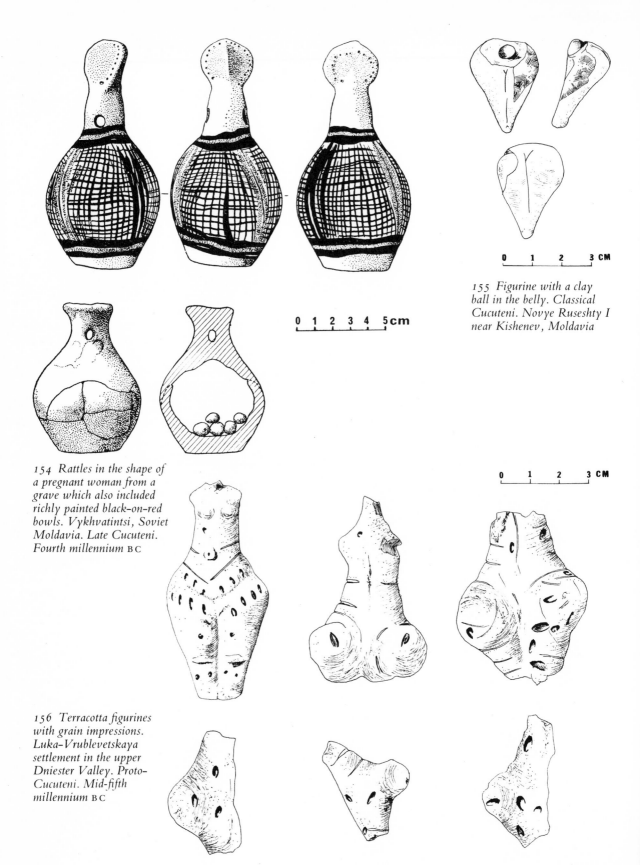

155 *Figurine with a clay ball in the belly. Classical Cucuteni. Novye Ruseshty I near Kishenev, Moldavia*

154 *Rattles in the shape of a pregnant woman from a grave which also included richly painted black-on-red bowls. Vykhvatintsi, Soviet Moldavia. Late Cucuteni. Fourth millennium* BC

156 *Terracotta figurines with grain impressions. Luka-Vrublevetskaya settlement in the upper Dniester Valley. Proto-Cucuteni. Mid-fifth millennium* BC

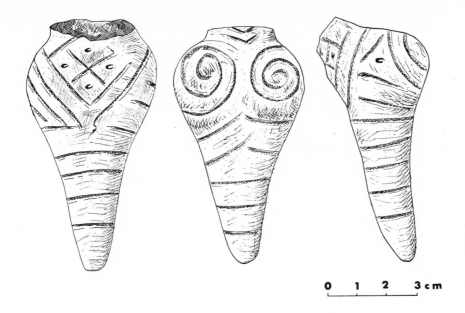

157 Lower half of female figurine with a dotted quartered lozenge in front and snakes winding over buttocks from Luka Vrublevetskaya, upper Dniester valley. c. late fifth millennium BC

THE DOT (SEED) AND THE LOZENGE (SOWN FIELD)

The dot, representing seed, and the lozenge, symbolizing the sown field, appear on sculptures of an enthroned pregnant goddess and are also incised or painted on totally schematized figurines. A lozenge with a dot or dash in its centre or in the corners must have been the symbolic invocation to secure fertility. Less abstract are the Early Cucuteni figurines from the western Ukraine where the entire body, particularly the abdomen and buttocks, were impressed with real grain. During the subsequent Classical Cucuteni phase the idea of pregnancy was expressed by the insertion of clay balls into the belly of a fat figurine (Fig. 155).

A lozenge is often the most pronounced feature, the rest of the female body serving only as a background to the ideographic concept. The idea of pregnancy as opposed to sterility is expressed by a dot in the centre of a lozenge or within each of the panels of a quartered lozenge. This ideogram, already present on seventh-millennium stamp-seals from Çatal Hüyük (Mellaart 1967: Pl. 121), is encountered throughout Old Europe both on Neolithic and Chalcolithic figurines. A lozenge and dot or a quadripartite lozenge is a very common motif on schematic Early and Classical Cucuteni (Tripolye) figurines. One or two snakes wind above the belly with its incised lozenge or surround sacred protuberances, most notably the buttocks. The repetition or multiplication of lozenges and their association with snakes or spirals was obviously meant to render the figurines or amulets more effective. Compositions of alternating lozenges and spirals are frequent on figurines and pots and also on clay plaques which may symbolize loaves of bread.

156

157–160
203–206

204, 205, 157

206, 160

161

205

203 Figurine with a dotted lozenge incised on the belly. Gladnice near Priština, southern Yugoslavia. *c.* 6000 BC

204, 205 Classical Cucuteni figurine. The elaborate incised design includes a quartered lozenge above the abdomen. Cucuteni, northern Moldavia. Mid-fifth millennium BC

206 Pregnant woman with a multiple lozenge design on the belly from Kolekovats, central Bulgaria. *c.* 4500 BC. The chair or (throne) was found separately but belongs to the same period

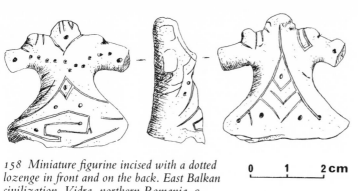

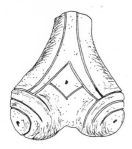

158 Miniature figurine incised with a dotted lozenge in front and on the back. East Balkan civilization. Vidra, northern Romania. c. 4500 BC

0   1   2 cm

159, 160 Highly schematic figurines (or charms) from Sitagroi, Macedonia. First half of the fifth millennium BC

0 1 2 3 CM

161 Loaf-shaped clay plaque incised with lozenges and spirals. Vinča settlement at Vršac, eastern Yugoslavia. c. 5000 BC or early fifth millennium BC

0 1   2   3 cm

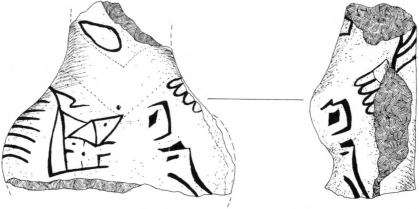

162 Fragment of the middle part of a figurine with designs of dotted lozenges and triangles and an egg (upper left) painted in black on red. Sitagroi. Macedonia. East Balkan civilization. c. 4500 BC

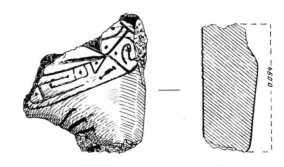

163 Fragment of a figurine incised with complicated design including dotted lozenges and triangles from the mound of Tangîru, lower Danube, Romania, c. 4000 BC or late fifth millennium BC

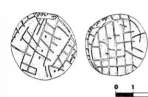

164 Black polished disc with white encrusted lines and dots. Ploskata Mogila near Plovdiv, central Bulgaria. East Balkan civilization. c. 4000 BC

A series of Gumelniţa and Cucuteni figurines have on the abdominal area a more complicated design consisting of interconnected lozenges and triangles usually containing a dot. Since this same composite design also recurs on round discs which are probably amulets or stamps from Gumelniţa settlements, this must be an established ideogram. It suggests the sacredness of sown fields.

THE ENTHRONED PREGNANT GODDESS

210, 211
207–209

Lozenges are typical embellishments of the garments of enthroned goddesses. The finest examples from various regions of Old Europe include the vessel-shaped Lady of Kökénydomb in southeastern Hungary and the 'Lady of Pazardžik' from central Bulgaria. The former wears over the lower part of the body a garment made up of panels of various sizes, many of which show a lozenge design; the latter is decorated with flowing incised lines interspersed with

209

lozenges. On each buttock are incised two large lozenges – placed here not as decoration, but to stress the functions of the earth-fertility goddess who is responsible for the germination, sprouting, growing and ripening of plants. The vessel shape and the lugs in the lower part of the Kökénydomb Lady suggest she was put to ritual use, (filled with water?), and carried over the fields. The Pazardžik Lady is a classical example of the Pregnant Goddess. Her centre of gravity in the abdomen draws her downward toward the earth of which she is a part. Her ample proportions, the essence of this sculpture, are symbolic of the fertile earth. She wears a round mask with a prominent nose and six holes for the lower lip. Her hands rest royally on the abdomen.

212

An impressive statuette of an enthroned, heavily-draped goddess wearing an ornate mask with slanted bulbous eyes and a medallion suspended on a thong was discovered in Priština, southern Yugoslavia. Snakes are incised on her belly to form an angular composition, above which there is an ideogram made of one horizontal and four vertical lines.

208

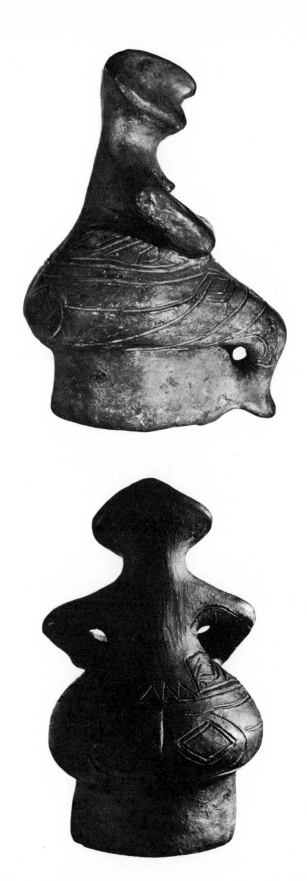

207-209 'The Lady of Pazardžik',
central Bulgaria. East Balkan
civilization, *c.* 4500 BC

210, 211 Anthropomorphic vessel, probably a portrayal of Pregnant Vegetation Goddess. Tisza settlement at Kökénydomb, southeastern Hungary. *c.* 5500 – 5000 BC

212 Enthroned Goddess from Predionica, southern Yugoslavia. Vinča. Mid-fifth millennium BC

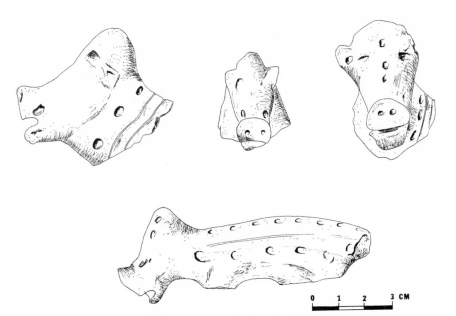

165 Fragments of figurines of pigs impressed with grain. Luka Vrublevetskaya in the upper valley of Dniester, USSR. Mid-fifth millennium B C

THE PIG, THE SACRED ANIMAL OF THE GODDESS OF VEGETATION

The curious connection between the Vegetation Goddess and pigs as known from Classical Greek times goes back to the Neolithic era. Sculptures of pigs are known from all parts of Old Europe and date from every period. In number they equal the representations of dogs, bulls and he-goats. The fast-growing body of a pig will have impressed early agriculturists; its fattening must have been compared to corn growing and ripening, so that its soft fats apparently came to symbolize the earth itself, causing the pig to become a sacred animal probably no later than 6000 B C.

An early Vinča Pregnant Vegetation Goddess wears a pig's mask, while the sacredness of the pig's body is indicated by the Cucuteni pig sculptures which have traces of grain impression on them. Grain was impressed on the body of the pig just as it was impressed on the body of the Vegetation Goddess. These figurines and the pig masks imply that the pig was a double of the Pregnant Vegetation Goddess and was her sacrificial animal.

213

165

Beautiful sculptures of entire pigs were found in the mound of Nea Makri in central Greece. The Vinča civilization has left us a masterpiece in the form of a pig's head from Leskovica near Štip in Macedonia. A well modelled early example comes from the Starčevo settlement of Donja Branjevina at Deronj in northwestern Yugoslavia (Karmanski 1968). Vessels or their handles were often shaped in the likeness of a pig's head or body and must have symbolized the goddess herself in the same way as other vessels did the Bird Goddess or the Great Goddess. The site of Vinča, in which the sculptures

215

211

213 Pig-masked Goddess of Vegetation. Rastu, Early Vinča site in western Romania

214 Head of a pig. Terracotta from the site of Leskavica, eastern Macedonia. Vinča civilization. *c.* mid-fifth millennium BC

215 Pig from Nea Makri, Neolithic Proto-Sesklo settlement in Attica, Greece. *c.* 6000 BC

216 Snout of a life-size suckling pig from Anza, eastern Macedonia. *c.* 5300-5100 BC

217 Head of a pig with perforated ears for ear-rings. Dalboki near Stara Zagora, Bulgaria. *c.* 4000 BC

218 Handle of a cult vase or rhyton from Vinča in the form of a pig's head. Early fifth millennium BC

appeared in many strata, yielded one exceptionally well sculpted head as well as a rhyton made of a thin red clay decorated with bands painted in black, in the shape of a pig's head. In the Vinča layer of the stratified site of Anza a life-size pig made of unbaked clay was discovered during the author's excavation in 1970. The Vinča layer was in a plough zone and the pig had been partly destroyed; much of the rest disintegrated as soon as it was touched, but its snout and one leg were preserved. There can be no doubt that the pig played an important cult role in East Balkan civilization. In addition to smaller and larger figurines of pigs, a pig's head from central Bulgaria had perforated ears for ear-rings! Stout vases, half anthropomorphic and half zoomorphic to resemble the hind parts of a pig, and small containers with pig's heads or incised stylized motifs of a pig's hind-quarters, were probably used for sacrifices or for votive offerings. Pigs, it is worth noting, were still being portrayed in Minoan Crete (Zervos 1956: Figs. 580, 582), and during the Classical and Hellenistic age in Greece and southern Italy. A true masterpiece of the fifth-fourth century BC is a lamp in the shape of a pig which was found in the cemetery of Camarino in Sicily. A lozenge and a floral design appear in the middle of the body (Sep. 833: Syracuse Archaeological Museum).

218

216

217

ALLUSIONS TO DEMETER, KORE AND PERSEPHONE IN GREEK MYTHOLOGY

Through her association with the pig, the beautifully draped Demeter with bare breasts, the queen of corn, the bread-giver and the queen of the dead (manifested as her daughter Persephone) can be connected with her predecessor, the prehistoric Vegetation Goddess. Persephone was even called *Pherrephata*, 'killer of suckling pigs', by the Athenians (V. Georgiev 1937: 22f.). Suckling pigs played a very prominent part in the cult of Demeter and Persephone. The festival of *Thesmophoria*, which occurred at the autumn sowing of the new crops in October in honour of Demeter, was one of the most important festivals in Greece. It was performed solely by women and lasted for three days. Women now brought suckling pigs, which three months before the festival had been thrown into subterranean caves to rot, and placed them on altars of *Thesmophoroi* – the name by which Demeter and her double or daughter Kore were called during the festival – with other gifts; they were then mixed with the seeds to be used for sowing (Nilsson 1957; 312; Simon 1969: 92). Herodotus describes a similar rite among the Egyptians: the inhabitants of the Nile delta let pigs trample on the seeds and press them into the earth (Herodotus 2, 14). The same is known from Egyptian paintings of Dynasty XVIII (Newberry 1928: Plate 19). The importance of the pig in Neolithic

214

and Chalcolithic Old Europe, particularly the association of pig and grain, suggests that the *Thesmophoria* and other similar festivals had their origin in early antiquity. This does not necessarily mean, however, that the Egyptians brought this custom to Greece, as Herodotus believed. At threshing time another festival, called *Skirophoria*, took place in Ancient Greece. Young virgins were clad in white robes and at night given sacred objects called *skira*. These objects were figurines of suckling pigs and cakes made in the shape of serpents. After the festival they were deposited in the sanctuary of Demeter. In the goddess' sanctuary at Lykosura, offerings made to Demeter were listed in inscriptions: oil, honeycomb, barley, figurines, poppy seeds, lamps, incense. Among the terracotta figurines portrayed in the marble reliefs found in the sanctuary were female examples with animal heads or animal legs including those of a pig (Nilsson 1957: 312ff.). The pig as an animal essential in purification rites played a major role in the Eleusinian Mysteries. So important was it, that when Eleusis was permitted to issue her autonomous coinage in 350–327 BC, the pig was chosen as the sign and symbol of her Mysteries (Harrison 1961: 153).

10   The Year-God

The whole group of interconnected symbols – phallus (or cylinder, mushroom and conical cap), ithyphallic animal-masked man, goat-man and the bull-man – represents a male stimulating principle in nature without whose influence nothing would grow and thrive. This family of symbols goes back in its origin to the early agricultural era, to the same period when the Goddess of Vegetation was born and when goat- and cow-herds existed. Charging bulls, bull heads or horns alone, bovine heads with human eyes and ithyphallic men are already known to the Proto-Sesklo and Starčevo cultural complexes, *i.e.* no later than the seventh millennium BC. Shrines of Çatal Hüyük include large bull figures in wall frescoes and sculptured bull heads and horns. Around the Mediterranean the bull and he-goat played a prominent part in religion from the seventh millennium onwards. So did the phallus, recognizable as a high cylindrical neck of androgynous figurines, as a stand, or the stem of a cup.

The phallus and bison are known from the Aurignacian and Magdalenian era of the Upper Palaeolithic. Isolated representations of phalli were found in the cave of Laussel, Dordogne. A bison-man playing upon a musical instrument in the engraving from La Pasiega, Santander, and another hybridized bison-man in the same cave (Giedion 1962: 193) illustrate that the image of a half-animal, half-human creature and the connection of man with the wild bull occurred early. The symbolic context, however, was different; the bison-man of the Upper Palaeolithic was not a year-god of an agricultural society. Phallic figurines from the Natufian and Pre-Pottery sites in Palestine demonstrate the persistent importance of phallic symbolism in pre-agricultural and agricultural societies.

THE PHALLUS

Representations of phalli are found in all phases and cultural groups of Old Europe with a wider variety in Neolithic Greece and Yugoslavia, particularly the Adriatic seaboard. They were fashioned in all sizes from the miniature to the exaggerated. Their decoration and shape range from naturalistic to fantastic: some have a 'cap' or a circumcision and an opening on top; others are geometrically decorated by painting or incision; still others spiral upwards like snakes. The clay phallus from Tsangli, a large Sesklo site in Thessaly, is painted cream, its naturalism enhanced by reddish-brown bands and has a broad incision at the top. From later Neolithic Sesklo comes an enormous marble phallus painted with red meanders top and bottom (National Museum, Athens 5936; Zervos, 1963: 398). The Vinča and Lengyel clay or bone phalli were decorated with bands of horizontal incisions and white encrusted patterns of dots symbolizing snakes. The East Balkan and Cucuteni phalli are usually undecorated.

Danilo, Butmir and Vinča settlements yielded hundreds of 'wine cups' with phallus-shaped stems. Many of them have plain, pointed stems, but others are charmingly decorated and masterfully shaped sculptures. Most interesting are those phalli imitating snakes, indicated by incision or in relief. In some instances two heads of snakes or of frogs appear on the top; others have human facial features, such as a protruding nose, while others again are geometrically decorated with striated zigzag bands or triangles. Cylindrical cups modelled as human heads also occur, and dishes and bowls of the Late Vinča complex have a phallus standing in the middle (Pločnik site: Archaeol. Museum Niš, Inv. 490).

Another category of phallic representations is made up of stands with human, animal or amorphous facial characteristics. Simple clay cylinders with a flattened base are frequent in the Starčevo and Early Vinča complexes of the central Balkans. Some have human facial features and female breasts; others have male genitals. We have already discussed the phallic aspect of the long cylindrical necks of the Bird Goddess and Great Goddess of the seventh and sixth millennia BC. The combining of female and male characteristics in one figurine did not completely die out after the sixth millennium BC.

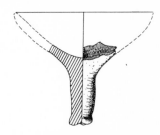

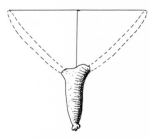

166 Phallic stems of 'wine cups'. Smilčić at Zadar, Dalmatia. c. late sixth millennium BC

168 Phallic stand with male genitals from Pavlovac, Early Vinča site in the upper Morava Valley

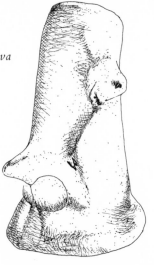

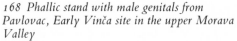

167 Anthropomorphic figurine in a shape of a phallus with a flat base. Crnokalačka Bara, southern Yugoslavia. c. early sixth millennium BC

217

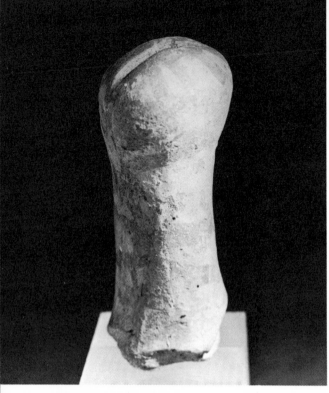

219 Clay phallus from Tsangli, Thessaly. Painted in reddish-brown on cream. Central Balkan Neolithic. c. 6000 BC

221 Two clay phalli from a Late Cucuteni site at Frumusica, northern Moldavia. Fourth millennium BC

220 Bone phallus from Bohuslavice, a Lengyel site in Moravia. The spiral design was executed by drilling pitted lines

222 Stem on cup with snake-like spirals. Smilčic at Zadar, Dalmatia. Danilo culture

223-225 Mushroom-shaped objects of light green stone from the Vinča site

226 Phallus-shaped vase decorated with running spirals in relief from Butmir near Sarajevo. Mid-fifth millennium BC

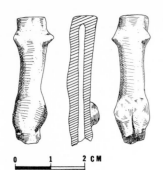

0 1 2 CM

169 Terracotta figurine with anthropomorphic features and a canal down the middle. Truşeşti site, northern Moldavia.

Many of the East Balkan female figurines have a canal through the whole length of the body. Since the canals are about 2 mm. in diameter it seems that they were not made for a practical reason but were simply imitations of the phallic canal.

Dwelling areas at Vinča yielded a number of mushrooms carved out of light green rock crystal which may have stood on domestic altars or possibly been used as studs for hip belts. Mushrooms are universally known as aphrodisiacs, and the swelling and growing of a mushroom must have been noticed by the Old Europeans causing it to be compared to the phallus. The fact that mushrooms were carved out of the best available stone alone speaks for the prominent role of the mushroom in magic and cult. The Indo-Europeans in the days of the Rigveda made their miraculous Soma drink from fly-agaric (Wasson 1971), and it is possible that the Vinča mushrooms were connected with intoxicating drinks; at all events they are imitations of phalli (*cf.* the mushroom cap in Pl. 225, right). The shape of a mushroom or phallus occurs frequently in sculptural art as a human cap on figurines, and a phallic form can be inferred in the beautiful Butmir vases which are decorated in running spirals and stand on cylindrical legs which support a globular bowl. Magical power was obviously attributed to phallic objects and conferred an appropriate benefit.

226

THE ITHYPHALLIC MASKED GOD

The ecstatic dancer, goat- or bull-masked, as seen in the Vinča sculptural repertory, can be interpreted as a representation of either an archetypal Dionysus or an excited worshipper of the Great Goddess. A most remarkable example is the sculpture from Fafos, in which he appears in human shape, probably to perform at a festival. His anthropomorphic portrayals show him also in a standing position with both hands holding his genitals, or with the right arm held across his breast and a red painted phallus in the left hand. More often he is seated on a throne, naked and ithyphallic. This posture recurs in all phases of Old European history, depicted rather clumsily in the Proto-Sesklo (two enthroned ithyphallic figurines were unearthed at Elateia and are housed in the Chaeronea museum, central Greece: Weinberg 1962) and Starčevo complexes, but more articulately in those of Vinča, Sesklo and Dimini. The head, when preserved, usually wears the mask of a horned animal with large human eyes.

227

228

229, 230

231

233–235

227 Ithyphallic masked male figure
from Fafos II, a Vinča site at
Kosovska Mitrovica, Yugoslavia.
Probably second half of fifth
millennium BC

228 Standing male figure holding
genitals. Sesklo, Thessaly

229, 230 Masked (and originally
horned) man holding red-painted
penis with the left hand.
Crnokalačka Bara, Classical Vinča
settlement near Niš, southeastern
Yugoslavia

231 Ithyphallic figure of an enthroned god from Porodin, southern Yugoslavia. Early sixth millennium BC

232 Ithyphallic figure of a seated man from Dimini near Volos, Thessaly. *c.* Mid-fifth millennium BC

233 Ithyphallic figurine wearing a goat mask with exaggerated horns and eyes. Fafos I near Kosovska Mitrovica, southern Yugoslavia. *c.* 5300–5000 BC

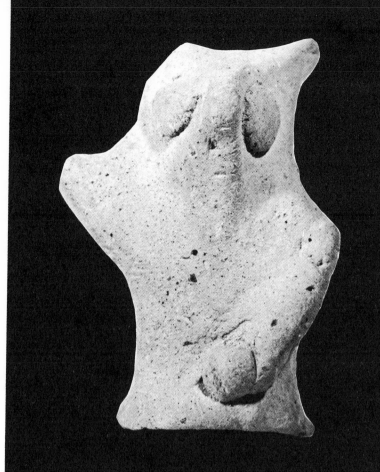

234 Animal-headed (masked) male figurine holding genitals with the left hand. From Vinča. Mid-fifth millennium BC

235 Head of a figurine wearing goat mask. Crnokalačka Bara, southern Yugoslavia. Vinča, mid-fifth millennium BC

234

235

233

236

239, 240, *170*

240–242

239, *170*

The male god's principal epiphany was in the form of a bull. The enthroned male figurines of Late Vinča, wearing an enormous mask, have vigorous shoulders which are shaped like a bull's rump or horns; quite frequently, too, the entire body is that of a bull. The god may also be represented as a vessel in the shape of a bull, but with the animal's head showing human characteristics: large wise eyes or ears with perforations for ear-rings or other decorations. The bull's strength is shown to be concentrated in his rump; both buttocks are enormous and snakes are incised upon them. Standing firmly on short legs, he conveys the impression of monumentality. This peculiar amalgam of animal and man, typical of Balkan Chalcolithic art, expressed the *Mysterium Fascinans*, something that cannot be described in terms of normal experience. It was a major factor in the inspiration and creation of these extraordinary sculptures. A human head grafted onto a bull's body reaches a culmination of power through symbiosis: the wisdom and passions of man merged with the physical strength and potency of the bull. Such hybrid creatures must have been regarded as possessing a greater potential than either a man or a bull alone.

Representations of a bull, he-goat or ram often appear on small ritual vessels. These horned heads embodying virile forces could have played their part in festivals, or in the worship of both the male and the female divinity. Vessels with horned animal-head protomes were encrusted or painted in white, red and black.

170 Black-on-red painted cult vase, probably a lamp, in the form of a stylized bull. The cylindrical container on top is broken. From the mound of Sitagroi near Drama, northeastern Greece. East Balkan civilization. c. 4500 BC

236 Man in a seated position wearing a large mask. Late Vinča site at Valač near Kosovska Mitrovica, southern Yugoslavia

237 Human-headed (masked) bull from Fafos II at Kosovska Mitrovica, southern Yugoslavia. Mid-Vinča, 5000 – 4500 BC

238 Human-headed (masked) bull from Valač, southern Yugoslavia. Late Vinča, 4500 – 4000 BC

239 Bull-legged terracotta tripod with a hole in the central cylinder. From Medvednjak, classical Vinča site at Smederevska Palanka southeast of Belgrade

240 Crouching bull wearing human mask. Vase from the mound of Gumelniţa. East Balkan civilization. *c.* 4500 BC

241 Terracotta head (mask) of a bull with human-like eyes. Sitagroi, Macedonia. East Balkan civilization. *c.* 4500 BC

242 Terracotta head of a bull, with horns broken off. Sitagroi, Macedonia. East Balkan civilization. *c.* 4500 BC

239

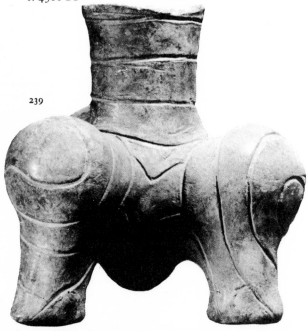

240

241
242

Dionysus is a pre-Indo-European god of great antiquity in spite of his composite name (dio-nysos, 'god of Nysa or Nysai'; the latter probably is a pre-Indo-European place name). His cult in Greece is evidenced by temples, sculptures of phalli and descriptions of processions carrying huge phalli as late as the second century BC, and the persisting tradition of Dionysiac festivals even into later times is attested by a group of mythical images having strong roots in the local (southeast European-western Anatolian) soil. Discussions about the origin of the Greek Dionysus – whether he came to Greece from Thrace, Crete or western Asia Minor – are pointless, since all these lands originally belonged to the same Mother Culture. Dionysus was a bull-god, god of annual renewal, imbued with all the urgency of nature. Brimming with virility, he was the god most favoured by women.

The abundance of phalli in Dionysiac festivals, in sculptures near the temples, on herms used as signposts on the roads and before the doors of houses suggests that the ancient Greeks were no less obsessed by phallic magic than were the Old Europeans. The bull-god was also alive in many areas of Greece and particularly in Macedonia in the time of Euripides whose *Bacchae* abounds in bull epiphanies:

> *A Horned God was found*
> *And a God with serpents crowned*
>
> (Euripides, *Bacchae*, 99;
> cited by Harrison [19030] 1961: 432).

In the Orphic mystery, the worshipper ate the raw flesh of the bull before he became 'Bacchos'. The ritual of Dionysus in Thrace included 'bull-voiced mimes' who bellowed to the god. The scholiast on Lycophron's *Alexandra* says that the women who worshipped Dionysus Laphystios wore horns themselves, in imitation of the god, for he was imagined to be bull-headed and is so represented in art (ref. in Harrison *ibid.*: 433). Plutarch gives more particulars: 'Many of the Greeks represent Dionysus' image in the form of a bull. The women of Elis in their prayers invoke the god to come to them with his bull-foot. And among the Argives there is a Dionysus with the title Bull-born. They summon him by their trumpets out of the water, casting lambs into the depths to the Door-keeper' (Plutarch *de Js. et Os.* XXXV, cited by Harrison *ibid.*: 433). Dionysus also manifested himself as the bull Zagreus, in which guise he was torn to pieces by the Titans.

The key to a more complete understanding of the male god and the Bull God of Old Europe lies in the Dionysiac festivals – Anthesteria, Lenaia and the Greater Dionysia. In these festivals, which have assimilated elements of deep antiquity, Dionysus appears as a year-god. The idea of renewal is predominant throughout the festivals of winter and spring. Each re-enacts an orgiastic agricultural scenario with phalli, phallus-shaped cups, ladles and cult dishes and the bull-man (Dionysus) marrying the queen (goddess).

The *Lenaia* festival held in January was preceded by a *Rural Dionysia* in which phalli were carried in procession amid general merrymaking to promote the fertility of the autumn-sown seed, and of the soil during the winter recess. Offerings were made before the image of Dionysus (including pouring porridge with a ladle), and priapic and goat songs were sung. The purpose of the Lenaia festival was to arouse the slumbering vegetation (Deubner 1956; James 1961: 142–43). The *City Dionysia* festival in March was also designed to ensure fertility. To this festival the cities of the Athenian empire sent the grossest kind of fertility emblem, the phallus, as part of their tribute (Webster 1959: 59). *Anthesteria* was a Festival of Flowers in honour of Dionysus as the god of spring, and included drinking and rejoicing. The second day of the festival was called *Choes*, the Day of the Cups. The wine was taken from the jars and brought to the sanctuary of Dionysus in the marshes, where it was silently distributed in small jugs among all citizens over the age of four. After everyone had drunk, the wife of the magistrate was married to Dionysus in the *Bukoleion* or Ox-stall, attended by women who had taken vows of chastity in the service of Dionysus. Thither the image of Dionysus, possibly in bovine form, or an actor wearing horns and a hide, was brought on a boat-like structure on wheels to complete the nuptial rites (James 1961: 140).

A sanctuary of Dionysus, which can be traced back to the fifteenth century BC, has been discovered on the island of Keos (Caskey 1964: 326). It yielded more than twenty terracotta figurines portraying women in a dancing posture, dressed in festive attire, with exposed breasts, 'snake collars and belts'. They may represent maenads, the devotees and ecstatic dancers in the Dionysiac festivals. The sanctuary was used for more than one thousand years, up to the Hellenistic period.

Since many elements of the year-god's festivals are represented in the sculptural art of Old Europe, it seems not unreasonable to assume that festivals took place in Neolithic and Chalcolithic Europe. Possibly the central idea of ritual drama, the 'Sacred Marriage', the ritual coition of the male god and a female goddess, is reflected in the little sculpture from Căscioarele. The statuette belongs to the East Balkan Chalcolithic Gumelniţa complex and is the only one of its kind, but this does not necessarily mean that there were no portrayals of the 'Sacred Marriage' in other areas and periods of Old Europe. The presence of the masked ithyphallic god also implies a festival at which a wedding ceremony is enacted, the male god marrying the

243

243 The Gumelniţa 'lovers', possibly a portrayal connected with the
ritual of 'sacred marriage'. Căscioarele. East Balkan civilization. Late fifth
millennium BC

Great Goddess. From the Căscioarele figurine it is seen that she is not a pregnant goddess, but a youthful virgin. She is portrayed in the nude and has a large pubic triangle.

When was the drama of hierogamy introduced into Europe? Was it at the very beginning of the Neolithic period, or on the advent of advanced agriculture? It seems unlikely to have been later than *c.* 6500 B C, when the 'phallic obsession' became manifest through representations of phallic stands, cups and ithyphallic gods.

THE 'SORROWFUL GOD'

We have considered until now the youthful, strong, creative aspect of the primeval Dionysus. Is there anything in the sculptural art of Old Europe to indicate his other aspect – the peaceful ancient? There

244, 245
248–252

are figures of a squatting or seated man on a stool or throne; his arms either rest peacefully on his lap, or they are propped on his knees to provide a support for his head. He shows no signs of emotion and is not animal-masked; his attitude and the facial expression of the mask he wears imply contemplation and worry. We may call him, therefore, the 'sorrowful god'. There are not enough data to reveal his functions, but we may suppose that he is either a god of vegetation, an old year-god who must die in order to be reborn the following spring, or a god of death, consort of the Great Goddess in her aspect of Death. The wide temporal and geographical distribution of this type of god speaks for his established position in the pantheon of Old Europe. His importance is stressed by the fact that the sculptures of a 'sorrowful god' are frequently produced with extreme care, some ranking as masterpieces of Neolithic art. Among these are the Vulkaneshti and Hamangia (Cernavoda) men in a leaning position seated on a small stool. Both are nude and in them we find the best portrayals of the male body dating from the fifth millennium B C. The back of the Vulkaneshti figure is perfectly rendered; one feels on it the touch of the god-maker's fingers. Unfortunately it is badly damaged and all that remains intact is its back; legs, arms and half of its head are missing. In Gerasimov's reconstruction, this man has his

246

elbows on the knees. One of the most celebrated sculptures of the Balkan Neolithic is the Hamangia 'Thinker' (so named after Rodin's 'Thinker'), a man sitting on a stool, leaning forward, holding his head on columnar arms with elbows on the knees. His legs are massive and as stable as those of a throne. The facial features are only

248–250

roughly indicated and no attempt has been made to model his hands. The head is definitely masked: it is flat and has perforations in the upper corners. The back is neatly curved and well proportioned. The Hamangian 'sorrowful god' was placed in a grave with a female

247

figurine, probably representing the Great Goddess. She is also of

230

244, 245 Enthroned male god from Pyrasos, Thessaly. Sesklo culture. Sixth millennium BC

246 Torso (seen from the back) of seated old man from Vulkaneshti, Soviet Moldavia. East Balkan civilization. Late fifth millennium BC

247

248

249

250

247 The Great Goddess of Hamangia
found together with 'Thinker' in
a grave of the cemetery of Cernavoda

248–250 The 'sorrowful god' or
'Thinker' of Hamangia. From a
grave in the cemetery of Cernavoda,
eastern Romania. *c.* 5000 BC

251, 252 The 'sorrowful god'
of Tirpeşti, Moldavia. *c.* mid-fifth
millennium BC

unique workmanship, portrayed in a seated position with her arms resting on one leg which is drawn up. She has a large pubic triangle and a massive cylindrical neck. Her face, a mask with deep triangular incisions for eyes, like that of the male figurine, is just as sorrowful as his. Both figurines are of the same style, size and colour and were probably made by the same gifted sculptor. In addition to the pair of gods, this grave in the Cernavoda cemetery yielded three schematic white marble figurines of the Great Goddess type. A figurine portrayed in almost the same posture, but made in a Cucutenian style, was unearthed in the settlement of Tirpeşti in northern Moldavia. From the artistic point of view the Tirpeşti sculpture is not a masterpiece, but again the value of the sculpture lies in the peculiar tension it conveys through its crouching posture and the crude head (a mask) held between the long arms and inarticulate hands.

We shall conclude this survey with the illustration of a 'Thinker' from Vidra, within the East Balkan Gumelniţa complex. He sits with his right arm resting on his lap and the left supporting his chin – a natural position for ruminating. The relationship of his gesture to that of the Great Goddess, as portrayed on the vessel of Sultana (see Pl. 155) and on many other figurines, suggests he has powers similar to those of the Great Goddess. A conspicuous feature of the Vidra man is his single eye, which may symbolize magical and chthonic characteristics. In the Late Cucuteni civilization almost all known male sculptures are one-eyed.

251, 252

171 The 'sorrowful god' of Vidra, lower Danube. East Balkan civilization. c. late fifth millennium BC–4000 BC

THE DIVINE CHILD

The Year-God cycle starts with the birth of the Divine Child. The masked goddess in the shape of a bear, snake or bird nurses the baby (see Pls. 132, 189, 193–195; Figs. 26, 96). The infant appropriately appears in the shape of a cub, baby snake, baby bird – all symbols of young life in nature. Masked figurines holding and feeding babies, or figurines with sacks on the back or with a hump – probably a schematic representation of a sack (see Pl. 26) – and their portrayals as parts of ritual vases, (see Pls. 26, 132, 189, 190) occur frequently enough to attest a ritual re-enactment of the myth of the birth and nurturing of the Infant.

There is a striking similarity between the Old European Divine Child and the infant Erichthonios, Hyakinthos, and Cretan Zeus in the ancient Greek myths, which have a pre-Greek origin. The Divine Child represents the awakening or a new-born spirit of vegetation. Erichthonios appears as a snake or a half snake, half human. A scene on a Greek amphora shows him emerging from a chest guarded by two snakes by which Athena also stands (British Museum, E.418); on other vases, Ge (Earth) holds out the small

234

Erichthonios to Athena. According to legend Athena hid the child in a chest together with snakes and gave the chest to the three maidens, Aglauros 'the Bright one', Pandrosos 'the all Dewy one', and Herse 'dew', to guard. The oldest literary testimony, the Catalogue of the Ships of the Iliad, says that the corn-yielding Earth bore him and Athena fostered him. In the Eleusinian Mysteries, the holiest and most ancient cult of Ancient Greece, the Divine Child Ploutos (*i.e.* Erichthonios) is given to others to rear. Erichthonios' association with the snake recalls the prominent place the snake occupies in the Eleusinian cult and in the festival of Thesmophoria. During the latter, mysterious sacred objects were in use, made of wheat dough in the shape of snakes and men (Nilsson 1950: 558–63). Hyakinthos and Cretan Zeus represent the same god of young vegetation under different names. Hyakinthos' connection with the vegetation cult is further evidenced by his name which denotes a flower (*id.*: 558 with a ref. to Machteld J. Mellink, *Hyakinthos*, Diss., 1943). Cretan Zeus, the Holy Babe born in the Cave of Dikte, has only an Indo-European (Greek) name, but is no other than the pre-Greek Minoan-Old European Divine Child. And it is significant that this child was not reared by the mother (Ge, Rhea, the Indo-European Earth Goddess), but by Artemis, the Mistress of Animals, Demeter or Athena.

As a symbol of the perpetuation of life the Divine Child was at the heart of the whole complex of images of an agrarian religion, and represents the most traditional of motifs. The chances are that rites similar to the Eleusinian Mysteries were performed in Old Europe.

A ritual hymn of invocation commemorating the birth of the Infant dating from the second or third century AD was found engraved on a stone stele at Palaikastro in eastern Crete. Surely its origins must lie in Old European symbolism, transmitted through the agency of Minoan culture.

'Io, Kouros most Great, I give thee hail, Kronian, Lord of that is wet and gleaming, thou art come at the head of thy Daimones. To Dikte for the Year, O, march, and rejoice in the dance and song, that we make to thee with harps and pipes mingled together, and sing as we come to a stand at thy well-fenced altar.
For here the shielded Nurturers took thee, a child immortal, from Rhea and with noise of beating feet hid thee away.
And the Horai began to be fruitful year by year and Dikte to possess mankind, and all wild living things were held about by wealth-loving peace.
Io, Kouros, the Great . . .
To us leap for full jars, and leap for fleecy flocks, and leap for fields of fruit, and for hives to bring increase. Io, Kouros, the Great . . .'
(Quoted in original and translation and analyzed by Harrison,
Themis, 1912, 1962 edition: 1–29).

Conclusions

In figurine art and pictorial painting the agricultural ancestors recreated their mythical world and the worship of their gods. Primordial events, principal personalities of the pantheon with their innumerable epiphanies, worshippers and participants in ritual ceremonies, all seem to have a life of their own in their various representations.

Myths and seasonal drama must have been enacted through the medium of the idol (the figurine), each with a different intention and with the invocation of appropriate divinities. The multiplicity of purpose and design is shown by sanctuaries, sacrifices, festive attire, masks, figures in dancing or leaping postures, musical instruments, shrine equipment, ladles and drinking cups, and other numerous and varied representations of objects and events which made up the context of these religious festivals. In making images of gods, worshippers and actors of the drama, man assured the cyclic returning and renewal of life. Many figurines were ex-votos and like the words of prayer were dedicated to the Great Goddess, the Bird or Snake Goddess, the Vegetation Goddess, or the Male God, a prototype of Dionysus, the daemon of vegetation.

Female snake, bird, egg, and fish played parts in creation myths and the female goddess was the creative principle. The Snake Goddess and Bird Goddess create the world, charge it with energy, and nourish the earth and its creatures with the life-giving element conceived as water. The waters of heaven and earth are under their control. The Great Goddess emerges miraculously out of death, out of the sacrificial bull, and in her body the new life begins. She is not the Earth, but a female human, capable of transforming herself into many living shapes, a doe, dog, toad, bee, butterfly, tree or pillar.

The task of sustaining life was the dominating motif in the mythical imagery of Old Europe, hence regeneration was one of the foremost manifestations. Naturally, the goddess who was responsible for the transformation from death to life became the central figure in the pantheon of gods. She, the Great Goddess, is associated with moon crescents, quadripartite designs and bull's horns, symbols of continuous creation and change. The mysterious transformation is most vividly expressed in her epiphany in the shape of a caterpillar, chrysalis and butterfly. Indeed, through this symbolism our ancestor proclaims that he believes in the beauty of young life. The ubiquity of phallic symbols connotes the glorification of the spontaneous life powers. Phallicism certainly had no obscene allusion; in the context of religious ritual it was a form of catharsis, not of symbolic procreation. There is no evidence that in Neolithic times mankind understood biological conception.

With the inception of agriculture, farming man began to observe the phenomena of the miraculous Earth more closely and more intensively than the previous hunter-fisher had done. A separate deity emerged, the Goddess of Vegetation, a symbol of the sacral nature of the seed and the sown field, whose ties with the Great Goddess are intimate.

Significantly, almost all Neolithic goddesses are composite images with an accumulation of traits from the pre-agricultural and agricultural eras. The water bird, deer, bear, fish, snake, toad, turtle, and the notion of hybridization of animal and man, were inherited from the Palaeolithic era and continued to serve as avatars of goddesses and gods. There was no such thing as a religion or mythical imagery newly created by agriculturists at the beginning of the food-producing period.

In Old Europe the world of myth was not polarized into female and male as it was among the Indo-European and many other nomadic and pastoral peoples of the steppes. Both principles were manifest side by side. The male divinity in the shape of a young man or a male animal appears to affirm and strengthen the forces of the creative and active female. Neither is subordinate to the other; by complementing one another, their power is doubled.

The central theme in re-enaction of myths obviously was the celebration of the birth of an infant. The baby as the symbol of a new life and the hope of survival is hugged by masked goddesses, Snake, Bird and Bear. Masked Nurses bearing a sack (the 'hunch-back' figurines) seem to have played a role as protectresses of the child who later matures and becomes a young god. The male god, the primeval Dionysus is saturated with a meaning closely related to that of the Great Goddess in her aspect of the Virgin Nature Goddess and Vegetation Goddess. All are gods of nature's life cycle, concerned with the problem of death and regeneration, and all were worshipped as symbols of exuberant life.

The pantheon reflects a society dominated by the mother. The role of woman was not subject to that of a man, and much that was

237

created between the inception of the Neolithic and the blossoming of the Minoan civilization was a result of that structure in which all resources of human nature, feminine and masculine, were utilized to the full as a creative force.

The Old European mythical imagery and religious practices were continued in Minoan Crete. The Minoan culture mirrors the same values, the same manual aptitude in artistic endeavour, the same glorification of the virgin beauty of life. The Old Europeans had taste and style – whimsical, imaginative and sophisticated; their culture was a worthy parent of the Minoan civilization.

Some scholars did in the past classify European prehistory and early history into matriarchal and patriarchal eras respectively. 'The beginning of the psychological-matriarchal age', says Neumann, 'is lost in the haze of prehistory, but its end at the dawn of our historical era unfolds magnificently before our eyes' (Neumann 1955: 92). It is then replaced by the patriarchal world with its different symbolism and its different values. This masculine world is that of the Indo-Europeans, which did not develop in Old Europe but was super-imposed upon it. Two entirely different sets of mythical images met. Symbols of the masculine group replaced the images of Old Europe. Some of the old elements were fused together as a subsidiary of the new symbolic imagery, thus losing their original meaning. Some images persisted side by side, creating chaos in the former harmony. Through losses and additions new complexes of symbols developed which are best reflected in Greek mythology. One cannot always distinguish the traces of the old since they are transformed or distorted. And yet it is surprising how long the Old European mythical concepts have persisted. The study of mythical images provides one of the best proofs that the Old European world was not the proto-Indo-European world and that there was no direct and unobstructed line of development to the modern Europeans. The earliest European civilization was savagely destroyed by the patri-archal element and it never recovered, but its legacy lingered in the substratum which nourished further European cultural develop-ments. The Old European creations were not lost; transformed, they enormously enriched the European psyche.

The teaching of Western civilization starts with the Greeks and rarely do people ask themselves what forces lay behind these begin-nings. But European civilization was not created in the space of a few centuries; the roots are deeper – by six thousand years. That is to say, vestiges of the myths and artistic concepts of Old Europe, which endured from the seventh to the fourth millennium BC were trans-mitted to the modern Western world and became part of its cultural heritage.

238

Abbreviations

AAASH: *Acta Archaeologica Academiae Scientiarum Hungaricae*, Budapest.

AJA: *American Journal of Archaeology*, New York.

Banner, *Kökénydomb*: J. Banner, 'Anthropomorphe Gefässe der Theisskultur von der Siedlung Kökénydomb bei Hödmezövásárhely (Ungarn)', *Germania*, XXXVIII: 14–35, 1959.

BCH: *Bulletin de Correspondance Hellénique*, Athens-Paris.

Berciu, *Contribuţii*: D. Berciu, *Contribuţii la problemele neoliticului in Rominia in lumina noilor cercetări.* Bucharest, 1961.

BRGK: *Berichte der Römisch-Germanischen Kommission.*

BSA: *Annual of the British School at Athens.* London.

BU: Belgrade University.

Czalog, *Szegvár-Tüzköves*: Jósef Czalog, 'Die anthropomorphen Gefässe und Idolplastiken von Szegvár-Tüzköves', *Acta Archaeologica*, XI: 7–38. Budapest, 1959.

Dacia: Recherches et découvertes archéologiques en Roumanie I–XII, 1924–47. Dacia Revue d'archéologie et d'histoire ancienne, N.S. I–XV, 1957–1972.

Dombay, *Zengövárkony*: János Dombay, 'Die Siedlung und das Gräberfeld in Zengövárkony'. *Archaeologia Hungarica*, 37. Budapest, 1960.

Dumitrescu, *L'art Romanie*: V. Dumitrescu, *L'art néolithique en Romanie.* Bucharest, 1968.

Dumitrescu, *Traian*: V. Dumitrescu, 'La station préhistorique de Traian; fouilles de 1936, 1938 et 1940', *Dacia*, N.S. IX–X (1941–44). 1945.

Evans, *Palace of Minos*: Sir Arthur Evans, *The Palace of Minos, a comparative account of the successive stages of the Early Cretan Civilization as illustrated by the discoveries at Knossos.* London. vol. I–1921; vol. II–1928; vol. III–1930; vol. IV–1935.

Galović, *Predionica*: R. Galović, *Predionica: Neolitsko Naselje Kod Prištine* (German translation: Predionica: Äneolithische Ansiedlung bei Priština). Priština. 1959.

Garašanin, *Religija*: D. Garašanin, 'Religija i kult neolitskog choveka na Centralnom Balkanu', *Neolit Centralnog Balkana*, 1968.

Gaul, *Neolithic Bulgaria*: J. H. Gaul, 'The Neolithic period in Bulgaria; early food producing cultures in Eastern Europe', *American School of Prehistoric Research*, Bulletin 16. 1948.

Georgiev-Angelov, *Ruse*: Georgi I. Georgiev and N. Angelov, 'Razkopki na seliśtnata mogila do Ruse prez 1948–1949 god', *Izvestija.* Bulgarska Akad. na Naukite, Archeol. Inst. XVIII (1952): 119–194 and XXXI (1957).

Georgiev, *Beiträge*: Georgi I. Georgiev, 'Beiträge zur Erforschung des Neolithikums und der Bronzezeit in Südbulgarien', *Archaeologia Austriaca*, XLI–XLII: 90–144. 1967.

Godishnik, Plovdiv: *Annuaire de Musée National Archéologique.* Plovdiv (in Bulgarian).

Grbić, *Pločnik*: M. Grbić. *Pločnik äneolithische Ansiedlung.* Belgrade, 1929.

Grbić, *Porodin*: M. Grbić et al., *Porodin, kasnoneolitsko naselje na Tumbi kod Bitolja.* Bitola, 1960.

Gulder, *Maissau*: Alois Gulder, 'Die urnenfelderzeitliche Frauenkröte von Maissau in Niederösterreich und ihr geistesgeschichtlicher Hintergrund', *Mitteilungen der Prähistorischen Kommission der Österreichischen Akademie der Wissenschaften.* X:1–157. 1960–62.

Hesperia: *Hesperia Journal of the American School at Athens.* Athens-Princeton.

IPEK: *Jahrbuch für Prähistorische und Ethnographische Kunst.* Berlin.

Izvestija: *Bulgarska Akademija na Naukite. Izvestija na Arkheologicheskija Institut.*

JHS: *Journal of Hellenic Studies.* London.

Kalicz, *Dieux*: Nándor Kalicz, *Dieux D'Argile. L'âge de pierre et de cuivre en Hongrie.* Budapest, 1970.

Kandyba, Schipenitz: O. Kandyba, *Schipenitz. Kunst und Geräte eines neolithischen Dorfes.* Bücher zur Ur- und Frühgeschichte, V. 1937.

Korošec, *Prehistorijska plastika*: Josip Korošec, 'Prehistorijska glinena plastika u Jugoslavija (Prehistoric plastic art in Yugoslavia)', *Archeološki Radovi i Rosprave*, I (1959), 61–117; II (1962), 103–174.

KSIIMK: *Kratkie Soobshchenija o Dokladakh i Polevykh Issledovanijakh Instituta Istorii Materialnoj Kultury*. Moscow.

Mellaart, *Çatal*: James Mellaart, '1962 excavations at Çatal Hüyük. Second preliminary report', *Anatolian Studies*, XIII: 43–103. 1963.

MIA: *Materialy i Issledovanija po Arkheologii SSSR*. Moscow-Leningrad.

NAM Bucharest: National Antiquities Museum, Institute of Archaeology of the Academy of Sciences. Bucharest.

Nikolov, *Gradešnica*: Bogdan Nikolov, 'Glinena pločka s pismeni znaci ot s. Gradešnica, Vračanski okryg' (Résumé in French: Plaque en argile avec des signes d'écriture du village Gradešnica, dép. de Vraca), in joint article with Vladimir I. Georgiev, 'Debuts d'écriture de Chalcolithique dans les terres bulgares', *Archaeologija*, XII, 3: 1–9. 1970.

NM Belgrade: National Museum Belgrade.

NM Belgrade *Catalogue* (1955): Norodni Muzej Beograd, Praistorija II. Katalog Keramike I (1955). Includes: B. Stalio, Zlokučani-Gradac, R. Galović, Lipovac – 'Dizaljka', and Sremski Karlovci – 'Karas'. With German translation.

Passek, *Céramique tripolienne*: T. S. Passek, La Céramique tripolienne. Izvestija Gosudarstvennoj Akademii Istorii Materialnoj Kul'tury. Leningrad-Moscow, 1935.

Petrescu-Dîmboviţa, *Truşeşti*: M. Petrescu-Dîmboviţa, 'Die wichtigsten Ergebnisse der archäologischen Ausgrabungen in der neolithischen Siedlung von Truşeşti (Moldau)', *Prähistorische Zeitschrift*, XLI: 172–186. 1963.

PZ: *Prähistorische Zeitschrift*. Berlin.

RGK: Römisch-Germanische Kommission.

Rosetti, *Vidra*: Dinu V. Rosetti, 'Săpăturile de la Vidra', *Materiale şi Cercetări Archeologie*, VII: 71–78. 1961.

Roska, *Torma Collection*: Marton Roska, *Die Sammlung Zsófia von Torma in der numismatisch-archäologischen Abteilung der Siebenbürgischen National Museum*. Kolozvàr-Cluj, 1941.

Rybakov, *Cosmogony*: B. A. Rybakov, 'Cosmogony and mythology of the agriculturalists of the Eneolithic', *Soviet Anthropology and Archaeology*, IV, 2: 16–36 and 3:33–51. 1965–66. Translation from Russian, originally published in *Sovetskaja Arkheologija*, 1965, 1 and 2.

SA: *Sovetskaja Arkheologija*.

SCIV: *Studii şi cercetări de Istorie Veche*, Akademia Republicci Populare Romine, Institutul de Arheologie.

Sheffield *Catalogue* 1969: C. Renfrew *The arts of the first farmers*, Sheffield City Museum. 1969.

Tasić, *Valač*: N. Tasić, 'Praistorisko naselje kod Valača' (Prehistoric settlement at Valač), *Glasnik Muzeja Kosova i Metohije*, II, IV, V:45. 1957.

Tasić-Tomić, *Crnokalačka Bara*: N. Tasić and E. Tomić, *Crnokalačka Bara Naselje Starčevačke i Vinčanske Kulture*, Dissertationes, VIII. Krusevac, 1969.

Todorović-Cermanović, *Banjica*: Jovan Todorović and Aleksandrina Cermanović, *Banjica'naselje vinčanske kulture*. (Banjica, Siedlung der Vinča-Gruppe). Belgrade, 1961.

Tsountas, *Diminiou kai Sesklou*: Ch. Tsountas, *Ai proistorikai akropoleis Diminiou kai Sesklou*. Athens, 1908.

UCLA: University of California at Los Angeles.

Vasić, *Vinča*: Miloje M. Vasić, *Praistorijska Vinča*, I–IV. Belgrade, 1932–36.

Vildomec, *Strzelitz*: F. Vildomec, 'Ein jungsteinzeitliches Gefäss mit eingestochenen Menschengestalten und Tierplastiken Strzelitz (Südmähren)', *Wiener prähistorische Zeitschrift*, XXVII: 1–6. 1940.

Vulpe, *Izvoare*: R. Vulpe, *Izvoare: Sapaturile din 1936–1948*. Summaries in Russian and French: Izvoare: Les Fouilles de 1936–1948). Biblioteca de Arheologie I. Bucharest, 1941.

Zervos, *Crète*: C. Zervos, *L'Art de la Crète, Néolithique et Minoenne*. Paris, 1956.

Zervos, *Naissance*: C. Zervos, *Naissance de la civilization en Grèce*. Paris, 1962–63.

Details of sites including radiocarbon dates

Achilleion, near Farsala, Thessaly, Greece, a stratified tell of the Sesklo culture with continuous habitation from *c.* 6600 BC to *c.* 5800 BC. The superimposed villages yielded domestic shrines and cult places centered around the ovens in the courtyards, over 200 anthropomorphic and zoomorphic figurines of clay and stone, removable masks, mask-decorated vases, stamps, altar tables, thrones, lamps and other cultic equipment. Dated by forty radiocarbon dates, Achilleion is a backbone for the study of the Sesklo economic, architectural, ceramic, and art developments. The average dates are: Phase I (Early Ceramic and Proto-Sesklo) $7470 \pm 70 - 7380 \pm 40$ B.P., true age around 6500 BC; Phase II (Early Sesklo) $7310 \pm 30 - 7262 \pm 50$ B.P., true age *c.* 6300 BC; Phase III (transitional) $7221 \pm 50 - 7160 \pm 40$ B.P., true age *c.* 6200 BC; Phase IV (classical Sesklo) 7040 ± 70:—6900 B.P., true age 6000 – 5900 BC (the uppermost level, IV *b*, was not radiocarbon dated). Finds in the Larisa archaeological museum. Publ. Gimbutas 1974; Ferguson, Gimbutas and Suess 1976. The final report to appear in 1983 in *Monumenta Archaeologica*, Institute of Archaeology, University of California, Los Angeles. Excavated 1973–74 by the author.

Anza, at the village of Anzabegovo between Titov Veles and Štip, East Macedonia, southeast Yugoslavia. Stratified Central Balkan Neolithic site beginning with the earliest painted pottery complex related to Proto-Sesklo in northern Greece (Anza I) continuing throughout the whole Neolithic (Anza II and III), and ending with Early Vinča (Anza IV). Excavated 1960 by J. Korošec and 1969–70 by the joint Yugoslav-American team, M. Garašanin and M. Gimbutas. Museum: Štip. Publ. Marija Gimbutas *Archaeology*, 25, 2, 1972; 1976.

C14 dates for Anza I: 7340 ± 250 BP, true age *c.* 6400/6300 BC (LJ 2180); 7210 ± 100 BP, true age *c.* 6400/6300 BC (LJ 2330/31); 7140 ± 250 BP, true age *c.* 6400/6300 BC (LJ 2332); 7120 ± 100 BP, true age *c.*

6400/6300 BC (LJ 2337); 7080 ± 100 BP, true age *c.* 6000 BC (LJ 2339); 7070 ± 100 BP, true age *c.* 6000 BC (LJ 2342); 7030 ± 320 BP, true age *c.* 6000 BC (LJ 2157); 6880 ± 250 BP, true age *c.* 6000 BC (LJ 2333).

Anza II: 6980 ± 80 BP, true age *c.* 5900/5800 BC (LJ 2409); 6900 ± 80 BP, true age *c.* 5900/5800 BC (LJ 2405).

Anza III: 6700 ± 80 BP, true age *c.* 5700/5600 BC (UCLA 1705C); 6560 ± 120 BP, true age *c.* 5700/5600 BC (UCLA 1705B): 6565 ± 250 BP, true age *c.* 5700/5600 BC (LJ 2185).

Anza IV: 6250 ± 100 BP, true age *c.* 5300 BC (LJ 2329); 6200 ± 200 BP, true age *c.* 5300 BC (LJ 2411).

Argissa, or Gremnos, near Larisa, Thessaly, Greece. A stratified Neolithic and Bronze Age tell. In over 8.5 m. of cultural material, fifteen strata were observed, representing the following sequence: pre-ceramic Neolithic, early ceramic, Proto-Sesklo, Dimini, and Mycenaean. Excavated 1955–58 by V. Milojčić. Publ. Milojčić 1955, 1958, 1965; Milojčić-Boessneck-Hopf, 1962. Museum: Larisa.

C14 dates. Pre-ceramic Neolithic; 8130 ± 100 BP, true age *c.* 7150 BC (UCLA 1657A); 7990 ± 95 BP, true age *c.* 7000 BC, (UCLA 1657D).

Early ceramic: 7500 ± 90 BP, true age *c.* 6500 BC (GrN 4145).

Ariuşd, district south of Gheorghe, region of Braşov. A stratified settlement of the Classical and Late Cucuteni civilization. Excavated 1907–8, 1910–12 and 1925. Publ. F. Laszlo *Dacia* I (1924).

Aszód, located northeast of Budapest, Hungary. A site and cemetery of the Lengyel culture. Excavated 1960–66 by N. Kalicz. Museum: Aszód.

C14 dates: 5100 ± 105 BP, true age 4200–3800 BC (UCLA 1225).

Azmak, near Stara Zagora, central Bulgaria. Large tell site which yielded a complete sequence of the East Balkan or

'Karanovo' civilization. Excavated 1960–63 by G. I. Georgiev. Museum: Stara Zagora. Publ. Georgiev 1961, 1962, 1963, 1965, 1969.

C14 dates for the Karanovo I phase: 7303 ± 150 BP, true age *c.* 6350 BC, (Bln 293); 7158 ± 150 BP, true age *c.* 6200 BC (Bln 291); 6878 ± 100 BP, true age *c.* 5900 BC (Bln 292); 6768 ± 100 BP, true age *c.* 5800 BC (Bln 294); 6779 ± 100 BP, true age *c.* 5800 BC (Bln 296); 6720 ± 100 BP, true age *c.* 5750 BC (Bln 295); 6812 ± 100 BP, true age *c.* 5850 BC (Bln 299); 6675 ± 100 BP, true age *c.* 5700 BC, (Bln 297); 6540 ± 100 BP, true age *c.* 5550 BC (Bln 298); 6652 ± 150 BP, true age *c.* 5700 BC (Bln 224); 6483 ± 100 BP, true age *c.* 5500 BC, (Bln 301); 6426 ± 150 BP, true age *c.* 5450 BC (Bln 300); 6279 ± 120 BP, true age *c.* 5300 BC (Bln 430).

Karanovo V phase: 5840 ± 100 BP, true age *c.* 4800 BC (Bln 136); 5737 ± 150 BP, true age *c.* 4550 BC (Bln 143); 5630 ± 150 BP, true age *c.* 4450 BC (Bln 150); 5829 ± 100 BP, true age *c.* 4750 BC (Bln 151); 5760 ± 150 BP, true age *c.* 4600 BC (Bln 148); 5803 ± 150 BP, true age *c* 4700 BC (Bln 142); 5697 ± 100 BP, true age *c.* 4550 BC (Bln 137); 5219 ± 150 BP, true age *c.* 4200–4000 BC (Bln 147).

Karanovo VI phase: 5888 ± 100 BP, true age *c.* 4850/4800 BC, (Bln 149); 5390 ± 100 BP, true age *c.* 4350 BC (Bln 145); 5035 ± 150 BP, true age *c.* 4200/3800 BC (Bln 146); 5717 ± 100 BP, true age *c.* 4550 BC (Bln 131); 5703 ± 100 BP, true age *c.* 4550 BC (Bln 139); 5597 ± 120 BP, true age *c.* 4450 BC (Bln 144); 5700 ± 100 BP, true age *c.* 4550 BC (Bln 135); 5621 ± 200 BP, true age *c.* 4500 BC (Bln 138); 5620 ± 100 BP, true age *c.* 4550 BC (Bln 141); 5520 ± 200 BP, true age *c.* 4400 BC (Bln 134).

Banjata, central Bulgaria near Kapitan Dimitrijevo at Pazardžik. Tell site with remains of East Balkan Karanovo I–II, III, V and VI phases. Excavated 1947–48 by P. Detev. Museum: Plovdiv. Publ. Detev, 1950.

Banjica, northeast of Belgrade. Stratified Vinča site with 4 m. of cultural remains. Five phases have been noted. Excavated

1955–57 by J. Todorović and A. Cermanović and published in 1961.

C14 dates: 5710 ± 90 BP, true age *c.* 4550 BC (GrN 1542) for the Late Vinča horizon.

Berești, at Bujor, eastern Romania. Classical Cucuteni (Cucuteni A) settlement. Museum: Galați. Publ. Ion T. Dragomir *Danubius* I (1967).

Bernovo Luka, western Ukraine, middle Dniester. Early Cucuteni (Tripolye) settlement. Excavated 1952 by T. S. Passek *et al.* Publ. Passek *Doklady* VI, Inst. Arch. Kiev (1953).

Bilcze Zlote, south of Tarnopol, upper Dniester Basin. A Late Cucuteni cave site. Excavated at the end of the nineteenth–early twentieth century by G. Ossowski and W. Demetrykiewicz. Museum: Arch. Mus. Cracow, Poland.

Blagoevo, at Razgrad, Bulgaria. East Balkan civilization, Chalcolithic, Karanovo VI period. Find place of marble figurine, Fig. 102, chapter VIII.

Bodrogkeresztúr, northeast Hungary. Name of the cultural group and period of the Hungarian Copper Age following the Tiszapolgár complex; includes a cemetery of 50 excavated graves. Excavated 1921–26 by L. Bella, J. Hillebrand and F. V. Tompa. Publ. Bella *Jb. der Urg. Arch. Ges.* (1923), Hillebrand *WPZ* 13 (1926).

Boian, island in Lake Boian north of the Danube, between Oltenița and Calarași, southeast Romania. Eponymous site of the Boian variant synchronous with Karanovo IV and V of the East Balkan civilization. Excavated 1924 by V. Christescu; 1956–59 by E. Comșa. Museum: NAM Bucharest. Publ. Christescu *Dacia* II (1925); Comșa *Mat. Cerc. Arh.* 5–8 (1959–62).

Bordjoš, near Novi Bečej, northern Yugoslavia. Find place of figurine, Pl. 94, Ch. VII. Tisza settlement.

Borets, near Plovdiv, central Bulgaria. East Balkan civilization, Chalcolithic.

Borsod, near Miskolc, northeastern Hungary. A Neolithic Bükk site in the Sajó

Valley. Excavated 1926–30 by A. Leszik, J. Hillebrand and F. Tompa; 1948 by J. Korek and P. Patay. Museum: Miskolc. Publ. Tompa 1929; Korek and Patay *Regeszeti Füz*, II, 2 (1958).

Brnč, Nitra, Slovakia, Czechoslovakia. Lengyel settlement defended by a strong palisade. The site belongs to the Brodzany and Ludanice phases of the Lengyel culture. The Ludanice phase is represented by seventeen children's burials. Excavated 1961–62 by J. Vladár. Museum: Nitra. Publ. J. Vladár 1969.

Butmir, near Sarajevo, Yugoslavia. Eponymous site of the Butmir complex. The settlement was stratified into three habitation horizons representing continuous development. Excavated 1893–96. Museum: Zemaljski Muzej, Sarajevo. Publ. Radimský 1895; Fiala 1898.

Bylany, near Kutná Hora. Kolin, Bohemia, Czechoslovakia. Large settlement of the Linear Pottery culture, followed by a settlement of the Chalcolithic Lengyel culture. Excavated 1953–61 by B. Soudský. Museum: Bylany and Prague. Publ. Soudský 1958, 1959, 1960, *Antiquity*, XXXVI (1962), 1966.

C14 dates for the Early phase: 6320 ± 230 BP, true age *c.* 5350 BC (M1897); 6250 ± 230 BP, true age *c.* 5300 BC (M1896).

Mid-phase: 6270 ± 65 BP, true age *c.* 5300 BC (GrN 454); 6170 ± 45 BP, true age *c.* 5100 BC (GrN 4752).

Late phase: 6180 ± 145 BP, true age *c.* 5100 BC (GrN 4755); 5810 ± 65 BP, true age *c.* 4700 BC (GrN 4751).

Calomfireşti, dist. of Teleorman, southern Romania. East Balkan civilization, Chalcolithic. Museum: NAM, Bucharest.

Capri, Grotta delle Felci, Naples, Italy. Chalcolithic and Bronze Age settlement with ceramic ware of the Capri, Ripoli and Diana groups. Excavated 1921 by V. Rellini. Museum: Museo di Capri. Publ. Rellini *Monumenta Antiqua* 29 (1923).

Căscioarele, southern Romania near Oltenița, an island in the lower Danube. A stratified Chalcolithic site including late

Boian and Gumelniţa settlements of the East Balkan civilization. The former yielded the sanctuary with two pillars, the latter a clay model of an edifice. Excavated 1925 by Gh. Stefan; 1962–69 by H. and V. Dumitrescu. Museum: NAM, Bucharest. Publ. V. Dumitrescu 1965, 1970; H. Dumitrescu 1968.

C14 dates of the Boian-Spanţov settlement: 5570 ± 100 BP, true age *c.* 4400 BC (Bln); 5860 ± 100 BP, true age *c.* 4800 BC, (Bln); 5980 ± 100 BP, true age *c.* 4900 BC (Bln).

Gumelniţa settlement: 5618 ± 120 BP, true age *c.* 4450 BC, (Bln); 5485 ± 120 BP, true age *c.* 4350 BC (Bln).

Čavdar, 60 km. east of Sofia, Bulgaria. Neolithic, East Balkan tell of the Karanovo I period. Excavation 1970 by R. Katinčarov. Museum: Sofia.

Cernavoda, northwest of Constanţa, Danube delta, Romania. Cemetery site of the Hamangia culture. Excavated 1957 by D. Berciu. Museum: NAM, Bucharest. Publ. Berciu, 1966. Pls. 247–250, Ch. X.

C14 dates for Hamangia III: 5880 ± 70 BP, true age *c.* 4800 BC (GrN 1986).

Cernica, located at Bucharest, Romania. Cemetery of the East Balkan civilization. Chalcolithic, Early Boian phases. 340 burials uncovered. Excavated 1960–67 by G. Cantacuzino and S. Morintz. Museum: NAM, Bucharest. Publ. Cantacuzino 1967.

Chaeronea, Boeotia, central Greece. Settlement with 6 m. of cultural material, basically Proto-Sesklo with red-on-white painted ware. Excavated 1902–7 by G. Sotiriadis. Museum: Chaeronea. Publ. Sotiriadis *Athen. Mitt.* 30 (1905); *Ephem. Arch.* (1908); *Rev. Etudes Grèques* 25 (1925).

Corinth, Peloponnese, Greece. Contains several layers of Neolithic settlements found under classical remains. Excavated since 1896. Publ. S. Weinberg *Hesperia* 6 (1937); 17 (1948); 29 (1960); *AJA* (1939), 51 (1947); V. Milojčić *Gnomon* 22 (1950).

Crnokalačka Bara, near Niš, 20 km. southeast of the mouth of the Morava, southern Yugoslavia. Stratified Central Balkan Neolithic (Starčevo II) and Chalcolithic Vinča site. The Vinča culture consists of three phases. Excavated 1936 by M. Marković; 1951 by M. and D. Garašanin; Museum of Kruševac and NM of Belgrade (R. Galović) 1959–60 and 1967. Publ. Tasić and Tomić 1969.

Crvena Stijena, near Petrovići, Montenegro, Yugoslavia. Cave site with evidence of settlement in the Palaeolithic, Mesolithic, and Early Neolithic. Excavated 1954–57 by A. Benac and M. Brodar. Publ. Benac and Brodar *Glasnik Sarajevo Arh.* 12 (1957); 13 (1958).

Csepa, southeast Hungary. Neolithic Central Balkan Starčevo (Körös) settlement. Museum: Szarvas, southern Hungary. Publ. F. Krecsmárik *Arch. Ert.* 32 (1912).

Cucuteni, near Tîrgu-Frumoş, district of Iaşi, Moldavia, northeast Romania. Stratified settlement with Cucuteni A, A–B, and B phases which gave its name to the Cucuteni civilization in Moldavia. Evidence of copper from the earliest phases. Excavated 1909–10 by H. Schmidt; 1961–68 by M. Petrescu-Dîmboviţa. Museum: Berlin and Bucharest, Iaşi and Bîrlad. Publ. Schmidt *Cucuteni* 1932; Petrescu-Dîmboviţa *Cucuteni* 1966.

Cuina Turcului, located on bank of the Danube at the Iron Gates, district of Turnu Severin, Romania. Central Balkan Neolithic Starčevo site with three consecutive phases. Excavated 1967–72. Museum: NAM, Bucharest.

Danilo, near Šibenik, Yugoslavia. Eponymous site of the Danilo culture. Excavated 1952 by D. Rendić-Miocević; 1953–55 by J. Korošec. Museum: Šibenik. Publ. Korošec 1964.

Dikili-Tash, at Philipi, Macedonia, Greece. Eponymous site of the Macedonian variant of the East Balkan civilization. Stratified mound with cultural strata parallel to Sitagroi. Excavated by J. Deshayes and D. Theocharis 1965; 1968–70. Publ. J. Deshayes, *Bulletin de Correspondance Hellénique*, volf. 86, Pt 2: 912–33.

Dimini (Dhimeni), near Volos, Thessaly, Greece. Eponymous site of the Late Neo-lithic Dimini group. Excavated 1908 by Ch. Tsountas. Museum: Athens and Volos. Publ. Tsountas 1908.

C14 date: 5630 ± 150 BP, true age *c.* 4450 BC (GrN).

Divostin, near Kragujevac, central Yugoslavia. Central Balkan Neolithic Starčevo and Late Vinča settlement. Excavated 1968–69 by the joint Yugoslav-American team, A. McPherron and D. Srejović. Museum: Kragujevac.

C14 dates for the Starčevo phase: 6950 ± 100 BP, true age *c.* 6000 BC (Bln 896) and for the same pit, thermoluminescence dating (Aitken's Oxford Lab.) yielded a value of 6190 ± 800 BC. Other Starčevo dates: 7080 ± 180 BP (Bln 823); 7020 ± 100 BP (Bln 826); 6970 ± 100 BP (Bln 824); 6910 ± 100 BP (Bln 827); 6995 ± 100 BP (Bln 862); 7060 ± 100 BP (Bln 866); 7200 ± 100 BP (Bln 899). True age *c.* 6000 BC.

Vinča phase: dates for Pit 121 were 5860 ± 100 BP, true age *c.* 4820 BC (Bln 898); 5247 ± 100 BP, true age *c.* 4300 BC (BM 574); thermoluminescence measurement yielded a value of 4920 BC ± 700 for the same pit. Other Vinča dates: 5825 ± 100 BP, true age *c.* 4800 BC (Bln 863); 6020 ± 100 BP, true age *c.* 5000 BC (Bln 865).

Dončova Mogila (Bikovo), central Bulgaria. Tell of the Chalcolithic East Balkan civilization of Karanovo V and VI periods. Excavated 1948–49 by P. Detev. Museum: Plovdiv. Publ. Detev, *Godishnik* 1 (1954).

Donja Branjevina, near Deronj, northern Yugoslavia. Central Balkan Neolithic Starčevo settlement. Excavated and published by S. Karmanski 1968. Museum: Odžaci.

Dudeşti, southeast of Bucharest, Romania. Stratified site with remains of the East Balkan Karanovo III and Early Vinča materials which succeeded the Starčevo (Criş) culture. Excavated 1954–56 by E. Comşa. Museum: NAM, Bucharest. Publ. Comşa *SCIV* 7 (1956); *Kongress* (1958).

Dvory Nad Žitavou, near Nove Zamky, western Slovakia. Cemetery of the Linear Pottery culture, Želiezovce group. Museum: Nitra. Excavated and published by J. Pavúk *Slov. Arh.* XXI, 1 (1964).

Elateia (Drakhmani), Phokis, Greece. Two Neolithic tell sites. Excavated 1909–10 by G. Sotiriadis and 1959 by S. Weinberg. Museum: Chaeronea. Publ. Sotiriadis *Athen. Mitt.* 30 (1905), 31 (1906); *Ephem. Arch.* (1908); *Rev. Etudes Grèques* 25 (1912); Wace and Thompson *Prehistoric Thessaly* 1912; Weinberg *AJA* 65 (1961); *Hesperia* 31 (1962).

Horizons with the earliest monochrome pottery: 7480 ± 70 BP, true age *c.* 6500 BC (GrN 2973); 7360 ± 90 BP, true age *c.* 6400 BC (GrN 3037); 7190 ± 100 BP, true age *c.* 6200 BC (GrN 3041).

Following horizon with painted pottery: 7040 ± 130 BP, true age *c.* 6050 BC (GrN 3502).

Fafos, at Kosovska Mitrovica, southern Yugoslavia. Fafos I–Early and Fafos II–Late Vinča settlements. Excavated 1956 and 1959–61 by B. Jovanović and J. Glišić. Museum: Priština.

Frumusica, near Moldavia. Classical Cucuteni settlement. Excavated and published 1946 by C. Matasă. Museum: Piatra Neamţ.

Ghelaeşti (or Nedeia near Ghelaeşti), district Neamţ, northeastern Romania, a Cucuteni A/B-B₁ settlement, *c.* 4000 – 3600 BC, noted for the discovery of a central structure with a ritual find. In an egg-shaped vase four figurines (two unpainted and two with black-painted heads and feet) had been placed at the cardinal points. Six vases, painted with snake and double-seed bands, were arranged in a circle around it. The assemblage probably was instrumental in rituals dedicated to the resurgence of plant life. Excavated in 1970 by Niţu, Cucoş and Monah, publ. 1971; Cucoş 1973. Finds in the museum of Piatra Neamţ.

Gladnice, near Priština, southern Yugoslavia. Central Balkan Neolithic Starčevo settlement. Excavated 1960 by J. Glišić. Museum: Priština.

Goljamo Delchevo, a Neolithic, Chalcolithic and Copper Age tell and a cemetery of 30 graves in the valley of R. Luda Kamchija, northeastern Bulgaria, excavated by D. Zlatarski 1931 and H. Todorova 1968–71.

The site yielded exquisite graphite painted pottery, anthropomorphic and zoomorphic vases, over 100 figurines, a.o. cult objects. The Chalcolithic period (Karanovo V, Sava variant) dated by radiocarbon: Level III (Bln) 5940 ± 100 B.P. and Level IV (Bln 924) 5840 ± 100, true age *c.* 4800 – 4700 BC. The Copper Age (later Karanovo VI); Level IX (Bln 921) 5515 ± 100 and Level XII (Bln 920) 5590 ± 100, (Bln 920a) 5640 ± 100, true age *c.* 4400 – 4300 BC. Finds in the Varna archaeological museum. Publ. Todorova, Ivanov, Vasilev, Hopf, Quitta, and Kohl 1975.

Gomolava, on the River Sava, Vojvodina, northern Yugoslavia. A stratified tell with the Mid-Vinča layer below Baden-Kostolac, Middle and Late Bronze Age, La Tène II and III, Roman and Medieval cultures. Excavated since 1904 by J. Brunsmed, 1953 by R. Rašajski and S. Nagy, 1965–71 by B. Brukner and B. Jovanović. Museum: Novi Sad.

Gorni Pasarel, central Bulgaria. Chalcolithic settlement of the East Balkan civilization. Excavated 1952–53 by N. Petkov. Museum: Plovdiv. Publ. Petkov 1957.

Gorza, at Hódmezövásárhely, southeastern Hungary. Settlement and burials of the Chalcolithic Tisza group. Excavated 1956–63 by G. Gazdapusztai. Museum: Hódmezövásárhely. Publ. Gazdapusztai *Móra Fer. Muz. Évkönyve* 1963.

Gradešnica (Gradeshnitsa) near Vraca, northwestern Bulgaria, Neolithic and Chalcolithic tell, excavated by B. Nikolov 1964–73. The Neolithic site of three successive horizons parallels Starčevo II Karanovo I, *c.* 5800 – 5600 BC, 16 houses of timber uprights and wattle and daub uncovered, some with geometric decoration on interior walls and included richly symbolically decorated polichrome painted globular and anthropomorphic vases. The three Chalcolithic levels run parallel with early Vinča, around 5000 BC 63 houses excavated arranged in streets. Houses are 6 to 9 m. long, rectangular, some of several rooms with ovens and pitched roofs. Horizon B yielded a temple model with symbols and signs

245

arranged in panels on the roof and walls and a shallow dish with inscriptions. More than a dozen vases were inscribed. Over 200 schematic anthropomorphic figurines collected, some inscribed with signs.

Grotta Scaloria, Manfredonia, Foggia, Italy. Adriatic civilization: Neolithic cave site with flint and obsidian tools, red painted and impresso wares. Excavated 1930 by Q. Quagliati. Museum: Foggia. Publ. by U. Rellini *La più antica ceramica dipinta in Italia* 1934; *BPI* LVI–LVII (1936–37). *See* Scaloria.

Gumelniţa, near Olteniţa, southern Romania. The type site of the Chalcolithic East Balkan civilization, synchronous with Karanovo VI in central Bulgaria. The settlement has been divided into two main phases corresponding with Gumelniţa II and III. Excavated 1925 and 1960 by V. Dumitrescu. Museum: NAM, Bucharest. Publ. V. Dumitrescu *Dacia* II (1925), VI/VIII (1937/40), IV N. S. (1960); *Archaeology* (1966).

C14 dates: 5865 ± 50 BP, true age *c.* 4800 BC (Bln); 5675 ± 80 BP, true age *c.* 4500 BC (Bln); 5400 ± 120 BP, true age *c.* 4350 BC (Bln); 5715 ± 70 BP, true age *c.* 4550 BC (GrN 3025); 5400 ± 90 BP, true age *c.* 4350 BC (GrN 3028).

Habaşeşti, near Tîrgu-Frumoş, Moldavia, northeast Romania. A classical Cucuteni settlement. Cucuteni A complex. The settlement was fortified by two defensive ditches. Excavated 1949–50 by V. Dumitrescu. Museum: NAM, Bucharest. Publ. V. Dumitrescu 1954. C14; 5330±80 BP true age 4360 BC (GrN 1985).

Hluboke Mašůvky, near Znojmo, Moravia, Czechoslovakia. Settlement of the Linear Pottery and Střelice group of the Chalcolithic Lengyel culture. Excavated 1927–39 by F. Vildomec; 1949–50 by J. Neustupný. Publ. Vildomec and Salm *IPEK* 11 (1931–37); *Obzor Prehist.* 13 (1946); Neustupný *Arch. Rozhl.* 2 (1950); 3 (1951); *Časopis Nar. Mus. Prag.* (1948–50).

Hurbanovo, near Hurbanovo, Komarno, southern Slovakia. Neolithic settlement with ceramic remains attributed to the Linear Pottery Želiezovce variant, Lengyel, Tisza and Bükk cultures. Excavated 1953–

58. Museum: Nitra. Publ. C. Ambros and B. Novotný *Arch. Rozhl.* 5 (1953); P. Čaplovic *Arch. Rozhl.* 8 (1956); B. Novotný *Počiatky vytvarneho prejavu na Slovensku* (1958); H. Quitta *PZ* 36 (1960).

Hvar, island, cave site located at Grapčeva spilja. Adriatic civilization, Chalcolithic period. Excavated and publ. by G. Novak 1955. Museum: Zagreb.

Ilonapart, near Szentes, southeastern Hungary. Linear Pottery settlement, excavated by J. Czalog in the early sixties. Museum: Szentes.

Izvoarele, near Bacău, Moldavia, northeastern Romania. Settlement of the Early Cucuteni civilization on the River Bistriţa. Five horizons have been identified as belonging to the Proto-Cucuteni and Cucuteni A. Excavated 1936–48 by R. Vulpe. Museum: NAM, Bucharest. Publ. Vulpe 1957.

Jasatepe, Plovdiv, Bulgaria. Tell site of the East Balkan civilization containing Karanovo III, V and late VI characteristics. Excavated 1945, 1950–59 by Detev. Museum: Plovdiv. Publ. Detev *Godishnik* 1 (1948), 3 (1959).

Kakanj, near Visoko, Bosnia, Yugoslavia. Late Central Balkan Starčevo settlement with Adriatic (Danilo) elements. Excavated 1954 by A. Benac and 1968 by G. Sterud. Museum: Zemaljski Muzej, Sarajevo. Publ. Benac *Glasnik Sarajevo Arh.* NF 11 (1956).

Kalojanovec, 18 km. southwest of Stara Zagora, central Bulgaria. Settlement of the East Balkan civilization, Karanovo IV period. Museum: Stara Zagora.

Kapitan Dimitrievo, central Bulgaria, *see* Banjata.

Karanovo, near Nova Zagora, central Bulgaria. Large tell and eponymous site of the Karanovo culture which provides the backbone of the East Balkan cultural sequence. Contains the major phases: Karanovo I and II (parallel to Starčevo), III (Veselinovo), IV, V (Marica phase), VI (Gumelniţa), VII (Early Bronze Age). Excavated 1936–57 by V. Mikov and G. I. Georgiev. Museum: Nova Zagora and Sofia. Publ. Mikov *Izvestija* 5 (1937), *Antiquity* XIII (1939), *SA*

I (1958), Mikov, Georgiev and Dzambazov *Vodac za Arch. Muz.* I (1952), Gaul *BASPR* 16 (1948).

C14 dates from the Karanovo II phase: 6807 ± 100 BP, true age *c.* 5850 BC (Bln 152); 6573 ± 100 BP, true age *c.* 5600 BC (Bln 201); 6300 ± 150 BP, true age *c.* 5550 BC (Bln 234).

Karanovo III phase: 6360 ± BP, true age *c.* 5400 BC (Bln 158).

Karanovo VI phase: 5840 ± 230 BP, true age *c.* 4800 BC (Bln 236).

Karbuna, Čimisli district, Soviet Moldavia, USSR, yielded a hoard of 852 objects in a vase attributed to the Pre-Cucuteni (Tripolye A) culture. Over half the objects were of copper and over 250 were of shell. The vase was uncovered in an unexcavated settlement. Publ. Sergeev *SA* (No. 1, 1962).

Kato Ierapetra, located on the southern coast of Crete. Middle Neolithic settlement. Museum: Heraklion, Crete (Giamalakis Collection).

Kazanlik, located at Kazanlik, central Bulgaria. A large tell which yielded a complete sequence of the Neolithic East Balkan civilization. Excavated 1966–70 by G. I. Georgiev and R. Katinčarov. Museum: Kazanlik.

Kenezlö, near Tokaj, northeastern Hungary. Neolithic Bükk and Chalcolithic Tisza settlement. Excavated by N. Fettich. Museum: Nyíregyháza. Publ. Tompa 1929.

Kodžadermen, near Šumen, northeastern Bulgaria. A 7 m.-high tell of the East Balkan civilization with remains of the Boian culture followed by Gumelniţa. Excavated 1914 by R. Popov. Museum: Sofia. Publ. Popov *Izvestija* 6 (1916–18); Gaul *BASPR* 16 (1948).

Kökénydomb, in Hódmezővásárhely, southeastern Hungary. Settlement and cemetery of the Tisza culture. Excavated 1929, 1940–42 and 1944 by J. Banner. Museum: Hódmezővásárhely. Publ. Banner, *Kökénydomb*.

Kolomijshchina, at Khalepje, south of Kiev, Ukrainian SSR. Settlement of the Classical Cucuteni (Tripolye) culture. Ex-

cavated 1934–38 by T. S. Passek. Museum: Moscow, Inst. Arch. Publ. Passek 1949.

Kopancs, in Hódmezővásárhely, southeastern Hungary. Comprises several Neolithic and Chalcolithic settlements including the Central Balkan Starčevo (Körös) succeeded by the Tisza complex. Excavated by J. Banner. Museum: Hódmezővásárhely. Publ. Banner *Dolgozatok* 8 (1932); 9–10 (1933–34); 13 (1937).

Koszylowce (Koshilovce), near Zališčiki, western Ukraine. Late Cucuteni (Tripolye) settlement. Excavated 1906–13. Museum: Lvov (Lwów), Publ. K. Hadaczek, *La colonie industrielle de Koszylowce* (Cracow 1915).

Kotacpart, at Hódmezővásárhely, southeastern Hungary. A Central Balkan Neolithic Starčevo (Körös) settlement including eight burials in rubbish pits. Excavated 1933–34 by G. Banner. Museum: Hódmezővásárhely. Publ. Banner *Dolgozatok* 8, 9–10 (1932, 1933–34).

C14 date: 6450 ± 100 BP, true age *c.* 5500 BC (Bln 115).

Krynichka, district of Balta, Podolia, west Ukraine. Late Cucuteni settlement excavated during the nineteenth century, private col. E. N. Antonovich-Melnik, Kiev. Publ. Makarenko *IPEK* (1927).

Kukova Mogila (Duvanli), near Plovdiv, central Bulgaria. Settlement of the East Balkan civilization, Karanovo III period. Excavated 1928–30 by B. Filov. Museum: Plovdiv.

Lang-Enzersdorf, located at Korneuburg, eastern Austria. Settlement of the Lengyel culture. Excavated 1952 by H. Ladenbauer-Orel. Museum: Vienna, Naturhistorisches Museum. Publ. Ladenbauer-Orel *IPEK* 19 (1954–59); *Jb. Landeskd. Niederösterreich* 36 (1964).

C14 dates: 5950 ± 130 BP, true age *c.* 4850 BC (Neustupný 1969); 5880 ± 120 BP, true age *c.* 4800 BC (Neustupný 1969).

Larga-Jijiei, district of Iaşi, Moldavia, northeastern Moldavia. Multiple settlement site with Linear Pottery, Early ('Pre-Cucuteni') and Late Cucuteni (Cucuteni B) material. Excavated and published by A. D. Alexandrescu, *Dacia* V (1961) and *SCIV* XII, 2 (1961).

Lengyel, near Szekszárd, Tolna, Hungary. Eponymous settlement and cemetery of the Lengyel culture. The Early Chalcolithic cemetery includes 90 graves. Excavated 1882–88 by M. Wosinszky. Museum: Szekszárd. Publ. Wosinszky *Das prähistorische Schanzwerk von Lengyel* 1888; *Tolnavarmegye törtenete* 1896.

Lepenski Vir, on the bank of the Danube at the Iron Gates, Yugoslavia. A village of trapezoidal houses, probably originally subterranean, including rectangular stone-walled sunken hearths and plastered floors. Fifty-four large egg-shaped stone sculptures were found. Contemporary with the Neolithic Early Starčevo complex, but includes local Danubian Mesolithic elements, especially in the physical type of people, massive Crô-Magnon. Excavated 1965–69 by D. Srejović and Z. Letica. Museum: University, Belgrade. Publ. Srejović 1969.

Chronology: end seventh–early sixth millennium BC.

C14 dates: 6560 ± 100 BP, true age *c.* 5600 BC (Bln 655); 6630 ± 100 BP, true age *c.* 5650 BC (Bln 654); 6820 ± 100 BP, true age *c.* 5850 BC (Bln 650); 6620 ± 100 BP, true age *c.* 5650 BC (Bln 652); 6820 ± 100 BP, true age *c.* 5850 BC (Bln 576); 6845 ± 100 BP, true age *c.* 5850 BC (Bln 647); 6860 ± 100 BP, true age *c.* 5900 BC, (Bln 575); 6800 ± 100 BP, true age *c.* 5850 BC (Bln 649); 6900 ± 100 BP, true age *c.* 5950 BC (Bln 678); 6900 ± 100 BP, true age *c.* 5950 BC (Bln 379); 7040 ± 100 BP, true age *c.* 6050 BC (Bln 653); 6984 ± 94 BP, true age *c.* 6000 BC (Z 115); 7300 ± 124 BP, true age *c.* 6350 BC (Z 143); 7310 ± 100 BP, true age *c.* 6350 BC (Bln 740a); 7360 ± 100 BP, true age *c.* 6400 BC (Bln 740b); 6970 ± 60 BP, true age *c.* 6000 BC (UCLA).

Lerna, near Argos, eastern Peloponnese, Greece. Settlement consisting of two Neolithic cultural layers followed by Early Bronze Age remains. The upper Late Neolithic layer consists of eight building horizons. Excavated 1956–59 by J. L. Caskey.

Museum: Argos. Publ. Caskey *Hesperia* 23 (1954), 25 (1956), 26 (1957), 27 (1958), 28 (1959).

Leţ (Varheghiu), at St Gheorghe, Transylvania, Romania. The site consists of various Neolithic and Chalcolithic settlements. The earliest stratum belongs to the Central Balkan Starčevo ('Criş') culture divided into two phases, followed by the East Balkan Boian and Cucuteni-Ariuşd Chalcolithic complexes. Excavated 1949–55 by Z. Szekely, I. Nestor and E. Zaharia. Museum: NAM, Bucharest. Publ. Zaharia *Dacia* N.S. VI (1962).

Lipovac, near Arandjelovac, 60 km. southeast of Belgrade. Late Vinča site. Excavated 1911 by M. Vasić; 1930 by M. Grbić and 1931 by V. Fewkes. Museum: NM Belgrade.

Lisičići, near Konjic, Hercegovina, Yugoslavia. A settlement of the Adriatic (Hvar) civilization, which is divided into three living horizons. Excavated 1952–54 by A. Benac. Museum: Zemaljski Muzej, Sarajevo. Publ. A. Benac *Neolitsko naselje u Lisičićima kod Konjica* 1958.

Lovets, near Stara Zagora, Bulgaria. East Balkan civilization of the Chalcolithic period (Karanovo VI–Gumelniţa type). Museum: Stara Zagora.

Luka-Vrublevetskaya, located in the upper Dniester Valley, district of Kamenec-Podolski, Ukraine, USSR. Early Cucuteni ('Tripolye A') settlement. Excavated 1946–50 by S. N. Bibikov. Museum: Moscow, Inst. Arch. Publ. Bibikov 1953.

Matera, Basilicata, Italy. Several Neolithic sites of the Adriatic civilization, Matera-Capri complexes, contemporaneous with the Sesklo and Dimini groups of Greece. Excavated 1912 by D. Ridola. Museum: Matera, Publ. D. Ridola *La Grotta dei Pipistrelli e la Grotta Funeraria in Matera* 1912.

Medvednjak, at Staro Selo, near Smederevska Palanka, central Yugoslavia. Large settlement of the classical Vinča civilization. Excavated 1968–70 by R. Galović sponsored by the Smederevska Palanka Museum. Unpublished.

C14 date for carbonized grain sample: 6100 ± 100 BP (LJ 2521), true age *c.* 5000 BC.

Megara Hyblaea, Syracuse, Sicily. Neolithic settlement of the Adriatic Impresso culture, Stentinello group. The site was surrounded by a defensive ditch. Excavated 1917 by P. Orsi; 1950 by F. Villard. Museum: Museo di Siracusa. Publ. P. Orsi *Monumenta Antiqua* 27 (1921); Vallet and Villard *Boll. Aete* 45 #3 (1960).

Mohelnice, Zábreh, Šumperk, Moravia, Czechoslovakia. Linear Pottery settlement followed by a Lengyel settlement. Excavated 1953 by R. Tichý. Museum: Brno. Publ. Tichý *Arch. Rozhl.* 8 (1956); *Sbornik Arch. Ust. Brno* I (1960); 2–3; *Prehled Výzkumu Brno* 1960; 1962; *Pam. Arch.* 49 (1958); 53 (1962).

Molfetta, Bari, Puglia, Italy. Impresso settlement. Fifty burials excavated. Graphite and painted ware similar to the Serra d'Alto complex were found. Excavated 1908–10 by A. Mosso and M. Gervasio. Museum: Museo Archeologico di Bari and Seminario di Molfetta. Publ. Mayer *Le Stazioni preistoriche di Molfetta* 1904; Messo *M.A.L.* XX (1910).

Muldava, central Bulgaria. Tell site with a rich layer of the Neolithic East Balkan (Karanovo I type) civilization. Excavated and publ. by Detev, *Godishnik* VI (1968). Museum: Plovdiv.

Murgecchia, Matera, Basilicata, Italy. Neolithic settlement of the Adriatic Matera culture. Site surrounded by two concentric ditches. Excavated 1898 by D. Ridola. Museum: Matera. Publ. Ridola *BPI* 44 (1924); 45 (1925).

Murgia Timone, Matera, Basilicata, Italy. Adriatic civilization, Matera complex. Museum: Matera. Excavated 1897 by D. Ridola and G. Patroni. Publ. Ridola *BPI* 44 (1924).

Nea Makri, Marathon, Attica, Greece. Settlement consisting of Early Neolithic (Proto-Sesklo) and Late Neolithic layers. Both contain rectangular houses with stone

foundations. Aegean civilization. Excavated 1954 by D. R. Theocharis. Museum: Volos. Publ. Theocharis *Athen. Mitt.* 71 (1956).

Nea Nikomedeia, near Verroia, Macedonia, Greece. Early Neolithic (Proto-Sesklo) of two levels and Late Neolithic settlements. Excavated 1961–63 by R. J. Rodden. Museum: Verroia. Publ. Rodden *PPS* 28 (1962); *Scientific American* (1965, April).

C14 dates for the first Early Neolithic building horizon: 8180 ± 150 BP, true age *c.* 7200 BC (Q 655); 7780 ± 270 BP, true age *c.* 6800 BC (GX 679). Following horizon: 7557 ± 91 BP, true age *c.* 6600 BC (P 1202); 7281 ± 74 BP, true age *c.* 6300 BC (P 1203A).

Nebo, near Travnik, Bosnia, Yugoslavia. A Butmir settlement. Ceramics are Classical and Late Butmir in style. Excavated 1948–49 by A. Benac. Museum: Zemaljski Muzej, Sarajevo. Publ. Benac *Prehistorijsko naselje Nebo i Problem Butmirske Kulture* 1952; *Glasnik Sarajevo Arh.* NF 8 (1953).

Nitra, Slovakia, Czechoslovakia. Within the city the following sites were excavated: an early Linear Pottery site with 77 graves located on the left bank of the River Nitra; a Lengyel site with houses of the Ludanice type. Excavated by J. Lichardus and J. Vladár. Publ. Vladár *Slov Arch.* 18–2 (1970).

Nitriansky Hrádok, Nové Zámky, Slovakia, Czechoslovakia. Settlement of the Lengyel culture. Middle Danube civilization. Excavated 1957–59 by A. Točík. Museum: Nitra. Publ. Točík *Referáty Liblice* 13 (1959); Lichardus. *Pam. Arch.* 57 (1966).

Nosa, at Subotica, northern Yugoslavia. Neolithic Starčevo (Körös) settlement with remains of rectangular houses. Excavated 1967–58 by D. Garašanin and L. Szekeres. Museum: Subotica. Publ. D. Garašanin *Berichte Röm. – Germ. Kom.* 39 (1958).

Novye Ruseshty I, near Kishenev, Moldavia, USSR. Classical Cucuteni settlement. Excavated by V. I. Markevich in the sixties. Museum: Kishenev. Publ. Markevich 1970.

Obre I, near Kakanj, Bosnia, Yugoslavia. Settlement consists of four habitation horizons, the earliest representing Starčevo complex with geometrically painted black-on-red ware. The upper three belong to an end phase of the same Central Balkan Neolithic culture, locally called 'Kakanj'. Excavated 1968 by A. Benac and M. Gimbutas. Museum: Zemaljski Muzej, Sarajevo and Cultural History Museum, UCLA, Los Angeles. Publ. Marija Gimbutas *Archaeology*, 23, 4 (1970).

C14 dates for the lowest horizons (Phase A): 7240 ± 60 BP, true age *c.* 6250 BC (UCLA 1605 I); 6795 ± 150 BP, true age *c.* 5780 BC (Bln Lab. 636); 6710 ± 60 BP, true age *c.* 5750 BC (UCLA 1605G).

Middle phase (Phase B): 6430 ± 60 BP, true age *c.* 5450 BC (UCLA 1605F).

Upper horizons (Phase C): 6230 ± 80 BP (Bln 659), true age *c.* 5150 BC; 6150 ± 70 BP, true age *c.* 5060 BC (UCLA 1605H).

Obre II, near Kakanj, Bosnia, Yugoslavia. Most important site of the Butmir culture. Nine habitation horizons have been established and three developmental phases. Excavated 1967–68 by A. Benac and M. Gimbutas. Museum: Zemaljski Muzej, Sarajevo. Publ. M. Gimbutas *Archaeology* 23–24 (1970); A. Benac *Obre II, Neolitsko naselje butmirske grupe na Gornjem Polju* (Sarajevo 1971).

C14 dates for the lowest layer (Butmir I): 6175 ± 80 BP, true age *c.* 5100 BC (Bln 639); 6075 ± 100 BP, true age *c.* 5000 BC (Bln 792); 6110 ± 60 BP, true age *c.* 5000 BC (GrN 5683); 6010 ± 60 BP, true age 4950 BC (GrN 5684); 5925 ± 80 BP, true age 4850 BC (Bln 657).

Middle layer (Butmir II): 5875 ± 60 BP, true age *c.* 4840 BC (UCLA 1605C).

Upper layer (Butmir II): 5740 ± 80 BP, true age *c.* 4550 BC (UCLA 1605B). Other dates show the same period.

Otzaki, near Larisa, Thessaly, Greece. Large tell site with four main cultural layers beginning with Proto-Sesklo, followed by Pre-Sesklo, Classical Sesklo, and Late Neolithic. Excavated 1953–55 by V. Milojčić. Museum: Larisa. Publ. Milojčić *Arch. Anzeiger* 1954, 1955, 1959; *Jb. Römisch-Germ. Zentral Museum* 1959.

Ovcharovo near Trgovište, northeastern Bulgaria, a Neolithic Starčevo-Criş site with semi-subterranean dwellings and a Chalcolithic-copper age tell with thirteen habitation levels, excavated by H. Todorova 1971–72. The later parallels Karanovo IV–VI. Extraordinary discoveries were made in Karanovo VI levels. Level 9 yielded a cultic scene of 26 miniature cult objects including four figurines with upraised arms and decorated with meanders and parallel lines, three temple façades or altar screens, nine chairs, three miniature tables, three vessels with lids, two large dishes, and three drums suggesting the ritual use of music. The group was in association with a shrine model including an altar and oven. Quantities of schematic figurines, other shrine models, anthropomorphic vases, graphite-painted pottery, and ceramic workshops came to light. Finds in Trgovište museum. Publ. Todorova 1976.

Padina, Iron Gate Gorge, northern Yugoslavia. Central Balkan Neolithic settlement, Danubian regional group with Starčevo elements. Related to Lepenski Vir. Excavated 1968–71 by B. Jovanović, sponsored by the Belgrade Arch. Institute. Publ. Jovanović *Arh. Pregl.* 10 (1968); *Stare Kulture u Djerdapu* (1969): *Arch. Iugoslavica* 9 (1971).

Parţa, south of Timisoare, western Romania. Early Vinča settlement. Museum: Timişoara.

Pazardžik (Junacite), central Bulgaria. Tell site of the Chalcolithic East Balkan civilization, followed by a Bronze Age layer. Excavated 1939 by V. Mikov. Museum: Plovdiv.

Perieni, near Bîrlad, northern Moldavia, Romania. Neolithic settlement of the Central Balkan Starčevo ('Criş') type, followed by a layer of the Linear Pottery culture of 'Music Note' type. Excavated 1949 and 1955 by M. Petrescu-Dîmboviţa. Museum: Iaşi, Moldavia. Publ. Petrescu-Dîmboviţa 1957; *Acta Arch. Acad. Sc. Hung.* 9 (1958).

Pianul de Jos, near Sibiu, Hunedoara, Romania. Settlement of the Chalcolithic

Petreşti group. Excavated 1963 by Iuliu Paul. Museum: Sibiu. Publ. Paul 1965.

Pietrele, near Bucharest, Romania. East Balkan Chalcolithic settlement with remains of Late Boian and five phases of Gumelniţa complexes. Excavated 1943–48 by D. Berciu. Museum: NAM, Bucharest. Publ. D. Berciu *Mat. Cerc. Arh.* 2 (1956).

Pločnik, southern Yugoslavia at Prokuplje. Large Late Vinča site with *c.* 3 m. of cultural deposits. Excavated 1927 by M. Grbić; 1968–70 by B. Stalio. Museum: NM Belgrade. Publ. Grbić 1929.

Porodin, near Bitola, southern Yugoslavia. Central Balkan Neolithic settlement. Starčevo complex, Macedonian variant. Excavated 1953–54 by M. Grbić *et al.* Publ. Grbić 1960.
C14 dates: 7110 ± 170 BP, true age *c.* 6150 BC (H 1486/987).

Predionica, in Priština, southern Yugoslavia. Vinča site of several periods, Early and Late, the latter half of the two phases. Excavated 1955–56 by R. Galović. Museum: Priština. Publ. Galović 1959.
C14 dates for Early Vinča: 6279 ± 80 BP, true age *c.* 5300 BC, (Bln 435).

Pyrasos, located at Nea Anchialos near Volos, Thessaly, Greece. Stratified tell site with the following succession of Thessalian Neolithic: Proto-Sesklo, Sesklo, Arapi-Dimini, Larissa and Rakhmani. Excavated 1956 by D. R. Theocharis. Publ. Theocharis *Thessalika* 2 (1959).

Radingrad near Razgrad, northeastern Bulgaria, a tell with several phases, parallel to Karanovo IV, V, excavated by Totju Ivanov in 1974–78. Unpublished. The most remarkable discovery was a two-storey temple. Its first floor had a ceramic workshop with a large oven and tools for pottery making and decoration, the second floor comprised the temple proper with a clay altar 75 cm. high, vertical loom, figurines, and temple models.

Ripoli, Corropoli, Terano, Abruzzi e Molise, Italy. Eponymous settlement and cemetery site of the Adriatic Ripoli complex. Excavated 1910 by A. Mosso; 1913–1915 by I. Dall'Osso and 1961 by A. M.

Radmilli. Publ. Rellini *La piu antica ceramica dipinta in Italia* 1934; Radmilli *RSP* 16, (1961); 17 (1962).

Röske-Ludvár, south of Szeged, southern Hungary. Central Balkan Starčevo (Körös) Neolithic settlement. Excavated 1965 by O. Trogmayer. Museum: Szeged.

Rudnik Kosovski, near Prizren, southern Yugoslavia. Central Balkan Neolithic Starčevo settlement. Excavated 1966–69 by J. Glišić. Museum: Priština.

Rug Bair, near Sv. Nikole, eastern Macedonia, southeastern Yugoslavia. Central Balkan Neolithic Starčevo and Early Vinča stratified site. Excavated 1970 by American (UCLA) and Yugoslav (Naroden Muzej, Štip) teams (M. Gimbutas and V. Sanev). Museum: Štip.

Ruginoasa, district of Iaşi, Moldavia, northeastern Romania. Settlement of the Classical Cucuteni (Cucuteni A) culture. Museum: NAM, Bucharest. Publ. H. Dumitrescu *Dacia* III–IV (1927–32).

Ruse, northern Bulgaria. East Balkan civilization, Chalcolithic site. (Karanovo VI–Gumelniţa period). Excavated 1950–53 by G. I. Georgiev and N. Angelov. Museum: Ruse. Publ. Georgiev-Angelov *Ruse*.

Sabatinovka II, Proto-Cucuteni (Early Tripolye) settlement near Uljanov, district of Kirovograd, western Ukraine. Excavated 1947–49 by M. L. Makarevich. Museum: Odessa. Publ. by Makarevich in *Arkheol. Pamjatki Ukrainskoj RSR*, vol. IV (1952) and Makarevich 1960b.

Salcuţa, near Craiova, southwestern Romania. Type site of the Salcuţa variant of the East Balkan civilization with seven phases of development. Follows the Central Balkan Neolithic Starčevo ('Criş') civilization. Excavated 1916–20 by I. Andriesescu; 1947 by H. Dumitrescu; 1951 by D. Berciu. Museum: NAM, Bucharest. Publ. Berciu 1961.

Sarvaš, near Osijek, northern Yugoslavia. Lowest horizons of this stratified site included a Central Balkan Starčevo layer, followed by the Lengyel and then Baden and Vučedol cultures. Excavated 1942–43 by R. R. Schmidt. Museum: Osijek and Arheol. Muzej, Zagreb. Publ. Schmidt *Vučedol* (1945).

Scaloria (*see also* Grotta Scaloria), a cave site at Manfredonia, south of Gargano, southeastern Italy, excavated by Marija Gimbutas and Shan Winn 1978–80. The upper cave yielded habitation remains and 140 burials, most of which were probably sacrificial; in the lower cave with stalagmites and stalactites, a sacred well, and quantities of vases were found. Total of *c.* 1500 symbolically decorated vases, inscribed bone and clay artifacts, and very rich flint industry was uncovered from the main period of the cave, *c.* 5600 – 5300 BC, based on six radiocarbon dates: (LJ-4980) 6800±160; (LJ-4649) 6720±100 B.P.; (LJ-4981) 6620±380 B.P.; (LJ-4650) 6490±140 B.P.; (LJ-4651) 6330±90 B.P.; (LJ-4983) 6050±130 B.P. The report due to appear in *Monumenta Archaeologica*, Institute of Archaeology, University of California, Los Angeles, 1984. On water cult in the lower cave *see* Tine 1972. Finds are in the archaeological museum of Manfredonia and Foggia.

Selevac, 15 km. west of Smederevska Palanka, central Yugoslavia. Settlement of early classical Vinča type. Excavated 1969–70 by R. Galović and R. Milošević and in '70s by R. Tringham. Museum: Smederevska Palanka.

Serra d'Alto, Matera, Basilicata, Italy. Settlement and cemetery site of the Adriatic Matera-Capri culture and type site of the Serra d'Alto complex. Site surrounded by a defensive ditch. Graves were excavated outside the settlement. Excavated 1919 by D. Ridola and U. Rellini. Museum: Museo di Matera. Publ. Mayer *Molfetta und Matera* 1924; Rellini *Not. Sc.* 50 (1925).

Sesklo, near Volos, Thessaly, Greece. Eponymous site of the Sesklo culture, represented by the middle layer. Preceded by the Pre-pottery, Earliest Pottery and Proto-Sesklo and followed by Dimini and Post-Dimini complexes. Excavated 1901–2 by Ch. Tsountas; 1957– by D. R. Theocharis. Museum: Volos. Publ. Tsountas 1908; Theocharis *Praktika* 32 (1957); *Thessalika* I (1958).

C14 dates for Pre-pottery period: 7755 ± 97 BP (P-1681), true age *c.* middle of the seventh millennium BC.

Early Pottery period: 7611 ± 83 (P-1679), 7427 ± 78 (P-1678), 7300 ± 93 (P-1680), true age of all three dates is within the second half of seventh millennium BC.

Classical Sesklo: 6964 ± 92 (P-1674), 6741 ± 103 (P-1677), 6694 ± 87 (P-1675), true age within the first half of seventh millennium BC. Late Classical 6504 ± 85 (P-1672), true age *c.* middle of sixth millennium BC.

Dimini Period: 5622 ± 80 (P-1671), true age *c.* middle of fifth millennium BC.

Sipintsi (Schipenitz), northwest of Chernovitsi, on the bank of the River Prut, western Ukraine (Bukovina), USSR. Late Cucuteni settlement. Publ. Kandyba *Schipenitz* 1947. Vienna, Naturhistorisches Museum.

Sitagroi, Plain of Drama, northeastern Greece. Large tell of the East Balkan civilization with 12 m. of cultural debris. Five periods, I–V. I and II, Late Neolithic synchronous with Karanovo III and IV; III, Chalcolithic synchronous with Karanovo VI, followed by periods IV and V of the Early Bronze Age Balkan-Danubian culture. Excavated 1968–69 by A. C. Renfrew and M. Gimbutas. Publ. Colin Renfrew *Proc. Preh. Soc.* 36 (1970).

C14 dates for Phase I: 6625 ± 170 BP, true age *c.* 5650 BC, (Bln 779); 6425 ± 100 BP, true age *c.* 5450 BC (Bln 778).

Phase II: 5920 ± 120 BP, true age *c.* 4850 BC (Bln 777); 5720 ± 100 BP, true age *c.* 4550 BC (Bln 776); 6240 ± 100 BP, true age *c.* 5300 BC (Bln 884); 5904 ± 66 BP, true age *c.* 4850 BC (BM 649).

Phase III: 5795 ± 100 BP, true age *c.* 4650 BC (Bln 882); 5555 ± 100 BP, true age *c.* 4400 BC (Bln 881); 5545 ± 100 BP, true age *c.* 4400 BC (Bln 883); 5100 ± 100 BP, true age *c.* 4200–3800 BC (Bln 774).

Smilčić, near Zadar, Dalmatia, Yugoslavia. Contains an early level of the Adriatic Impresso culture overlaid by a horizon of the Danilo complex. Excavated 1957–59; 1962 by Š. Batović. Museum: Zadar. Publ. Batović *Diadora* 2 (1960–61); 1966.

Souphli, at Larisa, Thessaly, Greece. Stratified tell including Pre-ceramic, Proto-Sesklo, Sesklo, and Late Neolithic Post-Dimini phases. Excavated 1956 by D. R. Theocharis. Museum: Larisa Publ. Theocharis *Thessalika* 1 (1958).

Staraja Buda, upper Siniukha Valley, western Ukraine. Late Cucuteni settlement. Publ. Passek *Céramique tripolienne* 1935.

Starčevo, near Belgrade, Yugoslavia. Eponymous site of the Neolithic Central Balkan Starčevo culture. Excavated 1930 by M. Grbić; 1931–32 by V. Fewkes, H. Goldman and R. W. Ehrich. Museum: NM Belgrade. Publ. V. Fewkes *Bull. Am. School Preh. Research* 9 (1936); D. Arandjelović-Garašanin, *Starčevačka Kultura* (1954).

Stentinello, Syracuse, Sicily. Eponymous site of the Stentinello group. Defended by a ditch and stone wall. Excavated 1890, 1912, 1920 by P. Orsi; 1961 by S. Tinè. Museum: Museo di Siracusa. Publ. Orsi *BPI* 16 (1890); 36 (1910); Tinè *Arch. Stor. Siracusano* 7 (1961).

Střelice, Jevišovice, Znojmo, southern Moravia, Czechoslovakia. Contains several sites of the Chalcolithic Střelice group of the Lengyel culture. Excavated by Palliardi and J. Vildomec at the end of the nineteenth–early twentieth century. Museum: Boskovštejn near Znojmo and Brno. Publ. J. Palliardi *MPC*, I (Vienna 1897); *WPZ* I (1914); Vildomec *OP* 7/8 (Prague, 1928/29); 12 (Prague, 1940); Neustupný *AR* 3 (1951).

Sulica, near Stara Zagora, central Bulgaria. Chalcolithic site, Karanovo VI period of the East Balkan civilization. Museum: Stara Zagora. Publ. Gaul *Neolithic Bulgaria*.

Sultana, located on the shore of Lake Mostiştea, district of Olteniţa, southern Romania. Belongs to the East Balkan civilization. Museum: Olteniţa. Publ. Marinescu-Bîlcu *Dacia* XI (1967).

Szegvár-Tüzköves, at Szentes, southeastern Hungary. Settlement and cemetery of the Tisza culture. Excavated 1956–57 by J. Czalog. Museum: Szentes. Publ. Czalog *Szegvár-Tüzköves*.

Tangîru, near Giurgiu, lower Danube, Romania. Stratified tell with twelve levels of Boian and nine of the Gumelniţa periods of the East Balkan civilization. Excavated 1933–35; 1956; 1957 by D. Berciu. Publ. Berciu 1961.

Tecić, near Kragujevac, central Yugoslavia. Central Balkan Neolithic Starčevo settlement and two burials. Excavated 1960 by R. Galović. Museum: NM Belgrade. Publ. Galović 1964.

Tirpeşti, district of Tg. Neamţ, region of Bacău, northeastern Romania. An Early Cucuteni ('Pre-Cucuteni III') settlement. Excavated by V. Dumitrescu and J. Marinescu-Bîlcu in the early sixties. Museum: NAM, Bucharest and Bacău.

Tiszapolgár-Basatanya at the village of Polgár near Tiszalök, southeastern Hungary. Eponymous cemetery site of the Chalcolithic period (or Early and Middle Copper Age of the Carpathian Basin). 166 graves excavated. Excavated 1929 by F. Tompa and 1946 by I. Bognár-Kutzián. Museum: NM Budapest. Publ. I. Bognár-Kutzián 1963. In the same area, tells with Neolithic-Chalcolithic remains are known: Tiszapolgár - Csöszhalom, Tiszapolgár-Folyrás-Szilmeg and others.

C14 dates: 6940 ± 100 BP, true age *c.* 4700 BC (Bln 513); 5845 ± 60 BP, true age *c.* 4700 BC (GrN 1934); 5775 ± 100 BP, true age *c.* 4700–4600 BC, (Bln 512). Later level: 5575 ± 100 BP, true age *c.* 4400 BC (Bln 509).

Traian, northern Moldavia, northeastern Romania. The site of several Neolithic settlements: 1, Dealul Fîntinilor including Linear Pottery, Early and Classical (Cucuteni A–B) remains and 2, Dealul Viei with a single layer belonging to the Early Cucuteni ('Pre-Cucuteni I') civilization. Excavated 1951–59 by H. Dumitrescu. Museum: NAM, Bucharest. Publ. H. Dumitrescu *SCIV* III (1952); IV (1953); V (1954); VI (1955); *Mat. Cerc. Arh.* III (1957) and V (1959); H. and V. Dumitrescu *Mat. Cerc. Arh.* VI (1959).

Tripolye, near Kiev, western Ukraine. Classical Cucuteni settlement and name used for the Cucuteni civilization in Soviet Moldavia and western Ukraine. Excavated 1899 by V. V. Khvojka (Chvojka). Museum: Kiev. Publ. Khvojka *Trudy XI Arkh. sjezda*, Kiev 1901.

Truşeşti, near Botoşani, northern Moldavia, Romania. Large habitation site in which 98 houses were uncovered, most of which belonged to the Classical Cucuteni (Cucuteni A) period. Excavated 1951–59; 1961 by M. Petrescu-Dîmboviţa. Museum: Iaşi. Publ. Petrescu-Dîmboviţa *Truşeşti*.

Tsangli, Thessaly, Greece. Neolithic settlement of the Sesklo culture. The uppermost layer associated with the Early Helladic Bronze Age. Excavated 1905 by Ch. Tsountas; 1910 by A. J. B. Wace and M. S. Thompson. Museum: Athens. Publ. Wace and Thompson 1912.

Tsani, Thessaly, Greece. Stratified Neolithic tell including remains of Pre-Sesklo (red monochrome pottery), classical Sesklo, Dimini and Late Neolithic characterized by a coarse grey ware and Urfirnis ware. Excavated 1909 by A. J. B. Wace and M. S. Thompson. Museum: Athens. Publ. Wace and Thompson 1912.

Turdaş (Tordoš), La Lunca locality on the bank of the River Mureş, Transylvania, region of Huneodara, Romania. Early Vinča settlement. Unsystematic excavation, end of the nineteenth century. Museum: Institute of History, Cluj. Publ. Roska, *Torma Collection* 1941.

Vădastra, near Corabia, Oltenia, southwestern Romania. Eponymous site of the Vădastra variant of the East Balkan civilization; contemporary with Boian. Preceded by a late middle Aurignacian Palaeolithic layer; overlain by a layer of the Salcuţa complex. Excavated 1926 by Vasile Christescu; 1934 by D. Berciu; 1946–62 by C. Mǎteescu. Museum: NAM, Bucharest. Publ. Christescu *Dacia* III–IV (1927–33); Mǎteescu *SCIV* 6 (1955); *Cerc. Arh.* 5–6 (1959); *Arch. Rozhl.* 14 (1962).

Valač, near Kosovska Mitrovica, southern Yugoslavia. Late Vinča settlement with cultural stratum 0.90–1.20 m. thick. Excavated 1957 by N. Tasić and J. Glišić. Museum: Kosovska Mitrovica. Publ. Tasić 1959; 1961.

C14 dates: 5895 ± 80 BP, true age *c.* 4850 BC (Bln 436). Corresponds to 4 m. depth at the Vinča site.

Valea Lupului, district of Iaşi, northeastern Romania. Large Late Cucuteni (Cucuteni B) settlement on the terrace of River Bahlui. Excavated 1953–57 by M. Petrescu-Dîmboviţa and M. Dinu. Museum: Iaşi. Publ. Petrescu-Dîmboviţa *SCIV* V (1954); Dinu Marin *Materiale Cerc. Arh.* 3 (1957); 5, G (1959).

Varna, a Copper Age cemetery of *c.* 4500 BC (Karanovo VI period) near the town of Varna on the Black Sea coast in Bulgaria. Discovered in 1972 and excavated in 1973–77 by Ivan Ivanov, the cemetery is particularly noted for quantities of gold and copper artifacts, marble rhytons, gold-painted vases, and life-size funerary clay masks with gold attributes. Finds in the Varna archaeological museum. Publ. by Gimbutas 1977 *a* and *b* and Ivanov 1978.

Varvarovka, near Kishenev, Soviet Moldavia. Late Cucuteni (Tripolye) settlement. Excavated 1967 by V. I. Makarevich. Museum: Kishenev.

Veselinovo, district of Jambol, eastern Bulgaria. Tell of the Late Neolithic, Karanovo III period, East Balkan civilization. Excavated by V. Mikov. Publ. Mikov *Izvestija* 13 (1939).

Vidra, near Giurgiu, southeast of Bucharest, Romania. Settlement of the East Balkan civilization particularly noted for its figurine and plastic art. Lowest level belongs to the Boian-Giuleşti phase and is followed by the Boian-Vidra, then the Gumelniţa layer. Excavated 1931–33 and 1958 by V. Rosetti. Museum: Bucharest City. Publ. V. Rosetti *Săpăturile de la Vidra* 1934; Publ. *Muz. Municip. Bucureşti* 1–2 (1935–36); *IPEK* 12 (1938); *Mat. Cerc. Arh.* 7 (1961).

Vinča, 14 km. southeast of Belgrade on the Danube, locality of Belo Brdo, Yugoslavia. Mound 10.5 m. deep. The two earliest settlements (below 8 m.) belong to the

Central Balkan Neolithic Starčevo culture, above which were 7 m. of deposits characteristic of the Vinča civilization. The Vinča civilization has been subdivided into four consecutive phases. Excavated 1908–12, 1924, 1928–32 by M. Vasić. Museum: BU and NM Belgrade. Publ. M. Vasić *Preistoriska Vinča* I–IV (1932–36).

C14 dates for Early and Mid-Vinča: 6190 ± BP, true age *c*. 5100 BC (GrN 1546); 5845 ± 160 BP, true age *c*. 4800 BC (GrN 1537).

Vladimirovka, Southern Bug Valley, western Ukraine. Classical Cucuteni (Tripolye B) settlement with about 200 houses. Excavated 1927–28 by B. Bezvenglinski; 1940 by T. S. Passek. Publ. Passek *Céramique Tripolienne* 1935; Passek 1949; E. K. Chernysh *KSIIMK* 40 (1951).

Vršnik, north of Štip, Macedonia, southeastern Yugoslavia. Central Balkan Neolithic stratified site of four main developmental phases, parallel to Anza I–IV. Begins with the earliest Starčevo (or Anza I) and ends with Early Vinča. Excavated 1958 by M. and D. Garašanin. Museum: Štip. Publ. by the excavators 1959 and 1961 in Štip Mus. Publ.

C14 for Vršnik III: 6865 ± 150 BP, true age *c*. 5900 BC (H 595/485).

Vulkaneshti, Soviet Moldavia. Chalcolithic (Gumelniţa) site of the East Balkan civilization. Excavated by T. S. Passek. Museum: Kishenev. Publ. Passek and Gerasimov, 1967.

Vykhvatintsi, district of Rybnica, upper Dniester, Soviet Moldavia, USSR. Late Cucuteni (Tripolye) cemetery. Excavated 1952 by T. S. Passek and E. K. Chernysh. Before this excavation, several graves were uncovered by M. V. Voevodskij and A. E. Alikhova in 1947. Excavated again in 1951 by I. G. Rosenfeldt. Publ. Passek 1954.

Zelenikovo, near Skopje, Macedonia, Yugoslavia. Located near the River Vardar. Two phases: the Central Balkan Neolithic Starčevo civilization and the Late Vinča civilization. Excavated 1950–53 by R. Galović. Museum: Gradskij Muzej, Skopje. Publ. Galović 1964.

Zengövárkony, near Pécs, Baranya, southwestern Hungary. Large settlement and cemetery of the Lengyel culture. The cemetery included 368 burials most of which were single inhumations containing grave goods. Excavated 1936–48 by J. Dombay. Museum: Pécs. Publ. Dombay 'A Zengövárkonyi öskori telep és temetö', *Arch. Hung.* 23 (1939); 37 (1960).

Zhvanets, district of Kiev, Ukraine, USSR. Late Cucuteni (Tripolye) settlement. Excavated by T. G. Movsha *Arkheologija* XIX (1965).

Bibliography

ALEXIOU, STYLIANOS, 1958. *E Minoike thea meth' ypsomenon cheiron*, Heraklion.

—, 1969. *Minoan Civilization*. Heraklion.

ANDRIESESCU, I., 1924. 'Les fouilles de Sultana', *Dacia*, I: 51–107.

ANGELOV, N., 1958. 'Die Siedlung bei Hotnica', *Studia in Honorem Acad D. Dečev*: 389.

—, 1961. 'Atelier d'idoles plates en os dans le tell près du village Hotnica', *Archeologija* (Sofia), III: 34.

ANISIMOV, A. F., 1959. *Kosmogonicheskie predstavlenija narodov severa*. Moscow and Leningrad.

BACHOFEN, J. J., 1861. *Das Mutterrecht. Eine Untersuchung über die Gynaikokratie der alten Welt nach ihrer religiösen und rechtlichen Natur*. Stuttgart.

BANNER, J., 1959. *Kökénydomb*.

BARNETT, R. D., 1956. 'Oriental influences on Adriatic Greece', *The Aegean and the Near East* (S. S. Weinberg, ed.), 222.

BASS, GEORGE G., 1959. 'Neolithic Figurines from Thespiai', *Hesperia*, XXVIII: 344–349.

BATOVIĆ, ŠIME, 1962. 'Neolitsko nalazište u Smilčicu (French résumé: Station Néolithique à Smilčić)', *Diadora* (Zadar Archaeological Museum): 31–115.

BATOVIĆ, ŠIME, 1966. *Stariji Neolit u Dalmaciji*. Zadar.

—, 1968. 'Problem kulta phallosa u Danilskoj kulturi (résumé in English: 'The problem of the phallus cult in Danilo culture'), *Diadora* (Zadar), IV: 5–51.

BAUMANN, H., 1955. *Das doppelte Geschlecht. Ethnologische Studien zur Bisexualität in Ritus and Mythos*. Berlin.

BENAC, ALOJZ, *Studien zur Stein- und Kupferzeit im Nordöstlichen Balkan* (Berichte der Römisch-Germanischen Kommission, no. 42, Berlin 1961).

BENNETT, E. L., 1955. *The Pylos Tablets*. Princeton.

BERCIU, D., 1956. *Cercetări și Descoperiri Arheologice in Regiunea București*. Bucharest.

—, 1959. 'Săpăturile arheologice de la Tangiru (r. Giurgiu, reg. București)', *Materiale și Cercetări Arheologice*, V: 143–154.

—, 1960. 'Neolithic figurines from Rumania', *Antiquity*, XXXIV, No. 136: 283–284, 4 ills.

—, 1961. *Contribuții*.

—, 1966. *Cultura Hamangia*. Bucharest.

—, 1966. 'Manifestation d'art néolithique en Roumanie. Le "couple" de Cernavoda', *IPEK* XXI (1964/1965): 42–45.

—, 1967. *Romania before Burebista*. London.

BERTLING, C. T., 1954. *Vierzahl, Kreuz und Mandala in Asien*. Amsterdam.

BIBIKOV, S. N., 1953. 'Poselenie Luka-Vrublevetskaja', *MIA* No. 38.

BIEBER, MARGARETTE, 1939. *The History of the Greek and Roman Theater*. Princeton.

BIELENFELD, E. 1954–55. 'Götterstatuen auf Vasenbildern', *Wissenschaftliche Zeitshrift der E. Moritz Arndt Universität Greifswald*, IV, Gesellschafts- und Sprachwissenschaftliche Reihe, IV, V.

BIESANTZ, H., 1954. *Kretisch-mykenische Siegelbilder*. Marburg.

BITTEL, K., 1950. 'Einige Idole aus Kleinasien', *PZ* 34/35 (1949/50), II: 135–144.

BOARDMAN, J., 1967. *Pre-classical, From Crete to Archaic Greece*. Harmondsworth.

BOGAEVSKIJ, B. L., 1937. *Orudija proizvodstva i domashnie zhivotnye Tripol'ja*. Moscow and Leningrad.

BOGNÁR-KUTZIÁN, I., 1944, 1947. *The Körös culture*. Budapest.

—, 1963. *The Copper Age Cemetery of Tiszapolgár-Basatanya*, Budapest, Akadémiai Kiadó.

—, 1972. *The Early Copper Age Tiszapolgár culture in the Carpathian Basin*. Budapest.

BRANIGAN, KEITH, 1969. 'The genesis of the Household Goddess', *Studi Micenei ed Egeo-Anatolici* 8: 28–38.

BRIFFAULT, ROBERT, 1927. *The Mothers*. London and New York.

BRUKNER, BOGDAN, 1964. 'Praistorijsko naselje na potesu Beletinci kod Obreža. – Prähistorische Siedlung auf der Flur "Beletinci" bei Obrež', *Rad Vojvodjan-*

skih Muzeja, XI (1962); 89–122.

BURKERT, WALTER, 1966. 'Greek tragedy and sacrificial ritual', *Greek, Roman and Byzantine Studies*, VII.

BURR, D., 1933. 'A geometric house and protoattic votive deposit', *Hesperia*, II: 604.

CALLIMACHUS, 1955. *Hymns and Epigrams*. London.

CANTACUZINO, GH., 1967. 'La nécropole préhistorique de Cernica et sa place dans le néolithique de Roumanie et d'Europe dans le cadre des dernières découvertes archéologiques', *Studii şi Cercetări Istorie Veche*, XVIII, 3: 379–400. Bucharest.

CASKEY, J. L., 1962. 'The Goddess of Ceos', *Archaeology*, 15: 223–26.

—, 1964. 'Excavations in Keos, 1963', *Hesperia*, XXXIII: 314–335.

CASKEY, J. L. and M. A. ELLIOT, 1956. 'A neolithic figurine from Lerna', *Hesperia*, XXV: 175–77.

CASSIRER, ERNST, 1925. *Das mythische Denken*. Philosophie der symbolischen Formen, II. Berlin.

CEHAK, H., 1933. 'Plastyka eneolitycznej kultury ceramiki malowanej w Polsce' (résumé in French: L'art plastique dans la culture énéolithique de la céramique peinte en Pologne), *Światowit* XIV: 164–250.

CHIKALENKO, LEVKO, 1953. 'The origin of the palaeolithic meander', *The Annals of the Ukranian Academy of Arts and Sciences in the U.S.*, III, 1 (7): 518–34.

COLDSTREAM, J. N., 1973. *Demeter*. London.

COMŞA, EUGEN, 1969. 'Quelques données nouvelles sur la phase de transition de la civilisation de Boian a celle de Gumelniţa', *Študijné Zvesti*, XVII: 73–87.

CONTENEAU, G., 1927. 'Idoles en pierre provenant de l'Asie Mineure', *Syria*, VIII: 193–200.

CONTENSON, HENRI de, 1971. 'Tell Ramad, a village of Syria of the 7th and 6th millennia BC', *Archaeology*, 24, 3: 278–85.

COOK, ARTHUR BERNARD, *Zeus a Study in Ancient Religion*, Cambridge University Press. 1914. 'Zeus God of the Bright Sky', Vol. I. 1925. 'Zeus God of the Dark Sky (Thunder and Lightning)', Vol. II parts I and II. 1940. 'Zeus God of the Dark Sky (Earthquakes, Clouds, Wind, Dew, Rain,

Meteorites)', Vol. III parts I and II.

CRAWFORD, O. G. S., 1958. *The Eye Goddess*. London.

CZALOG, JÓZSEF, 1959. *Szegvár-Tüzköves*.

—, 1960. 'Das Krummschwert des Idols von Szegvár-Tüzköves', *Acta Archaeologica*, XII: 57–68.

DALES, GEORGE F., 1963. 'Necklaces, bands and belts on Mesopotamian figurines', *Revue d'Assyriologie et d'Archaeologie Orientale*, LVII: 21–40.

DAWKINS, R. M., 1910. 'Excavations at Tsangli and Rakhmani', *Journal of Hellenic Studies*: 360.

—, 1929. *The Sanctuary of Artemis Orthia*. London.

DELVOYE, C., 1946. Rites de fécondité dans les religions pré-helléniques. *Bulletin de Correspondance Hellénique*, XL: 120–31.

DEMARGNE, P., 1964. *Aegean Art: the origins of Greek art*. London.

DESHAYES, J., 1968. 'Chronique des fouilles et découvertes archéologiques en Grèce en 1967', *Bulletin de Correspondance Hellénique*, XCII: 1069.

DESHAYES, JEAN and D. THEOHARIS, 1962. 'Dikili Tach', *Bulletin de Correspondance Hellénique*, LXXXVI, 2: 912–33.

DETEV, P., 1950. 'Le tell Baniata près de Kapitan Dimitrievo', *Godishnik, Plovdiv*, II: 1–24.

—, 1952. 'Arkheologicheski vesti', *Izvestija*, Series 2, XVIII: 331–41.

—, 1959. 'Matériaux de la préhistoire de Plovdiv', *Godishnik, Plovdiv*, III: 3–80.

—, 1960. 'Vorgeschichtliche Gefässe mit menschen- und tierähnlichen Darstellungen in Bulgarien', *Archäologischer Anzeiger*, I:

—, 1965. 'Modèles de décoration de l'énéolithique', *Archaeologija* (Sofia), VII, 4: 65–73.

—, 1968. 'Praistoricheskoto selischche pri selo Muldava', *Godishnik, Plovdiv*, VI: 9–48.

DEUBNER, L., 1932. *Attische Feste*, Berlin.

DIETERICH, A., 1925. *Mutter Erde. Ein Versuch über Volksreligion*. Berlin-Leipzig. First ed. 1905.

DIMITRIJEVIĆ, S., 1968. *Sopotsko-Lendjelska kultura*. Monographiae Archaeologicae, I (résumé in German: 112–23). Zagreb.

DIMITRIJEVIĆ, STOJAN, 1969. *Starčevačka*

257

kultura u Slavonsko-srijemskom prostoru i problem prijelaza ranog u srednji neolit u srpskom i hrvatskom podunavlju (with résumé in German: Die Starčevo-Kultur im Slawonisch-Syrmischen Raum und das Problem des Übergangs vom älteren zum Mittleren Neolithikum im serbischen und kroatischen Donaugebiet) Gradski Muzej, Vukovar.

DIMITROV, M., 1962. 'Kostena choveshka figurka ot s. Lovets, Starozagorsko', *Arkheologija*, IV, 1: 65–68.

DOMBAY, JÁNOS, 1960. *Zengövárkony*.

DOUGLAS, VAN BUREN, E., 1930. *Clay figurines of Babylonia and Assyria*. New Haven.

DOUMAS, CHRISTOS, 1968. *The N. P. Goulandris collection of Early Cycladic Art*. Athens.

DRAGOMIR, I. T., 1967. 'Săpături arheologice la Tg. Bereşti, r. Bujor, reg. Galati', *Danubius* I: 41–57.

DROPPA, ANTON, 1961. *Domica – Baradla, jaskyne predhistorického človeka*. Bratislava.

DUMÉZIL, G., 1929. *Le problème des Centaures*. Paris.

DUMITRESCU, HORTENSIA, 1960. 'Antropomorfnye izobrazhenija na sosudakh iz Traian', *Dacia*, N.S. IV: 31–32.

—, 1961. 'Connections between the Cucuteni-Tripolie cultural complex and the neighboring eneolithic cultures in the light of the utilization of golden pendants', *Dacia*, N.S. V: 69–93.

—, 1968. 'Un modèle de sanctuaire découvert dans la station énéolithique de Căscioarele', *Dacia*, N.S. XII: 381–94.

DUMITRESCU, VLADIMIR, 1934. 'La plastique antropomorphe en argile de la civilisation énéolithique Balkano – Danubienne de type Gumelniţa', *IPEK* (1932/1933): 49–72.

DUMITRESCU, V., 1945. *Traian*.

—, 1954. *Habaşeşti*. Bucharest.

—, 1956. 'Semnificaţia şi Originea Unui Tip de Figurina Feminina Descoperita la Rast' (summaries in Russian [pp. 116–17] and French: Signification et Origine d'un Type de Figurine Féminine Découverte à Rast, pp. 117–18), *SCIV*, XII, 1–2: 95–118.

—, 1959. 'La civilisation de Cucuteni', *Berichten van de rijksdienst voor het oudheidkundig bodemonderzoek*, IX: 7–48.

—, 1965. 'Căscioarele', *Archaeology*, 18: 34.

—, 1966. 'New discoveries at Gumelniţa', *Archaeology*, 19, 3: 162–72.

—, 1968. *L'art Roumanie*.

—, 1970. Édifice destiné au culte découvert dans la couche Boian-Spanţov de la station-tell de Căscioarele', *Dacia*, XIV: 5–24.

ELIADE, M., 1952. *Images et symboles*. Paris.

—, *Patterns in Comparative Religion*. New York.

—, 1958. *Birth and Rebirth. The religious meanings of initiation in human culture*. New York.

—, 1958. *Patterns in Comparative Religion*. London.

—, 1960. *Myths, Dreams and Mysteries. The Encounter Between Contemporary Faiths and Archaic Realities*. New York.

—, 1969. *Myths and Symbols: studies in honor of M. Eliade*.

EVANS, A. J., 1906. 'The Prehistoric Tombs of Knossos', *Archaeologia*, LIX: 391–562.

—, 1914. 'The Tomb of the Double Axes', *Archaeologia*, LXV: 1–94.

—, 1925. 'The Ring of Nestor: A Glimpse into the Minoan After-World', *Journal of Hellenic Studies*, XLV: 1–75. London.

—, 1921–35. *The Palace of Minos*.

EVANS, J. D., 1964. 'Excavations at Knossos, 1957–1960', *Annual of the British School of Archaeology*: 132–240.

FARNELL, L. R., 1903. *The Cults of the Greek States* III. Oxford.

—, 1927. 'Cretan Influence in Greek Religion', *Essays in Aegean Archaeology presented to Sir Arthur Evans*. Oxford.

FIALA, FR. and M. HOERNES, 1898. *Die neolithische Station von Butmir*, II. Vienna.

FONTENROSE, J., 1959. *Python. A Study of Delphic Myth and Its Origins*. Los Angeles.

FRANKFORT, H., 1964. *Cylinder Seals. A documentary essay on the art and religion of the Ancient Near East*. London. (First edition 1939).

GALBENU, D., 1962. 'Aşezarea neolitica de la Hirşova', *SCIV*, XIII, 2: 285–306.

GALOVIĆ, R., 1959. *Predionica*.

—, 1964. 'Neue Funde der Starčevo-Kultur in Mittelserbien und Makedonien', *Bericht der Römisch-Germanischen Kommission*: 3–28.

—, 1966. 'The monumental prehistoric clay figures of the Middle Balkans', *American Journal of Archaeology*, LXX 4: 370–71.

—, 1969. 'Die Starčevokultur in Jugoslawien', *Fundamenta, Monographien zur Urgeschichte*, ed. H. Schwabedissen, Reihe A Band 3: *Die Anfänge des Neolithikums vom Orient bis Nordeuropa*, Part II.

GARAŠANIN, D., 1968. *Religija*.

GARAŠANIN-ARANJELOVIĆ DRAGA, 1951. 'Die Steinidole des serbischen Neolithikums', *Starinar*, N.S., II: 7–12.

—, 1954. *Starčevačka Kultura*. Ljubljana.

GARAŠANIN, M., 1958. 'Neolithikum und Bronzezeit in Serbien und Makedonien', *Bericht der Römisch-Germanischen Kommission* (Deutches Archäologisches Institut, Berlin), XXXIX: 1–130.

GASTER, THEODOR H., 1961. *Thespis, Ritual, Myth and Drama in the Ancient Near East*. Garden City.

GAUL, J. H., 1948. 'The Neolithic period in Bulgaria; early food producing cultures in Eastern Europe', *American School of Prehistoric Research*, Bulletin 16.

GEORGIEV, GEORGI I., 1955. 'Mramorna statuetka ot Blagoevo, Razgradsko', *Izvestija*, XIX: 1–13.

—, 1961. 'Kulturgruppen der Jungstein- und Kupferzeit in der Ebene von Thrazien (Südbulgarien)', *L'Europe à la Fin de l'Âge de la Pierre*: 45–100.

—, 1962. 'Azmashkata selishchna mogila, kraj Stara Zagora', *Arkheologija*, IV, 1: 59–65.

—, 1963. 'Glavni rezultati ot razkopkite na Azmashkata selishchna mogila prez 1961 r.', *Izvestija*, XXVI: 157–76. (German summary: 174–76).

—, 1965. 'The Azmak mound in southern Bulgaria', *Antiquity*, XXXIX:

—, 1969. 'Die äneolithische Kultur in Südbulgarien im Lichte der Ausgrabungen vom Tell Azmak bei Stara Zagora', *Študijne Zvesti*, XVII: 141–58.

—, 1967. *Beiträge*.

GEORGIEV-ANGELOV, *Ruse*.

GEORGIEV, VLADIMIR I., 1937. *Die Träger der kretisch-mykenischen Kultur, ihre Herkunft und ihre Sprache*. Sofia.

—, 1969. 'Un sceau inscrit de l'epoque chalcolithique trouvé en Thrace', *Studi Micenei ed Egeo-Anatolici*: 32–35.

—, 1970. 'Pismenostta v'rkhu glinenata pločka ot s. Gradešnica' (résumé in French: 'L'écriture sur la plaque en argile du village Gradešnica'). In a joint article with Bogdan Nikolov 'Débuts d'écriture du chalcolithique dans les terres bulgares', *Archaeologija*, XII, 3: 7–9.

GIEDION, S., 1962. *The Eternal Present: The Beginnings of Art*. New York.

GIMBUTAS, M., 1970a. 'Obre, Yugoslavia. Two neolithic sites', *Archaeology*, 23, 4: 287–97. New York.

—, 1970b. 'Proto-Indo-European Culture: The Kurgan culture during the fifth, fourth and third millennia B.C.', *Indo-European and Indo-Europeans*: 155–97. Philadelphia.

—, 1972a. 'Excavations at Anza, Macedonia', *Archaeology*, 25, 2: 112–23. New York.

—, 1972b. 'The Neolithic cultures of the Balkan Peninsula', *Aspects of the Balkans*: 9–49. The Hague.

—, 1973. 'Old Europe *c*. 7000–3500 BC: The earliest European civilization before the infiltration of the Indo-European peoples', *Journal of Indo-European Studies*, I, No. 1: 1–21.

GLIŠIĆ, J., JOVANOVIĆ, B., 1957. 'Praistorisko naselje na Gladnicama kod Gračanice (Eine vorgeschichtliche Ansiedlung am Gladnice bei Gračanica)', *Glasnik Muzeja Kosova i Metohije*, II: 223–33.

—, 1964. 'Stratigraphie der Vinča Gruppe Siedlung bei der Spinnerei in Priština', *Glasnik Muzeja Kosova i Metohije*, VII–VIII.

GOLDMAN, BERNARD, 1963. 'Typology of the Mother-goddess figurines', *IPEK*, 20: 8–15, pls.

GRAZIOSI, P., 1956. *L'Arte dell' antica età della pietra*. Florence.

—, 1971. 'Le pitture preistoriche delle Grotte di Porto Badisco e S. Cesarea', *Accademia Nazionale dei Lincei, Rendiconti della Classe di Scienze morali, storiche e filologiche*, Serie VIII, vol. XXVI, fasc. 1–2: 1–7, pl. I–VII.

GRBIĆ, M., 1929. *Pločnik*.

GRBIĆ, M. *et al.*, 1960. *Porodin*.

GREIFENHAGEN, ADOLF, 1965. 'Schmuck

und Gerät eines lydischen Mädchens', *Antike Kunst*, VIII: 13–20.

GRUNDMANN, K., 1953. 'Figürliche Darstellungen in der neolithischen Keramik Nord- und Mittel-Griechenlands', *Jahrbuch des Deutschen Archäologischen Institutes*, Berlin. LXVIII: 1–37.

GULDER, ALOIS, 1960–62. *Maissau*.

GUTHRIE, W. K. C., 1961. *The Religion and Myth of the Greeks*. The Cambridge Ancient History, II. Cambridge.

HAMPE, R., 1936. *Frühe griechische Sagenbilder in Böotien*. Athens.

HARDING, ESTER, 1955. *Woman's mysteries. Ancient and Modern*. Pantheon, Los Angeles.

HARRISON, JANE E., 1894. *Mythology and Monuments of Ancient Athens*. New York and London.

—, 1927. *Themis: A Study of the social origins of Greek religion*. 2nd ed. Cambridge.

—, 1961. *Prolegomena to the study of Greek religion*. 3rd ed. Cambridge.

HAZZIDAKIS, J., 1921. *Tylissos à l'époque minoenne*. Paris.

HELCK, WOLFGANG, 1971. 'Betrachtungen zur grossen Göttin und den ihr verbundenen Gottheiten', *Religion und Kultur der alten Mittelmeerwelt in Parallelforschungen*, 2.

HELLER, JOHN L., 1961. 'A labyrinth from Pylos?', *American Journal of Archaeology*, 65: 57–62.

HENTZE, CARL, 1932. *Mythes et symboles lunaires*. Anvers.

HEUBECK, A., 1966. *Aus der Welt der Frühgriechischen Lineartafeln*. Göttingen.

HEURTLEY, W. A., 1939. *Prehistoric Macedonia*. Cambridge.

HIGGINS, R. A., 1967. *Greek Terracottas*. London.

HIMNER, M., 1933. 'Etudes sur la civilisation prémycénienne', *Światowit*, XIV (1930–31): 17–163.

HÖCKMANN, OLAF, 1968. 'Zu Formenschatz und Ursprung der schematischen Kykladenplastik', *Berliner Jahrbuch für Vor- und Frühgeschichte*, VIII: 45–75.

—, 1969. 'Die menschengestaltige Figuralplastik der südeuropäischen Jungsteinzeit und Steinkupferzeit', *Münst. Beiträge zur Vorgeschichtsforschung*, 3.

HOGARTH, D. G., 1927. 'Aegean Sepulchral Figurines', *Essays in Aegean Archaeology Presented to Sir Arthur Evans* (Oxford): 55–62.

HÖHN, KARL, 1946. *Artemis, Gestaltwandel einer Göttin*. Zürich.

HULTKRANTZ, A., 'Religious Tradition', *Comparative Religion and Folklore*. Ethnos. Stockholm.

IMMERWAHR, SARA ANDERSON, 1971. *The Athenian Agora*. Vol. XIII. Princeton.

JACOBSEN, THOMAS, W., 1969. 'Frangthi cave: a Stone Age site in Southern Greece', *Archaeology*, 22, 1: 4–9.

JACOBSEN, THORKILD, 1965. 'Formative Tendencies in Sumerian religion', *The Bible and the Ancient Near East. Essays in honor of W. F. Albright*. 353–68.

JAMES, E. O., 1958. *Myth and Ritual*. London.

—, 1961. *Seasonal feasts and festivals*. London.

JOCKEL, RUDOLPH, 1953. *Götter und Dämonen*. Darmstadt-Genf.

JOVANOVIĆ, B., 1967. 'La signification de certains elements de culte du groupe de Starčevo', *Starinar*, 18: 11–20.

JOVANOVIĆ, BORISLAV and GLIŠIĆ, JOVAN, 1961. 'Eneolitsko naselje na Kormadinu kod Jakova (Station énéolithique dans la localité de Kormadin près de Jakov)', *Starinar* (1960): 113–42.

JUCKER, INES, 1963. 'Frauenfest in Korinth', *Antike Kunst*, VI, A.2: 47–61.

JUNG, CARL G. et al., 1964. *Man and his symbols*. Garden City.

JUNG, C. G. u. K. KERÉNYI, 1951. *Einführung in das Wesen der Mythologie. Das göttliche Kind. Das göttliche Mädchen*. 4th ed. Leipzig.

KAHIL, G.-, LILLY, 1965. 'Autour de l'Artemis attique', *Antike Kunst*, VIII: 20–34.

KALICZ, NÁNDOR, 1970. *Dieux*.

KANDYBA, O., 1937. *Schipenitz*.

KENNA, V. E. G., 1968. 'Ancient Crete and the use of the cylinder seal', *AJA*, LXXII (4): 321–36.

KERÉNYI, K., 1952. *Die Jungfrau und Mutter der griechischen Religion. Eine Studie über Pallas Athene*. Albae Vigiliae, 12.

—, 1956. 'Herkunft der Dionysosreligion', *Arbeitsgemeinschaft Nordrhein-Westfalen*, Heft 58.

—, 1961. *Der frühe Dionysos*. Oslo.

KHAVLJUK, P. I., 1959. 'Novye dannye o kultovykh izobrazhenijakh v Tripole',

Sovetskaja Arkheologija, 1959, 3: 206–8.

KOREK, JÓZSEF, 1959. 'Zu den anthropomorphen Darstellungen der Bükker Kultur', *Folia Archaeologica*: 104.

KOROŠEC, JOSIP, 1959. *Prehistorijska plastika*.

—, 1964. *Danilo i Danilska Kultura* (German translation: Danilo und die Danilo-Kulturgruppe, 89–105). Ljubljana.

KRAPPE, A. H., 1952. *La Genèse des mythes*. Paris.

KRAUS, TH., 1960. *Hekate. Studien zu Wesen und Bild der Göttin in Kleinasien und Griechenland*. Heidelberg.

KRISS, R., 1930. 'Die Opferkröte', *Bayerischer Heimatschutz*: 107.

KRISTENSEN, W. BREDE, 1926. *Het Leven Uit Den Dood, Studien over Egyptischen en Oud-Griekschen Godsdienst*. Haarlem.

KÜBLER, K., 1943. *Kerameikos* IV. Berlin.

KUHN, HERBERT, 1951. *Das Problem des Urmonotheismus*. Akad. d. Wiss. und der Literatur, Mainz Abh. d. Geistes und Sozialwissentschaftlichen Klasse, 1950, XXII: 1639–72.

KUSURGASHEVA, A. P., 1970. 'Antropomorfnaja plastika iz poselenija Novye Ruseshty I', *KSIIMK* 123: 69–76.

LAUMONIER, A., 1958. *Les cultes indigènes en Carie*. Bibl. des Ecoles Franc., d'Athènes et de Rome.

LEAHU, V., 1962. 'Săpăturile arheologice de salvare de la Giuleşti-Sirbi', *Cercetări Arheologice in Bucureşti*: 179–219.

LEEUW, G. VAN DER, 1933. 2nd edition 1955. *Phänomenologie der Religion*. Tübingen.

—, 1963. *Sacred and profane beauty. The holy in art*. London.

LEROI-GOURHAN, ANDRÉ, 1967. *Treasures of prehistoric art*. New York.

LEVY, RACHEL G., 1963. *Religious conceptions of the Stone Age and their influence upon European thought*. New York. (Originally published in 1948 as *The Gate of Horn*.)

LÉVY-BRUHL, L., 1938. *L'expérience mystique et les symboles chez les primitifs*. Paris.

LICHARDUS, JAN, 1962. 'Die Bükker Kultur in der Slowakei und ihre Stellung im Karpatenbecken', *Študijne Zvesti*, IX: 47–62.

LLOYD, SETON and J. MELLAART, 1957. 'Beycesultan excavations', Fourth preliminary report *Anatolian Studies*, VIII: 93–126.

LUKAS, FRANZ, 1894. 'Das Ei als kosmogonische Vorstellung', *Zeitschrift für Verein für Volkskunde*, IV: 227–43.

MACKENZIE, DONALD A., *Myths of Crete and Pre-Hellenic Europe*. London.

MAJEWSKI, K., 1935. *Figuralna plastyka cykladzka. Geneza i rozwój form*. Lwów.

MAKARENKO, N. E., 1927. 'Sculpture de la civilisation tripolienne en Ukraine', *IPEK*: 119.

MAKAREVICH, M. L., 1960a. 'Issledovanija v rajone s. Stena na Srednem Dnestre', *Kratkie Soobshchenija Instituta Arkheologii*, 10: 23–32.

—, 1960b. 'Ob ideologicheskikh predstavlenijakh u tripolskikh plemen', *Odesskoe arkheologicheskoe obshchestvo. Zapiski*. Odessa, I (34): 290–301.

MAKKAY, J., 1962. 'Die balkanischen sogenannten kopflosen Idole – ihr Ursprung und ihre Erklärung', *Acta Archaeologica*, XIV: 1–24.

—, 1964. 'Early Near Eastern and South East European Gods', *Acta Archaeologica*, XVI: 3–64.

—, 1969. 'Die neolithischen Funde von Bicske', *Študijné Zvesti*, XVII: 253–70.

MALINOWSKI, B., 1926. *Myth in primitive psychology*. London.

MALLOWAN, M. E. L., 1947. 'Excavations at Brak and Chagar Bazar', *Iraq*, IX: 1–254.

MALTEN, LUDOLF, 1928. 'Der Stier in Kult und mythischen Bild', *Jahrbuch des Deutschen Archaeologischen Instituts*, XLIII: 90–139.

MARINATOS, S., 1945. 'La Stéatopygie dans la Grèce Préhistorique', *Praktika*: 1ff.

—, 1968a. 'Αἰώρα', *Antichthon*, Journal of the Australian Society for Classical Studies II: 1–14.

—, 1968b. 'Die Eulengöttin von Pylos', *Mitteilungen des deutschen archäologischen Instituts*, LXXXIII: 167–74.

—, 1971. 'Thera Anaskaphai 1970', *Athens Annals of Archaeology*, part 1.

MARINATOS, S. and M. HIRMER, 1960. *Crete and Mycenae*. London.

MARINESCU-BÎLCU, SILVIA, 1964. 'Reflets des rapports entre les civilisations de Hamangia et de Précucuteni dans la plastique Précucuténienne de Tirpeşti', *Dacia*, VIII: 307–12.

—, 1967. 'Die Bedeutung einiger Gesten und Haltungen in der jungsteinzeitlichen Skulptur der ausserkarpatischen Gebiete Rumäniens', *Dacia*, N.S. XI: 47–58.

MARINESCU-BÎLCU, SILVIA and BARBU IONESCU, 1968. *Catalogue sculpturilor eneolitice din Muzeul raional Olteniţa.* Olteniţa.

MARKEVICH, V. I., 1970. 'Mnogoslojnoe poselenie Novye Ruseshty I', *Kratkie Soobshchenija Instituta Arkheologii*, CXXIII: 56–68.

MARSHAK, ALEXANDER, 1972. *The roots of civilization. The cognitive beginnings of man's first art, symbol and notation.* New York.

MATASĂ, C., 1946. *Frumuşica. Village préhistorique a céramique peinte dans la Moldavie du Nord.* Bucharest.

—, 1964. 'Aşezarea eneolitica Cucuteni B de la Tîrgu Ocna-Podei (raionul Tîrgu Ocna, reg. Bacău)', *Arheologia Moldovei*, II–III: 11–66.

MATEESCO, C. N., 1957. 'Fouilles archéologiques à Cruşovu', *Materiale şi Cercetări Archeologie*, III: 103.

—, 1965. 'Contribution à l'étude de la civilisation de Vădastra. Phase Vădastra II (d'après les nouvelles fouilles de Vădastra)', *Atti del VI Congresso Internazionale delle Scienze Preistoriche e Protostoriche*, 1962 (II Comunicazioni, Sezioni I–IV): 258–63.

MATZ, FRIEDRICH, 1958. *Göttererscheinung und Kultbild im Minoischen Kreta.* Akad. d. Wiss. u. d. Lit. Abhandlungen d. Geistes u. Sozwiss. Klasse VII. Wiesbaden.

—, 1962. *Kreta und Frühes Griechentum.* Holle, Baden-Baden. English ed.

—, 1962. *Crete and Early Greece.* London.

McPHERRON, A. and D. SREJOVIĆ, *Divostin.* Belgrade (in preparation).

MEGAW, J. V. S., 1968. 'The earliest musical instruments in Europe', *Archaeology*, 21 2: 124–32.

MELLAART, JAMES. 1960. 'Hacılar – fourth preliminary report', *Anatolian Studies* X: 39–74.

—, 1963. 'Deities and Shrines of Neolithic Anatolia', *Archaeology*, 16, 1: 29–38.

—, 1964. '1963 excavations at Çatal Hüyük. Third preliminary report', *Anatolian Studies*, XIV: 39–119.

—, 1965. *Earliest Civilizations of the Near East.* London.

—, 1967. *Çatal Hüyük, a neolithic town in Anatolia.* London and New York.

—, 1970. *Excavations at Hacılar I* (text), II (illus.). Edinburgh.

METZGER, H., 1965. *Recherches sur l'Imagerie Athénienne.* Paris.

MEULI, K., 1945. 'Griechische Opferbräuche', *Phyllobolia für Peter von der Mühll zum 1. 8. 1945.* Basel.

MICHAUD, J.-P., 1970. 'Chronique des fouilles en 1968 et 1969', *BCH*, 94: 1049.

MIKOV, V., 1939. 'Tell près du village de Veselinovo', *Izvestija Arkheol. Instituta, Bulgarska Akad. na Naukite*, XIII: 195.

—, 1959. 'The Prehistoric Mound of Karanovo', *Archaeology*, 12, 2: 88–97.

MILOJČIĆ, VLADIMIR, 1950. 'Die Askoskanne und einige andere ägäischbalkanische Gefässformen', *Mitteilungen des deutschen archäol. Instituts* III: 107–18.

—, 1955. 'Vorbericht über die Ausgrabungen auf den Magulen von Otzaki, Arapi und Gremnos bei Larissa', *Archäologischer Anzeiger*: 182–231.

—, 1959. 'Ergebnisse der deutschen Ausgrabungen in Thessalien 1953–58', *Jahrbuch des Römisch-Germanischen Zentralmuseum, Mainz.* VI: 10–56.

—, 1965. 'Ausgrabungen in Thessalien', *Neue deutsche Ausgrabungen im Mittelmeergebiet und im Vorderen Orient*: 225–236.

MILOJČIĆ, V., J. BOESSNECK and M. HOPF, 1962. *Die deutschen Ausgrabungen auf der Argissa-Magula in Thessalien. 1: Das präkeramische Neolithikum sowie die Tier- und Pflanzenreste.* Beiträge zur ur- und frühgeschichtlichen Archäologie des Mittelmeer-Kulturraumes, Bonn.

MOVSHA, T. G., 1964. 'Trippil'ske pokhovannja v s. Tsviklivtsi', *Arkheologija*, XVI: 213–22.

—, 1969. 'Ob antropomorfnoj plastike tripol'skoj kul'tury', *Sovetskaja Arkheologija*, II: 15–34.

—, 1971. 'Svjatilishcha tripol'skoj kul'tury', *Sovetskaja Arkheologija*, 1971, 1: 201–5.

MÜLLER, V., 1929. *Frühe Plastik in Griechenland und Vorderasien. Ihre Typenbildung* von der neolithischen bis in der griechisch-archaischen Zeit. 3000–600 v. Chr. Augsburg.

MÜLLER-KARPE, H., 1968. *Handbuch der Vorgeschichte. Jungsteinzeit* (Bd. 2), I and II. Munich.

MYLONAS, G. E., 1956. 'Seated and multiple Mycenaean figurines in the National Museum of Athens, Greece', *The Aegean and the Near East: Studies presented to Hetty Goldman* (New York): 110–22.

—, 1961. *Eleusis and Eleusinian Mysteries*. Princeton.

—, 1966. *Mycenae and the Mycenaean Age*. Princeton.

NANDRIS, JOHN, 1969. 'Early neothermal sites in the Near East and Anatolia. A review of material, including figurines, as a background to the Neolithic of temperate south east Europe', *Memoria Antiquitatis*, I: 11–66.

—, 1970. 'The development and relationships of the earlier Greek neolithic', *Man*, V, 2: 191–213.

Neolit centralnog Balkana (Les Régions Centrales des Balkans à l'époque néolitiques). National Museum, Belgrade, 1968.

NEUMANN, ERICH, 1955. *The Great Mother*. New York.

NEUSTUPNÝ, E., 1968b. 'Absolute chronology of the Neolithic and Aeneolithic periods in central and south-eastern Europe', *Slovenska Archeologia*, XIV, 19: 19–56.

—, 1969. 'Der Übergang vom Neolithikum zum Äneolithikum und der Ausklang der Lengyel-Kultur', *Študijné Zvesti*, XVII: 271–91.

NEUSTUPNÝ, J., 1956. 'Studies on the Eneolithic plastic arts', *Sbornik Narodn. Mus. Praze*, X: 24–101.

NEWBERRY, P. E., 1928. 'The pig and the cult-animal of Set', *Journal of Egyptian Archaeology*, XIV: 211–26.

NIKOLOV, BOGDAN, 1968. 'Praistoricheskoto selishche pri s. Okhoden, Vračanski okryg', *Archeologija*, I: 65–75.

—, 1970. *Gradešnica*.

—, 1970. 'Idolnata plastika ot s. Gradešnica' (résumé in French: 'La plastique des idoles du village Gradešnica'), *Archeologija*, XII–4: 56–68.

—, 1970. 'Praistoricheskoto selishte Kaleto pri s. Gradešnica, Vračanski okryg', *Izvestija na Arkheol. Institut* (Bulletin de l'Institut d'Arch.), XXXII: 231–53.

NILSSON, MARTIN P., 1921. 'Die Anfänge der Göttin Athena', *Det K. Danske Videnskaberns Selskab, Hist,-filol. Medd.*, IV: 7.

—, 1950. *The Minoan-Mycenaean religion and its survival in Greek religion*. Lund.

—, 1957. *Griechische Feste von religiöser Bedeutung*. Leipzig. (1906 first ed.).

NIŢU, A., 1968a. 'Reprezentari umane pe ceramica Criş şi liniara din Moldova', *SCIV*, XIX, 3: 387–395.

—, 1968b. 'Tema plastica a venenei Calipige pe ceramica neolitica Carpato Balcanica', *Sesiuneu ştiencifica a Museelor*. Bucharest.

—, 1969. 'Cu privire la derivatia unor motive geometrice in ornamentatia ceramicii Candate', *Arheologia Moldavei*, VI: 7–41.

—, 1972. 'Reprezentările zoomorfe plastice pe ceramica neo-eneolitică Carpato-dunăreană, *Arheologia Moldovei*, VII: 9–96.

NOVAK, G., 1955. *Predhistorijski Hvar*. Zagreb.

NOVOTNÝ, BOHUSLAV, 1958. *Počiatky vytvarného prejavu na Slovensku (Die Anfänge der bildenden Kunst in der Slowakei)*.

—, 1958. *Slovensko v mladšej dobe kamennej* (= Die Slowakei in der Jungsteinzeit). Bratislava.

ORSSICH DE SLAVETICH, A., 1940. 'Bubanj, eine vorgeschichtliche Ansiedlung bei Niš', *Mitteilungen der Prähistorischen Kommission*, IV/1–2. 1–46.

OSTROWSKA, E., 1949. 'Neolityczne figurki gliniane na Śląsku', *Z otchłani wieków*, XVIII: 152–54.

OTTO, W. F., 1947. *Die Götter Griechenlands*, 3 ed. Frankfurt.

—, 1954. *The Homeric gods: the spiritual significance of Greek religion*. London. (English translation of *Die Götter Griechenlands*, 1929).

—, 1965. *Dionysus: myth and cult*. Bloomington.

OVCHAROV, DIMIT'R, 1968. 'Novi eneolitni choveshki figurki ot Tyrgovischchki okryg', *Archeologija*, III: 38–45.

PALLIS, SV. AA., 1926. *The Babylonian Akitu festival*. Copenhagen.

PALMER, L. R., 1965. *Mycenaeans and Minoans*. London.

PASSEK., T. S., 1935. *Céramique tripolienne*.

—, 1949. 'Periodizatsija tripolskikh poselenii', *Materialy i Issledovanija po Arkheologii SSSR*, No. 10.

—, 1965. 'Kostjanye amulety iz Floresht', *Novoe v Sovetskoj Arkheologii*: 77–84.

—, 1954. 'Itogi rabot v Moldavii v oblasti pervobytnoj Arkheologii', *KSIIMK*, 56: 76–97.

PASSEK, T. S. and M. M. GERASIMOV, 1967. 'Novaja statuetka iz Vulkaneshti', *KSIIMK*, 111: 38–41.

PAUL, E., 1959. *Die böotischen Brettidole*. Leipzig.

PAUL, IULIU, 1965a. 'Ein Kulttisch aus der jungsteinzeitlichen Siedlung von Deutschpien (Pianul de Jos)', *Forschungen zur Volks- und Landeskunde*, VIII, 1: 69–76.

—, 1965b. 'Un complex de cult descoperit in asezarea neolitica de la Pianul de Jos. – Ein in der neolithischen Niederlassung von Pianul de Jos entdeckter Kultkomplex', *Studii şi Comunicari*: 5–20.

PAULY, AUGUST FRIEDRICH VON, 1894–19—. *Pauleys Realencyclopädie der klassischen Altertumswissenschaft; neue Bearbeitung ... unter Mitwirkung zahlreicher Fachgenossen hrsg. von G. Wissova*. Stuttgart.

PAVÚK, JURAJ, 1965. 'Nové nálezy lengyelskej kultúry zo Slovenska. Neue Funde der Lengyel-Kultur in der Slowakei', *Slovenská Archeológia*, XIII, 1: 27–50.

PAVÚK, JURAJ and STANISLAV ŠIŠKA, 1971. 'Neolitské a eneolitské osídlenie Slovenska' (German summary: Neolithische und äneolithische Besiedlung der Slowakei), *Slovenská Archeológia*, XIX, 2: 319–64.

PESTALOZZA, U., 1942–43. 'L'aratro e la donna nel mondo religioso Mediterraneo', *Rendiconti, Reale Instituto Lombardo di Scienze e Lettere*, LXXVI, 2: 324.

—, 1952. *Religione Mediterranea*. Milano.

PETKOV, N., 1950. 'Classification des idoles płates en os de la civilisation énéolithique balkano-danubienne', *Godishnik, Plovdiv*, II: 25.

PETRESCU-DÎMBOVIŢA, M., 1963. *Truşeşti*.

—, 1957. 'Sondajul stratigrafic de la Perieni', *Materiale şi Cercetări Arheologice*, III: 65–82.

—, 1965. 'Evolution de la civilisation de Cucuteni à la lumière des nouvelles fouilles archéologiques de Cucuteni-Baiceni', *Rivista di Scienze Preistoriche*, XX, 1: 157–81.

—, 1966. *Cucuteni. Monumentele Patriei Noastre*. Bucharest.

—, 1969. 'Einige Probleme der Cucuteni-Kultur im Lichte der neuen archälogischen Grabungen', *Študijné Zvesti*, XVII: 361–74.

PETTAZZONI, R., 1954. 'Myths of beginnings and creation-myths', *Essays on the History of Religion* (Leiden): 24–36.

PETTERSON, OLOF, 1967. 'Mother Earth. An analysis of the Mother Earth concepts according to Albrecht Dieterich', *Scripta Minora*, 1965–66, 3: 1–100.

PICKARD-CAMBRIDGE, A. W., 1927. *Dithyramb, tragedy, and comedy*. Oxford.

—, 1953. *Festivals – The dramatic festivals of Athens*, Oxford.

PICARD, CH, 1944–45. 'Statues et ex-voto du "Stibadeion" dionysiaque de Delos', *Bulletin Correspondance Hellénique*, 68–69: 240–70.

—, 1948. *Les religions préhelléniques*. Paris.

PIGGOTT, STUART, 1965. *Ancient Europe, from the beginnings of agriculture to classical antiquity*. Edinburgh and Chicago.

PLATON, N., 1949. 'Nouvelle interprétation des idoles-cloches du Minoen Moyen I', *Mélanges d'Archéologie et d'Histoire offerts à Charles Picard*: 833–46.

—, 1966. *Crète*. Clèveland.

PODBORSKÝ, VLADIMIR, 1970. 'Současný stav výskumu kultury s moravskou malovanou keramikou (résumé in German: Der gegenwärtige Forschungsstand der Kultur mit mährischer bemalter Keramik)', *Slovenská Archeológia*, XVIII, 2: 235–311.

POPOV, R., 1911. 'Idoli i životinski figuri od predistoričeskata mogila pri "Kodžadermen"', *Izvestija na Balgarskoto Arkheologičesko Družestvo*, II: 70–80.

—, 1918. 'Kodža-Dermenskata mogila pri gr. Šumen', *Izvestija na Bulgarskoto Arkheologičesko Družestvo*, VI (1916–18): 71–155.

POPOVITCH, VLADISLAV, 1965. 'Une civilisation égéo-orientale sur le moyen Danube', *Revue Archéologique*, II: 1–56.

PRENDI, FRANCO, 1966. 'La civilisation préhistorique de Maliq', *Studia Albanica*, No. 1: 255–80.

PRINZ, H., 1915. *Altorientalische Symbolik.* Berlin.

PROTOPOPESCO-PAKE, MATEESCO, CORNELIUS, N. and GROSSU, AL. V., 1969. 'Formation des couches de civilisation de la station de Vădastra en rapport avec le sol, la faune malacologique et le climat', *Quartär*, XX: 135–62.

PRZYLUSKI, J., 1939. 'Ursprung und Entwicklung des Kultes der Mutter-Göttin', *Eranos-Jahrbuch*, VI: 11–57.

QUITTA, H., 1957. 'Zur Deutung und Herkunft der bandkeramischen "Krötendarstellungen" ', *Varia Praehist.*, II: 51.

—, 1971. 'Der Balkan als Mittler zwischen Vorderem Orient und Europa', *Evolution und Revolution im Alten Orient und in Europa.*

RADIN, PAUL, 1957. *Primitive Man as Philosopher.* New York. First edition, 1927.

RADIMSKÝ, V. and M. HOERNES, 1895. *Die neolithische Station von Butmir.* Part I. Part II, 1898, prepared by Fr. Fiala and M. Hoernes. Vienna.

RADUNCHEVA, ANA, 1970. *Praistorichesko izkustvo v Bulgarija.* Sofia.

—, 1971. 'Za prednaznachenieto na njakoi glineni eneolitni zhivotinski figurki' (Sur la signification de certaines figurines animales en argile de l'Enéolithique) *Arkheologija* (Sofia), 2: 58–66.

RAISON, JACQUES, 1969. *Le grand palais de Knossos.* Rome.

RANSOME, HILDA M., 1937. *The Sacred Bee in ancient times and folklore.* Boston and New York.

REITLER, RUDOLPH, 1949. 'A theriomorphic representation of Hekate-Artemis', *American Journal of Archaeology*, LIII: 29–31.

—, 1963. 'Neolithische Statuetten aus Cypern' *IPEK* 1960/63: 22–27.

RENFREW, COLIN, 1969. 'The Autonomy of the Southeastern European Copper Age', *Proceedings of the Prehistoric Society* for 1969, XXXV: 12–47.

—, 1969. 'The development and chronology of the Early Cycladic figurines', *AJA*, 73: 1–32.

—, 1972. *The Emergence of Civilization: The Cyclades and the Aegean in the Third Millennium B.C.*, London.

RENFREW, C. and J. D. EVANS, 1966. 'The Fat Lady of Saliagos', *Antiquity*, XL, 159: 218–19.

RENFREW, C., J. R. CANN, and J. E. DIXON, 1965. 'Obsidian in the Aegean', *Annual of the British School of Archaeology at Athens*, No. 60: 225.

RODDEN, ROBERT J., 1965. 'An Early Neolithic village in Greece', *Scientific American*, 212, 4: 82–93.

ROSE, H. J., 1906–10. 'Sanctuary of Artemis Orthia at Sparta', *Journal of Hellenic Studies.*

ROSETTI, D., 1938. 'Steinkupferzeitliche Plastik aus einem Wohnhügel bei Bukarest', *IPEK*, XII: 29–50.

ROSETTI, DINU V., 1961. *Vidra.*

ROSKA, MARTON, 1941. *Torma Collection.*

ROUSE, W. H. D., 1902. *Greek votive offerings.* Cambridge.

RYBAKOV, B. A., 1965. *Cosmogony.*

RYNDINA, N. V., 1969. 'Rannetripol'skaja obrabotka medi'. (Copper manufacture during the Early Tripolye period), *Sovetskaja Arkheologija*, 3: 21–41.

SAKELLARIOU, A., 1958. *Les cachets minoens de la Collection Giamalakis*, Paris.

SANDARS, N. K., 1968. *Prehistoric art in Europe.* Harmondsworth and Baltimore.

SCHACHERMEYR, FRITZ, 1964. *Das ägäische Neolithikum.* Studies in Mediterranean Archeology, 6.

—, 1967. *Ägäis und Orient.* Österreichische Akademie der Wissenschaften. Vienna.

SCHEFOLD, KARL, 1964 (2nd ed.). *Frühgriechische Sagenbilder.* Munich. English translation by A. Hicks: *Myth and Legend in Early Greek Art*, London 1966.

—, 1965. 'Heroen und Nymphen in Kykladengräbern', *Antike Kunst*, VIII: 87–91.

SCHMIDT, HUBERT, 1932. *Cucuteni in der oberen Moldau.* Berlin-Leipzig.

SEGER, H., 1928. 'Der Widder von Jordansmühl', *IPEK*: 13–17.

SERGEEV, G. P., 1962. 'Rannetripol'skij klad u s. Karbuna' (Early Tripolye hoard near the village of Karbuna), *Sovetskaja Arkheologija*, 1962, 1: 135–51.

SIFAKIS, G. M., 1967. *Studies in the history of hellenistic drama*. London.

—, 1971. *Parabasis and Animal Choruses, a contribution to the history of Attic comedy*. London.

SIMON, ERIKA, 1969. *Die Götter der Griechen*. Munich.

ŠIŠKA, S., 1964. 'Pohrebisko tiszapolgárskej kultúry v Tibave (German summary: Gräberfeld der Tiszapolgár-Kultur in Tibava)', *Slovenská Archeológia*, Ročník XII, 2: 295–356.

SOUDSKÝ, BOHUMIL, 1966. 'Interprétation historique de l'ornement linéaire', *Památky Archeologické*, LVIII, 1: 91–125.

SPIESS, K. V., 1914. 'Die Kröte, ein Bild der Gebärmutter', *Mitra*: 209.

SREJOVIĆ, DRAGOSLAV, 1963. 'Versuch einer historischen Wertung der Vinča-Gruppe', *Archaeologia Iugoslavica*, IV: 5–17.

SREJOVIĆ, DRAGOSLAV, et al., 1969. *Lepenski Vir. Nova praistorijska kultura u Podunavlju* (with résumé in French). Belgrade. English ed. 1972: *Europe's First Monumental Sculpture: New Discoveries at Lepenski Vir*. London.

STANČEVA, M., and M. GAVRILOVA, 1961. 'Čoveski glineni figurki o neolitnoto selište v Sofiia', *Arkheologija* (Sofia), III–3: 73–76.

TASIĆ, N., 1957. *Valač*.

TASIĆ, N. and TOMIĆ, E., 1969. *Crnokalačka Bara*.

TAYLOUR, WILLIAM (LORD), 1969. 'Mycenae 1968', *Antiquity*, XLIII: 91–97.

—, 1970. 'New light on Mycenaean religion', *Antiquity*, XLIV: 270–279.

TELEGIN, D. JA., 1968. *Dnipro-donets'ka kul'tura*. Kiev.

THEOCHARIS, D. R., 1956. 'Nea Makri: eine grosse neolithische Siedlung in der Nähe von Marathon', *Mitteilungen des Deutschen Archäologischen Instituts, Athenische Abteilung*, LXXI, 1: 1–29.

—, 1958. 'Thessalie précéramique. Exposé provisoire des fouilles (en grec)', *Thessalika*, I: 70–86.

—, 1959. 'Pyrasos', *Thessalika*, B: 29–67.

—, 1962. 'From Neolithic Thessaly (I) (in Greek with an English summary). *Thessalika*, D: 63–83.

—, 1967. *The prehistory of Thessaly*. Tessalika Leletimata Volos.

THILENIUS, G., 1905. 'Kröte und Gebärmutter', *Globus*, LXXXVII: 105.

THIMME, JÜRGEN, 1965. 'Die religiöse Bedeutung der Kykladenidole', *Antike Kunst*, VII: 71–87.

THOMPSON, H. A., 1960. 'Activities in the Athenian Agora, 1959', *Hesperia*, XXIX: 367.

TICHÝ, R., 1970. 'Zu einigen neolithischen Kultgegenständen aus Mohelnice', *Sbornik Československé Společnosti Archeologické*, IV: 7–19.

TINÈ, SANTO, 1972. 'Gli scavi del villaggio neolitico di Passo di Corvo', *Atti della XIV Riunione Scientifica dell'Istituto Italiano di Preistoria e Protoistoria in Puglia 13–16 Ottobre 1970*: 313–31.

TODOROVIĆ, JOVAN and CERMANOVIĆ, ALEKSANDRINA, 1961. *Banjica*.

TOMPA, F., 1929. 'Die Bandkeramik in Ungarn. Die Bükker- und die Theiss-Kultur', *Arch. Hung.*, V–VI, Budapest.

TROGMAYER, OTTO, 1966. 'Ein neolithisches Hausmodellfragment von Röszke', *Acta Arch. Acad. Hung.*: 11–26.

TRUMP, DAVID H., 1966. *Central and Southern Italy before Rome*. London.

TSCHILINGIROW, A., 1915. 'Zwei Marmorfiguren aus Bulgarien', *Prähistorische Zeitschrift*, VII: 219.

TSOUNTAS, CH., 1908. *Diminiou kai Sesklou*.

TULOK, M., 1971. 'A late Neolithic idol of comical type', *AAASH*, 23: 3–17.

UCKO, P. J., 1962. 'The Intepretation of Prehistoric Figurines', *Journal of the Royal Anthr. Inst.* 92. London.

—, 1968b. *Anthropomorphic figurines of predynastic Egypt and Neolithic Crete with comparative material from the prehistoric Near East and Mainland Greece*. London.

VALLOIS, R., 1922. 'L' "agalma" des Dionysius de Delos', *Bulletin de Correspondance Hellénique*, XLVI: 94–112.

VASIĆ, MILOJE M., 1932–36. *Vinča*.

VILDOMEC, F., 1940. *Strzelitz*.

VIZDAL, JAROSLAV, 1964. 'Nález bukovohorského idolu na neolitickom sidlisku v Lastovciach – Fund eines Idols der Bükker-Kultur auf der neolithischen

Siedlungsstätte in Lastovce'. *Archeologické Rozhledy*, XVI: 427–32.

VLADÁR, JOZEF, 1969. 'Frühäneolithische Siedlung und Gräberfeld in Branč', *Študijné Zvesti Archeologického Ústavu Slovenskej Akadémie Vied*, Vol. 17, Nitra.

VLASSA, N., 1963. 'Chronology of the Neolithic in Transylvania, in the light of the Tartaria settlement's stratigraphy', *Dacia*, N.S., VII: 485–94.

—, 1970. 'Kulturelle Beziehungen des Neolithikums Siebenbürgens zum vorderen Orient', *Acta Musei Napocensis*, VII: 3–39.

VRIES, JAN DE, 1967. *The study of religion, a historical approach*. New York.

VULPE, R., 1941. 'Les fouilles de Calu', *Dacia*, VII–VIII: 13–68.

—, 1957. *Izvoare*.

WACE, A., 1949. 'Prehistoric stone figurines from the mainland', *Hesperia*, Supplement 8.

WACE, A. J. B. and M. S. THOMPSON, 1912. *Prehistoric Thessaly*. Cambridge.

WASSON, GORDON R., 1971. 'The Soma of the Rig Veda: What was it?', *Journal of the American Oriental Society*, XCI, 2: 169–88.

WEBSTER, T. B. L., 1958. 'Some thoughts on the prehistory of Greek drama', *Bulletin of the Institute of Classical Studies*, V. London.

—, 1959. 'Die mykenische Vorgeschichte des griechischen Dramas', *Antike und Abendland*, VIII: 7–14.

—, 1959. *Greek art and literature 700–530 BC*. London.

WEINBERG, S. S., 1951. 'Neolithic Figurines and Aegean Interrelations', *AJA*, LV, 2: 121–33.

—, 1962. 'Excavations at prehistoric Elateia, 1959', *Hesperia*, XXXI: 158–209.

—, 1965a. 'Ceramics and the supernatural: cult and burial evidence in the Aegean world', *Ceramics and Man*. Viking Fund Publications in Anthropology, XLI: 187–201.

—, 1965b. 'Relative Chronology of the Aegean', *Relative Chronologies in Old World Archeology*: 285–320.

—, 1965. *The Stone Age in the Aegean*, Cambridge Ancient History, Fasc. 36.

WEINBERG, S. S. and ROBINSON, H. S.,

1960. 'Excavations at Corinth 1958', *Hesperia*, XXIX: 225–54.

WILAMOWITZ-MOELLENDORFF U. VON, 1959. *Der Glaube der Hellenen*, I and II, 3rd ed. Darmstadt.

WILLETS, R. F., 1962. *Cretan cults and festivals*. London.

ZAHARIA, EUGENIA, 1964. 'Considerații despre cultura Criş, pe baza sondajelor de la Leţ' (Considérations sur la civilisation de Criş à la lumière des sondages de Leţ), *Studii şi Cercetări de Istorie Veche*, XV: 19–44.

ZERVOS, C., 1935. *L'art de la Mésopotamie de la fin du 4e. millenaire au 15e. siècle avant notre ère. Elam, Sumer, Akkad*. Paris.

—, 1956. *Crète*.

—, 1957. *L'art des Cyclades*. Paris.

—, 1962–63. *Naissance*.

ZIMMER, HEINRICH, 1946. Myths and symbols in Indian art and civilization. New York.

ZGIBEA, MIOARA, 1962. 'Figurine gumelniţene de pe teritoriul oraşului şi regiunii Bucureşti (Figurines de la civilisation de Gumelniţa trouvées sur le territoire de la ville et de la région de Bucharest)', *Cercetări Arheologice in Bucureşti*: 271–300.

ZIOMECKI, JULIUS, 1959. 'Plastika figuralna z Bulgarii', *Archeologia*, IX (Warsaw-Wrocław): 35–61.

New entries added for this edition

ARNAL, JEAN, 1976. *Les statues-menhirs, hommes et dieux*. Paris.

BENAC, ALOJZ, 1973. 'Obre II and Obre I', *Wissenschaftliche Mitteilungen des Bosnisch-Herzegowinischen Landesmuseums*, Band III, Sarajevo.

BOSINSKI, G. and G. FISCHER, 1974. *Die Menschendarstellungen von Gönnersdorf der Ausgrabung von 1968*. Wiesbaden.

CASTIGLIONI, OTTAVIO CORNAGGIA and GIULIO CALEGARI, 1975. 'I pendagli "a busto ginemorfo" del paleolitico superiore centro-occidentale Europeo, con un inventario ragionato dei reperti italiani', *Museo Civico di Storia Naturale di Milano*, 66, 1–2: 25–52.

CHOLLOT-VARAGNAC, MARTHE, 1980. *Les origines du graphisme symbolique. Essai*

d'analyse des écritures primitives en Préhistoire, Paris.

COMŞA, EUGENE, 1974. Istoria communităţilor
culturii Boian (L'histoire des communautés de
la culture Boian). Bucharest.

CRISMARU, ARISTOTEL, 1977. Drăguşeni.
Contribuţii la o monograrie archeologică.
Botoşani (Comitetul Judeţean de Cultură
şi Educaţie Socialista, Muzeul Judeţean de
Istorie Botoşani).

CUCOŞ, ŞT, 1973. 'Un complex ritual
cucutenian descoperit la Ghelăeşti (jud.
Neamţ),' Studii şi Cercetări de Istorie Veche
24, 2 (Bucharest), 207 ff.

—, 1973. Céramique néolithique du musée
archéologique de Piatra Neamţ. Piatra
Neamţ (Acta Musei Petrodavensis. Bib-
liotheca Memoriae Antiquitatis)

—, 1975. 'Două vase zoomorfe eneolitice,'
Carpica (Muzeul Judeţean de Istorie şi Artă
Bacău), VII: 7–14.

CZALOG, JÓZSEF, 1972. 'Thronendes Frau-
enidol von Szegvár-Tüzkövez', Idole,
prähistorische Keramiken aus Ungarn,
Vienna (Naturhistorisches Museum,
N.F,7): 20–23, Taf. 17–20.

D'ANNA, A., 1977. Les statues-menhirs et stèles
anthropomorphes du midi méditerranéen.
Paris.

DAMES, MICHAEL, 1976. The Silbury Treasure. The Great Goddess Rediscovered.
London.

DELPORTE, H., 1979. L'Image de la femme dans
l'art préhistorique. Paris.

DUMITRESCU, VLADIMIR, 1974. Arta preistorică
în România. Bucharest.

EKENVALL, ASTA, 1978 'Batrachians as
Symbols of Life, Death, and Women,'
Kvinnhistoriskt arkiv. 14 (Göteborg).

GIMBUTAS, MARIJA, 1974. 'Achilleion: a
Neolithic Mound in Thessaly; Preliminary Report on 1973 and 1974 Excavations', Journal of Field Archaeology, vol.
I: 277–302.

—, 1976. 'Figurines', Neolithic Macedonia as
Reflected by Excavation at Anza, Southeast
Yugoslavia, M. Gimbutas, ed. Mon-
umenta Archaeologica I (the Institute of
Archaeology of the University of Califor-
nia, Los Angeles): 198–241.

—, 1976. 'Ideograms and symbolic Design
on Ritual Objects of Old Europe (Neolithic and Chalcolithic Southeast Europe)',

To Illustrate the Monuments, ed. J. V. S.
Megaw: 77–98. London.

—, 1977. 'Gold Treasure at Varna', Archaeology 30, I (New York): 44–51. Also:
'Varna, a sensationally rich cemetery of
the Karanovo civilization about 4500 BC,'
Expedition 19, 4 (Philadelphia): 39–47.

—, 1977. 'The First Wave of Eurasian Steppe
Pastoralists into Copper Age Europe,' The
Journal of Indo-European Studies, V, 4:
277–339.

—, 1980. 'The Temples of Old Europe',
Archaeology (New York): 41–51.

—, 1980. 'The Kurgan Wave #2, c.
3400–3200 BC in "The Transformation of
European and Anatolian Culture at
4500–2500 BC", The Journal of Indo-
European Studies, VIII, 3–4: 273–317.

GOLDMAN, GYÖRGY, 1978 'Gesichtsgefässe
und andere Menschendarstellungen aus
Battonya', A Békés Megyei Múzeumok
Közleményei (Békés) 5: 13–60.

GRAZIOSI, PAOLO, 1975. 'Nuove manifes-
tazioni d'arte mesolitica e neolitica nel
riparo Gaban presso Trento', Rivista di
Scienze Preistoriche (Florence), XXX, 1–2:
237–78.

FERGUSON, C. W., M. GIMBUTAS and H. E.
SUESS 1976. 'Historical Dates for Neolithic
Sites of Southeast Europe' Science 191:
1170–72.

FLORESCU, MARILENA 1979. 'Contribuţii la
cunoaşterea concepţilor despre lume şi
viaţa a comunităţilor tribale monteorene',
Carpica (Bacău, Romania), XI: 57–134.

FRIEDRICH, PAUL, 1978. The Meaning of
Aphrodite. Chicago and London.

IVANOV, I. S., 1978. 'Les fouillés archéologiques de la nécropole chalcolitique à
Varna, 1972–1975' Studia Praehistorica,
1–2 (Sofia): 13–26.

—, 1978. Sakrovishchata na Varnenskija
khalkoliten nekropol. Sofia.

KALICZ, NÁNDOR and JÁNOS MAKKAY, 1972.
'Gefässe mit Gesichtsdarstellungen der
Linienbandkeramik in Ungarn', Idole,
prähistorische Keramiken aus Ungarn,
Vienna (Naturhistorisches Museum, N.F.
7): 9–15, Taf. 11, 12.

—, 1977. Die Linienbandkeramik in der grossen
ungarischen Tiefebene. Budapest.

KARMANSKI, SERGEJ, 1977. Katalog antropom-
orfne i zoomorfne plastike iz okoline Odžaka.

Odžaci.

KOVÁCS, TIBOR, 1973. 'Askoi, bird-shaped vessels, bird-shaped rattles in Bronze Age Hungary', *Folia Archaeologica*, XXIII: 7–28.

LO SCHIAVO, FULVIA, 1978. 'Figurazioni antropomorfe nella Grotta del Bue Marino-Cala Gonone, Dorgali', *Sardegna Centro-Orientale dal Neolithic alla Fine Mondo Antico* (Sassari): 53–55, pls.

MAKKAY, JÁNOS, 1972. 'Eingeritzte und plastische Menschendarstellungen der transdanubischen Linienbandkeramik', *Idole, prähistoriche Keramiken aus Ungarn*, Vienna (Naturhistorisches Museum, N.F. 7): 16–19, Taf. 13–15.

MARINESCU-BÎLCU, SILVIA, 1974. *Cultura Precucuteni pe teritoriul României*, Bucharest (Institute of Archaeology of the Academy of Sciences of SR Romania), Biblioteca de arheologie XXII.

—, 1974. 'La plastica in terracotta della cultura precucuteniana', *Rivista de Scienze Preistoriche* (Florence), XXIX, 2: 399–436.

MARSHACK, A., 1978. 'The Meander as a System: the Analysis and Recognition of Iconographic Units in Upper Palaeolithic Compositions', *Form in Indigenous Art*, Canberra (Australian Institute of Aboriginal Studies): 286–317.

—, 1979. 'Ukrainian Upper Palaeolithic Symbol Systems: A Cognitive and Comparative Analysis of Complex Ritual Marking', *Current Anthropology*, June 1979.

NICA, MARIN, 1976. 'Cîrcea, cea mai veche aşezare neolithică de la sud de Carpaţi (with résumé in French: Cîrcea, le plus ancien établissement néolitique au sud des Carpates)', *Studii ş Cercetări de Istorie Veche*, vol. 27, 4 (Bucharest).

NIKOLOV, BOGDAN, 1974. *Gradechintza*. Sofia.

—, 1975. *Zaminets*. Sofia.

NIŢU, A., ŞT. CUCOŞ and D. MONAH, 1971. 'Ghelăeşti (Piatra Neamţ), I. Săpaturile din 1969 in Aşezarea Cucuteniană Nedeia', *Memoria Antiquitatis*, III: 11–64.

RACZKY, PAL, 1980. 'A Körös kultúra ujabb figurális ábrázolásai a Középtiszavidékröl és törteneti összefüggéseik' (with summary in English: "New Figural Representations of the Körös Culture from the Middle Tisza Region and their Historical Connections'), *A Szolnok Megyei Múzeumok Évkönyve 1979–1980*, Szolnok: 5–33.

ROBBINS, MIRIAM, 1980. 'The Assimilation of Pre-Indo-European Goddesses into Indo-European Society', in 'The Transformation of European and Anatolian Cultures at 4500–2500 BC', ed. M. Gimbutas, *The Journal of Indo-European Studies*, VIII, 1–2: 19–31.

THEOCHARIS, D. R., ed. 1973. *Neolithic Greece*, Athens (National Bank of Greece).

THIMME, JÜRGEN, ed., 1976. *Art and Culture of the Cyclades* (Pat Getz-Preziosi, trans. and editor of the English edition). Karlsruhe.

TINÈ, SANTO, 1972. 'Un culto neolitico nelle acque nella grotta Scaloria,' *Symposium sulla Religioni della Preistorica*, Valcamonica.

TODOROVA, HENRIETA, 1974. 'Kultszene und Hausmodell aus Ovčarovo, Bez. Targovişte', *Thracia* (Sofia) III: 39–46.

—, 1976. *Ovčarovo*, Sofia.

—. 1978. *The Eneolithic Period in Bulgaria in the Fifth Millennium BC*, London.

TODOROVA, H., ST. IVANOV, V. VASILEV, M. HOPF, H. QUITTA, and G. KOHL, 1975. *Selishchnata Mogila pri Goljamo Delchevo*, Sofia

TROGMAYER, OTTO, 1972. 'Frühneolithische anthropomorphe Gefässe', *Idole, prähistorische Keramiken aus Ungarn*, Vienna (Naturhistorisches Museum, N.F. 7): 7–8, Taf. 1–4.

Catalogue

1 Terracotta torso. H. 8.75 cm. Fine brown fabric. Black lines about the abdomen indicate decoration by painting. Hip-belt shown by application. Found 6.9 m. deep in Vinča mound. Vasić's excavation. BU Collection, 4971. Publ. Vasić, *Vinča*, I: Fig. 95; Vol. III: Fig. 152.

2 Terracotta figurine of fine fabric with white-encrusted incisions indicating dress. Classical Vinča. Potporanj, Kremenjak locality, settlement south of Vršac, north-eastern Yugoslavia. Regional Museum Vršac. Excavated at end of nineteenth century. F. Milleker, *Die steinzeitliche Funde von Potporanj bei Vršac* (Vršac 1934): 1–23.

3 Dark-red terracotta figurine. H. 11.3 cm. Eroded surface. Found 7.8 m. deep in Vinča mound. Vasić's excavation. BU Collection, inv. 948. Publ. Vasić, *Vinča*, III: Fig. 131.

4 Seated terracotta female figurine from the settlement of Banjica near Belgrade. H. 9.2 cm. Head and part of stool broken off. Dark-grey fabric. White-encrusted incisions. Front and middle part of back painted black. Two perforations on each arm stump. Knees and contours of legs indicated although legs shown merged with those of throne. Excavated 1955–57 by J. Todorović and A. Cermanović. Publ. J. Todorović–A. Cermanović, *Banjica*: Pl. VIII, *2,3*.

5 Terracotta torso of a Late Vinča female figurine. Dark-grey fabric, white-filled incisions. Found 4.1 m. deep in Vinča mound. H. 5.2 cm. Vasić's excavation. NM Belgrade. Publ. Vasić, *Vinča*, III: Fig. 419.

6 Terracotta torso of a female figurine wearing a skirt indicated by incised vertical and horizontal lines. H. 10 cm. Gradac settlement at Zlokuchani, Morava Valley, excavated 1909 by Vasić. NM Belgrade, inv. 785. Publ. Vasić, *Glas Serb. Köngl. Akademie* (1911). B. Stalio, Zlokučani-Gradac, NM Belgrade *Catalogue* II (1955): Pl. XVI, *3a,b*.

7 Terracotta torso wearing a checkerboard skirt indicated by white-filled incised lines and dots. H. 7.6 cm. Lower part in form of a cylinder. Classical Vinča. Found 5.6 m. deep in Vinča mound, Vasić's excavation. NM Belgrade. Publ. Vasić, *Vinča*, I: Fig. 144.

8 Terracotta female torso with incisions indicating dress. H. 11 cm. Grey fabric, medium coarse. Mid-Vinča. Found 6.7 m. deep in Vinča mound. Vasić's excavation. NM Belgrade 976. Publ. Vasić, *Vinča*, III: Fig. 168.

9 Lower part of terracotta figurine from Beletinci at Obrež, district of Sremska Mitrovica, northern Yugoslavia. Black burnished. Decorated by white-encrusted incisions and dots. Traces of black paint. H. 7 cm. Excavation of Vojvodjanski Muzej, Novi Sad, by B. Brukner, 1961. Vojvodjanski Muzej, Novi Sad. Publ. B. Brukner, 'Praistorisko naselje na potesu Beletintsi kod Obreža', *Rad Vojvodjanskikh Muzeja*, II (1962): 108, Pl. VIII: *1*.

10 Terracotta figurine of a man with a chest-band, hip-belt and dagger indicated in relief. Orange-red fabric. Head and portions of legs broken off. H. 7.2 cm. Cucuteni A settlement at Berești near Bujor, district of Galați, eastern Romania. Regional Museum of History, Galați. Publ. Ion T. Dragomir, 'Săpături arheologice la Tg. Berești (r. Bujor, reg. Galați)', *Danubius*, I (1967): 41–57.

11 Terracotta figurine of a seated man from Valač at Kosovska Mitrovica, Kosovo Metohije province, Yugoslavia. Found 1.26 m. deep in this Late Vinča settlement. Dark-grey fabric, smooth surface. Head broken off. H. 7.8 cm. White-filled incrustations indicate trousers, blouse and fingers. Broad, V-shaped collar painted red. 1955 excavation by N. Tasić. National Museum, Kosovska Mitrovica. Publ. Tasić, *Valač*: Pl. IX, Fig. 3.

12 Representation of a decorated shoe, part of a sculpture. Gumelnița B-I phase from the

Vidra mound, lower Danube region, 29 km. southeast of Bucharest. Excavated 1931–33 by Dinu V. Rosetti. Bucharest City Museum. Publ. D. Rosetti, *IPEK*, 12 (1938): Pl. 23, *2*.

13 Cylindrical terracotta head with incisions indicating hair and eyes. Nose in relief. H. 3.3 cm. Starčevo settlement at Pavlovac, locality Čukar. NM Belgrade and Archaeological Institute NM Belgrade, 15035 excavations of 1955. Publ. M. Garašanin in 39. *BRGK* 1958, I, 2. NM Belgrade *Catalogue* (1968): 34

14 Terracotta masked head with incisions indicating hair divided into two sections. H. 7.2 cm. Fine grey fabric, polished surface. Mid-Vinča. Found 6.5 m. deep in Vinča mound. Vasić's excavation. BU Collection, 363. Publ. Vasić, *Vinča*, III: 28, Fig. 179.

15 Terracotta head of a masked woman from the settlement of Crnokalačka Bara at Rujište near Ražanj, 20 km. southeast of the mouth of Southern Morava river, southeastern Yugoslavia. Late Vinča. H. 6 cm. Black-baked, polished, lustrous surface. Pentagonal mask shows well modelled eyes, brow-ridges and nose. Top of head at back incised to indicate hair. 1959–60 excavations of Kruševac museum carried out by E. Tomić and N. Tasić. Publ. Tasić–Tomić, *Crnokalačka Bara*: Pl. X, *1*.

16 Female figurine in terracotta from Late Cucuteni (Cucuteni B) settlement at Krynichka, district of Balta, Podolia, Ukrainian SSR. H. 10.5 cm. Naturalistically rendered nude body with long hair indicated by incision ending in a flat disc which apparently portrays a large round coil. Face flat with distinct contours of a mask. Figure in a slightly stooping position. Arms held beneath long breasts. Nineteenth-century excavation. Owned by E. N. Antonovich-Melnik, Kiev. Publ. N. E. Makarenko 'Sculpture de la civilization tripolienne en Ukraine', *IPEK* (1927): 119.

17 Terracotta masked head with a conical cap found 5 m. deep in Vinča mound. Mid-Vinča. H. 5 cm. Light-brown fabric. Vasić's excavation. BU Collection, 868. Publ. Vasić, *Vinča*, III: Fig. 573.

18 Mask and phallic stand found in Phase IV at Achilleion, near Farsala, Thessaly, Greece. Grey clay with traces of white slip. Forehead damaged. Excavated 1973 by M. Gimbutas. H. of removable mask 3 cm., of stand 6 cm.

19 Five masks from different periods: *i*, Vinča found 8.5 m. deep (Starčevo). Publ. Vasić, *Vinča*, III: Fig. 50, Vinča collection, inv. 874; *ii*, Vinča, found 7.3 m. deep (Early Vinča). Publ. Vasić, *Vinča*, II, 94, Fig. 187; *iii*, Vinča, found 6.5 m. deep (Mid-Vinča). Publ. Vasić, *Vinča*, II: Fig. 340, inv. 538; *iv*, Vinča, found 4.2 m. deep (early Late Vinča). Publ. Vasić, *Vinča*, I: Pl. XXXVI; *v*, Valač at Kosovska Mitrovica (Late Vinča). Publ. Tasić, *Valač*.

20 Terracotta head wearing broad triangular mask. H. 6.4 cm. Seven pairs of perforations in back of head and one at each upper corner. Found 4.6 m. deep in Vinča mound. Vasić's excavation. Publ. Vasić, *Vinča*, III: Fig. 366.

21 Baked clay model of a sanctuary with bird-goddess' image above the round opening and plumage indicated by incision. L. 20 cm. Dark-brown fabric. Derives from unsystematic excavations of end of nineteenth century at La Luncă county of Turdaş (Tordoš) on the bank of R. Mureş (Maroš), Transylvania, Romania. Early Vinča culture, early fifth millennium BC. Arch. Museum of the Institute of History, Cluj. Publ. Roska, *Torma Collection*.

22 Clay model of a shrine. Izvoarele, Gumelniţa site, lower Danube. NAM Bucharest.

23 Clay model of a shrine from Popudnia, upper Dniester region, western Ukraine. Late Cucuteni. After M. Himner, 'Étude sur la civilisation prémycénienne', *Światowit*, XIV (1933): Pl. XVIII.

24, 31 Plan and decorative detail of the Căscioarele shrine, after V. Dumitrescu 'Édifice destiné au culte decouvert dans la couche Boian – Spanţov de la station – tell de Căscioarele', *Dacia*, XIV (1970): 20, Fig. 8 and colour plate.

25, 26 Plan of a shrine and figurines found on its altar. From Early Cucuteni (Tripolye) settlement at Sabatinovka, Southern Bug Valley, Soviet Moldavia. After Makarevich, 1960.

27, 28 Contents of the shrine at Gournia (27); perforated vessels from Knossos (28). After Nilsson 1950: 80.

29 Zoomorphic stand with angular perforations from Turdaş, Transylvania. Early Vinča period c. 5000 BC. Museum of Cluj.

30 Plan of a shrine from the Palace of Knossos (detail). After A. J. Evans, *BSA* VIII (1901–2): 95–102.

32 Gold ring from Mycenae. After Nilsson 1950: 81.

33 Terracotta chairs or thrones from the settlement of Ruse on the Danube, northern Bulgaria. Gumelniţa complex, East Balkan civilization. After Georgiev-Angelov, *Ruse*: 93, Fig. 53.

34 Reconstruction of a cult table with vases from the settlement of Pianul de Jos, Petreşti II phase, excavated 1963 by Iuliu Paul. Scale of vases is about 1:8, of jar under the table 1:16. Reconstruction after Iuliu Paul, 'Ein Kulttisch aus der jungsteinzeitlichen Siedlung von Deutschpien (Pianul de Jos)', *Forschungen zur Volks- und Landeskunde*, VIII, 1 (1965): 69–76.

35 Minoan seal depicting a priestess with triton shell beside an altar. After R. R. Schmidt, *Cucuteni* (1932): Fig. 21; also S. Alexiou, *Minoan Civilization* (1969): Fig. 49.

36 Late Vinča terracotta figurine. Drawing from photograph by Zervos reproduced in *Naissance*, II: 460, Fig. 734.

37 Inscribed terracotta figurine from 'the Middle Minoan palace of Tylissos. *After* Evans, *Palace of Minos*, I: 634, Fig. 472.

38 Cylindrical Late Vinča figurine in terracotta incised with ideograms and script signs. Light-brown fabric. H. 11.6 cm. Found 3 m. deep in Vinča mound. Vasić's excavation. NM Belgrade. Publ. Vasić, *Vinča*, III: 89, Fig. 455.

39 Terracotta figurine. Early Vinča. H. approx. 5 cm. Light-brown fabric. From Vinča mound. NM Belgrade. After Popovitch, *Revue Archéologique*, II (1955).

40 Miniature terracotta vessels from the Vinča site. Early Vinča period. After Z. Letica, 'Minijature suḋovi iz Vinča', *Zbornik National Museum Belgrade*, V (1967): 77–126.

41 Terracotta spindle-whorl from the mound of Dikilitash near Philipi, Macedonia. After Deshayes, *BCH*, XCII (196): 1072.

42 Inscribed vessels from Gradešnica near Vraca, western Bulgaria. After B. Nikolov, 'Plaque en argile avec des signes d'écriture du village Gradešnica, dép. de Vraca' and Vladimir I. Georgiev, 'L'écriture sur la plaque en argile du village Gradešnica', *Arkheologija*, XII, 3 (1970): 1–9, Figs. 6, 7.

43 Burnt clay tablets, figurines, clay 'anchor' or figurine, and Spondylus bracelet found in the ritual pit of the Early Vinča layer at Tărtăria near Cluj, Transylvania, western Romania. After N. Vlassa, 'Chronology of the Neolithic in Transylvania in the light of the Tărtăria settlement's stratigraphy', *Dacia*, N.S. VII (1963): Fig. 7.

44 Inscribed clay objects from Sukoró-Tóradülö, east of Székesfehérvár. Early Vinča (Bicske type) settlement contemporary with Linear Pottery culture. After J. Makkay, 'The Late Neolithic Turdaş group of signs', *Alba Regia* (Székesfehérvár 1969): I, *2,3*.

45 Dishes from the Gumelniţa layer of the Tangîru mound, locality 2, lower Danube, Romania. Diam. 16.5 cm. and 17.2 cm. Painted with graphite. Excavation by D. Berciu, 1959. NAM Bucharest. D. Berciu, *Tangiru* (1959): Fig. 8; and *Contribuţii*: 434, Fig. 211.

46 Signs incised on inside and outside of Bylany and other Linear Pottery dishes and jars in Czechoslovakia. After B. Soudský–I. Pavlů, 'Interpretation historique de l'ornement linéaire', *Památky Archeologické*, LVII–1 (1966): 91–125.

47 Terracotta figurine with a flat crown bearing a quartered incised design. Arms are reduced to stumps and legs to a pointed cone. H. 4.5 cm. Fine reddish-brown fabric.

Found in the inside of a clay silo dug in the earth. Medvednjak at Smederevska Palanka, southeast of Belgrade. Excavated 1969 by R. Milošević of the Naroden Muzej in Smederevska Palanka. Housed in this museum, Inv. M 23. Courtesy of the Smederevska Palanka Naroden Muzej.

48 Terracotta stamp with incised quartered design. Ruse, northern Bulgaria. Gumelniţa complex. After Georgiev-Angelov, *Ruse*: Fig. 48, *3*.

49 Terracotta miniature horns of consecration. *1*, *2*, from the Ruse mound on the Danube in northern Bulgaria. After G. Georgiev and N. Angelov, *Izvestija*, XXI (1957): 90, Fig. 50, *4*, *5*. *3*, Vinča, after J. Korošec, *Acta et Dissertationes* II (1962, Zagreb): Pl. XXXIX, *2*.

50 Cucuteni vase with profile indicated (left side) (a) and exploded drawing of the decoration (b). Cucuteni A phase from the settlement of Hăbăşeşti, northern Moldavia. After V. Dumitrescu, *Hăbăşeşti* (1954): 289, Pl. LXVII.

51 Decorative motifs on Cucuteni B vases from Sipintsi on River Prut, 15 km. northwest of Chernovitsi (Czernowitz), Bukovina. Excavated at the end of the nineteenth century by J. Szombathy *et al.*

52 Terracotta cult vessel. Porodin. Reconstructed. After Grbić, *Porodin* (1960): Pl. XXVIII: 4.

53 Classical Cucuteni vase and exploded drawing of decoration from Vladimirovka, Southern Bug Valley, western Ukraine. 1927–28 excavations by B. Bezvenglinski. After T. S. Passek, *Céramique tripolienne*: Pl. XXI.

54 Two dishes with black-on-red painted decoration from Tomashevka, northeast of Uman, western Ukraine. Late Cucuteni (Tripolye C). Excavated 1924–27 by P. P. Kurinny. *1*, 1:10; *2*, 1:5. After T. S. Passek, *Céramique tripolienne*: Pl. XXXIII.

55 Gumelniţa vase from Tangîru, southern Romania. H. 10.8 cm. Graphite-painted. Excavation by D. Berciu, NAM Bucharest. Publ. Berciu, *Contribuţii*: 441, Fig. 202.

56, 57 Painted geometric designs on Late Cucuteni vases from Sipintsi. After Kandyba, *Schipenitz* (1946).

58 Exploded drawing of decoration on a vase from Dimbul Morii, a settlement of Cucuteni A–B phase at Cucuteni in northern Moldavia. Excavated 1909–10 by R. R. Schmidt and from 1961 on by M. Petrescu-Dîmboviţa. Historical Museum of Moldavia, Iaşi. Publ. by M. Petrescu-Dîmboviţa, *Cucuteni* (1966): Fig. 36.

59 *Askos* from the Early Vinča layer of the Anza site between Sv. Nikole and Štip, eastern Macedonia, Yugoslavia. Grey fabric. Burnished dark grey or black. H. approx. 60 cm. Lower part reconstructed. Naroden Muzej, Štip. Excavation by M. Gimbutas Publ. 1972 and 1976.

60 Vase with bird and egg design. Knossos, temple repository. After Evans, *Palace of Minos*, Vol. I: Fig. 405, *d*.

61 Vase with bird design. Phylakopi III, Melos. After Evans, *Palace of Minos*, Vol. I: Fig. 405, *f*.

62 Hollow anthropomorphic-ornithomorphic terracotta figurine. Starčevo complex. Cylindrical head broken off. Spiraliform channelling around the buttock-shaped posterior. Fine light-brown fabric. H. 7.5 cm. Excavation by S. Karmanski, at Donja Branjevina near Deronj. Archaeological section, Museum at Odžaci, northern Yugoslavia. Publ. by S. Karmanski, *Žrtvenici, statuete i amuleti sa lokaliteta donja Branjevina kod Deronja*, (Odžaci 1968): Fig. 1.

63 Terracotta figurine from Karanovo I deposit at the tell of Čavdar, *c.* 60 km., east of Sofia in central Bulgaria. The figurine is flat in front, has a broad and high neck, pinched nose and horizontally incised eyes. Buttocks were probably formed around a bird's egg. Stands on a cylindrical base. Excavated 1970 by R. Katinčarov. Archaeological Museum of the Bulgarian Academy of Sciences, Sofia.

64 Neolithic terracotta figurines with exaggerated buttocks from: *1*, Lepenski Vir, northern Yugoslavia, Starčevo complex;

2, Crete; *3*, Karanovo I at Stara Zagora, central Bulgaria. *1*, after D. Srejović, *Lepenski Vir* (1969): Fig. 43; *2*, after P. Ucko, *Anthropomorphic figurines* (1968): No. 55; *3*, after G. Georgiev, 'Kulturgruppen der Jungstein- und der Kupferzeit in der Ebene von Thrazien', *L'Europe à la fin de l'âge de la pierre*, Prague (1961), Pl. XXXII, 2.

65 Upper part of a cult vase on the neck of which the flattened mask of a Bird Goddess is portrayed in relief, from Sultana at Olteniţa, lower Danube, southwestern Romania. Accidentally discovered in 1957. H. 18.18 cm. Reddish-brown clay. Fine fabric with some admixture of mica and chalk. The original shape of the vessel was roughly biconical. The neck is graphite-painted with 'rain torrent' and 'spiral snake' motifs in negative design. The goddess' arms indicated in relief on the shoulders. Olteniţa Museum. Publ. by S. Marinescu-Bîlcu and B. Ionescu, *Catalogul sculpturilor eneolitice din.* Museul raional Olteniţa (1968).

66, 67 Pots from Tomashevka and Staraja Buda, upper Siniukha Valley, Late Cucuteni (Tripolye) sites in the western Ukraine. After Passek, *Céramique tripolienne*.

68 Decorative motifs on Cucuteni B (Late Tripolye) vases, painted in black. Sipintsi (Schipenitz), Bukovina, the upper Dniester Valley. After Kandyba, *Schipenitz*.

69 Designs painted in dark-brown on orange on a footed vase from the Neolithic settlement of Anza, central Macedonia. Anza III ('geometric' phase) which equates with Late Starčevo in central and northern Yugoslavia. Author's excavation of 1970. Publ. M. Gimbutas, 'Excavation at Anza, Macedonia', *Archaeology*, 25, 2, 1972; 1976.

70 Beaker from Tsangli, Thessaly. After K. Grundmann, 'Figürliche Darstellungen in der neolithischen Keramik Nord und Mit-telgriechenlands', *Jahrbuch des Deutschen Archäologischen Instituts*, 28 (1953): Abb. 28.

71 Designs painted in black on a red background on Late Starčevo vases from Gornja Tuzla, Bosnia, Starčevo at Belgrade and Vinkovci at Vukovar. Based on: S. Dimi-trijević, *Starčevačka Kultura u Slavonsko-srijemskom prostoru*, Vukovar, 1969.

72 Neolithic clay stamp seals: *1*, Starčevo culture from Grabovac, southern Yugoslavia. Publ. in *Arheološki Pregled*, 9, Pl. I; *2*, *3*, *5*, Karanovo I culture from Čavdar, 60 km. east of Sofia, Bulgaria, courtesy G. Georgiev, Archaeological Museum in Sofia; *4*, Rug Bair at Sveti Nikole, eastern Macedonia, Yugoslavia. Author's excavation (UCLA and Štip Museum) 1970, Archaeological Museum of Štip.

73 Terracotta lid from Early Vinča settlement at Parţa, district of Timişoara, western Romania. H. approx. 20 cm. Muzeul Banatului, Timişoara. Courtesy of this Museum.

74 Fragment of a terracotta lid with eyes, beak, incised chevrons and 'water streams'. Fine fabric, coloured red. H. 13.5 cm., W. 11 cm. Radacje, Malča near Niš, southern Yugoslavia. Early Vinča settlement, excavated from 1956 onwards by D. Krstić. National Museum of Niš, Inv. No. 4511. Publ. in: *Les civilisations préhistoriques de la Morava et de la Serbie orientale*. National Museum Niš, Catalogue of 1971 exhibit, No. 76.

75, 76 Terracotta figurines from the Sitagroi mound, Drama Plain, northeastern Greece. Sitagroi III. East Balkan civilization, Chalcolithic. M. Gimbutas (UCLA)–A. C. Renfrew (Sheffield Univ.) excavation 1968. Philipi Museum.

77 Fragment of a terracotta figurine: head of Bird Goddess incised with chevrons and parallel lines on top. Lozenge-shaped eyes. All incisions white-encrusted. H. 3.5 cm. Fine dark-grey fabric. Rug-Bair at Sveti Nikole, central Macedonia, Yugoslavia. 1960 excavations, Archaeological Museum of Skopje, Inv. No. 90. Publ. by National Naroden Museum in Štip: *Les civilisations préhistoriques de la Macedoine*, Catalogue of the exhibit 1971, No. 71.

78 Terracotta figurine probably part of a small cult vessel. Grey fabric. H. 5.3 cm. Incised, white-encrusted. Found 8.5 m. deep in the Vinča site. Early Vinča. Vasić's excavation.

NM Belgrade. Vasić, *Vinča*, II: 159, Fig. 330.

79 Terracotta double-headed stand vertically perforated, from the Early Vinča settlement at Crnokalačka Bara near Ražanj, south-eastern Yugoslavia. H. 5 cm. Light-brown fabric. Polished. Shows contours of a mask. White-encrusted incisions. Kruševac Museum excavations 1959–60. Tasić-Tomić, *Crnokalačka Bara*: Pl. XIV.

80 Terracotta seal from Predionica, Priština. Diam. 6.9 cm. Brick-red, fine fabric. 1955 excavations of Priština and NM Belgrade. National Museum Priština, Kosovo Metohije, Yugoslavia. R. Galović, *Predionica*: Pl. 79: *1, 2*.

81 Terracotta lid with anthropomorphic features and incisions. H. approx. 20 cm. Fine fabric, grey in colour. Early Vinča settlement at Parţa, south of Timişoara, western Romania. Approx. 1:2. Museul Banatului, Timişoara.

82 Terracotta head of a Classical Vinča figurine decorated with incised and white encrusted meanders and parallel lines. H. 10:0 cm. Kremenjak at Potporanj, south of Vršac, northeastern Yugoslavia. Excavated 1957 by R. Rašajski of the National (Narodni) Museum of Vršac, Inv. No. 81223. Publ. in *Praistorijska nalazišta Vojvodine*, Catalogue of the exhibit in Novi Sad, 1971: No. 7.

83 Upper part of crude terracotta figurine of grey fabric, showing masked head tilted upwards. Large meander incised over neck, mask, arm stumps and chest. Potporanj at Vršac. Early Vinča settlement. Vršac museum excavation. Courtesy of this Museum.

84 Terracotta figurine of a bird with meander incised on the back and wings. Starting below the beak, a hole runs through to the back. Found 6.2 m. deep in Vinča mound. Classical Vinča. H. 3.8 cm. Grey fabric. Vasić's excavation. BU Collection, 614 (1279). Vasić, *Vinča*, III: Pl. CXXXI, Fig. 614.

85 Stylized Early Vinča terracotta figurine with incised eyes, meanders and necklaces. Light-brown fabric. H. 4.2 cm. Z. Torma

Collection from Turdaş, Mureş River valley, western Romania. Archaeological Museum of the Institute of History, Cluj, M. Roska, *Torma Coll.*: Pl. CXXXIX: *4*.

86 Fragment of cylindrical terracotta figurine. Light-brown fabric. Vinča site at Agino Brdo, Grodska, near Belgrade. Belgrade City Museum, Inv. 3829. Courtesy of this Museum.

87 Terracotta figurine from Vinča. Bottom part of a female figure on a throne. H. 6.5 cm. Broken off at waist. Vasić's excavation. NM Belgrade, Inv. 9232.

88 Terracotta lid decorated with design of meanders, chevrons and parallel lines; white-encrusted incisions. Lower part broken off. H. 9 cm. Fine grey fabric. Early Vinča. Aiud, Transylvania. Courtesy of History Museum, Cluj.

89 Ellipsoid plaque with a flat base. Meander design surrounded by chevrons and semi-circles. L. 15.5 cm., W. 9.1 cm. Light-brown fabric. One end reconstructed. Vinča settlement at Banjica near Belgrade. Excavation of Belgrade City Museum by J. Todorović. Belgrade City Museum, Inv. 1944.6. Publ. J. Todorović–A Cermanović, *Banjica*: Pl. XIII: *5*.

90 Clay tablet with a labyrinth design (Cn 1287.v) from Pylos, western Greece. After L. J. D. Richardson, 'The labyrinth'. In Palmer, Chadwick, eds. *Cambridge Colloquium on Mycenaean studies* (1966): 286.

91 Clay model of a temple dedicated to the Bird Goddess. Excised, white-encrusted meander pattern over entire front part. Rectangular gate in centre has a polished surface. Necklaces indicated in relief. H. with the head (not preserved) about 38 cm., W. 28 cm. Vădastra, dist. of Corabia, southeast of Oltenia, Romania. Publ. C. N. Mateesco, 'Un maestru al desenului arheologic Dionisie pecuraru', *Studii şi cercetări de Istoria Arte*, Seria Arta Plastica, XVII, 2 (1970): Fig. 2.

92 Details of vase decoration and a decorated vase from Traian (Dealul Fintînilor), Cu-

275

cuteni A–B layer of the settlement in northern Moldavia, northeastern Romania. After Hortensia Dumitrescu, *Dacia*, N.S. IV (1960): 34, Fig. 2.

93 Upper Palaeolithic figurines of bone with engraved meanders and chevrons from Mezin on the River Desna, western Ukraine. After A. Salmony, 'Some Palaeolithic ivory carving from Mezine', *Artibus Asiae*, 12, No. 1/2 (1949): 107, Figs. 1 and 2; and I. G. Shovkopljas *Mezinskaja stojanka*, Kiev (1965), Pl. 48.

94 Proto-Sesklo terracotta figurine in form of a bird-phallus hybrid. Hole on top. Bird-like wings and tail indicated. Broken at bottom. Light-brown fabric. H. 10 cm. Tsangli, Thessaly. Excavated and published by A. J. B. Wace and M. S. Thompson, *Prehistoric Thessaly* (1912). Archaeological Museum in Volos, Thessaly.

95 Large vase from Anza, central Macedonia, Yugoslavia. Anza IV period, Early Vinča. H. 92 cm. The pithos with bird's face indicated on the neck (24 cm. high) was discovered broken into many small fragments. The body of the vase except for the bottom part is decorated with bands painted alternately in cream and red. A red band slants down on either side of the beak. Necklace with two pendants at the ends shown in relief. UCLA (author's) and Štip Naroden Museum excavation of 1970. Housed (unreconstructed) in Naroden Muzej, Štip. Publ. M. Gimbutas 'Excavations at Anza, Macedonia', *Archaeology*, 25, 2, 1972. Also 1976.

96 Terracotta figurine of a woman seated on a tabouret holding a baby. Head broken off. Painted in brown on cream in horizontal, vertical and spiral bands. Dimini period at Sesklo near Volos, Thessaly. Excavated and published by Tsountas, 1908. Athens National Museum: 36, Inv. 5937. Zervos, *Naissance*, Vol. II: 305, Fig. 395.

97 Painted figure of a Snake Goddess on the leg of an altar-table from Phaistos, southern Crete. H. 18 cm. Proto-palatial period. Heraklion, Archaeological Museum, Gallery III, Case 42, No. 10576.

98, 99 Terracotta figurines from Hacılar, Konya Plain, central Anatolia. *98*, H. (reconstructed) 10.2 cm.; *99*, 9.2 cm. After J. Mellaart, 'Excavation at Hacılar', *Anatolian Studies*, XI (1961): Figs. 11 and 14.

100 Cycladic figurine of white marble with a massive phallus-shaped head. Protruding nose, but no eyes. Breasts slightly indicated and held by hands. Almost conical legs. Rounded, well proportioned buttocks. H. 12.9 cm. After Marie Luise and Hans Erlenmeyer, 'Von der frühen Bildkunst der Kykladen', *Antike Kunst*, VIII, 2 (1965): Pl. 18: 6 and 7.

101 Fragments of seated marble figurine with folded arms from the settlement of Ruse, northern Bulgaria. Gumelniţa complex (Karanovo VI). Excavated between 1948 and 1953. Publ. by Georgiev-Angelov, 107, Fig. 64.

102 Marble figure with folded arms from near the village of Blagoevo, region of Razgrad, Bulgaria. H. approx. 32 cm. Found in fragments in the area of the settlement mound. Oval head with nose, eyes (pupils shown with little pits), and ears. The ears have four perforations each, to which copper earrings were attached. Other features include an arm-band on the right arm, a small pit for the navel, a pubic triangle, depressions for *trigonum lumbale* on the buttocks and back of the knees. Traces of red colouring on the eyes and ears. After cutting with flint, the figure was smoothed with sandstone, and the pits were made with a bone tool, sand and water. Publ. by G. Georgiev, 'Eine Marmorstatuette aus Blagoevo, Bezirk Razgrad'. *Izvestija*, 19 (1955), 11–13.

103 Flat figurines of bone from the settlement of Ruse on the lower Danube, northern Bulgaria. Discovered in the settlement area. Excavations of 1950–53 by Georgiev-Angelov, *Ruse*.

104 Inventory from a single grave in the cemetery of Vykhvatintsi, Soviet Moldavia. See ref. 149, 150 (half-tone plates).

105 Anthropomorphic vase, known as 'Goddess of Vidra', from the Gumelniţa settlement at Vidra, district of Giurgiu south of Bucharest, lower Danube basin. The vase is

42.5 cm. high and its lid (not recovered) probably portrayed the Goddess' face. A gold pendant was found on her chest between the breasts. Gumelniţa B (or Gumelniţa III in D. Berciu's classification). Incised lines, circles and lozenges encrusted with white colour. D. Rosetti's 1934 excavation. Publ. Rosetti, *Vidra; Idem*, 'Steinkupferzeitliche Plastik aus einem Wohnhügel bei Bucharest', *IPEK*, 12. Bucharest City Museum.

106 Pottery dish from Pietrele, county Giurgiu, district of Ilfov, area of Bucharest. Graphite-painted. Diam. 46.3 cm. Gumelniţa complex. East Balkan civilization. Excavated 1943–48 by D. Berciu. NAM Bucharest. Publ. by D. Berciu in *Materiale Cercetări Arheol.* 2 (1956): Fig. 42.

107 Pottery dish from Petreni, western Ukraine. Painted in chocolate-brown on ochre-red. Diam. 51 cm. After Passek, *Céramique tripolienne*.

108 Double-egg (or buttock)-shaped pottery bowl. Pietrele. Gumelniţa complex. Diam. 15.8 cm. Graphite painted on outside. Source as *106*.

109, 110 Figurines with the upper part broken off, showing double-eggs in the inside of the belly. Novye Ruseshty I settlement. Classical Cucuteni (Tripolye). After V. I. Markevich, 'Mnogoslojnoe poselenie Novye Ruseshty I', *KSIIMK*, 123 (1970): 64.

111 Anthropomorphic vase in shape of female buttocks with two small lugs on top. Painted white on red. H. 10.1 cm. Cucuteni A phase. Izvoare at Piatra Neamţ, district of Bacău, northeastern Romania. Excavations of the Institute of Archaeology of the Academy of Sciences, Bucharest, by R. Vulpe 1936–48. NAM Bucharest. Publ. Vulpe, *Izvoare*: Figs. 106, 107.

112 Black-on-red painted design on inside of a bowl. Koszyłowce, western Ukraine. Late Cucuteni (Cucuteni B) period. After Rybakov, *Cosmogony*: Fig. 24.

113 Exploded drawings of shoulder decoration motifs on large amphoras from the Cucuteni B settlement of Sipintsi (Schipenitz),

northwest of Chernovitsi, Bucovina in western Ukraine. After Kandyba, *Schipenitz*: 57, Figs. 41 and 42.

114–116 Late Minoan decorative drawings. After Evans, *Palace of Minos*. *114*: Vol. II, b, Fig. 456; *115*: Vol. IV, 1, Fig. 291; *116*: Vol. II, b, Fig. 368.

117 Vessel in the shape of a dog. H. 8.2 cm. Found 7.8 m. deep at the Vinča site. Shoulders have perforations for a string or chord to be drawn through. Vasić's excavation. BU Collection. Publ. by Vasić, *Vinča*, II: Pl. XCI, 347.

118 Lid handle of a pot in the shape of a masked dog. H. 4.5 cm., L. 5 cm. Discovered during the excavation of 1952–53 in Goljamata Mogila at Gorni Pasarel, central Bulgaria, together with graphite-painted pottery. Flat face with a pronounced conical nose – obviously representing a mask. Notches on the back and on the front legs. East Balkan Karanovo VI. Excavation of the Institute of Archaeology of the Bulgarian Academy of Sciences, carried out by N. Petkov. Publ. N. Petkov, 'Zhivotinski dekorativen element v eneolitnata keramika pri Gorni Pasarel', *Izvestija*, XXI (1957): 291–94.

119 Lid of a steatite pyxis with a handle on top in the form of a dog. From Mochlos, Early Minoan II settlement, eastern Crete. Reproduced from R. Dussaud, *Les civilisations préhelléniques dans le bassin de la mer Egée* (Paris 1914, 2nd ed.): 38, Fig. 20.

120 Stylized dog in a menacing attitude, painted in black on a very large, ochre-red vase of Cucuteni B period from the settlement of Varvarovka near Kishenev, Soviet Moldavia. Excavated 1967 by V. I. Markevich. Archaeological Museum of the Institute of History of the Academy of Sciences of the Moldavian S.R., Kishenev.

121 Black-on-red painted vase from Krutoborodintsi, western Ukraine. Late Cucuteni civilization. Reproduced from Rybakov, *Cosmogony* (1965).

122 Painted vase from Valea Lupului, northern Moldavia, Romania. H. 52.8 cm. Black and red on cream background. Cucuteni B

period. After M. Petrescu-Dîmboviţa, *SCIV*, VI: 704, Fig. 14, *1*.

123 Potsherds with representations of a tree in association with dogs, from Sipintsi, 15 km. northwest of Chernovitsi, Bukovina. After Kandyba, *Schipenitz*: 75.

124 Patterns on large conical bowls, between 30 and 50 cm. in diameter, from Cucuteni B settlements in the western Ukraine. Black or chocolate-brown painted on ochre red. *1, 2, 4, 5, 7* after Passek, *La céramique tripolienne* (1935): VII; *3, 6, 8* after Kandyba, *Schipenitz*: 84–87.

125 Orange-coloured bowl shaped like a modern salad bowl, with abstract design on inside. Dog, inner crescents and leaves around the edge painted red, rest of design black. Diam. 41 cm. Bilcze Zlote, south of Tarnopol in western Ukraine. Late Cucuteni. Courtesy of Archaeological Museum, Cracow.

126 Oval containers with stylized zoomorphic design. Sipintsi, Late Cucuteni site between the upper Prut and upper Dniester. Reproduced from Kandyba, *Schipenitz*: 89, Figs. 123 and 124.

127 Terracotta figurine from Hacılar, Konya Plain, central Anatolia, north of Kizilkaya. L. 7 cm. Found in House Q5 of the Late Neolithic village (early sixth millennium BC). Hacılar VI period. After J. Mellaart, 'Excavations at Hacılar', *Anatolian Studies*, XI (1961): 59, Fig. 20.

128 Female figure in relief on a potsherd of a large vase of Starčevo type from Sarvaš, Vlastelinski brijeg, district of Osijek, River Drava basin, northwestern Yugoslavia. Found in the lowest layer of this stratified site known for its Lengyel and Vučedol settlements above the Starčevo, during R. R. Schmidt's excavation of 1942–43. Osijek Museum. Publ. by R. R. Schmidt, *Die Burg Vučedol* (Zagreb 1945). Drawing after author's photograph in 1968.

129 Shrine from Çatal Hüyük, Konya Plain, central Anatolia. Reconstruction by J. Mellaart, Level VI A, showing restored north and west walls. C14 dates with half-life of 5730 from this level range from 5850 ± 94 to 5781 ± 96. After Mellaart, *Çatal*: 127, Fig. 40.

130 Figure incised on a globular vase from the settlement at Borsod, Bükk culture. Miskolc, Hermann Otto Museum. Excavation by A. Leszik, J. Hillebrand and F. Tompa 1926–48. F. Tompa, *Die Bandkeramik in Ungarn*, Budapest (1929): Pl. XVIII, 5.

131 Anthropomorphic figure engraved on a sherd from the base of a dish of early Linear Pottery culture. Settlement of Kolešovice, district of Rakovnik, Bohemia, Czechoslovakia. After H. Quitta, *Forschungen zur Vor- und Frühgeschichte*, Leipzig (1957), 2, 81. 2. Pot from the Linear Pottery settlement of Prague-Bubenec, after A. Stocký, *La Bohême Préhistorique*, I, *L'âge de Pierre*, Prague (1929): 183.

132 Painted amphora. H. 12.5 cm. First Palace of Phaistos, southern Crete. Middle Minoan I. After Zervos, *Crète*: Fig. 346.

133 Bronze toad. L. 8.2 cm. Peloponnese. Exact provenience not known, but Corinth is highly probable. Inscription Αμων Σωνόον Βοασοvι, as reconstructed by Fränkel, is connected with the name of the worshipper. Dated 'not later than the early part of the fifth century BC'. Berlin, Museum of the Archaeological Institute. After M. Fränkel, 'Geweihter Frosch', *Jahrbuch des Kaiserlich Deutschen Archäologischen Instituts*, Bd. I (1887): 48–53.

134 Terracotta figurine of a toad. A face, breasts and vulva are indicated on the underside. Found in a cremation grave in the cemetery of Maissau, lower Austria. After Gulder, *Maissau*: 101, Abb. 56, 2.

135 Amber toad from Vetulonia, discovered by I. Falchi in 1894. L. 3.5 cm. After Gulder, *Maissau*: 53. Reproduced from I. Falchi, *Not. d. scavi* 1895: 316, Fig. 33.

136 Ivory figurines from the sanctuary at Orthia at Sparta. After R. M. Dawkins, 'Excavation at Sparta', *Annual of the British School at Athens*, No. XIII, Session 1906–7, and H. J. Rose, 'The Sanctuary of Artemis Orthia at Sparta', *JHS* 1906–10: Pl. CXV.

137 Modern 'folk' toads made of wax from the Austrian Alpine region. *1, 2*, after R. Kriss 'Die Opferkröte', *Bayerischer Heimatschutz* (1930): 107; *3*, after K. Spiess, 'Die Kröte, ein Bild der Gebärmutter', *Mitra* (1914): 209.

138 Terracotta hedgehog from Cāscioarele, Gumelniţa layer, southern Romania. H. 6.1 cm. NM Bucharest. Publ. Dumitrescu, *L'art Roumanie*: Pl. 109.

139 Onyx gem from Knossos, *c.* 1500 BC. Reproduced from Zervos, *Crète*: Fig. 629.

140 Design on one face of three-sided bead seal from Kasteli Pedeada, southeast of Knossos, Crete. After Evans, *Palace of Minos*, vol. III: R4, Fig. 93 A, *d*.

141 Design on a painted Boeotian amphora. After *Efemeris Archeol.* (1892): Pl. 10, *1*.

142 Masked figure painted in cherry-red on white Proto-Sesklo vase (shown in black; other similar figures reconstructed). Lower layer of the Otzaki Magula, 8 km. north of Larissa, Thessaly. Excavated 1954 by Vladimir Milojčić. Larissa Museum. Publ. by V. Milojčić, 'Ausgrabungen in Thessalien', *Neue deutsche Ausgrabungen in Mittelmeergebeit und in Vorderen Orient*: 226, 228–29, Abb. 2. Typological relationships to other Proto-Sesklo sites (Argissa, Nea Nikomedeia) place the Proto-Sesklo phase at Otzaki within the period of 6500 – 6300 BC.

143 Relief of a schematized Bee Goddess on a Linear Danubian potsherd from Holašovice. After V. Karger. Publ. by Gulder, *Maissau*.

144 Potsherd with a relief portraying a figure with upraised arms and outspread legs flanking a triangular protuberance. Classical Cucuteni (Cucuteni A₂ phase) settlement of Truşeşti-Tuguieta, northern Moldavia, Romania. Publ. by M. Petrescu-Dîmboviţa, 'Einige Probleme der Cucuteni-Kultur im Lichte der neuen archäologischen Grabungen', *Študijne Zvesti*, No. 17 (1969): 368.

145 A Mycenaean gem, after G. E. Mylonas, *Mycenae and the Mycenaean age* (1966): 125, No. 27.

146 Gold ring from a grave at Isopata, north of Knossos. Diam. 2.6 cm. Redrawn from the photograph in C. Zervos, *Crète*: Fig. 632.

147, 148 Mycenaean gold chrysalis and Minoan seal impression. Reproduced from Arthur Evans, 'The Ring of Nestor', *JHS*, XLV, Part I (1925): Figs. 45, 47.

149 Representation, on a mould, of goddess holding butterflies (double-axes). After Zervos, *Crète*: 451, Fig. 746.

150 Butterfly signs engraved on inside and outside of jars and dishes from the Linear Pottery sites of Bylany and elsewhere in Bohemia, Czechoslovakia. After B. Soudský and I. Pavlů, 'Interprétation historique de l'ornement linéaire', *Památky Archeologické*, LVII, 1 (1966): 91–125.

151 Mycenaean krater from Salamis, Cyprus (Enkomi). British Museum. First published by Arthur Evans in *JHS*, XXI (1901): 107, Fig. 3.

152 Detail of a Middle Minoan III vase from Knossos, painted with a zone of double-axes. After Zervos, *Crète*: 304, Fig. 440.

153 Painted motif on a Late Minoan I vase from Mochlos. After A. B. Cook, *Zeus*, vol. II, 1: 527, Fig. 395 (republished from G. B. G[ordon], 'The double-axe and some other symbols', University of Pennsylvania: *The Museum Journal* 1916, VII, 48: Fig. 38).

154 Terracotta rattles containing clay balls, in shape of a pregnant goddess, found in a grave. The rattles are perforated through the neck. Painted black on red. Cucuteni B period. Vykhvatintsi cemetery in Soviet Moldavia, child's grave No. 13. After T. S. Passek, *KSIIMK*, 56 (1954): 94, 95.

155 Broken-off lower portion of terracotta figurine, with a clay ball within the belly. Novye Ruseshty I settlement near Kishenev, upper Dniester region, Soviet Moldavia. After A. P. Kusurgasheva, 'Anthropomorfnaja plastika iz poselenija Novye Ruseshty', *KSIIMK*, 123 (1970): Fig. 74.

156 Terracotta figurines with grain impressions. Luka-Vrublevetskaja, Proto-Cucuteni (Early Tripolye) settlement in Dniester

valley. After Bibikov, Luka-Vrublevetska-ja, *MIA*, 38 (1958): Pls. 77, 78, 82.

157 Lower part of terracotta figurine from Luka Vrublevetskaja, Proto-Cucuteni (Early Tripolye) site, western Ukraine. H. 8 cm. Light-brown fabric, white-filled incisions. Quadripartite lozenge with a dot in each section incised above belly, snake spirals on buttocks. Tapering legs totally schematized and incised with horizontal lines. Museum of Ethnology, Leningrad. Publ. Bibikov, *MIA*, 38 (1958): 400, Pl. 108.

158 Schematic terracotta figurine from Vidra, southern Romania. Gumelniţa A phase. Bucharest City Museum. After D. Rosetti, 'Steinkupferzeitliche Plastik aus einem Wohnhügel bei Bukarest', *IPEK*, 12 (1938): Pl. 12.

159, 160 Schematic terracotta figurines from the Sitagroi mound, Macedonia, Greece. H. approx. 5 cm. Period II of this mound (fifth millennium BC). Light-brown fabric. *159*: SF 3130; *160*: SF 498. Philipi Museum.

161 Terracotta plaque with incised and white-encrusted lozenges and spirals. Vinča settlement at Potporanj (upper layer of this site) near Vršac, northeastern Yugoslavia. 13.4 × 7.9 cm. Narodni Muzej Vršac, Inv. No. 1233. After *Praistorijska nalazišta Vojvodine*, Novi Sad (1971), Fig. 6.

162 Fragment of a terracotta figurine. Red-slipped, and with black-painted design. Period III of Sitagroi tell: Gumelniţa culture. Excavated 1968 by A. C. Renfrew (Sheffield University) – M. Gimbutas (UCLA), Philipi Museum.

163 Fragment of a figurine comprising abdominal area and part of a thigh. Geometrical patterns of white-encrusted incised lines and dots. Gumelniţa A (or I) phase from the Tangîru mound, lower Danube region. Max. dimension 9.4 cm. Excavation by the Institute of Archaeology of the Academy of Sciences of the Romanian P.R. by D. Berciu. NAM Bucharest. After D. Berciu, 'Sur les résultats du controle stratigraphique à Tangiru et à Petru Rareş', *Dacia*, 1959: 65, Fig. 5, 7.

164 Black polished disc with white encrustation.

Diam. approx. 4 cm. Tell of Ploskata Mogila, Zlati trap near Plovdiv, central Bulgaria. Gumelniţa culture. Plovdiv Museum. Publ. P. Detev, *Izvestija*, Series 2, Vol. 18 (1952): 337, Fig. 333.

165 Fragments of terracotta figurines portraying pigs impressed with grain from the Proto-Cucuteni (Early Tripolye) settlement of Luka Vrublevetskaja, upper Dniester basin. After Bibikov, *MIA*, 38 (1958): 406, Fig. 114. Leningrad, Museum of Ethnology of the Academy of Sciences.

166 Phallus-shaped clay artifacts, possibly used as stems for 'wine cups', as reconstructed by Š. Batović. Danilo settlement at Smilčić near Zadar. Excavated 1958 by S. Batović. Archaeological Museum in Zadar. After Š. Batović, 'Problem kulta phallosa u Danilskoj kulturi', *Diadora*, 4 (1968): Fig. 3, Pl. IV, *3*.

167 Cylindrical terracotta figurine with pinched-up nose, incised eyes, and breasts. Incisions around the top. Widening base. H. 5.5 cm. Crnokalačka Bara at Rujište near Ražanj. Found in Starčevo layer of the stratified settlement. Excavated 1959 by R. Galović. NM Belgrade. Publ. R. Galović, 'Die Starčevo-kultur in Jugoslawien', *Die Anfänge des Neolithikums von Orient bis Nordeuropa*, II: Pl. 13, 4.

168 Phallus-shaped terracotta stand with male genitals. Broken at neck and at arm stumps. Pavlovac (locality called 'Čukar'), upper Morava basin, southern Yugoslavia. Early Vinča. H. 5.2 cm. Fine light-grey fabric. NM Belgrade and Archaeological Institute excavation of 1955. NM Belgrade, Inv. No. 14923. Publ. M. and D. Garašanin in *Starinar* (1956–57): 398.

169 Terracotta figurine from the habitation site of Truşeşti-Tuguieta, district of Iaşi, northern Moldavia, Romania. 'Cucuteni A' phase. Light brown fabric. H. 3.2 cm. Excavated 1953 by M. Petrescu-Dîmboviţa and Adrian C. Florescu. Archaeological Museum Iaşi. Publ. A. and M. Florescu, 'Santierul arheologic Truşeşti', *Materiale si Cercetări Arheologice*, VII: 81, 82, Figs. 2 and 3.

170 Stylized bull of red baked clay, burnished and well fired. Probably used as a lamp.

Perforations above each leg and through nose and tail for suspension. Painted black on red. H. 10.6 cm., L. 16.44 cm. Sitagroi mound, Drama Plain, eastern Macedonia, Greece. Period III of Sitagroi. Dikilitash (Gumelniţa) variant of East Balkan civilization. Discovered in 1968 during M. Gimbutas (UCLA)–A. C. Renfrew (Sheffield Univ.) excavations. Philipi Museum, SF 1207.

171 Terracotta figurine of a nude seated 'Thinker' wearing a large mask with six perforations for attachments. Fine brown fabric. H. 7 cm. Vidra, Gumelniţa settlement, lower Danube. 1934 excavation by D. Rosetti. Bucharest City Museum. Publ. V. Rosetti, *IPEK*, 12 (1938): 29–50.

HALF-TONE PLATES

1 Bird Goddess from Achilleion, near Farsala, Thessaly, Greece. H. 6.1 cm. Orange-pink clay, originally white-slipped. Incised 'coffee-bean' eyes. The head is that of a beaked bird but the hair-do is human and made. to resemble a bun. The cylindrical neck damaged during recovery. Excavated 1973 by M. Gimbutas.

2 Terracotta schematized figurine found in the lowest layer of the Vinča mound. Starčevo complex. Hair incised on top of cylindrical upper portion. Fine brown fabric. Excavated 1931 by Vasić. H. 10.6 cm. BU Collection, No. 856. Publ.: Vasić, *Vinča*, II: Pl. 22, Figs. *54a,b*; III: Fig. 36; NM Belgrade *Catalogue* (1968): *44*. Sheffield *Catalogue* (1969): *48*.

3, 4 Early Vinča schematic figurine found 8.4 m. deep in Vinča mound. Vasić's excavations. H. 12.4 cm. Baked clay, pale red. Normal breasts, conical belly, pronounced buttocks. Stumps for arms. Triangular head indicates mask. BU Collection, 885. Publ. Vasić, *Vinča*, I: Pl. XVIII, Fig. 92.

5 Marble figurine from the site of Gradac, near Leskovac, southern Yugoslavia. H. 6.5 cm. Excavated 1909 by Vasić. NM Belgrade, 861. NM Belgrade Catalogue (1955), I: 22, II, Pl. 17, Fig. 5.

6 Bone figurine. No head, globes for arms. Emphasized abdominal area. Legs reduced to a cone. H. 4.8 cm. Discovered in a grave of the cemetery of Cernica – Căldăraru, distr. of Ilfov, near Bucharest, Romania. Early Boian complex. Excavated 1961–67 by Gh. Cantacuzino. NAM, Bucharest. Publ. Gh. Cantacuzino, 'The prehistoric necropolis of Cernica and its place in the neolithic cultures of Romania and of Europe in the light of recent discoveries', *Dacia*, N.S. XIII (1969): 53, Fig. 5, *30*.

7, 8 Terracotta figurine of a seated nude female from Thessaly, assigned by D. R. Theocharis to the Sesklo period. Isolated find. H. 8 cm. Fine light-brown fabric. Three panels of hair indicated in relief. 'Coffee-bean' eyes. Pronounced nose. Pointed buttocks. Archaeological Museum Volos, Thessaly. Publ. D. R. Theocharis, *Bakalakis' Festschrift* (1971).

9 Classical Vinča terracotta figurine with flattened upper, and rounded lower part. Pentagonal (masked) head. Two perforations in each arm stump. From the site of Selevac near Smederevska Palanka, southeast of Belgrade. Fine grey fabric. H. 12 cm. 1969 excavations of NM Belgrade and Smederevska Palanka Museum by R. Galović. National Museum, Smederevska Palanka. Courtesy of this museum.

10 Terracotta squatting figurine with a smooth grey surface. Incisions and punctate design indicate dress. Late Vinča. Found 5.1 m. deep in Vinča mound. H. 7.9 cm. BU Collection, 1197. Vasić, *Vinča*, II: 150, Fig.

313a,b,c; III: Fig. 499; NM Belgrade Catalogue (1968): No. 154.

11, 12 Terracotta figurine of a squatting man. Hands on tightly drawn-up knees. Fafos I at Kosovska Mitrovica. Early Vinča period. H. 6.8 cm. Fine dark-grey fabric. Excavated 1959 by J. Glišić and B. Jovanović. Regional Museum Priština, Inv. F-I-7c-d/2250. NM Belgrade Catalogue (1968): 62; Sheffield Catalogue (1969): 66, Pl. 13.

13, 14 Terracotta figurine from the Cucuteni B period of the Sipintsi (Schipenitz) settlement 15 km. northwest of Chernovitsi in the upper Prut Valley, Bukovina, USSR. Orange-red fabric, polished surface. H. 11 cm. Female body schematically rendered. Perforations for eyes. Head flat at the back, protruding nose, no arms, a cone for legs. Breasts and navel indicated. White-filled incisions for necklaces, belt and fringes in front. On the back, a lung-shaped design, probably symbolic. Excavated 1893 by J. Szombathy et al. Naturhistorisches Museum, Vienna. Publ. O. Kandyba, Schipenitz: 151, Fig. 51.

15 Terracotta figurine. H. 12 cm. Impressed dots form necklaces and hip-belt and border pubic triangle. Arm stumps and hips perforated. Head broken off. Legs shown as a cone. End of skirt indicated by two rows of circles. Fine light-brown fabric. Burnished. Bilcze Zlote. Late Cucuteni settlement, upper Dniester basin. Courtesy Cracow Archaeological Museum.

16 Upper part of a large terracotta figurine. H. 28.7 cm. Fafos II, at Kosovska Mitrovica, Kosovo Metohije, Yugoslavia. Late Vinča. Fine dark-grey fabric. Incisions over mask and body. Eyes and medallion in raised relief. Hands on hips. Excavated 1959 by J. Glišić and B. Jovanović. Regional Museum, Priština, F-II-2B/263. NM Belgrade Catalogue (1968): 97; Sheffield Catalogue: 104.

17 Terracotta figurine, originally seated on a throne (now lost). Orange-red fabric with white-filled incisions. H. 25 cm. Surface find from Bariljevo near Gazimestan, district of Priština, Kosovo Metohije province of Yugoslavia. Late Vinča. First published by N. Slavković-Djurić: Glasnik Muzeja Kosova i Metohije, VII–VIII: Fig. 3. Regional Museum Priština, Ba-SN/1. NM Belgrade Catalogue (1968): 105; Sheffield Catalogue (1969): Pl. 15.

18, 19 Terracotta figurine from Late Vinča settlement of Crnokalačka Bara at Rujište near Ražanj, north of Niš, Yugoslavia. H. c. 14 cm. Head missing. Brown fabric, burnished, white-encrusted incisions indicating dress. Two perforations in each shoulder. Navel indicated by depression. NM Belgrade excavations of 1959 by R. Galović. Courtesy of NM Belgrade.

20 Terracotta seated figurine from Čaršija at Ripen, central Yugoslavia. Fine grey fabric, polished surface. H. 16.1 cm. Head, arms and feet broken off. One side and buttocks damaged. Otherwise well preserved. Breasts, navel, hip-belt, apron, and leg bindings indicated by white-encrusted incisions. Excavated 1906 by Vasić and published by him in Glas Sprske Kraljevske Akademije, LXX: Pl. X and XI, Fig. 14. NM Belgrade, 765. NM Belgrade Catalogue (1968): 141.

21 Lower part of terracotta statuette from Late Vinča settlement of Crnokalačka Bara at Rujište near Ražanj, north of Niš. Light brown fabric with white-encrusted incisions, polished surface. H. 13 cm. NM Belgrade, inv. 20945. R. Galović, Archeološki Pregled (1960).

22 Legs of a large terracotta statuette found 5.1 m. deep in Vinča mound. H. 6.9 cm. Diagonal incisions over calves. Toes indicated by incision. Red paint on toes. Black fabric, smooth, lustrous surface. Vasić's excavation. BU Collection, 4.1213. Publ. Vasić, Vinča, I: Pl. XI, Fig. 36.

23 Upper part of a Late Vinča figurine of a masked man from Pločnik near Prokuplje, Yugoslavia. H. 18 cm. Incised and red-painted bands on chest and neck. Fine dark-grey fabric. Excavated 1927 by M. Grbić. NM Belgrade, 2257. On display. Publ. M. Grbić, Pločnik: 80, Pl. 7.

24, 25 Terracotta figurine of fine dark-grey fabric from Fafos at Kosovska Mitrovica, discovered in layer Ib. Classical Vinča. H. 20

cm. Contours of roughly triangular mask with large nose and plastically modelled eyes clearly indicated. The figure leans forward slightly. Protruding belly and buttocks indicate padded knickers. Knickers and V-necked blouse rendered by incision. Hands broken off. Excavated 1959 by J. Glišić and B. Jovanović. Regional Museum, Priština, F-I-17C/1251. NM Belgrade *Catalogue* (1968): 60; Sheffield *Catalogue* (1969): 64 (misleadingly called a 'woman').

26 Terracotta figurine from the Vinča mound. Grey fabric. Arms broken. Hump on the back. Originally part of a large vessel. Pentagonal mask considerably larger than head. No facial features. Vasić's excavation. BU Collection, 4403. Museum: Kosovska Mitrovica (H1-V0-80). Sheffield *Catalogue* (1969): 178, Pl. 13.

27 Masked head found 5.7 m. deep in Vinča mound. Ears are indicated protruding from below the mask. Dark-red terracotta. Remains of red paint on top of head and over the ears. H. 9.6 cm. Vasić's excavation. BU Collection, 4956. Publ. Vasić, *Vinča*, III: Pl. XXVIII, Fig. 139.

28 Masked head of fine dark-grey fabric on cylindrical neck. Late Vinča. H. 7.7 cm. Surface find during 1955–56 NM Belgrade excavation by R. Galović. Regional Museum, Priština, inv. 162. Publ. R. Galović, *Predionica*: Pl. 16: 1; NM Belgrade (1968): 100; Sheffield *Catalogue* (1969): Pl. 13: 107.

29 Red terracotta head from Crnokalačka Bara at Rujište near Ražanj, north of Niš, southern Yugoslavia. Large semicircular eyes, ridge nose and rows of incisions on the cheeks. Spiraliform ears are cut on the mask. Hair indicated in relief. H. 9 cm. NM Belgrade excavation by R. Galović, 1968. Courtesy of NM Belgrade and the excavator.

30 Neck of pottery vessel of fine brown fabric from Gladnice by the monastery of Gračanica, Kosovo Metohije, Yugoslavia. Starčevo. Large ears at sides of well delineated contours of mask. 'Coffee-bean' eyes. H. 10.4 cm. Excavated 1960 by J. Glišić. Regional Museum, Priština G-2E (1246 a). NM Belgrade *Catalogue* (1968): 26. Publ. Sheffield *Catalogue* (1969): Pl. 5.

31 Terracotta animal head of grey fabric from Vinča site at Gradac, upper Morava Valley. H. 5.5 cm. Excavated 1909 by Vasić. NM Belgrade, inv. 783. B. Stalio: NM Belgrade *Catalogue* (1955), I: 22, II Pl. XVIII, 5.

32 Stylized animal mask of terracotta from Pločnik near Prokuplje. Late Vinča. Fine grey fabric. Semi-globular eyes shielded by brow ridges. Flat cheeks with three radial incisions. Vertical incisions along the upper part of forehead. Excavated 1927 by M. Grbić. NM Belgrade exhibit. Publ. Grbić, *Pločnik*.

33 Large figurine of dark grey fabric, burnished, with pentagonal mask made in a mould. Beaked nose, raised semi-spherical eyes and bow-shaped brow ridges. Depression below nose. Ears and hair indicated. Perforations through shoulders. Navel and hip-belt indicated. Crown of head and nape painted red. Protruding buttocks in imitation of bird's body. H. 30.6 cm. Classical Vinča. Found 6.2 m. (7.445 m.) deep in Vinča mound. Vasić's excavation. BU Collection, No. 999. Publ. Vasić, *Vinča*, II: Pl. LXXIX and LXXX, Fig. 301a–d; III: r. 33, Fig. 203; D. Srejović, 1965: Pl. 18, 3.

34 Cylindrical model of a masked goddess, originally attached to the roof of a sanctuary. Hollow inside. H. 20.8 cm. Fine brown fabric. Porodin mound near Bitola, southern Yugoslavia. Radiocarbon date from Porodin: 5300 BC. True age: end of the seventh millennium BC. Excavation by M. Grbić, et al., 1953. Archaeological Museum Bitola, 68. Publ. Grbić, *Porodin*; NM Belgrade *Catalogue* (1968): 19.

35 Terracotta masked and crowned head on a cylindrical neck from the Porodin mound near Bitola, southern Yugoslavia. Excavated 1953–54 by M. Grbić, et al. Archaeological Museum, Bitola. Publ. Grbić, *Porodin*, Pl. XXX: 2.

36 Terracotta masked Vinča head, black polished with white-filled incisions. Red-painted at corners and centre. Perforations at upper corners. Medvednjak near Smederevska Palanka, southeast of Belgrade. Excavation of NM Belgrade by R. Galović 1969. Smederevska Palanka Museum.

37 Head and shoulders of dark-grey burnished terracotta figurine with perforations through mask and shoulders from Crnokalačka Bara near Ražanj, north of Niš, southern Yugoslavia. Late Vinča. H. 10 cm. Excavation by R. Galović, 1959. NM Belgrade, inv. 16009. R. Galović, *Arkheološki Pregled* 2 (1960): 24; NM Belgrade *Catalogue* (1968): 124; Sheffield *Catalogue* (1969): Pl. 17, 131.

38 Ornamented Vinča mask from Predionica at Priština, Kosovo Metohije, southern Yugoslavia. Fine dark-grey fabric, burnished. H. 10 cm. Excavated 1955–56 by R. Galović sponsored by Kosovo Metohije Museum in Priština and NM Belgrade. Regional Museum Priština (157). Publ. R. Galović, *Predionica*: Pl. 16.

39 Monumental Vinča head with almond-shaped eyes from Predionica, near Priština. White-encrusted incisions above and below eyes. Fine light-brown fabric, burnished. H. 17.5 cm., W. 15 cm. Surface find. Kosovo Metohije Regional Museum Priština (158). Publ. Galović, *Predionica*: Pl. 1.

40 Clay model of a sanctuary from Vădastra (II), southeastern Oltenia, 14 km. northwest of Corabia, above the Danube. H. approx. 15 cm. Grey fabric deeply encrusted with white. Ram and bull heads on roofs of two temples painted red. 1959 excavation by Corneliu N. Mateesco. NAM Bucharest. Publ. CN. Mateesco: 'Sapaturi arheologice la Vădastra', *Materiale și Cercetări Arheologice* VIII (1962): 189, Fig. 2; *Idem. Acta VI Intern Congress of Pre- and Protohistoric Sciences*, Rome (1962).

41 Clay model of a sanctuary with T-shaped entrance and hole for a chimney-shaped figurine of the type shown in Pl. 34. Goddess' necklace indicated in relief. Protuberances at each corner of roof. H. 17.1 cm., L. 25.6 cm. Fine dark-brown polished surface. Porodin mound near Bitola, southern Yugoslavia. Radiocarbon date for Porodin (grain sample) 5300 BC (Berlin Lab.). Excavated 1953 by M. Grbić, *et al.* Bitola Arch. Museum, inv. 1, Publ. Grbić, *Porodin*: Pl. XXXIV, *1*; NM Belgrade *Catalogue* (1968): 10; Sheffield *Catalogue* (1969): *11*.

42 Baked clay model of edifice, coloured red, with originally well polished surface. H. 24.2 cm., L. (max.) 51 cm., W. 13 cm. Temples on top are approx. 8 cm. wide and 9 cm. high, forming a superstructure 49.8 cm. long. Discovered at Căscioarele, an island settlement of the Gumelnița culture, 20 km. west of Oltenița north of the lower Danube in southern Romania by Hortensia and Vladimir Dumitrescu. H. Dumitrescu, 'Un modèle de sanctuaire découvert dans la station énéolithique de Căscioarele', *Dacia*, N.S. XII (1968): 381–94.

43–45 Terracotta altarpieces from Trușești, Classical Cucuteni settlement in the district of Botoșani, northern Moldavia, excavated 1951–61 by M. Petrescu-Dîmbovița. 43: H. approx. 150 cm.; 44: H. 65 cm.; 45: 73 × 70 cm. NAM Bucharest. Publ. Petrescu-Dîmbovița, *Trușești*: 172–86.

46, 47 Seated masked male figure holding a sickle, from Szegvár-Tüzköves. Arm-rings shown in relief. Legs broken off below knees. Nose damaged. Belt indicated by incision of chevrons. Fine brown fabric. Tisza culture. H. 25.6 cm. Koszta József Museum in Szentes, southeastern Hungary. Czalog Collection, 59.1.1. Publ. Czalog, J., 'Die anthropomorphen Gefässe und Idolplastiken von Szegvár-Tüzköves', *Acta Archaeologica* (1959), 7–38; Kalicz, N, *Dieux*: 32–34.

48 Copper sickle from Zalaszentmihály, western Hungary. L. 54 cm., W. 5.7 cm. at top, 2.5 cm. at perforation. Balaton Museum, Keszthely. Publ. F. Czalog, 'Das Krummschwert des Idols von Szegvár-Tüzköves', *Acta Archaeologica*, 12: 58–59. Štip, Naroden Muzej, SF 1421. Publ. M. Gimbutas, 'Excavations at Anza, Macedonia', *Archaeology*, 25, 2, 1972.

49 Polychrome dish. Dark-brown and white on orange-red. Diam. 29 cm. Valea Lupului, 5 km. west of Iași, northern Moldavia, northeastern Romania. Cucuteni B settlement. Excavated 1953–57 by M. Petrescu-Dîmbovița *et al.* Iași Museum, Moldavia. Publ. V. Dumitrescu, *L'art Roumanie*: 50.

50 Polychrome Classical Cucuteni vase. Painted in red bordered with dark-brown

on cream. Cucuteni A phase. H. 32 cm. Truşeşti settlement, district of Botoşani, northern Moldavia. Excavation by M. Petrescu-Dîmboviţa 1951–61. NAM Bucharest, Inv. No. II. 2285. Publ. Dumitrescu, *L'art Roumanie*: 49.

51 Vase from Podei at Targu Ocna, northern Moldavia. Romania Cucuteni B settlement. H. 33 cm. W. (max.) 29 cm. Painted in dark-brown on white background. Bull's head and horns in relief. Archaeological Museum of Piatra Neamţ, Inv. 2790. Publ. C. Mătasă, 'Asezarea eneolitica Cucuteni B de la Tîrgu Ocna-Podei (raional Tîrgu Ocna, reg. Bacău)', *Arheologia Moldovei*, II–III (1964): 11–66.

52 Terracotta figurine in the shape of a horned stand with female breasts. One horn broken. Has a deep hole in the middle. H. 5.2 cm. Medvednjak, Vinča site at Smederevska Palanka. NM B excavation of 1970 by R. Galović. National Museum, Smederevska Palanka, No. 126. Courtesy of this museum.

53 Terracotta figurine of a bull with exaggeratedly large horns, broken at each side. L. 13.5 cm. W. (across horns) 8.5 cm., H. 9 cm. Fafos settlement at Kosovska Mitrovica: phase Ib (Mid-Vinča period). Archaeological museum of Kosovska Mitrovica. Source same as Pls. 24, 25.

54 Pottery snake of fine dark grey fabric decorated with zigzag incisions and puncturings. Diam. (max.) 3.7 cm. Predionica, Early Vinča settlement. Excavated 1955 by R. Galović. Regional Museum Priština, 76. Publ. R. Galović, *Predionica* (1959): Pl. 5.

55, 56 'Snake bowl' with holes between raised design on inside from Kukova Mogila (Duvanli) near Plovdiv, Bulgaria. Grey fabric. Diam. 20 cm. Excavated 1928–30 by B. Filov. Found associated with Karanovo III-Jasatepe type finds. Plovdiv Museum. Courtesy of Plovdiv Museum.

57 Rim sherd with a horned-snake relief. Brown, medium thick, unpainted vessel. Dibel at Šuplevec, north of Bitola. Courtesy of Archaeological Museum in Bitola.

58, 59 Thin-walled polished dish from the cemetery of Dvory nad Žitavou, Želiezovce

group of Linear Pottery culture. Snake application inside. Nitra Archael. Museum of the Institute of Archaeology. Publ. J. Pavůk, 'Grab des Želiezovce-typus in Dvory nad Žitavou', *Slovenská Arheologia*, XII–I (1964): Figs. 5, 6.

60 Detail of a Late Cucuteni piriform orangered vase with dark-brown painted design. Bilcze Zlote. Courtesy of Archaeological Museum in Cracow.

61, 62 Terracotta snake protomes: fragments of cult vessels. 61, approx. actual size; 62, L. 5 cm. Fine light-brown fabric. Porodin near Bitola, southern Yugoslavia. Archaeological Museum Bitola, Inv. 562, 175, 353, 631, 635.

63, 64 Pottery vessel with a horned head and snakes shown in relief. Brown fabric. H. 6.9 cm. Tell Azmak at Stara Zagora. Neolithic Karanovo I complex. Excavation by G. I. Georgiev 1962–65. Stara Zagora Museum. Publ. Georgiev, *Beiträge*.

65 Seated terracotta figurine with folded legs from Kato Ierapetra, Crete. Unusual for its state of preservation in the Aegean area. H. 14.5 cm. Triangular head with a prominent nose, crowned by a triangular cap or coiffure which flares out around the head. Massive cylindrical neck. Stubby arms, held close to sides of protruding, angular abdomen. Exaggerated buttocks. Hair indicated on the crown and the back of the neck. Eyes, fingers and toes rendered by incision. Lips shown plastically. Decoration or dress indicated above breasts, front shoulders, and along the spine at the back by two parallel lines of incision. Surface is of ashen colour tinged with red, well burnished. The core darker red with some impurities. Surface find at the Neolithic settlement presumed to belong to a period coinciding with the Middle Neolithic at Knossos. The collection of Dr Giamalakis in Heraklion. Publ. by S. S. Weinberg, 'Neolithic figurines and Aegean interrelations', *AJA*, vol. 55, No. 2 (April 1951): Pl. IA. Also by P. J. Ucko, *Anthropomorphic figurines*, London (1968): 246–48.

66 Zoomorphic lid found 7.2 m. deep in Vinča mound. Early Vinča. Fine light-

brown fabric. 12 × 10.5 cm. Tip of nose broken. Two holes below the nose indicate repair. BU Collection, 399. Vasić's excavation. Vasić, *Vinča*, II: Pl. XLV.

67 Late Cucuteni vase painted in dark brown on orange-red. The cosmogonical (snake, egg, plant) design covers the entire surface. Bilcze Zlote, western Ukraine, upper Dniester Valley.

68 Egg-shaped stone sculpture with an engraved design which probably portrays a vulva. Found at the corner of the hearth in house No. 51 at Lepenski Vir, northern Yugoslavia. In the classification of D. Srejović it belongs to the Ic phase of the site. L. 16 cm., W. 13 cm. D. Srejović, excavation of 1968. BU Collection, No. 19. Publ. D. Srejović, *Lepenski Vir* (1969): Pl. 48.

69, 70 Ornithomorphic vase found 2.3 m. (4.1 m.) deep at Vinča site. Late Vinča. Fine red fabric. L. 20.7 cm., H. 14 cm. Opening in the tail. Oval body. Channelled decoration. Head modelled in detail and showing zoomorphic features. Ears broken. Stands on a ring base. Classical Vinča. Vasić's excavation. BU Collection, Inv. 1913. Publ. Vasić, *Vinča* II: Fig. 356.

71 Ornithomorphic vase from Căscioarele, an island settlement in the lower Danube region, 20 km. west of Olteniţa, Gumelniţa layer. Excavation by H. and V. Dumitrescu (see 42). H. 13.2 cm. Fine fabric, burnished. NAM, Bucharest. Publ. Dumitrescu, *L'art Roumanie*: Fig. 109.

72, 73, 75, 76 Sandstone sculptures from Lepenski Vir, northern Yugoslavia. 73, Brown, 22 cm. × 14 cm. From House 40; 76, brown, H. *c.* 50 cm., lower part damaged. From House a/5; 75, brown, H. 50 cm. From House 44; 72, grey, H. 40 cm. From House 44, near the sculpture reproduced in Pl. 75. D. Srejović excavation 1965–68. BU Collection. Publ. D. Srejović, *Lepenski Vir* (1972): Pls. 24, 26, 31, 52, V, VII.

74 Potsherd in form of a fish from Mala Grabovnica near Leskovac, central Yugoslavia. Fine dark-grey fabric. L. 6.3 cm. Excavation 1953 by M. Garašanin. Narod-

ni Muzej Leskovac, Inv. 1391. Publ. NM Belgrade *Catalogue* (1968): 113.

77 Funnel-shaped vase found 4.3 m. deep in the Vinča mound. Divided by vertical and horizontal incisions into panels with clusters of vertical zigzag lines, dots, or a meander motif. H. 16 cm. Brown fabric. BU Collection, Inv. 744. Vasić, *Vinča*, II: Pl. CII, Fig. 367; IV, Pl. LVI.

78 Zoomorphic terracotta lid found 8.2 m. deep at the Vinča site. H. 17 cm. Fine fabric, grey colour. Decorated by incision filled in with white paste. Reconstructed portions plain white. Vasić's excavations. BU Collection, No. 410. Publ. Vasić, *Vinča*, II: Pl. LXI, 110.

79 Red terracotta lid found 4.2 m. deep at the Vinča site. Decorated by bands of incised parallel lines filled in with white paste. H. 5.5 cm. NM Belgrade, No. 1489. Publ. Vasić, *Vinča*, II: Fig. 154.

80, 81 Bear-shaped cult vessel from the settlement at Smilčić near Zadar, Adriatic coast of Yugoslavia. H. 10 cm. Archaeological Museum, Zadar. Excavated and published by S. Batović: 'Neolitsko nalezište u Smilčicu', *Radovi Instituta Jugosl. Akad. Znanosti i Umjestnosti u Zadru*, X: 83–138.

82 Terracotta paw of a bear with bands of incisions. Obre II, Sq. V, 2, depth 1.20–1.40 m. H. 9 cm. UCLA (M. Gimbutas)–Sarajevo Zemaljski Muzej (A. Benac) excavation of 1968. Publ. A. Benac, Obre II (1971): Pl. XXVIII, 2.

83, 84 Sesklo terracotta bust of a female figurine from M. Vrysi. Archaeological Museum of Volos. Publ. by Zervos, *Naissance*: 166, Fig. 104.

85 Upper part of a figurine with cylindrical head and bird's beak. Perforated ears. Deep hole for mouth. Three bosses applied below the hole on the neck. One breast and perforated arm stump preserved on the left side. H. 13 cm. Brown fabric. Porodin at Bitola, southern Yugoslavia. M. Grbić *et al.* excavation of 1953–54, sponsored by the Archaeological Institute of the Serbian Academy of Sciences, Belgrade. Archaeological Museum, Bitola. Publ. M. Grbić, *Porodin*: Pl. XXIX, 2.

86 Upper part of Early or Mid-Vinča double-headed figurine from Rastu, southwestern Romania, district of Dolj. H. 7 cm. Perforations through shoulders. V's and meanders incised below breasts. Heads damaged. Originally had prominent semicircular eyebrows and noses (beaks). Round holes below the noses. Fine grey fabric. Traces of red colouring all over. NAM Bucharest, Inv. No. 4833.

87 Vase from Kenézlö belonging to the Bükk group. Originally in the Archaeological Museum of Nyiregyháza, northeastern Hungary, lost during World War II. Publ. F. Tompa, *Über einige ungarische Denkmäler der prähistorischen Kunst* (1928), 23, Pl. *II*, 3; *idem*, 'Die Bandkeramik in Ungarn', *Archaeologia Hungarica*, 5/6 (1929): 41, Pl. 31, 1.

88 Jar with breasts and incised parallel-line decoration on central band. H. 8 cm. Painted white. Early Cucuteni ('Pre-Cucuteni III') settlement of Negreşti at Vaslui, northern Moldavia. History Museum of Moldavia, Iaşi.

89 Terracotta head of a Bird Goddess figurine with incised and white-encrusted chevrons above the beak. Eyes indicated by incised semicircular lines. W. 6 cm. Kalojanovec, 18 km. southwest of Stara Zagora. East Balkan civilization, Karanovo IV Period. Archaeological Museum of Stara Zagora, Inv. No. 181.

90 Terracotta figurine of a double-headed goddess found 6.1 m. deep in the Vinča mound. Mid-Vinča. H. 4.5 cm. Grey fabric. Incised on front and back. Remains of red paint over side panels of the larger head, around the neck, over the inside of V-sign in front, in the back of the neck and on the back of masks (contours of masks as they appear from the back). Vasić, *Vinča*, II: Pl. 86, Fig. 323.

91 Terracotta altar table of fine grey fabric, painted red, white-encrusted. Female figure broken off at waist. Cylindrical vessel partly damaged. H. 9 cm. L. 10.2 cm. Found 5.8 m. deep in Vinča mound. Mid-Vinča. Vasić's excavation. NM Belgrade, Inv. 1295. Vasić, *Vinča* III: 108, Fig. 512.

92 Altar table in form of seated woman with arms around a vessel, decorated with incised meandering bands alternately painted in red. Fafos I at Kosovska Mitrovica, southern Yugoslavia. H. 17.6 cm. Excavated 1959 by J. Glišić and B. Jovanović. Regional Museum Priština, F-I-3B-502. NM Belgrade Catalogue (1968): 54; Sheffield *Catalogue* (1969): 58.

93 Slightly tapering spouted pot. White-encrusted incisions. Settlement of Borsod, province of Borsod-Abaúj-Zemplén, northeastern Hungary. Tisza-Bükk border. Excavation by A. Leszik, J. Hillebrand and F. Tompa, 1926. F. Tompa, *Die Bandkeramik in Ungarn* (1929): Pl. XLIV, 5.

94 Terracotta figurine of a seated woman holding a shallow basin, from Bordjoš near Bečej, northern Yugoslavia. Fine red fabric. Surface find. NM Belgrade, Inv. 16281. Miodrag Grbić, 'A neolithic statuette from Bečej in Banat', *Archaeologia Yugoslavia*, I (1954): 16–17, Figs. 1–4.

95 Terracotta head of a figurine from Crnokalačka Bara at Rujište near Ražanj, north of Niš. Clear representation of a pentagonal mask decorated with vertical incisions and meanders above the right eye. Raised semicircular eyes, large nose, no mouth. Grey fabric. H. 6.8 cm. NM Belgrade excavations of 1959. NM Belgrade, Inv. 16006. Publ. R. Galović, *Arkheološki Pregled*, 2 (1960): 24. Sheffield *Catalogue* (1969): 124.

96 Terracotta masked head of fine grey fabric incised with meanders above and spirals below large raised eyes. H. 5.6 cm. Medvednjak near Smederevska Palanka. R. Galović (NM Belgrade) excavation of 1970. Courtesy of Smederevska Palanka National Museum.

97 Terracotta figurine with white-encrusted incisions found 2.5 m. deep in Vinča mound. Late Vinča. She wears a bird's mask. Arms broken off. Small breasts, between which is a raised medallion. Perforations through hips, sides of mask and crown of the head. H. 15.8 cm. Vasić's excavation. NM Belgrade Vasić, *Vinča*, I: Pl. XXXI, Fig. 141; III: 94, Fig. 467.

98 Half of a terracotta disc with incised spiral and meander patterns. Two broken projections in the middle. Light-brown fabric. Found 5.4 m. deep at the Vinča site. Vasić's excavation. BU Collection, Inv. 537. Vasić, *Vinča*, IV: Pl. LIV, Fig. 141.

99 Upper part of a Vinča terracotta figurine. Settlement of Medvednjak. Smederevska Palanka Museum excavations of 1969. National Museum Smederevska Palanka. Courtesy of this Museum.

100, 101 Double-headed terracotta figurine. Fine dark-grey fabric with white-encrusted incisions. Three perforations through each arm, four through each crown and one through the sides of the masks. Legs broken off. Vinča layer of the Gomolava mound on the River Sava, district of Sremska Mitrovica, northern Yugoslavia. 1965 excavation by Vojvodjanski Muzej, Novi Sad. Courtesy of this Museum.

102, 103 Seated goddess from Szegvár-Tüzköves at Szentes. Tisza culture. Head and legs broken off. H. *c.* 22 cm. Light-brown fabric. Decoration in form of incised panels of meanders and zigzags. Excavated 1956–57 by J. Czalog. Czalog, *Szegvár-Tüzköves*. Koszta József Museum, Szentes, Hungary.

104 Vessel on a pedestal from Szegvár-Tüzköves. H. 11 cm. Szentes, Koszta József Museum, Inv. 59.1.58. J. Czalog, 'Das Wohnhaus "E" von Szegvár-Tüzköves', *Acta Archaeologica Hungarica*, 9 (1958): Pl. I, Fig. 1. Kalicz, *Dieux*: 48.

105–107 Vase in the form of a seated goddess. Kökénydomb, Tisza culture. H. 33 cm. Light-brown fabric. Excavation by J. Banner, 1942. Tornyai János Museum, Hódmezővásárhely, Inv. 762/42. Banner: *Kökénydomb*: 14–35; Kalicz, *Dieux*: 37.

108, 109 Altarpiece of clay, 46 cm. high, 53 cm. wide at base, 18.5 cm. deep, from the settlement at Kökénydomb southeastern Hungary. Tisza culture. Excavated 1942 by J. Banner. Tornyai János Museum Hódmezővásárhely, Inv. 1089/42. J. Banner and J. Korek, 'Les campagnes IV et V des fouilles pratiquées en Kökénydomb de Hódmezővásárhely', *Archaeológiai Értesítö*, 76 (1949): 9–23, 24–25, Pl. VIII, Fig. 8–9. Kalicz, *Dieux*: 38–39.

110 Details of vase decoration and a decorated vase from Traian (Dealul Fîntînilor), Cucuteni A–B layer of the settlement in northern Moldavia, northeastern Romania. After Hortensia Dumitrescu, *Dacia*, N.S. IV (1960): 34, Fig. 2.

111 Crude cylindrical terracotta figurine with female breasts and male genitals. Conical abdomen and sharply protruding buttocks. Eyes indicated by deep incision. Painted nose. H. 5.5 cm. Light-brown fabric. Vinča. Vasić's excavation. BU Collection, Inv. 5.76. Publ. Vasić, *Vinča*.

112 Marble figurine from Attica, Greece. H. 22.5 cm. Typologically early Sesklo. Exact provenience not known. Museum of Eleusis. After Zervos, *Naissance*: 210, Fig. 203.

113–115 Terracotta figurine from Anza, eastern Macedonia, found above house wall built of convex bricks and associated with a barbotine sherd and a sherd with floral Central Balkan Neolithic II design. Beaked nose, slanting excised eyes, slight protrusions for wings, well modelled buttocks. Legs merge together ending in a conical tip. Buff-orange burnished. Remains of red-painted hip-belt. H. 4.11 cm. Author's excavation 1969. Naroden Muzej, Štip, SF21. Publ. M. Gimbutas, 'Excavation at Anza, Macedonia', *Archaeology*, 25, 2: 120.

116, 117 Cult vase in the shape of a crowned duck wearing a human mask found 7.05 m. deep at the Vinča site. Terracotta with very thin walls of light-brown fabric. Hollow. Has an opening in the tail. Rippled, polished surface. Decorated with bands of bituminous material. L. 36 cm., H. 20.8 cm. BU Collection, Inv. 2005. Vasić, *Vinča*, I: Pl. XXIV.

118 Vase in the likeness of Bird Goddess. Fine light-brown fabric, channelled surface. Mask shown in relief. Eyes and nose plastically rendered. Breasts and knees indicated. Two perforations in each arm stump. H. 32.5 cm., W. 15.5 cm. Vinča, Vasić's excavation. NM Belgrade, Inv. 1481. Publ. Vasić, *Vinča*, I (1932): 43, Pl. XVII.

119 Head of Bird Goddess modelled on the neck of a polychrome painted Cucuteni

vase. Eyebrows and beak form a letter T. Circular plastic eyes. Most of left side reconstructed. H. 11.4 cm. Classical Cucuteni ('Cucuteni A'), Ruginoasa, district of Iaşi. NAM Bucharest, II, 4681. Publ. V. Dumitrescu, *L'art Roumanie*: No. 80.

120 Terracotta female figurine wearing bird's mask from the Vinča mound. Surface find. In standing position with stump arms and two perforations in each. Small breasts. Large eyes, V-neck and skirt indicated by incision. Neck and upper top corner of the mask painted in red. Fine dark-grey fabric, burnished. H. 16 cm. NM Belgrade, 4654. NM Belgrade *Catalogue* 1968: 146.

121 Terracotta figurine from Supska near Čuprija, central Yugoslavia. Surface find. Fine reddish-brown fabric. H. 15 cm. National Museum, Čuprija, Inv. 300. NM Belgrade (1968): 129.

122, 123 Terracotta masked head in shape of a duck. Four perforations, one through each cheek and one above each eye. Deep and wide incisions for eyes and decoration. H. approx. 5 cm. The Vinča mound. Late Vinča. NM Belgrade, Inv. 1443.

124 Miniature bird-shaped head of a terracotta figurine. Two incised channels round the neck. Peaked crown. Excised dots for eyes. H. 1.9 cm. Fine light-brown fabric. Sitagroi mound, northeastern Greece. Early Gumelniţa culture. M. Gimbutas (UCLA)–A. C. Renfrew (Sheffield Univ.) excavation of 1968. Philipi Museum, Sitagroi, SF 412.

125 Upper torso of a terracotta figurine. H. 4.8 cm. Fine grey fabric. Excised and white-encrusted decoration, forming spiral and meander designs. Flat head indicates a mask with representation of Bird Goddess' face: eyebrows connected with the beak. Vădastra dist. of Corabia, Oltenia, Romania. MF 1948. NAM Bucharest.

126, 127 Heads of terracotta bird-headed figurines with double spiral curls. Three holes in front. Sitagroi mound, East Balkan civilization, as 124 above.

128 Early Tripolye (Proto-Cucuteni) terracotta figurine. Slightly forward-leaning posture. Cylindrical neck, upper part of body slender, fat hips and buttocks. Decorated with incisions. Six stabbings in front of neck. Female breasts slightly indicated. Short stumps for arms. H. 16.3 cm. Bernovo Luka site, western Ukraine. After P. P. Efimenko and I. G. Shovkoplias, 'Arkheologicheskie otkrytja na Ukraine za poslednie gody', *SA*, XIX (1954): 5–40.

129, 130 Terracotta figurine decorated with white-encrusted incisions all over the body. Forward-leaning posture. Fine fabric. Classical Cucuteni ('Cucuteni A') period, found in Moldavia, locality unknown. NAM, Bucharest, Inv. No. 5730. Publ. V. Dumitrescu, 'La civilisation de Cucuteni', *Berichten van de rijksdienst voor het audheidkundig Godemonderzoek*, 9 (1959): Fig. 10, 2.

131 Terracotta female figurine from the early Lengyel settlement at Střelice at Boskovštejn, district of Znojmo, Moravia. Fine light brown fabric. H. 15.5 cm. Five necklaces indicated by horizontal incisions around the neck. Eyes incised. Beak-nose. Hair rendered by application and incision. No indication of dress. Stumps for wings. F. Vildomec's excavation and collection. Moravian Museum, Brno, Czechoslovakia. Publ. by W. and B. Forman and J. Poulík, *Prehistoric Art* (in Czechoslovakia), London (undated, c. 1955): Fig. 47.

132 Baked clay figure of mother and child wearing bird masks attached to a burnished pottery fragment found 4.7 m. deep in the Vinča mound. Fine dark-grey fabric. H. 14.4 cm. Lower part damaged, child's mask broken off. Eyes, decoration of masks, dress and necklace indicated by white-encrusted incisions. Small stumps for arms, probably symbolizing wings. Masks are pentagonal. Mother's mask has two perforations on either side. Small breasts indicated. Vasić's excavation. BU Collection, Inv. 1233. Publ. Vasić, *Vinča*, II: Pl. LXXXV, Fig. 322.

133, 134 Terracotta head of a ram, broken off at the neck. Painted bright red with traces of white around eyes and between the lines of the horns. Fine fabric, orange clay. H. 3.9 cm. Anza, eastern Macedonia, Yugoslavia. Anza IV, Early Vinča. Found 1970 above the top floor of Vinča house during author's excavation of site. Štip Museum, SF 1691.

135 Terracotta head of a he-goat or ram that formed part of a vase. Horns broken off. Roughly triangular head with ridge down middle. Raised and slit eyes. Deep parallel lines incised round neck, encrusted with white. Red-painted neck between and below incisions. Black burnished surface. L. 10 cm., W. (of head) 5.4 cm. Sitagroi mound, eastern Macedonia, Greece, Period III. East Balkan civilization, Dikilitash complex. Discovered in the stratigraphic area during the 1968 excavation by C. A. Renfrew (Sheffield University)–M. Gimbutas (UCLA). Philipi Museum, SF 203.

136 Terracotta cult vessel in the shape of a ram. Horns connected with the rim. Fine light-grey fabric. H. 5.8 cm. Incisions of V's and chevrons encrusted with white paste. Traces of red paint. From the Vinča mound, Classical Vinča. Vasić's excavation. BU Collection, Inv. 1175. Publ. Vasić, *Vinča*, II: Pl. LXXVIII, Fig. 335.

137 Zoomorphic ritual vase, rectangular with a horned ram's head at one end. H. 10.5 cm., L. 16.5 cm. Grey fabric. Decorated with incised and white-encrusted concentric or parallel lines. Banjata at Kapitan Dimitrievo, district of Pazazdzik, central Bulgaria. Gumelniţa complex. Excavation by P. Detev 1947–48 of the Archaeological Museum Plovdiv. Publ. P. Detev, 'Le tell Baniata près de Kapitan Dimitrievo', *Godishnik*, Plovdiv (1950) II, 1f.

138 Clay sculpture of a female in standing position with cylindrical neck and folded arms. H. 17.5 cm. Grey fabric. Made in sections (head, torso and two legs) and then pegged together before they hardened. Incised eyes, pinched-up nose. Small breasts. Found within the house of the early phase of the Neolithic settlement of Nea Nikomedeia at Verroia, western Macedonia, Greece. Central Balkan Proto-Sesklo complex. 1961–63 excavations of Cambridge and Harvard Universities. Excav. and publ. by R. J. Rodden, 'An early neolithic village in Greece', *Scientific American*, Vol. 212, No. 4, April 1965.

139 Cylindrical head of a terracotta figurine with prominent pinched-up nose and slit eyes. Deep incisions near upper end. Canal ends in a hole on top. H. 4.7 cm. Fine grey fabric. Rudnik Kosovski near Prizren, Kosovo Metohije, southern Yugoslavia. Central Balkan Starčevo complex. Found in 1966. Later this settlement was excavated by J. Glišić. Regional Museum in Priština, RU-A3-VIII-IC. NM *Catalogue* (1968): 32.

140 Standing terracotta figurine with pillar-neck, phallus-shaped massive breasts, large abdomen and folded arms. Back is flat. H. 15.7 cm. Fine brown fabric. Cemetery of Cernavoda on the lower Danube, north-west of Constanţa. 1957 excav. by D. Berciu, sponsored by the Archaeological Institute of the Academy of Sciences, Romanian P. R. NAM Bucharest. Publ. D. Berciu, *Cultura Hamangia* (1966), I: Fig. 53.

141 Marble figurine found in the nineteenth century in the vicinity of Sparta. Publ. in *Athenische Mitteilungen* XVI: 52, Fig. 1. Later by Tsountas, *Diminiou kai Sesklou*: Fig. 311, and Zervos, *Naissance*: Fig. 114.

142 Marble figurine. Athens Nat. Museum, inv. 8772. H. approx. 13 cm.

143 Upper part of a terracotta figurine cupping breasts. From Sesklo, Thessaly. Sesklo complex. Tsountas excavation. Publ. 1908 Tsountas, *Diminiou kai Sesklou*: Fig. 14. Courtesy of Athens National Museum, inv. 5942.

144 White marble figurine. H. 7 cm. Tell Azmak, central Bulgaria. Karanovo I. Stara Zagora Museum. 1960–63 excavations by G. I. Georgiev and P. Detev. Publ. by G. I. Georgiev *Beiträge*: Abb. 12.

145 Terracotta torso with folded arms. Head and lower part not preserved. Fine brown fabric. H. 3.5 cm. Settlement of Pianul de Jos near Alba, Transylvania. 1962–63 excavation by Iuliu Paul. Petreşti group with strong Gumelniţa influences. Sibiu Museum. Publ. Paul, I, 'Der Forschungsstand über die Petreşti-Kultur', *Študijné zvesti*, 22: 331, Abb. 2: 10. *Idem*, 'Asezarea neo-eneolitica de la Pianul de Jos (Podei), Jud. Alba', *Studii şi communicari* (Sibiu, 1967): Pl. VI, 8.

146 Well preserved figurine from the tell of Sulica near Stara Zagora. Local grey marble. H. 13 cm. Wide head, semicircular eyes, pronounced nose. Five round depressions below the mouth, three in each ear. Breasts slightly indicated. Left hand covers the right. Short tapering legs. Stara Zagora Museum. Publ. Gaul, *Neolithic Bulgaria*, Pl. LX, *2*.

147 Figurine with folded arms, no breasts, legs together. Head broken off below neck. Borets (Topra-Asar) near Plovdiv, central Bulgaria. H. 10 cm. Local light-grey marble. Accidentally discovered by farmers in 1908. Plovdiv Archaeological Museum. Assigned to the period of Karanovo VI on typological grounds. Publ. Gaul, *Neolithic Bulgaria*: 189, Pl. LX, *3*.

148 Cycladic marble figurine from Syros. H. 21.6 cm. Red colouring preserved on chest. After Zervos, *Cyclades*: 188, Fig. 248.

149, 150 Slender schematized terracotta figurine. Breasts and buttocks emphasized, large incised pubic triangle. Punctate decoration around head, arm stumps and over hips. Holes for eyes, large nose. H. approx. 15 cm. Vykhvatintsi cemetery, grave No. 29. Cucuteni B – late Tripolye period. Arch. Museum of the Institute of History, Acad. of Sciences, Kishenev, Soviet Moldavia. Publ. I. G. Rozenfeld, 'Vykhvatinski mogil'nik po razkopkam 1951 goda', *KSIIMK*, 56: 98–104.

151 Flat figurine of bone with large incised pubic triangle and punctated decoration. Holes for eyes. One hole in middle of neck and two in the back below the waist. On the side of the head three pairs of holes for ear-rings (now broken). Perforations through arm stumps and feet. Copper plates above legs. H. 15 cm. Northern central Bulgaria, district of Stara Zagora. Museum of Stara Zagora, Bulgaria. Publ. M. Dimitrov, 'Kostena choveshka figurka at s. Lovets, Starozagorsko', *Arkheologija*, IV, 1 (1962): 65–68.

152 Terracotta figurine from Lerna near Argos, eastern Peloponnese. H. 18.2 cm. Found beneath the debris of third building level. Worn and slightly chipped. Head and lower part of right leg broken off. Hard fired and compact. Burnished. Fine fabric: light pink/buff surface, grey core. Floor of Late Neolithic house, Level 17. Argos Museum. Excavation by J. L. Caskey (University of Cincinnati) 1956. Publ. J. L. Caskey and M. A. Elliot, 'Neolithic figurines from Lerna', *Hesperia*, XXV (1956), 175–77; *Idem*, 'Where Hercules slew the Hydra: a neolithic sculpture of "classic beauty" and the relics of some 2500 years from Peloponnesian Lerna', *Illustrated London News*, January 1957: 68–71.

153 Schematized terracotta figurine with large, incised pubic triangle. Hole on top for insertion of a cylinder. Legs reduced to protruding feet. Fine greyish-brown fabric. Isolated find from Vinča. NM Belgrade, Inv. No. 5023. Publ. J. Korošec in *Archeološki Vestniki*, 3 (1952), 55 f. and *Prehistorijska plastika*.

154 Marble figurine in which the child stands on top of mother's head. H. 23 cm. Isolated find housed in Badisches Landesmuseum, Karlsruhe. Inv. 64/100, Neg. No. 6275. Publ. J. Thimme, *Antike Kunst*, VIII, Taf. 21: 2. Courtesy of Dr Jürgen Thimme, Badisches Landesmuseum, Karlsruhe.

155 Anthropomorphic vase, decorated with white paint on reddish-brown background. Slipped. H. 32.3 cm. Discovered in the settlement area of the East Balkan Gumelniţa culture at Sultana on the shore of Lake Mostistea. Acquired by Barbu Ionesar, director of the Olteniţa Museum. Publ. by S. Marinescu-Bîlcu, 'Die Bedeutung einiger Gesten und Haltungen in der jungsteinzeitlichen Skulptur der ausserkarpatischen Gebiete Rumäniens', *Dacia*, XI (1967): 47–58.

156, 157 Squatting woman with exaggerated buttocks and drawn-up legs. H. 7.6 cm. Face masked. Right hand at the mouth, left broken off. Fine black fabric, but not burnished. Excised lines encrusted with white paste include concentric circles with a dot in the middle, on back and side of each buttock and at knees. Narrow waist. Behind, there is a dot in the middle of the back and a lozenge below the waist. Medvednjak at Smederevska Palanka, central Yugoslavia. Classical Vinča. R. Milošević's excavation of 1969. Smederevska Palanka Naroden Museum, Inv. 944. Courtesy of this Museum.

158 A large pithos, with two large supernatural hands worked in relief on both sides of the upper, and two smaller ones on the lower part of the jar. The vessel, approx. 1 m. high, has a short cylindrical neck and three lugs. Lower part in barbotine, upper part brown burnished. Banjata at Kapitan Dimitrievo near Plovdiv, central Bulgaria. Gumelniţa complex. East Balkan civilization, Chalcolithic. Excavations of the Plovdiv Archaeological Museum by P. Detev in 1947–48. Plovdiv. Arch. Museum. Lit.: P. Detev 'Le tell Baniata près de Kapitan Dimitrievo', *Godishnik, Plovdiv* (1950): II, *1*.

159 Vase from Muldava, Neolithic settlement near Plovdiv, central Bulgaria. H. 11 cm. Karanovo I period. Plovdiv Archaeological Museum excavation by P. Detev. Publ. P. Detev, *Godishnik*, Plovdiv, III, 3 (1959).

160 Binocular vase. Ochre-red with chocolate-brown decorations. Cucuteni B. Bilcze Zlote, western Ukraine. Courtesy of Cracow Archaeological Museum.

161 Reclining terracotta animal, half fox, half dog. Fine brown fabric. Eyes and mouth white-encrusted. L. 6 cm. Gumelniţa site at Pietrele, district of Ilfov. NAM Bucharest I.3472. Publ. by D. Berciu, *Contribuţii*, and V. Dumitrescu, *L'art Romanie*: 103.

162 Dog-shaped handle – fragment of a pear-shaped, slightly biconical Cucuteni B vase. Fine fabric, ochre-red with traces of ornamentation in black paint which through weathering has lost its original lustre and colour. The animal figure was perpendicularly attached to the upper part of the vessel. The fragment measures 9.5 × 4.5 cm., the animal itself being 6.5 cm. long and 2.5 cm. high. Its firm attachment by legs and tail to the wall of the vase suggests that it served as a handle. The animal's head is rendered schematically, but the rest of the body is naturalistic, with even the tensed muscles showing. Found at Podei, located on a terrace of the River Trotus near the small town of Targu-Ocna, northeast of the Carpathian Mts in Moldavia, by I. Iacobovici, professor of the medical faculty at

Bucharest. First donated with other finds to the local museum of Targu-Ocna and later taken over by NAM Bucharest, Inv. 5714. The object was first published by R. Vulpe, 'Figurine thériomorphe de la civilisation Cucuteni B', *IPEK*, 12 (1938): 57–65, Pl. 33.

163 Dog's head carved from rock crystal. H. 4.3 cm., L. 6 cm. Crnokalačka Bara near Ražanj north of Niš, southern Yugoslavia. NM Belgrade (R. Galović) excavation of 1960. NMB Inv. No. 16071. Publ. NM Belgrade *Catalogue* 1968: 125.

164 Cucuteni B$_2$ vase from the settlement of Valea Lupului 5 km. west of Iaşi, northern Moldavia, Romania. H. 31.5 cm. Lower part of the vase is reconstructed. The design, executed in dark red, bordered with black on white, is applied to the cylindrical neck and extends over the shoulder (seen only on the other side of the photographed object). Between the metopes with a flying dog and caterpillars, winding snakes are to be seen. On the shoulder, below the toothed line, large eggs are painted in black bands (not visible in the photograph). Excavated 1953–57 by M. Petrescu-Dîmboviţa *et al.* History Museum of Moldavia, Iaşi. Publ. *SCIV* V (1954) and VI (1955). Also: V. Dumitrescu, *L'art Roumanie*: 52; Rybakov, *Cosmogony*: 42.

165 Detail of large ochre-red, pear-shaped vase showing frieze with black-painted design on the bulging upper part. This design includes large discs between two spiralling bands above which fly dogs stylized in Late Cucutenian fashion. The top of the frieze has a border of three parallel lines and a row of triangles. H. 36 cm., W. 33 cm. Animal figures 5 cm. long. Bilcze Zlote settlement, upper Dniester Valley, formerly Polish Galicia, now western Ukraine. Archaeological Museum in Cracow, Poland. Courtesy of this Museum.

166 Fragment of a storage vessel with figure of a stag in relief. H. 18 cm., W. 29 cm. Csépa, southeastern Hungary. An isolated find of the Starčevo (Körös) complex. Tessedik Sámuel Museum, Szarvaš. Publ. by Krecsmárik in *Archaeologiai Értesitö*, 32 (1912); 366–68; I. Kutzián, *The Körös Culture* (1944): Pl. II, *1*. N. Kalicz, *Dieux*: Pl. 8.

167, 168 Terracotta vase in the shape of a doe. L. 64 cm., H. 39 cm. Fine light-brown fabric, painted in white on red. Carefully modelled head and neck. Slit-eyes in raised relief. Round opening at mouth. Cylindrical neck to opening on back. Muldava mound, central Bulgaria. Found associated with the Neolithic pottery of Karanovo I type. Plovdiv Archaeological Museum. Excavated and published by P. Detev, 'Praistorichestoto Selishche pri selo Muldava', *Godishnik*, Plovdiv, VI (1968): 33, Fig. 26.

169 Vinča figurine of an erect toad found 7.1 m. deep in the Vinča mound. Vasić's excavation. BU Collection, Inv. 1281. Vasić, *Vinča*, vol. III: Fig. 616.

170 White marble figurine of a toad. H. 7.5 cm. Half of conical head missing. Starčevo layer of the stratified Neolithic settlement at Anza (Anzabegovo) near Štip, southeastern Yugoslavia. Naroden Muzej Štip, SF 2221. M. Gimbutas (UCLA)–Naroden Muzej Štip (M. Garašanin) excavation 1970.

171 Toad carved out of greenish blue serpentine from Nea Nikomedeia. Courtesy of the excavator, R. J. Rodden. See 138.

172 Part of Late Vinča vase with human figures and snakes in relief. 15.7 × 24.6 cm. Gomolava tell at Sremska Mitrovica, northern Yugoslavia. Red-brown fabric, polished surface. Found on the floor of Vinča house. Excavation of 1955 by Vojvodjanski Museum, Novi Sad. Vojvodjanski, Novi Sad, northern Yugoslavia, Inv. A 2185. Publ. S. Nagy, *Rad vojvodjanskikh muzeja*, 9 (1960): 119, Pl. IV, 2, NM Belgrade *Catalogue* (1968): 89.

173 Neck of a pithos, H. 11 cm. Diam. 20.5 cm. Handles in the shape of human arms. Incisions round rim. Designs include a face with eyes, mouth and raised nose above an M-sign, and deeply incised snake and meander patterns. Discovered at Szentes-Jaksorpart, eastern Hungary. Szakálhát complex of the Linear pottery culture. Housed in Koszta József Museum in Szentes, 54, 156, 31. Publ. G. Csallany, 'Gesichtsdarstellungen auf Gefässen der Theiss-Kultur', *Germania*, 23 (1939): Pl. XV, Fig. 2; Kalicz, *Dieux*: Pl. 25.

174 Terracotta figurine of a tortoise found on the surface at the Vinča site. L. 6 cm., W. 3.9 cm. Fine grey fabric. NM Belgrade, Inv. No. 4334 (bought by NM Belgrade from a farmer in 1934). NM Belgrade *Catalogue*, 1968: 72. Publ. Garašanin, *Religija*: 251, Fig. 23.

175 Terracotta head of a hedgehog from a classical Vinča site at Crnokalačka Bara, north of Niš, southern Yugoslavia. H. 6 cm. NM Belgrade by R. Galović 1969. NM Belgrade, Inv. 20195. Unpublished. Courtesy of the excavator.

176 Terracotta lid in the form of a hedgehog with an anthropomorphic face. Gumelniţa B settlement at Vidra, south of Bucharest, lower Danube basin. H. 5 cm. D. Rosetti's excavation of 1934. Bucharest City Museum. Publ. by D. Rosetti, 'Steinkupferzeitliche Plastik aus einem Wohnhügel bei Bukarest', *IPEK*, 12 (1938): 29–50. Repeated by V. Dumitrescu, *L'art Roumanie*: Pl. 100.

177 Terracotta hedgehog from Căscioarele, Gumelniţa layer, southern Romania. H. 6.1 cm. NM Bucharest. Publ. Dumitrescu, *L'art Roumanie*: Pl. 109.

178 Bull's head with large horns cut out of a flat piece of bone. Image of the goddess in the centre of the head is geometrically rendered by means of punctate lines. The figure is composed of two triangles meeting with their tips at the waist. Legs narrow down to a point. Head and navel portrayed by larger dots. Raised arms bifurcate halfway up. Punctate line also runs down middle of horns and along top of head. Perforations at each of the four corners and on top of the head probably were used for attaching it to some other object. Bilcze Złote (Polish), Bilche Zolotoe (Ukrainian), south of Tarnopol, on the Seret (N.) basin in the western Ukraine, upper Dniester, a Cucuteni (Tripolye) cave site excavated in the nineteenth and early twentieth centuries by G. Ossowski and W. Demetrykiewicz. Early Cucuteni B (Tripolye C II in the classification by T. Passek, 1949). Archaeological Museum, Cracow.

179 Bee Goddess on a gold plaque from Camiros, Rhodes. Seventh century B C. Courtesy

of Museum of Fine Arts, Boston (Neg. No. B2578). Publ. Ransom, *The Bee*, 1937: Pl. V.

180 Pottery fragment showing Bee Goddess in relief (part only). Kotacpart at Hódmezövásárhely, southeastern Hungary, a Starčevo (Körös) site. Museum of Tornyai János at Hódmezövásárhely, Inv. No. 748/32. Publ. by J. Banner, 'Die neolithische Ansiedlung von Hódmezövásárhely-Kopáncs und Kotacpart und die III periode der Theiss-Kultur', *Dolgozatok*, VIII (1932): 1–31, 32–48, Pl. XVIII, 2. Also in I. Kutzián, *The Körös culture* (1944): Pl. XLI, 1. In both publications the figure appears upside down.

181 Fragments of a bowl from Ilonapart at Szentes, southeastern Hungary, with a figure of the Bee Goddess painted in red on a white background. Discovered by J. Czalog 'Szentes-Ilonapart', *Acta Archaeologica* (Szeged 1966). Courtesy of Szentes Museum.

182 Brown-on-cream painted vase from a Cucuteni B settlement of Podei near Tîrgu-Ocna, district of Bacău. H. 19 cm. Diam. 22.5 cm. Piatra Neamţ Museum, Inv. 1514.

183 Animal-headed female figurine seated on a stool of red baked terracotta, decorated with deep incisions filled in with white. Navel indicated by hole within an encircled raised belly. Two perforations through arm stumps, hips and mask. Four perforations at back of crown. Found 4.1 m. deep in the Vinča mound. Vasić's excavation. NM Belgrade exhibit. Publ. Vasić, *Vinča*, I: 121, Figs. 139a,b,c; and III: 114, Figs. 541a,b,c.

184, 185 Terracotta figurine of a masked goddess, painted in black and red diagonal bands. Eyes, nose, centre of forehead and chin painted black. Perforations through the shoulders and arms and through the corners of the pentagonal mask. Lower part missing. Was originally seated on a throne. Left arm broken below the shoulder; right hand on left breast. H. 15.1 cm. Lustrous surface. Found 4.38 m. deep in Vinča mound. BU Collection, Inv. No. 1222. Vasić's excavation. Publ. Vasić, *Vinča*, I: Pl. XXXVI.

186, 187 Terracotta figurine (cylindrical stand) with head of a bear cub from Pavlovac (locality Čukar), upper Morava Valley, southeastern Yugoslavia. Small stumps for arms. H. 16.6 cm. Fine dark brown fabric. 1955 excavation of NM Belgrade and Archaeological Institute of Serbian Academy of Sciences. NM Belgrade, Inv. 15369. Publ. M. Garašanin in 39. *BRGK* (1958): Pl. 1, a, b. Assumed to be of Late Vinča (Vinča-Pločnik) period.

188 Terracotta figurine in half animal, half human form. Applied ears, pinched-up nose, eyes and mouth excised. Left arm and left breast broken off. Right hand on the abdomen. Lower part missing. H. 9.5 cm. Fine brown fabric. Starčevo complex. Porodin near Bitola, southern Yugoslavia. Excavated 1954 by M. Grbić et al. Archaeological Museum Bitola, Inv. No. 14. Publ. Grbić, *Porodin*, Pl. 39; Sheffield *Catalogue* (1969): Pl. 6.

189, 190 Terracotta sculpture of a seated mother holding a large child on her lap. V's, meanders and crescents incised on the back. Both heads missing. Legs and right arm of the mother broken off. H. 12.4 cm. Fine light-brown fabric. Early Vinča settlement at Rastu near Dolj, southwestern Romania. NAM, Bucharest. Publ. V. Dumitrescu, *Raport asupra activităţii ştiinţifice a Muzeului Naţional de Antichităţi în anii 1942 şi 1943* (Bucharest 1944); 84–87, Fig. 16.

191, 192 Terracotta figurine of fine dark-grey fabric from Supska near Ćuprija. H. 9.2 cm. Lower part and left arm missing. Perforations through shoulders and elbows. Incisions indicate eyes, blouse lines, constricted sleeves, fingers, navel and notched cord by which pouch on back was attached. Central section at front and back (between incisions) painted in black. Surface find. NM Belgrade 20196. NM Belgrade *Catalogue* (1968): 128.

193 Terracotta figurine of a bear-masked woman in a seated position holding a bear cub. Light-grey fabric. Impure clay. H. 5.7 cm. Excavated 1959 by J. Glišić and B. Jovanović. Fafos factory in Kosovska Mitrovica, Kosovo Metohije, Yugoslavia. Found in later horizon of the settlement, labelled Fafos II. National Museum, Kosovska Mitrovica, Inv. 2090. NM Belgrade *Catalogue* (1968): 96.

194 Terracotta figurine of mother holding baby. Head and legs missing. Was originally seated on a throne. Two perforations through each shoulder. Massive arms, fingers crudely incised. Dress indicated by white-encrusted incisions. H. 8 cm. Fine grey fabric. Vinča site at Gradac near Zlokučani, Morava Valley, excavated by M. Vasić in 1909, but the figurine is a surface find. NM Belgrade, Inv. 775. Publ. M. Vasić in *Glas Serb. Kralj. Akademie* (1911).

195 Mother and child plastically rendered on a pottery fragment from early Lengyel village of Zengövárkony near Pécs, province of Baranya, Hungary. Holes for eyes. Schematized animal-shaped head. Massive arms and hands. H. 5 cm. Excavation by J. Dombay in 1939. Janus Pannonius Museum in Pécs, Inv. 5.187.1939. Published by Dombay, *Zengövárkony*: 217, Pl. 87, Fig. 6; Pl. 114, Fig. 4a–b.

196 Terracotta standing figurine from Medvednjak near Smederevska Palanka, southeast of Belgrade. H. 15.7 cm. One arm stump and head broken off. Fine dark-grey fabric. Black polished with white-encrusted incisions indicating both dress and magical signs – a snake on the abdomen and meander on the back. Snake and meander bands are painted in red. Excavated 1970 by R. Milosjević, director of the Narodin Muzej Smederevska Palanka, Inv. 112. Courtesy of this museum.

197 Terracotta figurine of a seated pregnant woman with hands above the abdomen. Legs like cones. Head missing. H. 2.5 cm. Fine reddish-brown fabric. Porodin near Bitola as above, Inv. 1306. Publ. Grbić, *Porodin*: Pl. XXXI: 7.

198 Terracotta torso of a nude and pregnant woman holding her hands above the belly. Left arm broken. Head and lower portion missing. H. 5.25 cm. Fine reddish-brown fabric. Porodin mound near Bitola, western Macedonia. Excavated 1953 by M. Grbić *et al.* Central Balkan Neolithic, Starčevo complex. Bitola Archaeological Museum, Inv. 470. Publ. Grbić, *Porodin*, but object not illustrated.

199 Hamangia-type standing terracotta figurine with hands on the abdomen. Pillar head, feet and left shoulder reconstructed. Large breasts, very wide hips. H. 21.7 cm. Cernavoda cemetery, Dobruja. Light brown fabric. NAM Bucharest, Inv. V.22003. Excavation of 1957 by D. Berciu of the Institute of Archaeology, Academy of Sciences, Romanian P.R. Publ. D. Berciu, *Cultura Hamangia* (1966).

200, 201 Lower half of terracotta seated figurine, broken at waist and end of legs. Accentated abdominal part with wide hips and pregnant belly. Incised with white-encrusted lines, spirals and dots: double spiral on the belly, triangles with a dot inside each forming band on the back. Diagonal lines above the legs suggest skirt or trousers. Upper back plain except for two holes marking *Trigonum lumbale* and two holes at the back of the neck. Brown/grey fabric. H. 3.5 cm. Max. width 3.1 cm. 1968 excavation of Sitagroi mound by C. A. Renfrew (Sheffield) and M. Gimbutas (UCLA). Period III, equivalent to the East Balkan Gumelniţa civilization. Philipi Museum, Macedonia, Greece, SF 1276.

202 Schematized figurine of pregnant female with band of incised snakes around the belly. Orange/buff fine baked clay. White-encrusted incisions. H. 5.15 cm. Max. diam. 3 cm. Sitagroi mound (Period III), Greek Macedonia, Philipi Museum, SF 4489.

203 Terracotta figurine in a squatting position. H. 3.9 cm. Schematically rendered. Head broken off. Incised lines mark legs. Lozenge with a dot in the middle on belly. Gladnice, site at Gračanica near Priština in Kosovo Metohije, southern Yugoslavia, a Neolithic Starčevo settlement. J. Glisić's excavation of 1960. Regional Museum Priština, Inv. No. G-2E/1205. Belgrade 1968 *Catalogue*: 31.

204, 205 Terracotta figurine of a standing female incised all over with lines and magical signs. In front, in the very centre, a quadripartite lozenge with a dot in each section and a snake design above it on chest. Breasts not indicated. Arm stumps incised on front and back with parallel lines. V-line below the schematized head with pinched-up nose. Hair indicated by application of small lumps of clay. Fine reddish-brown baked clay. Polished surface. H. 15 cm. Cucuteni, northern Moldavia. Cucuteni A phase. NAM Bucharest.

206 Terracotta figurine in seated position, placed on a terracotta throne (not found together). The figurine, with a multiple lozenge design incised above the pregnant belly, from Selo Kalekovets near Plovdiv, central Bulgaria; the chair (throne) from Kapitan Dimitrievo. Both are of Karanovo VI-Gumelniţa type. H. approx. 10 cm. Plovdiv Archaeological Museum.

207–209 The seated goddess of Pazardžik at Plovdiv, central Bulgaria. H. approx. 15 cm. Polished surface, fine fabric. White-encrusted incised lines. Naturhistorisches Museum, Vienna. Publ. by M. Hoernes, *Urgeschichte Europas*, p. 204. Republished by E. Neumann, *The Great Mother* (1955), Pl. 6. Courtesy of Naturhistorisches Museum, Prähistorische Abteilung.

210, 211 Anthropomorphic red-painted vessel in the form of an enthroned goddess. Fine reddish-brown fabric. H. 23 cm. No head. Legs broken off below the knees. Small breasts. Schematic folded arms each wearing two bracelets and one arm-ring. Navel indicated by a semi-globular protuberance with a dot in the middle. Incised geometric design, originally white-encrusted, covers lower part of the body. Kökénydomb at Hódmezövásárhely on River Tisza in southeastern Hungary. Tisza culture. Tornyai János museum, Hódmezövásárhely, Inv. No. 761/42. Publ. J. Banner, *Kökénydomb*.

212 Enthroned goddess from Predionica, Vinča site at Priština Kosovo Metohije, southern Yugoslavia. H. 18.5 cm. Fine red fabric. Surface find during excavation. Regional Priština Museum, Inv. 161. Publ. by R. Galović, *Predionica*, Priština (1959): Pl. 3.

213 Upper portion of terracotta figurine of goddess with pig's head or mask. Fine grey fabric. H. 9 cm. Rastu, lower Danube region, western Romania. Early Vinča settlement. NAM Bucharest. Excavation by V. Dumitrescu in 1942 and 1943: V. Dumitrescu, *Raport asupra activităţii ştiintifice a Muzeului National de Antichităti in anii 1942 si 1943* (Bucharest 1944): 84–87.

214 Terracotta head of a pig from Vinča. Leskavica near Štip, Macedonia. Fine light-brown fabric. H. 19 cm. Surface find in the area of Vinča settlement. Naroden Muzej, Štip. Publ. NM Belgrade catalogue (1968): 93.

215 Naturalistically rendered terracotta pig from the Nea Makri mound, Attica Proto-Sesklo culture. Volos Museum. L. 6.5 cm. Fine reddish-brown fabric. Excavated 1954 by D. R. Theocharis. Publ. Theocharis in *Athenische Mitteilungen*, 71 (1956): 1ff.

216 Fragment (snout) of a life-size sculpture of a pig. Unbaked clay. From the Vinča layer of the stratified site of Anza between Titov Veles and Štip in eastern Macedonia. Discovered by the author during the season of 1970. With the exception of one leg, all other parts of the pig had completely disintegrated. Made of local orange clay with chaff temper and including some large quartz grains. Rough, buff-coloured, unpolished surface. Vertical cross-section of snout 3.9 cm. Test pit XIX, 5. Naroden Muzej, Štip.

217 Terracotta head of a pig. It has large ears with three perforations in each and deep holes in the snout. Plastically rendered eyes. L. 9.1 cm. Light-brown fine fabric. Dalbaki, 15 km. east of Stara Zagora, central Bulgaria. Marica-Gumelniţa culture. Courtesy of Stara Zagora Archaeological Museum.

218 Pig's head and neck of red baked terracotta, with polished and rippled surface. Hollow. Black-painted bands around the neck and eyes. Face (mask) sharply outlined. Perforations on both sides. Probably part of the cult vase (or a rhyton) found 7.6 m. (5.8 m.) deep in the Vinča mound, during Vasić's excavation. L. 7.8 cm. BU Collection. Publ. Vasić, *Vinča*, I: Pl. 27 and Figs. 118a,b; II: Pl. XCVII and Fig. 363. Vasić: *Illustrated London News*, 1930, October 18 as 'a rhyton of red clay in the form of a goat'.

219 One of the terracotta phalli found in the Proto-Seslko complex in the Tsangli mound, Thessaly. Excavation by A. J. B. Wace and M. S. Thompson: *Prehistoric Thessaly* (1912), cf. Figs. 74b, 76b, 77c, e, 91a, 109b, h, i, k, 141a–c. This phallus has a cream colour thickly applied and is painted with horizontal reddish-brown bands. The rounded top has a slit. H. 9 cm. Volos Museum, Thessaly, Greece. *c.* 6000 BC. After Zervos, *Naissance*, I (1962): 250, Fig. 283.

220 Bone phallus from Bohuslavice, a Lengyel settlement near Znojmo. The dotted snake pattern is white-encrusted. Brno Archaeological Museum, Inv. No. 2.637. Courtesy of this museum.

221 Phalli from the Cucuteni B settlement of Frumuşica, Moldavia, northeastern Romania. H. 13 and 7 cm. In both, a canal runs from top to bottom. Excavation by C. Matasă. Publ. Matasă, C. *Frumuşica* (Bucharest 1946). Archaeological Museum in Piatra Neamţ, Moldavia, Inv. 9081296.

222 Phallus-shaped clay artifacts, possibly used as stems for 'wine cups', as reconstructed by Š. Batović. Danilo settlement at Smilčić near Zadar. Excavated 1958 by Š. Batović. Archaeological Museum in Zadar. After Š. Batović, 'Problem kulta phallosa u Danilskoj kulturi', *Diadora*, 4 (1968): Fig. 3, Pl. IV, 3.

223–225 Mushroom-shaped studs or stands of light green marble. H. *a* 3.5 cm.; *b* 3 cm.; *c* 2.3 cm. Vinča site. Vasić's excavation. Belgrade Univ. Collection, 500, 543, 708.

226 Butmir vase. Butmir settlement, Bosnia, Yugoslavia. Fine dark grey fabric. H. 20.5 cm. Excavations of 1893–96 by V. Radimsky, F. Fiala and M. Hoernes. Sarajevo Zemaljski Muzej. Publ. V. Radimsky and M. Hoernes, *Die neolitische Station von Butmir*, I (1895). Date by analogy to Obre settlement near Kakanj: *c.* mid-fifth millennium BC.

227 Terracotta masked figurine of a nude ithyphallic man in a jumping or dancing posture. Hands on thighs. Legs broken off. Top of head rounded. Contours of mask visible. Eyes indicated by depression. Fragments of a belt (?) on waist. H. 12 cm. Fine light-brown fabric. Later layer of Fafos (Fafos II) at Kosovska Mitrovica, southern Yugoslavia. Mid-Vinča phase. Excavated 1959 by J. Glišić. Kosovska Mitrovica Archaeological Museum, 7-B-850. Publ. by R. Galović in *Review* magazine 1968.

228 Terracotta sculpture from Seslko, Thessaly. H. approx. 9 cm. Tsountas excavation. Publ. by Kh. Tsountas, *Dimeniou kai Sesklou* (1908); repeated by Zervos, *Naissance* (1962): Fig. 276. National Museum Athens, Inv. 5945. Photo: Courtesy of National Museum Athens.

229, 230 Masked ithyphallic and horned (horns broken off) man with the right hand over the left shoulder. Left hand holds penis which is painted red. H. 8 cm. Bracelets indicated by incision. Eyes incised. Light brown fabric. Late Vinča settlement of Crnokalačka Bara at Rujište near Ražanj, north of Niš, southeastern Yugoslavia. NM Belgrade, Inv. 20.942. Excavated 1959 by R. Galović. Publ. R. Galović *Archeološki Pregled* (1960).

231 Crude terracotta figurine of an enthroned male figure in an ithyphallic position. Cylindrical head with no facial features. Arms broken off. H. 5.3 cm. Grey fabric. From the Porodin mound. Excavated 1954 by M. Grbić *et al.* Archaeological Museum, Bitola, Porodin 629. Publ. M. Grbić, *Porodin*: Pl. XL.

232 Ithyphallic man seated on a stool from the area of Larisa, Thesaly. Terracotta. Raised right arm touching right ear. Mouth indicated by incision, nose broken off. Left arm on left knee. Tense posture. Engraved necklace around the neck. Radial incisions and two semicircles above the genitals. Penis broken. H. approx. 50 cm. National Museum Athens, Inv. 5894.

233 Ithyphallic terracotta figurine of a standing male with horned animal head (mask). Carefully modelled horns. Semi-spherical eyes. Folded arms with arm-rings on the upper arms indicated in clay. Legs fused into a narrow base. H. 4.3 cm. Fine brown fabric. Earliest layer of Fafos (Fafos Ia) at Kosovska Mitrovica, southern Yugoslavia.

Excavated 1959 by J. Glišić. Mid-Vinča period. Regional Museum, Priština, Inv. F-I-17c/1251. Publ. by R. Galović, *Review* 1968.

234 Schematized terracotta figurine of an ithyphallic man with animal head. Horns slightly indicated. Applied large circular eyes and a conical phallus. Left hand holding phallus. Right arm and horn damaged. Flat base. H. approx. 7 cm. Found 6.7 m. deep at the Vinča site. Vasić's excavation. BU Collection, Inv. 1251. Vasić, *Vinča*, III: 585.

235 Masked head of a terracotta figurine portraying a horned animal, painted in red and black, with incised white-encrusted lines. Large semicircular eyes. Horns broken. H. 7 cm. Crnokalačka Bara south of Niš, southern Yugoslavia. Excavated 1959 by R. Galović. NM Belgrade, Inv. No. 19110. Unpublished. Mentioned in *Arheološki Pregled* (1960) by R. Galović.

236 Terracotta figurine of a masked man in a seated position. Head (mask) and shoulders disproportionally large, the lower part compressed. Legs broken off below knees. Ornament by incision and white encrustation. Fine grey fabric. H. 22 cm. W. (across shoulders) 15.4 cm. Valač near Kosovska Mitrovica, southern Yugoslavia. Excavated 1957 by N. Tasić. Publ. N. Tasić, *Kosmet Glasnik*, 2 (1957): 44, Pl. 13a,b. Museum of Kosovska Mitrovica.

237 Terracotta figurine of a bull with a human head (mask) from later Fafos layer (Fafos II). Late Vinča. L. 12.3 cm., H. 5.6 cm. Fine grey fabric. Excavated 1959 by J. Glišić and B. Jovanović. Regional Museum, Priština, F II-2A-160. NM Belgrade *Catalogue* (1968): 95; Sheffield *Catalogue* (1969): Pl. 16.

238 Human-headed bull. Terracotta figurine from the site of Valač near Kosovska Mitrovica. Body and hind legs missing. Fine brown fabric, incised decoration white-encrusted and painted dark red and black. Eyes and middle parts of forelegs painted black. H. 10.5 cm. National Museum Kosovska Mitrovica Va-113/2. N. Tasić excavation: publ. N. Tasić, *Kosmet Glasnik* (1960): Fig. 4. NM Belgrade *Catalogue* (1968): 104. Sheffield *Catalogue* (1969: 111.

239 Bull-legged pottery tripod from Medvednjak near Smederevska Palanka. Fine red fabric. H. 11.5 cm. Vinča culture. Discovered by R. Milošević before the systematic excavations in 1969–70 together with two other tripods, one larger, another smaller, and a figurine (female, in festive attire and wearing a pentagonal mask, in a standing position). Narodni Muzej, Smederevska Palanka, M VIII 48. Publ. Sheffield *Catalogue* (1969): 181–84.

240 Vase in shape of a crouching bull with a half-human, half-bull mask attached to the neck. The mask has very large perforations. Opening at the top of the head. H. 11.4 cm. Decoration by graphite painting: five concentric circles below the head, three on each side of the body and two spirals on either side of the raised ridge representing the spine. Gumelniţa mound, lower Danube district of Ilfov, southern Romania (Walachia). Excavations by V. Dumitrescu of the Institute of Archaeology of the Academy of Sciences, Bucharest, 1925–60. Gumelniţa B period. NAM, I 3451. Publ. S. Marinescu, 'Doua vase zoomorfe din cultura Gumelniţa', *SCIV*, XII, 2 (1961): 345–56; Dumitrescu, *L'art Roumanie*: 107.

241 Head of a bull broken off at the neck. Pentagonal, flattened face suggesting a mask has large diamond-shaped eyes and line of incisions along the nose ridge and eyebrows. Two incised lines round neck, originally painted red. Reddish-brown burnished surface. H. 4.4 cm. W. (of mask) 4.6 cm. Sitagroi mound, Period III. Dikilitash variant (equals Gumelniţa). Discovered 1968 during M. Gimbutas (UCLA)–A. C. Renfrew (Sheffield University) excavation. Philippi Museum SF 1286.

242 Head of a bull that formed part of a cult vessel. Horns missing. Ears indicated. Well modelled semi-globular eyes. Distinct nose ridge. Brown burnished. H. (of face) 4.6 cm., W. 2.7 cm. Sitagroi mound, Period III. Philippi Museum SF 210.

243 The Gumelniţa 'lovers': conjoined female and male terracotta statuette. The male (ithyphallic) embraces the female, who is characterized by a large pubic triangle and small breasts. Both have pinched-up noses,

perforated ears (female, two holes; male, one hole) and the female has three holes in the mouth area. H. 6.8 cm. Fine light-brown fabric. Gumelniţa mound, district of Ilfov, lower Danube. Final Gumelniţa A, found at a depth of 0.90 m. below the present ground level. Excavated by V. Dumitrescu. Olteniţa Archaeological Museum. Publ. *Antiquity* (1964): Pl. XXXVIII a (note by V. Dumitrescu); V. Dumitrescu 'New discoveries at Gumelniţa', *Archaeology*, XIX (1966), 3: 162–72; *Idem, L'art Roumanie*: 90.

244, 245   Terracotta figurine of an enthroned male god. Head, right leg and two legs of the throne broken off. Hands on knees. H. 7 cm. Painted red on back and front. The Pyrasos mound at the modern village of Nea Anchialos, midway between Volos and Almyros. Found in second Neolithic stratum (from the bottom) from the Sesklo end of the Proto-Sesklo period. Excavated 1956 by D. R. Theocharis. Volos Archaeological Museum, Inv. 2429. Publ. D. R. Theocharis 'Pyrasos', *Thessalika* (1959): 29–68, Pl. III, *b*.

246   Terracotta torso of a seated man with a well modelled back. Vulkaneshti, Soviet Moldavia. Excavated by T. S. Passek. Archaeological Museum of the Institute of History of the Academy of Sciences of the Moldavian S.R., Kishenev. Publ. by T. S. Passek and M. M. Gerasimov, 'Novaja statuetka iz Vulkaneshti', *KSIIMK*, No. III (1967): 38–41.

247–250   Male and female gods from the cemetery of Cernavoda, northwest of Constanţa, in the area of the Danube delta. Hamangia culture. Fine brown fabric, polished dark-brown surface. H. (male) 11.5 cm., (female) 11.3 cm. Completely preserved. Both wear masks. Flat necks and backs. 1957 excavation by D. Berciu sponsored by Archaeological Institute of the Academy of Sciences of the Romanian P. R. NAM Bucharest, Inv. V 6496. Publ. by D. Berciu, 'Neolithic figurines from Romania', *Antiquity*, XXXIV, No. 136 (1960): 283–84. *Ibid.*, 'Mamifestation d'art néolithique en Roumanie. Le "couple" de Cernavoda', *IPEK*, 21 (1964/65): 42–45.

251, 252   Terracotta seated man with hands to his head from Tirpeşti, district of Tg. Neamţ, region of Bacău, Moldavia, Romania, an early Cucuteni ('Pre-Cucuteni III') settlement. H. 7.7 cm. Fine ochre-red fabric. Polished surface. Flattened back. Legs broken off. Long cylindrical neck and upper arms. Flat head, suggesting a mask. Excavated by V. Dumitrescu and S. Marinescu-Bîlcu. NAM Bucharest. Publ. by S. Marinescu-Bîlcu, 'Reflets des rapports entre les civilizations de Hamangia et de Précucuteni dans la plastique Précucuténienne de Tirpeşti', *Dacia*, VIII (1964); 307–12.

Index